Introduction to
United States Government
Information Sources

LIBRARY AND
INFORMATION SCIENCE TEXT SERIES

The School Library Media Center. 5th ed. By Emanuel T. Prostano and Joyce S. Prostano.

Library and Information Center Management. 5th ed. By Robert D. Stueart and Barbara B. Moran.

The Academic Library: Its Context, Its Purpose, and Its Operation. By John M. Budd.

Information Sources in Science and Technology. 3d ed. By C. D. Hurt.

The Social Sciences: A Cross-Disciplinary Guide to Selected Sources. 2d ed. Nancy L. Herron, General Editor.

Introduction to United States Government Information Sources. 6th ed. By Joseph Morehead.

The Economics of Information: A Guide to Economic and Cost-Benefit Analysis for Information Professionals. By Bruce R. Kingma.

Reference and Information Services: An Introduction. 2d ed. Richard E. Bopp and Linda C. Smith, General Editors.

Developing Library and Information Center Collections. 3d ed. By G. Edward Evans.

The Collection Program in Schools: Concepts, Practices, and Information Sources. 2d ed. By Phyllis J. Van Orden.

Introduction to Technical Services. 6th ed. By G. Edward Evans and Sandra M. Heft.

The School Library Media Manager. 2d ed. By Blanche Woolls.

The Humanities: A Selective Guide to Information Sources. 4th ed. By Ron Blazek and Elizabeth Aversa.

Introduction to Cataloging and Classification. By Bohdan S. Wynar. 8th ed. By Arlene G. Taylor.

Introduction to Library Public Services. 6th ed. By G. Edward Evans, Anthony J. Amodeo, and Thomas L. Carter.

A Guide to the Library of Congress Classification. 5th ed. By Lois Mai Chan.

The Organization of Information. By Arlene G. Taylor.

Systems Analysis for Librarians and Information Professionals. 2d ed. By Larry N. Osborne and Margaret Nakamura.

Introduction to United States Government Information Sources

Sixth Edition

Joe Morehead

1999
Libraries Unlimited, Inc.
Englewood, Colorado

LIBRARIES UNLIMITED, INC.
P.O. Box 6633
Englewood, CO 80155-6633
1-800-237-6124
www.lu.com

Library of Congress Cataloging-in-Publication Data

Morehead, Joe, 1931-
    Introduction to United States government information sources /
Joe Morehead. -- 6th ed.
    xxv, 491 p. 17x25 cm. -- (Library and information science text series)
    Includes bibliographical references and indexes.
    ISBN 1-56308-734-0 (cloth). -- ISBN 1-56308-735-9 (pbk.)
    1. Government information--United States. 2. Government
publications--United States. I. Title. II. Series.
ZA5055.U6M67   1999
015.73'053--dc21   99-35598
                                                       CIP

AHJ-7164

This book is dedicated to
Bebe Morehead,
my beloved co-conspirator in life.

CONTENTS

2—GOVERNMENT PRINTING OFFICE PROGRAMS AND SERVICES (continued)

LIST OF
ILLUSTRATIONS

PREFACE
TO THE SIXTH EDITION

The purpose of this text is to provide an account of the general and specialized sources, in print and non-print formats, that make up the bibliographic and textual structure of federal government information. Like the previous editions, the work serves as a text for library school students, a reference source for institutions that acquire public documents, a resource for information professionals and their clientele, and a guide for researchers who must access the immense amount of information produced by or for the federal establishment. The emphasis remains a contemporary one; the reader is encouraged to consult other historical or specialized studies I have noted in chapter 4 for more detailed information.

This edition has been extensively revised to reflect the many changes that have occurred in the production and dissemination of government products within the last five years of the final decade of the twentieth century. Information in electronic packages generally, and on the Internet particularly, has transformed the access to federal information as dramatically as it has other forms and categories of knowledge, information, and entertainment. The chapters contain not only descriptive data but critical and analytical commentary on the methods and merits of this transformation. While there might be an unfortunate tendency on the part of some government officials to harbor a naive enthusiasm about dissemination of government products in electronic form, saner voices have not yet repudiated the utility of the print medium. Today, the variety of formats offers more options than ever before to meet the needs of the most discriminating users; the danger is that we may ignore the inability to preserve certain short-lived technologies while indulging our giddy excitement about the latest gadget or existing upgraded creation. If technology is to remain our servant, we must not become promiscuously enthusiastic about that which represents a paradigm shift in society.

The narrative begins with an introductory overview of issues, themes, and problems associated with the migration of federal government information to the Internet. Chapters 2 and 3 describe the administrative machinery and information systems by which both the Government Printing Office and its network of designated depository libraries manage official products and services. Chapter 4 introduces the general checklists, indexes, and guides to retrospective and current government information. Chapters 5 through 8 discuss the prominent sources generated by or in support of the three constitutionally mandated branches of the federal establishment, as well as the independent agencies with regulatory powers and the advisory committees and commissions. The interrelationships among these entities constitute the grand dialectic that the framers of the Constitution envisaged.

Chapter 9 summarizes the numerous statistical sources created by or for the government, with an analysis of selected issues and problems facing the Census Bureau as it prepares for the millennial census. Chapter 10 deals with the major categories of intellectual property: trade secrets, patents, trademarks, and copyright. Chapter 11 involves a discourse on the functions of selected departments and agencies in certain critical disciplines: scientific research and development, education, declassified information, and audits and evaluations. Chapter 12 portrays the consequential role geographic information systems play in the creation and provision of maps, charts, and gazetteers. The appendix is a bibliography of the primary source materials generated in the impeachment and trial of William Jefferson Clinton, September 9, 1998, to February 12, 1999.

I question the necessity to provide a lengthy laundry list of executive branch agencies with their Web site addresses. This task is admirably performed for us at two splendid sites: The Louisiana State University (LSU) Pathway Service "List of Federal Agencies on the Internet" and the companion site of "Agency Links" to Laurie Andriot's *Internet Blue Pages.* Both sources are discussed in chapter 4. I have also tried to confine most of the Uniform Resource Locators (URLs) I have cited to the home page of the entity under discussion rather than to every sub-address, which is, in most instances, just a point and click away from the basic URL. Rather, I have displayed the URLs in boldface so they can be more easily distinguished for bookmarking or verification. I am well aware that URLs unfortunately change and disappear; and Web sites are redesigned with different bars, buttons, and links. The frustrations inevitably engendered by these inconsistencies may be mitigated by present and future developments in site management (chapter 2).

Regardless of the benefits, and difficulties, that present and future technologies confer upon the production and dissemination of government information products, and despite the bold vision of a PC with Internet access in every home, the public will continue to rely, probably more than ever, on the mediating expertise of documents librarians to help retrieve the vast and variegated body of government information in whatever format it is published. It is my hope that this book will better acquaint the reader with some of these diverse and unfailingly interesting sources.

ACKNOWLEDGMENTS

The best part of writing a book is that it gives me an excuse to phone, visit, or e-mail my many friends and colleagues and ask them to tell me what they know or can find out. I am never disappointed or surprised by their generous and unerring responses; their special talents and skills always make my task measurably easier. For their knowledge, advice, assistance, and cooperation, thanks to librarians Catherine M. Dwyer, Richard D. Irving, and Barbara J. Via, the University at Albany; Robert Emery, Albany Law School; and Mary Woodward, New York State Library. Thanks also to Christine Barber, Cathy Dwyer's administrative assistant. I am indebted to Robert Scardamalia, Chief Demographer, New York State Department of Economic Development and Director of the New York State Data Center, for his time and patience in explaining Census data to me and my students.

For their outstanding assistance in the preparation of this work, my thanks to managing editor Carmel Huestis, copyeditor Sharon DeJohn, and typesetter Kay Minnis, Libraries Unlimited. To my longtime friend and publisher, Dr. Bohdan S. Wynar, a large measure of appreciation for his wisdom and guidance throughout all the years and editions.

A special note of recognition goes to Mary Alingh, my graduate assistant from January 1998 to May 1999. In tasks small and large, I relied upon her combination of meticulous attention to detail, research skills, and creativity. Moreover, she is largely responsible for the careful and accurate organization of primary source materials in the appendix.

Any errors of commission or omission are, of course, my responsibility alone.

CHAPTER ONE

THE TRANSFORMATION OF GOVERNMENT INFORMATION

The old order changeth, yielding place to new.
—Alfred, Lord Tennyson

Be not the first by whom the new are tried,
Nor yet the last to lay the old aside.
—Alexander Pope

INTRODUCTION

The invention of movable type in the fifteenth century liberated us from the control of clerics and scribes. Numerous copies of the Bible, *Justinian's Code,* or *Plato's Republic* could be produced in identical form. Every literate person could have access to the same text and could interpret and judge it without benefit of the mediating authorities of church and state. About the time that Gutenberg was perfecting his printing press, the Vatican Library was formed; its first catalog listed some 2,500 volumes. Today, thanks to Gutenberg, any number of scholars have that many books or more in their home or office.

With the electronic revolution, the democratizing process that began with Gutenberg has ostensibly taken another leap forward. To continue the library analogy, not only is the catalog now digitized, but the computer can call up a variety of other catalogs and databases. In fact, from the comfort of our homes or offices we have bibliographic and, increasingly, textual access to so much knowledge that Erasmus would weep to know of this strange and wonderful gadget.[1]

When computer scientists talk about nanocomputers, digital ink, or "artificial life" software that works like biological organisms, skeptics may raise an eyebrow in disbelief. But these prophesies merely indicate that the computer is in its infancy, and our imaginations try to grasp what the computer will ultimately become and how that will affect our lives. It is doubtful that today's crystal-ball gazers will make a mistake of the magnitude of Kenneth Olsen, president and founder of Digital Equipment Corporation, who in 1977 said that "There is no reason for any individual to have a computer in their home." Besides being grammatically infelicitous, this howler is by no means uniquely foolish in retrospect. After all, it was the eponymous Lord Kelvin, Scottish mathematician and physicist, who said in 1897 that "Radio has no future."[2]

Before we become either promiscuously enthusiastic or depressingly cynical about this technology, it is well to stand aside and take a dispassionate view of what some have called that 800-pound gorilla in our midst. It is safe to say that the storage and retrieval of information generally, and government information in particular, in electronic formats will dominate the twenty-first century. This transformation assumes an inevitability, for the computer has become the ascendant metaphor and paradigm of the information age.

FROM ARPANET TO INTERNET

ARPANET is an acronym for Advanced Research Projects Agency Network, a packet-switched computer network to connect the Department of Defense (DoD) and corporate military suppliers together in a manner that if parts of the network were destroyed as a result of a nuclear attack, alternate paths would be available. The Agency decided to fund the establishment of a packet-switched network, connecting together various sites in the continental United States that were in receipt of ARPA grants. In early 1969, the contract for the network was awarded to a company in Cambridge, Massachusetts, the design for which was that each "host" computer was to be connected to a "dedicated minicomputer which formed part of the communications sub-network. These node computers were called IMPs and were later superseded by . . . terminal IMPs."[3] Concepts such as packet switching and dynamic rerouting, dispersed nodes, redundant connections, and TCP/IPs (Transport Control Protocols/Internet Protocols) to exchange data over the Internet made the ARPANET a viable enterprise.[4]

Initially, progress was sluggish in connecting government agencies and universities. The first, four-node experimental network was operational in early 1970. "By 1971 there were about nineteen nodes . . . with thirty different university sites that ARPA was funding." In 1983 ARPANET "became known as the ARPA Internet and the DoD divided it into two connected networks: MILNET, a network of military computers, and ARPANET, the network of research computers." Along came the National Science Foundation (NSF) and created a network of supercomputers called NSFNet, which in 1986 connected to ARPANET. NSFNet's superior communications technology resulted in the phasing out of ARPANET in the latter half of the decade, and by 1990 ARPANET ceased to exist. NSFNet was called the Internet Backbone and since 1995 has been replaced by private companies serving as Network Access Points.[5]

As to that perennial question, Who owns the Internet?, John Burke's summary is as well reasoned as any I have come across:

> It is somewhat true to say that everyone and no one owns the Net. What is more true is the fact that a combination of private and public organizations own parts of the Net. In the past, the U.S. government owned the supercomputers that controlled the flow of Net traffic, but this function has drifted over to private industry. The [federal] government is just one of dozens of players out there. Colleges and universities, private companies, nonprofit organizations, governments and individuals own the computers that are connected. Various groupings of public and private groups and organizations own the networks. The phone companies own the lines on which everything travels. In the end, no one group has control and no single set of rules has been established.[6]

Some rejoice in this diffusion, claiming that it exemplifies the very essence and purity of Athenian democracy (like Camelot, a romantic vision of a past that probably never was); others argue that the absence of a centralized presence and consistent standards engenders utter disarray.

The World Wide Web (known hereafter as the Web), a system for furnishing hypertext access to information wherever it is located on the Internet, was conceived at the European Laboratory for Particle Physics (CERN) and is a marvelous resource, but it too is a mere toddler. A reliable guess is that the average person in the year 2010 will look upon this generation of electronic hardware and software products as being as primitive as the Model T Ford or butter churns now seem to us. In the immediate future it is reasonable to assume that the Internet, and in particular the Web, will continue to grow in both bandwidth and number of users. But that's a no-brainer. When it comes to forecasting the rate of technological progress, my crystal ball is opaque. We do know this, however: The federal government has decreed that the Internet shall bear the burden of disseminating government information into the fore-seeable future.

THE INTERNET AND ITS METAPHORS

Every revolution begets its tribe of paraphrasts. The Internet, an international computer network of networks connected to one another using TCP/IP protocols, is one component in a congeries of communications networks named the "information highway." Whether accurate or not, this phrase has become the metaphor of choice, and it has spawned all sorts of ancillary similes. Transportation metaphors abound, of course, although it's difficult to imagine one "surfing" a highway, except during a heavy rain when your car hydroplanes the slippery streets. Users have discovered potholes on the highway, crowded entrances and exits, traffic jams, and the like. Metaphors also reflect the building trades (this site is "under construction"), navigational systems, the garment industry (buttons), and other clever descriptive words and phrases. Some pundits have found it necessary to disdain the information superhighway as a useful metaphor and devise analogies that, in their opinion, better clarify this grand achievement. John Perry Barlow, co-founder of the Electronic Frontier Foundation, calls the Internet "a great nervous system capable of turning human minds into human mud [but also the] most profound technological event since fire [that will bring about a] profound change in what it is to be human. The Internet is creating one social space where every single person may gather—and it's not defined like the physical world. [It is] going to cause the renegotiation of power on this planet."[7] Such overwrought emotions require a cold shower.

In 1962, Marshall McLuhan created a sensation when he averred that "the new electronic interdependence recreates the world in the image of a global village," even if most of us found it very difficult to understand the rest of his prescient but ponderously dense and philosophically abstruse *Gutenberg Galaxy*. "Instead of tending towards a vast Alexandrian library the world has become a computer, an electronic brain. . . . So, unless aware of this dynamic, we shall at once move into a phase of panic terrors, exactly befitting a small world of tribal drums, total interdependence, and superimposed co-existence."[8] Dr. Paul Resnick, chairman of the PICS (Platform for Internet Content Selection) working group of the World Wide Web Consortium, would disagree with McLuhan's metaphor of a global village. "The metaphor is misleading," he says. "Many cultures coexist on the Internet and at times clash. In its public spaces, people interact commercially and socially with strangers as well as with acquaintances and friends. The city is a more apt metaphor, with its suggestion of unlimited opportunities and myriad dangers."[9] Perhaps the metaphor of a city is more pertinent, but not New York; according to one wag, the Internet is comparable to the Big Apple, in that both feature "inexplicable traffic delays, random confrontations with lunatics, and easy, private, around-the-clock access to pornography."[10]

Despite its giddy enthusiasm, I rather fancy Barlow's symbol, that of a vast nervous system, forever changing and growing. In cybersurfing the Internet, I am continually amazed at the amount of information out there, but I often feel like Mickey Mouse hopelessly whisking with his little broom the tide of water sweeping into his master's den. The "Sorcerer's Apprentice," that classic orchestral scherzo of Paul Dukas immortalized in Walt Disney's *Fantasia,* personifies the Internet.

WHO WILL TAME THE INTERNET?

Resnick was one of several distinguished contributors to the March 1997 issue of *Scientific American* in which a special report on subduing the Internet beast invested librarians as the right people for the job because, in the words of the journal's editor in chief, "the Internet is made of information, and nobody knows more about how to order information than librarians, who have been pondering that problem for thousands of years."[11] However, Martin Dillon, Executive Director, OCLC Institute, in a May 1998 graduation speech to the University of North Carolina School of Information and Library Science, said, "It is clear to virtually all who use the Internet that chaos reigns there. What impact is the library profession having on this chaos? I would say that it is almost unnoticeable."[12] In the famous phrase commonly attributed to Mark Twain but actually the provenance of Charles Dudley Warner, who collaborated with the great humorist in the writing of *The Gilded Age,* "Everybody talks about the weather, but nobody does anything about it." This typifies the Internet, a gelatinous, pullulating organism, existing in a chaotic mix of the ephemeral and the substantive, the trivial and the important.

Stated in other terms, a major problem with the Internet is that one often has to dig through a great pudding of irrelevant material to extract small plums of apposite information. Those of us who spend much of our time searching for government information may have an advantage, if just to know that sometimes we can demarcate the boundaries. The reader will encounter the words "GPO Access" many times in the chapters ahead. Its Uniform Resource Locator (URL)—**http://www. access.gpo.gov**—with its manifold links and buttons, rewards us with a great deal of information; but we must keep this address in perspective. GPO Access is but a small part of the Internet. Virtually every department of the federal government has its own Web site, many of which predate GPO Access; and new agency sites are mounted every week. Moreover, Web directories such as *Yahoo! Government* and *GovBot* are helping to organize government information, and guides such as Laurie Andriot's Web site (**http://www.fedweb.com**) reduce research rage.

THE LOSS OF INFORMATION

"One of the great ironies of the information age is that, while the late twentieth century will undoubtedly record more data than have been recorded at any other time in history, it will also almost certainly lose more information than has been lost in any previous era." The information age appears to offer the historian a Holy Grail of instant and permanent access to virtually limitless amounts of information. But as the pace of technological change increases, so does the speed at which each new generation of equipment supplants the last. "Right now, the half-life of most computer technology is between three and five years," says Steve Puglia of the National Archives, in an interview held in 1999. In the 1980s the Archives transferred some 200,000 documents and images onto optical disks, the cutting edge of the new technology at the time. "I'm not sure we can still play them," Puglia says, because they depend on computer software and hardware that are no longer on the market.[13] The problem of losing information is just as crucial, perhaps more so, than the problem of information overload.

BEDAZZLED BY THE FUTURE

Perhaps we are not as concerned as we should be about information storage and preservation issues because we are bewitched by the sheer audacity of the technology that is already with us or on the drawing board. Speech recognition software, which came to fruition in 1998, has already freed us, if we wish, from the need to use the mouse or keyboard. "Continuous speech dictation," in which a computer transcribes everyday dialogue, is faster and easier than typing. A few days of regular use, less time than it takes to teach Rover to sit, and the 95 percent accuracy touted by the manufacturers is achieved. Several competitors are in the market: IBM, Dragon Systems, and Lernout & Hauspie are just a few of the companies vying for your allegiance and dollars. The advent of voice technology is particularly attractive to business, for it will provide a new distribution channel for reaching customers.[14] The Society for Automotive Engineers reports initiatives that focus on integrating communications, computers, and automobiles so that drivers and passengers can verbally request and listen to e-mail, locate a restaurant or hotel, ask for navigation help or for specific music or sports scores, and use voice-activated telephone services, "all done safely without interfering with driving."[15] This last quote from a respected journal may raise a few eyebrows. Our ingenuity will no doubt transcend this technology so that we can continue to drive badly and suffer accidents. And NASA's Jet Propulsion Laboratory has developed the technology for exchanging data, such as e-mail, between ground computers and remote spacecraft. Someday, colonists living on Mars will e-mail their earth-bound kith and kin.

Nicholas Negroponte, founding director of the Massachusetts Institute of Technology's avant-garde Media Lab, is not at all surprised at what wonders technology will effect. He envisages a future in which we will all have private multimedia "butlers" programmed by voice command to screen our telephone calls, schedule our days, and select our entertainment. Americans, he says, will spend more time on the Internet than on mingling with other people, a prophecy he seems not at all concerned about. Video-on-demand will have put videocassette rental stores out of business. The bits of information that stream into our living rooms will be converted into customized newspapers. Raw data about the weather or a football game will be converted at our discretion into a printout chart, a verbal report, a video picture, or a miniature re-creation. The world will be decentralized, globalized, harmonized.[16] People will be empowered and live happily ever after, and the brave new world that Miranda embraced in *The Tempest* is not tempered by the irony of an Aldous Huxley.

On the other hand, Clifford Stoll, an astronomer who penetrated and exposed a German spy ring on the Internet, is as gloomy as Negroponte is optimistic. But Stoll is a champion of librarians. Like the authors of the *Scientific American* issue I mentioned above, Stoll notes that librarians have "centuries of experience in dealing with books about weird topics. So answer me this: how come they're not consulted right in the beginning of the design of more databases?" In another passage, the author comments on something most librarians will attest to: "As computers invade libraries, librarians spend a lot of time learning how to operate them. Next time you need your library card renewed and you wonder where the librarian is hiding, check to see if he's taking a class in how to access some database."[17] Aside from Stoll's confusing clerical and professional tasks, his point may strike a responsive chord. But mainly he's ambivalent about computers; a kind of love-hate relationship emerges in his book. "Computer networks return answers—often the right ones—but they emphasize the product over the process. When I'm online, I sense the vast ocean of information available to me. But I'm alone, without a tutor or librarian."[18]

GOVERNMENT INFORMATION ISSUES

The articulation of problems and issues is necessarily the first step in attempting to resolve them. The Government Printing Office (GPO) has made an exemplary beginning in its 1996 *Study to Identify Measures Necessary for a Successful Transition to a More Electronic Federal Depository Library Program,* a report to Congress mandated by law. The study enunciates five "Principles for Federal Government Information"; each principle is succinctly stated, followed by an annotated explication. This is followed by a mission statement and seven goals, which precede the identification of eight "policy issues that impact publishing agencies, GPO, NARA, depository libraries, the public, and the private sector."[19]

Privatizing Government Information

Unfortunately, not all the principles are observed by federal agencies. For example, principle 2 proscribes, inter alia, the copyright of federal information; yet Wayne P. Kelley, a former Superintendent of Documents (1991–1997), notes that during his tenure he observed "a growing trend toward the transfer of federal information from the public domain to private ownership." This can happen in several ways, Kelley says. "The most direct approach is when the government simply transfers ownership or copyright to a private sector publisher"; Kelley uses the example of the privatization of formerly important publications such as the *U.S. Industrial & Trade Outlook* and the *Journal of the National Cancer Institute.*[20]

Preserving Government Information

Principle 4 concerns the government's obligation to "guarantee the preservation of Government information for future generations of Americans"; this information "in a meaningful format must be maintained in perpetuity to ensure the continued accountability of the Government to its present and future citizens."[21] When James Rhoads was

Archivist of the United States, he was asked by the chairman of the ANSI PH1-3 Task Group on Vesicular and Diazo Film to clarify the meaning of the term "archival." His answer, dated December 15, 1975, is worth quoting in part:

> Essentially the term "archival" is synonymous with "permanent" and the two are frequently used interchangeably. To us they have the same meaning: that is, forever. To say that we are going to keep forever everything that is now classified as archival or permanent is a rather positive statement and one which none of us can guarantee. Yet it does express our intention in relation to records which have been appraised as being of permanent value, or archival.[22]

Well, nothing is forever (except perhaps diamonds). But an overview of research on the longevity of the digital disk medium concludes that the archival life of a CD-ROM is anywhere from ten to twenty years. While there are well-established techniques of "error detection and correction," the price of special equipment to effect these restorations is high.[23] Other electronic products may not survive. In the mid-1990s, the National Archives informed Congress that the Census Bureau "reported to us . . . that they have over 4,000 reels of tape, containing permanently valuable data, which are difficult, if not impossible to use because they are in CENIO [Census Input/Output] format or because the files have been compressed on an ad hoc basis."[24] Horror stories like these abound. I mention this problem in chapter 3 as well as here, because its supreme importance bears iteration.

Stewart Brand, the creator of the famous *Whole Earth Catalog,* sounds the alarm by stating that because the world's work (the economy, knowledge in general, and so forth) has become digital, preservation

> is a civilizational issue. Information lives in two major dimensions—space and time. With digitization and the Internet, all information is now potentially global. The space dimension for data will keep exploding, but the time dimension is shrinking. The half-life of data is currently about five years. There is no improvement in sight because the attention span of the high-tech industry can only reach as far as next year's upgrade, and its products reflect that. But civilizational time is measured in centuries. A major disconnect is in progress. Loss of cultural memory has become the price of staying perfectly current.[25]

Under current regulations codified at 36 CFR 1228, the National Archives and Records Administration (NARA) accepts from GPO "one copy of every publication cataloged through the Cataloging and Indexing Program and/or distributed by GPO through the Federal Depository Library Program. GPO transfers a full collection to NARA after the completion of every four-year Presidential term." However, in recent years, "NARA has begun to accept for reference purposes only, without accessioning for preservation, CD-ROM discs and other electronic products that are software dependent and, therefore, not in archival format." Moreover, "NARA does not take extraordinary measures to ensure long-term access or preservation of the content, and such a transfer does not meet the publishing agency's obligation for transfer of the information to NARA for preservation." GPO's strategic plan calls for provision of electronic information to NARA "in formats acceptable for archival purposes"; but when that is not possible, legislative or regulatory activity will be needed to transfer information to NARA "in suitable archival formats."[26]

Society is not going to return to the days when print was the exclusive medium, nor should it. But it is interesting that Nicholas Negroponte, whose sanguinity about the future is almost risible, forthrightly identifies himself as "someone who does not like to read." Donald S. Lamm, the chairman of W. W. Norton & Company, wonders if the electronic revolution is going to be so stimulating that it will overcome what is referred to as *aliteracy,* defined as "the ability to read without the desire to do so." Even though the hour for the book may be late, it "will coexist with the computer, as it has had to coexist far earlier in [the 20th century] with movies and then television. Like symphony orchestras, however, books seem destined to move gradually—not today and not tomorrow—to the fringes of our culture. Their utility will not come to an end, even if books serve future generations mainly as beacons to the headlands of civilization."[27] This wry prediction is one that any literate person devoutly hopes will not come to pass. History and experience suggest that things are never quite as bad or quite as good as the haruspices of any epoch presage.

Public Access to Government Information

That the public has a "right to know" is a staple of politicians (and librarians). Principle 1 of the *Study to Identify Measures* speaks of "open and uninhibited access" as "a cornerstone of every democratic society." Wherever this ur-principle is limned, lofty phrases taken from James Madison and Thomas Jefferson are sure to follow. But the historical record belies the assumption that unfettered public access is universally accepted by and acceptable to government and governed alike. Over the decades the federal establishment has withheld information it has produced or acquired for any number of reasons: national security interests, budgetary constraints, internal decision-making activities, privacy, inadvertence, political mischief, outright deception.

The melancholy fact is that nothing inheres in the Constitution or the statutes granting the right to be informed. As constitutional law scholar Thomas I. Emerson pointed out in a 1977 law review article, "The Supreme Court has recognized in a number of cases that the first amendment embodies a constitutional guarantee of the right to know," but the High Court "has never clarified the right or pressed it toward its logical borders." Emerson states that "the greatest contribution that could be made in this whole realm of law would be explicit recognition by the courts that the constitutional right to know embraces the right of the public to obtain information from the government."[28] It is a matter of record that the federal appellate courts have been reluctant to embrace Emerson's suggestion. Over the decades, arguments postulating this right have skittered along the edges of the courts' consciousness but have never coalesced. Using WESTLAW and LEXIS-NEXIS, I examined appellate cases on point since 1977; although dicta were prevalent, I did not find any case law that clearly and unambiguously declared a constitutional right of access to government information.[29] Nor am I convinced that the migration of government information to the Internet will establish this perceived right as ratio decidendi in some future court case.

As if this were not bad enough, Representative Steny D. Hoyer (D-MD) entered into the *Congressional Record* of May 22, 1997, remarks citing estimates that "more than 50 percent of all tangible Government information products are not being made available to the Federal Depository Library Program."[30] These "fugitive documents" generated by federal departments and agencies without bibliographic accountability unless they reach a library by chance and are entered into the OCLC database are as lost to the public as if they never existed (see chapter 3).

Authenticity and Integrity of Government Information

Principle 3 states that "the obligation to provide long range assurances of authenticity will become increasingly important as more Government information moves to electronic formats." This is related to the need for permanent public access and will require cooperation from the producing agencies, GPO, depository libraries, and NARA "to establish authenticity, provide persistent identification and description of Government information products, and establish appropriate arrangements for its continued accessibility." The *Study* notes that "a greater degree of standardization than now exists" is desirable.[31] If you obtain your information from the GPO Access Web site, or a site, like a depository library, linked to GPO Access, or bona fide sites of agencies (unless there are serious disclaimers), the chances of the information being inauthentic are slight.

Government Information in the Public Domain

Principle 5 involves copyright and privatizing issues, discussed above. According to Wayne P. Kelley, government agencies "entering into agreements with private publishers create the opportunity for serious conflicts of interest, particularly if details of the agreement are secret. Agencies granting use of their names for commercial purposes undermine their own credibility."[32] Privatization, in short, is never warranted.

CONCLUSION

The principles, goals, and strategies set forth in the study document will furnish abundant work for the assiduous and dedicated staff at the Office of the Superintendent of Documents. Each issue involves many stakeholders and, ultimately, the public's right to information, whether or not that right is supported explicitly in constitutional law. The Internet is destined to become as ubiquitous as the telephone and the television; and perhaps someday it will be as easy to access information from it as it is to microwave a TV dinner. "The novelty of its usage will fade into the background. . . . [It] will become an indelible fixture of modern life, not so much because we can't live without it but because we won't want to live without it."[33] But, says Web archivist Brewster Kahle, at present the Web "has a 'memory' of about two months."[34] Perhaps inspired by the movie, Barbara Ceizler Silver, in her introductory comments to *Library Journal*'s annual "Notable Government Documents" column, says, "Archival problems seen mind-boggling, and documents librarians are debating the need to make paper copies of web sites before they disappear like the *Titanic*."[35] Stewart Brand employs *Titanic* imagery too:

> I have a fantasy that preservationists of the digital information age are like passengers who have wandered up on the deck of the *Titanic* and see the approaching iceberg. They run down

to the grand ballroom to warn everyone. There's a great party raging, and none of passengers really wants to hear about icebergs. . . . Finally, some in the festive crowd grudgingly concede the possibility of an iceberg ahead, but they confidently assure everyone that there's really nothing to worry about. The *Titanic*'s officers and crew have everything under control. And, in any case, the ship is unsinkable.[36]

Technological change is invariably threatening. All of us, government and citizen alike, face the great unknown, which is, and always will be, like stepping into a dark room.

NOTES

1. Gertrude Himmelfarb, "Revolution in the Library," *The Key Reporter* 62: 2–3 (Spring 1997).

2. "Cloudy Days in Tomorrowland," *Newsweek,* January 27, 1997, p. 86.

3. Adrian V. Stokes, *Concise Encyclopedia of Information Technology,* 2d ed. (Brookfield, VT: Gower, 1985), pp. 9–10.

4. Bernard Aboda, *The Online User's Encyclopedia* (New York: Addison-Wesley, 1993), pp. 527–29.

5. Allen C. Benson, *The Complete Internet Companion for Librarians* (New York: Neal-Schuman, 1995), pp. 3–4.

6. John Burke, *Learning the Internet: A Workbook for Beginners* (New York: Neal-Schuman, 1996), p. 2.

7. *AALL Spectrum,* September 1998, p. 14.

8. Marshall McLuhan, *The Gutenberg Galaxy* (Toronto: University of Toronto Press, 1962), pp. 31–32.

9. Paul Resnick, "Filtering Information on the Internet," *Scientific American* 276: 62 (March 1997).

10. David Owen, "Ripoff," *The New Yorker,* February 22/March 1, 1999, p. 76.

11. John Rennie, "Civilizing the Internet," *Scientific American* 276: 6 (March 1997).

12. Norman Oder, "Cataloging the Net: Can We Do It?" *Library Journal,* October 1, 1998, p. 47.

13. Alexander Stille, "Overload," *The New Yorker,* March 18, 1999, pp. 38, 42.

14. Glenn Carroll Strait, "Breaking the Voice Barrier," *World and I* 14: 1–6 (February 1999).

15. Richard Lind et al., "The Network Vehicle—A Glimpse into the Future of Mobile Multi-media," *Automotive Engineering International* 106: S3 (September 1998).

16. Nicholas Negroponte, *Being Digital* (New York: Knopf, 1995), passim.

17. Clifford Stoll, *Silicon Snake Oil: Second Thoughts on the Information Highway* (New York: Doubleday, 1995), pp. 211–12.

18. Ibid., p. 124.

19. *Study to Identify Measures Necessary for a Successful Transition to a More Electronic Federal Depository Library Program* (Washington: Government Printing Office, June 1996), pp. 4–7.

20. Wayne P. Kelley, "Keeping Public Information Public," *Library Journal,* May 15, 1998, p. 1.

21. *Study to Identify Measures,* p. 5.

22. Thomas A. Bourke, "Spaulding and Materazzi Revisited: A Ten Year Retrospect," *Microform Review* 17: 131 (August 1988).

23. Raymond J. Bouley, "The Life and Death of CD-ROM," *CD-ROM Librarian* 7: 10–17 (January 1992).

24. Stille, "Overload," p. 43.

25. Stewart Brand, "Escaping the Digital Dark Age," *Library Journal,* February 1, 1999, p. 46.

26. *Study to Identify Measures,* pp. 21, 22n.

27. Donald S. Lamm, "Life Outside Academe," *The Key Reporter* 60: 6–7 (Summer 1995).

28. Thomas I. Emerson, "Colonial Intentions and Current Realities of the First Amendment," *University of Pennsylvania Law Review* 125: 755, 762 (1977).

29. Joe Morehead, "The Myth of Public Access to Federal Government Information as a Constitutional Right," *The Serials Librarian* 26(2): 1–26 (1995).

30. Hoyer's remarks in the *Congressional Record* (daily edition), May 22, 1997, pp. E1045–46, republished in *Administrative Notes* 18: 14 (June 15, 1997).

31. *Study to Identify Measures,* pp. 5, 27–28.

32. Kelley, "Keeping Public Information Public," p. 37.

33. *Newsweek,* December 30/January 6, 1997, pp. 52–53.

34. Brand, "Escaping the Digital Dark Age," p. 48.

35. Barbara Ceizler Silver, "Coverage from Culture to Cloning," *Library Journal,* May 15, 1998, p. 48.

36. Brand, "Escaping the Digital Dark Age," p. 48.

CHAPTER TWO

GOVERNMENT PRINTING OFFICE PROGRAMS AND SERVICES

If you stand on Capitol Hill, at the top of the high flight of stairs leading into the Senate, and look straight north, you will see the Government Printing Office. It is in dreary contrast to the pure whiteness of the Capitol. A long rectangle of sooty brick, domineered by a scorched cupola, from whose apparent ashes rises the Phoenix of a gilt eagle. . . . The near exterior view is no better than the remote one. A huge factory of red brick, about 350 feet long, with the gables and one side facing separate streets, and the other side fenced up to enclose boiler houses, paper storehouses, wagon-sheds, wastepaper barracks, and an accessory wing for stereotyping and for a machine shop—this is all that a passing pedestrian knows of the GPO.

—John B. Ellis, *Sights and Secrets of the National Capital* (New York: U.S. Publishing Company, 1869)

A BRIEF HISTORY OF THE GOVERNMENT PRINTING OFFICE

The Printing Act of June 23, 1860 (12 Stat. 118) provided for the establishment of the Government Printing Office (GPO), which opened for business March 4, 1861, the same day Abraham Lincoln was inaugurated as the sixteenth president of the United States. It was located, as it is today, at the corner of H Street North and North Capitol Street, a stone's throw from the Capitol itself. In the mid-nineteenth century, the area around the building was known as Swampoodle. "H Street to the east was only on a map, with grading to the turnpike gate at Bladensburg Road completed in 1983. . . . H Street to the west had been graded and graveled to New Jersey Avenue in 1857. There may have been some form of transportation for GPO workers, but the H Street horse-cars did not run until 9 years later." The GPO "began its public printing career in relative obscurity." There was the "feverish excitement of Lincoln's inauguration and the imminence of civil war. . . . On April 12, Fort Sumter was fired upon."[1]

The establishment of the Government Printing Office followed several decades of unsatisfactory work by contract printers, who had been selected each Congress (or session) by both houses, a system acknowledged as failing to perform the job adequately. During this period, the commercial printers were typically newspaper publishers who had printing plants with enough capacity to handle the extra congressional work. In 1818, a congressional committee recommended the creation of a government printing agency, in order "to produce promptitude, uniformity, accuracy and elegance in the execution of public printing [for] the work of Congress . . . and that of the various departments." The current system of low bidder, the committee reported, created delays and a product "executed in such an inelegant and incorrect manner, as must bring disgrace and ridicule on the literature, and the press of our country."[2] But nothing came of the proposal, and more than forty years would pass before the federal government established its own public printer.

Despite a number of acts that Congress passed during the first half of the nineteenth century in an attempt to bring some integrity into the commercial printing of government documents, the modus operandi was increasingly beset with corruption and patronage. Profiteering, waste, and inefficiency flourished until the act of 1860 brought relief from the spoils system. The legislation created a Superintendent of Public Printing to manage the official printing and binding "authorized by the Senate and House of Representatives, the executive and judicial departments, and the Court of Claims." The officers of this new entity were enjoined not to "have any interest, direct or indirect, in the publication of any newspaper or periodical" or other binding, engraving, or procurement activities that would suggest a conflict of interest. If the new Superintendent were to "corruptly collude" with private publishers, a fine and penitentiary sentence awaited him.[3]

When the GPO was created, the Congress was the entity that generated most government publications. Executive branch work was used primarily as a filler when Congress was not in session. A General Accounting Office (GAO) study determined that, in 1861, GPO produced $510,000 worth of printing, of which only $40,000 was for the executive branch.[4] The agencies of the executive branch have since far outstripped the legislative branch in the number of publications issued. By the late 1980s, executive branch workload exceeded that of Congress by a 6 to 1 ratio, that of the judiciary by a 300 to 1 ratio. These figures do not include a large (and unknown) amount of "non-GPO" publications produced by the executive branch in over 200 field printing plants and a large number of duplicating facilities.[5]

THE GPO TODAY

The Government Printing Office is an agency of the Congress. Congressional work is performed in GPO's central office plant in Washington to provide Congress with immediate service by working jointly with a number of leadership offices, committees, and individual members and their staffs in both chambers to ensure that congressional documents are delivered in a timely manner for the effective conduct of legislative business. GPO also produces in-house executive branch work for the creation of core government documents such as the *Federal Register, Code of Federal Regulations,* and the *Budget of the United States Government* in its various editions. The GPO works in concert with the Small Business Administration to ensure the viability of contractual arrangements with commercial printers, a majority of whom are categorized as "small businesses." More than 70 percent of GPO printing and binding revenue covers reproduction services procured from commercial firms throughout the country. GPO competitively buys printing products and services from more than 10,000 private sector firms, and this activity is justified as good fiscal policy and good politics.[6] Moreover, the office is responsible for the dissemination of publications under international exchange agreements and the distribution of documents to recipients designated by law.

The head of the GPO is the Public Printer of the United States, an appointive position that requires Senate approval. The Congressional Joint Committee on Printing (JCP) acts as a Board of Directors of the GPO and derives its authority from the provisions of Title 44 of the United States Code. An organization chart of the Government Printing Office is published in each annual edition of the *United States Government Manual* (see chapter 6).

Fiscal Year Appropriations

For fiscal year (FY) 2000 (the federal fiscal year runs from October 1 to September 30), the Public Printer requested a total of $128,459,000, which included more than $82 million for the congressional printing and binding appropriation and slightly over $31 million for the Office of Superintendent of Documents. The $82 million includes everything from the publication of the quotidian *Congressional Record* ($22.1 million), which is produced overnight, to envelopes and franks, privileges accorded members of Congress to mail materials free of charge ($1.1 million).[7] Paying homage to their seigneurs, the members of Congress, is an annual ritual as the Public Printer, usually accompanied by the Superintendent of Documents, goes hat in hand before the House and Senate subcommittees on legislative appropriations to defend his budgetary requests for the upcoming fiscal year. The published hearings containing this testimony provide the best single source of information about the activities and plans of the GPO, and this testimony is available in print and online from several commercial and governmental sources (see chapter 5).

Computer-to-Plate Technology

Since 1998, the GPO has been gradually acquiring state-of-the-art computer-to-plate (CTP) technology, which makes it possible to send electronic text and image files directly to automated platemaking devices, eliminating the need for film negatives and the additional labor-intensive manual process of stripping and imposing those negatives onto goldenrod for conventional platemaking. As a result, GPO is able to deliver the same volume of quality print products to Congress, the executive branch departments and agencies, and the public at a significantly reduced labor cost. Moreover, by reducing the disposal or recycling of film and associated processing chemicals, CTP technology reduces environmental hazards.[8] The GPO has come a long way from the early days of the agency's existence when "gaslight etched the faces of a rank of printers as they plucked leaden characters, one by one, from a wooden case."[9]

GPO is required by law to recover its printing costs. 44 U.S.C. § 309 directs that GPO's revolving fund for departmental printing "shall be reimbursed for the cost of all services and supplies furnished . . . at rates which include charges for overhead and related expenses." In addition, 44 U.S.C. § 310 requires an ordering agency to pay GPO, upon its written request, all or part of the estimated or actual cost of the delivered work and for GPO to adjust its billing on the basis of actual cost when a customer pays for delivered work in advance.[10] Since 1965, GPO's Denver Field Printing Plant has been equipped and staffed to handle classified printing needs. Documents up to and including those at the level of "Secret" are produced at this facility. While GPO is a highly versatile printing establishment, it does not print money, bonds, or postage stamps. That work is done at the Bureau of Engraving and Printing, an agency within the Department of the Treasury. However, GPO does produce more than 7 million passports and nearly 300 million postal cards each year.[11] Regional printing procurement offices are located in several cities, including New York, Boston, Chicago, Dallas, and Atlanta.

GPO Access

GPO's official entry into electronic publishing was effected by passage, on June 8, 1993, of the Government Printing Office Electronic Information Access Enhancement Act of 1993 (PL 103-40; 107 Stat. 112; 44 U.S.C. § 4101 et seq.). Pursuant to Senate Bill 564, the legislation requires the GPO to disseminate government information products online. The Act is the basis of GPO Access, the agency's Internet information service. From modest beginnings in June 1994, the number of databases freely available to the public from GPO's Home Page (**http://www.access.gpo.gov**) has blossomed to more than seventy representing the three branches, a growing number of agency Government Information Locator Service (GILS) sites, partnerships with some depository libraries to enhance the capabilities of GPO Access, and links to a myriad of other federal government resources on the Web. These databases and others are discussed in detail in chapters 4 through 12 of this text. A direct link to the home page of GPO Access itself is **http://www.access.gpo.gov/su_docs/index.html**.

GPO has been rewarded for its achievement. In 1998 GPO Access was named one of the "Best Feds on the Web" by *Government Executive* magazine. The GPO site was one of only fifteen federal Web sites to be thus honored and the only Web site in the legislative branch to be selected. Earlier kudos include a 1994 Technology Leadership Award and the 1995 James Madison Award. In 1997, GPO Access and the Commerce Department jointly earned a Hammer Award from the Vice-President's National Performance Review for creating an electronic version of *Commerce Business Daily* called CBDNet. Usage also reflects the general public's interest. Since 1994 the public has downloaded from approximately 2 million documents per month to more than 10.5 million per month. For example, in 1997, "first-day GPO Access hits for the budget totaled 10,149. [In 1998] hits for the budget jumped to 64,428, an increase of 535 percent."[12]

A good example of the ingenuity of GPO Access is its "Core Documents of U.S. Democracy" page. The full text of publications in this ongoing series represents titles that, according to the site, are "vital to the democratic process and critical to an informed electorate. They support the public's right to know about the essential activities of their Government." Of interest to students of our heritage are publications such as the predecessors to the *Congressional Record, Maclay's Journal* (see chapter 5) and the *Federalist Papers.* The other titles link to the GPO Access home page offerings, such as the *United States Code,* Supreme Court decisions, the *Federal Register,* and the *Code of Federal Regulations.* This set can be visited through GPO Access or directly at **http://www.access.gpo.gov/su_docs/dpos/coredocs.html**.

Another example of GPO's public awareness attitude is the GPO News Releases series, the provenance of the agency's Office of Congressional, Legislative and Public Affairs. In 1998 these news releases were made available at **http://www.access.gpo.gov/aboutgpo/index.html**.

All is not sweetness and light, however. In 1998 testimony before the Senate Rules and Administration Committee, a key General Accounting Office official said that "based on the management audit Booz-Allen & Hamilton [a prestigious private-sector consulting firm] conducted in collaboration with [GAO], we believe that GPO has significant and persistent management problems, beginning with the lack of a clearly-defined strategic mission and plan for achieving it."[13] The report, titled "Management Audit of the Government Printing Office" (May 21, 1998), contained ninety-five recommendations for action affecting seven GPO areas. The Public Printer assured the House subcommittee on Legislative Appropriations for Fiscal Year 2000 that the GPO "will take action to address them as it deems necessary."[14]

Government Information Locator Service

The Government Information Locator Service (GILS) is a method of identifying, locating, and describing publicly available federal information resources, including electronic information resources. It can be accessed from the GPO home page or directly (**http://www.access.gpo.gov/su_docs/gils**). Because this collection is decentralized, the GPO provides a single point of entry to access, or link to, all federal GILS databases. The ways in which GILS can be accessed include (1) "Browse GILS Records by Agency," which furnishes the text of publications such as the *Budget of the United States Government* or committee prints issued by the House Ways and Means Committee; (2) "Browse Pathway GILS Records," designed to help depository libraries (chapter 3) and their clientele locate and access relevant information from departments and major independent agencies; and (3) "Browse

Pointer GILS Records," which consists of a list of departments and independent agencies that have mounted their GILS records on a server other than GPO Access, describing their holdings and containing links to these holdings.

THE OFFICE OF SUPERINTENDENT OF DOCUMENTS

The position of Superintendent of Documents (SuDocs or SOD) was established in the Department of the Interior by an act of March 3, 1869 (15 Stat. 292), with the responsibility of distributing public documents to depository libraries and to other institutions and officials authorized by law. The position was transferred to the GPO and renamed Superintendent of Documents by the Printing Act of 1895, which also expanded the Superintendent's responsibilities to include bibliographic control and sale of government publications. Sections 62 and 64 of the act required the preparation of three catalogs: a "comprehensive index of public documents," a "consolidated index of Congressional documents," and a "catalog of Government publications . . . which shall show the documents printed during the preceding month, where obtainable and the price thereof." The comprehensive index became the renowned *Document Catalog* (1893–1940). The consolidated index became the *Document Index* (1895–1933) and the *Numerical Lists and Schedule of Volumes* (1933–1980). The last became the *Monthly Catalog of United States Government Publications,* which in 1947 was declared by the Joint Committee on Printing to satisfy the statutory requirements of the comprehensive index. More detail on these seminal sources is provided in chapters 4 and 5.

Structure and Functions of the SuDocs Office

Within the GPO, the Office of Superintendent of Documents comprises six departments: documents sales service, information dissemination policy, office of electronic information dissemination, office of marketing, technical support group, and library programs service (LPS). This last consists of two major components: the Library Division and the Depository Distribution Division. In turn, the Library Division has subdivisions that manage cataloging, depository services, and depository administration; the last two are further discussed in chapter 3. Like any other bureaucracy, the GPO and the Office of Superintendent of Documents occasionally tinker with their internal organization, ever hoping that changes in its structure will effect greater operational success.

The major programs of the office include GPO Access; sales; cataloging and indexing of government materials; mailing of certain government publications for Congress and executive branch entities according to specific provisions of law ("by law") or on a reimbursable basis; the Federal Depository Library Program (FDLP, discussed in chapter 3); and the International Exchange Program. Under this last activity, pursuant to international compacts and codified at 44 U.S.C. § 1719, federal government publications are distributed to foreign libraries in exchange for copies of official publications of other nations, which are shipped to the Library of Congress. The FY 2000 budget estimated requirements for running these programs came to about $31.2 million, a minuscule sum in a federal budget that exceeds $1.7 trillion. Of this sum, the lion's share, $26.8 million, was earmarked for the FDLP. The cataloging and indexing operation cost $3.3 million, the by-law distribution, $0.6 million, and the international exchange activity, $0.5 million.[15]

The Sales Program

Operated by the Documents Sales Service (DSS), the inventory of the sales program consists of more than 12,000 products offered in a variety of formats: Print continues to predominate, but CD-ROM, magnetic tape, microfiche, and videos are also sales items. There has been a "gradual decline in traditional printed products as more Federal agencies place their products on their Web sites or publish in other electronic formats." Still, in FY 1998, the sales program "handled more than 653,000 orders and sold over 11 million copies of publications."[16] GPO is authorized to provide dissemination services at the least cost to the government. Prices are governed by 44 U.S.C. § 1708, a formula based on recovering only the incremental costs for reproducing and disseminating a product plus a legislated 50 percent surcharge. In addition, designated book dealers and educational institution bookstores are authorized to receive a 25 percent discount on the domestic price of a product when delivered to the dealer's normal place of business. No discount is allowed if the item is shipped to a third party, unless the quantity shipped for a single title equals 100 or more copies. These products are sold through a mail-order operation distributed from facilities in Laurel, Maryland, and Pueblo, Colorado; through some dozen consigned sales agents from other federal agencies; and in U.S. Government Bookstores.

The easiest way to purchase sales publications is to open a Deposit Account, which is a prepaid account with the SuDocs for customers, individual or institutional, who have a continuing interest in obtaining sales products. To open an account, submit a written request along with a minimum deposit of $50 by check, UNESCO coupons, or money order payable to the Superintendent of Documents, or by credit card (VISA, MasterCard, or Discover/NOVUS). You can mail or fax your request to the Superintendent of Documents, Deposit Accounts Section, Stop SSOR, Washington, DC 20402.

GPO Bookstores

The first federal government bookstore was opened in the GPO mail building in 1921. The first out-of-town bookstore opened in Chicago in 1967. Currently, twenty-four GPO bookstores are located in federal buildings, commercial office buildings, and even in shopping centers. A list of GPO Bookstores with addresses, phone, and fax numbers is found in sources such as The Subject Bibliography (SB) series, *U.S. Government Subscriptions,* the *Monthly Catalog* (see chapter 4), and online via GPO Access. This last can be accessed from the GPO home page by clicking on "GPO Sales" and "Locations of U.S. Government Bookstores." Each bookstore carries a selection of at least 1,500 of the most popular titles in print and electronic formats, including subscriptions to periodicals. Some of the bookstores have a street map for locating purposes. Figure 2.1, page 24, shows a printout from the Web page of the location of the bookstore at 26 Federal Plaza, New York City.

Current Awareness Sources

Several catalogs in print and on the Internet are the provenance of the Office of Superintendent of Documents. Although they are designed primarily to support the sales program, they can be used for acquisitions and reference or access services. It should be remembered that these sources list only those government materials available for sale through the Superintendent. Moreover, all the sales publications noted below have been assigned SuDocs classification numbers, and these symbols are published in the semiannual *List of Classes of United States Government Publications Available for Selection by Depository Libraries* (known by its short title *List of Classes*), which is in paper copy and on GPO Access. Also keep in mind that the GPO has assigned different titles to virtually the same sources published in print and on its Web site links. Print titles and their schedules are described below.

Figure 2.1. U.S. Government Bookstore, New York, New York.

Room 2-120, Federal Building
26 Federal Plaza
New York, NY 10278
      Hours: 8:15 a.m.-4:15 p.m., Monday through Friday,
          except Federal holidays
Phone: (212) 264-3825   Fax: (212) 264-9318

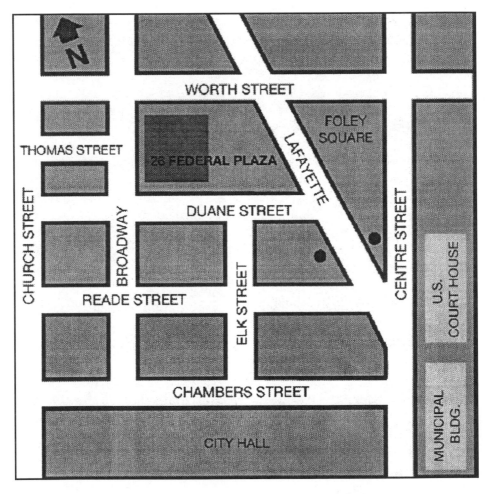

**http://www.access.gpo.gov/su_docs/sale/
abkst017.html**

United States Government Information

Subtitled "Publications, Periodicals, Electronic Products," this semi-annual periodical, formerly known as *U.S. Government Books* when it was published quarterly, contains patriotic (red, white, and blue) pages with annotations and ordering information. If you do not order at least one document from a current issue of *United States Government Information,* do not expect to see another catalog in the mail without re-subscribing all over again. But even depository libraries, which should receive this publication regularly (GP 3.17/5; • 556-A), experience a time lag between issues.

New Products from the U.S. Government

Subtitled "Publications, Periodicals and Electronic Information for Sale," this bimonthly is sometimes issued irregularly. Unlike its colorful cousin, *New Products* is a bland, black-and-white list organized by broad subjects (Agriculture, Business & Labor, and so forth) and then al-phabetically by title within each category. This too is a depository item, is free to customers, and is on GPO Access.

U.S. Government Subscriptions

A quarterly, this publication was once known as *Price List 36.* It lists dated periodicals, irregular issuances, and basic manuals with amendments, entries for which are marked by a bullet or black dot. Most entries are annotated and provide periodicity, price, Stock Keeping Unit, SuDocs class stem, and domestic and foreign subscription prices. Figure 2.2, page 26, shows a page from *U.S. Government Subscriptions.*

Consumer Information Catalog

The quarterly *Consumer Information Catalog* (CIC) consists of more than 200 free and low-cost federal publications of interest to con-sumers. Organized by broad subjects (cars, children, housing, money, travel, and so forth), ordering information is located in the back of the brochures. The CIC emanates from the Consumer Information Center, Pueblo, Colorado, which GPO manages for the General Services Ad-ministration (**www.pueblo.gsa.gov**). Figure 2.3, page 27, shows a typical page from an issue of the *Consumer Information Catalog.*

Figure 2.2. Page from *U.S. Government Subscriptions.*

●REPRESENTATION PROCEEDINGS CASE
HANDLING MANUAL.   LIST ID RCHM
Discusses representation case handling procedures and
provides procedural and operational guidance for the
General Counsel's staff with processing representation
cases filed under the Federal Service Labor Management
Relations Statute, pursuant to Section 7104(F).

Subscription-$70.00
S/N 963-001-00000-2   File Code 1S

Foreign Subscription-$87.50

Subscription service consists of a basic manual and
supplementary material for an indeterminate period.
In looseleaf form, punched for 3-ring binder.

●REPRESENTATION PROCEEDINGS HEARING
OFFICER'S GUIDE.   LIST ID RHOG
Designed to be used in conjunction with the
Representation Proceedings Case Handling Manual and
describes techniques of conducting hearings and
developing a complete record. The Substantive and
Employee Category sections are also useful in defining,
narrowing and resolving issues raised by petitions at any
stage prior to hearings.

Subscription-$67.00
S/N 963-002-00000-9 File Code 1S

Foreign Subscription-$83.75

Subscription service consists of a basic manual
and supplementary material for an indeterminate
period. In looseleaf form, punched for 3-ring
binder.

RESOURCES IN EDUCATION.   LIST ID RIE
Sponsored by the United States Department of Education,
Office of Educational Research and Improvement,
Educational Resources Information Center (ERIC).
Provides up-to-date information about educational research
sponsored by the Bureau of Research, Office of Education.
Designed to keep teachers, administrators, research
specialists, the public, and others in the educational
community informed about the latest significant findings
from educational research.

Subscription-$78.00/year; $27.00/copy (12 back issues)

Monthly   S/N 765-003-00000-8   File Code 2M
SuDocs Class Stem ED 1.310:

Foreign Subscription-$97.50/year; $33.75/copy (12 back
issues)

RURAL COOPERATIVES.   LIST ID NFC
Composed of articles on the news, views and research
relating to the cooperative sector.

Subscription-$11.00/year; $3.00/copy (3 back issues)
Bimonthly S/N 701-020-00000-6 File Code 2M
SuDocs Class Stem A 109.11:

Foreign Subscription-$13.75/year; $3.75/copy (3 back
issues)

RURAL DEVELOPMENT PERSPECTIVES.
LIST ID RDP
Covers factors influencing rural development, and
persistent and emerging problems.

Subscription-$7.50/year; $4.25/copy (2 back issues)
Triannually S/N 701-031-00000-8   File Code 2B
SuDocs Class Stem A 93.41/2:

Foreign Subscription-$9.40/year; $5.31/copy (2 back
issues)

Subscription service will be accepted for one or two
years.

SAMHSA NEWS.   LIST ID ADAN
Contains articles on agency-related issues, such as AIDS,
alcoholism, drug abuse, and mental health, and events of
the Substance Abuse and Mental Health Services
Administration.

Subscription-$8.50/year; $2.25/copy (2 back issues)
Quarterly S/N 717-002-00000-8 File Code 2E
SuDocs Class Stem HE 20.8026:

Foreign Subscription-$10.65/year; $2.81/copy (2 back
issues)

Figure 2.3. Page from *Consumer Information Catalog*.

Occupational Outlook Quarterly. Reviews new occupations, salaries, job trends, and much more. 1 year subscription, 4 issues. (DOL) **250F. $8.00.**

Resumes, Application Forms, Cover Letters, and Interviews. Tips on tailoring your resume for specific jobs and sample interview questions. 8 pp. (1987. DOL) **106F. $1.25.**

Sales Occupations. If you're interested in going into sales, this guide will help. It offers information on different types of sales positions and gives details on each specific position. 21 pp. (1998. DOL) **107F. $2.25.**

Tips for Finding the Right Job. Learn how to assess your skills and interests, prepare a resume, write cover letters, and interview for a job. 28 pp. (1996. DOL) **108F. $1.75.**

Tomorrow's Jobs. Discusses changes and trends in the economy, labor force, occupational growth, education and training requirements, and much more. 18 pp. (1998. DOL) **109F. $2.25.**

- *Also read "The Job Outlook In Brief, 1996-2006" on the previous page for more helpful career info.*

What You Should Know About Your Pension Rights. Explains your rights, benefits, payment schedules, protections, and more. 48 pp. (1995. DOL) **321F. 50¢.**

Your Guaranteed Pension. Answers 19 frequently asked questions about the security of private pension plans, including benefits and plan termination. 11 pp. (1998. PBGC) **519F. Free.**

FEDERAL PROGRAMS

The Americans with Disabilities Act: Questions and Answers. Explains how the civil rights of persons with disabilities are protected at work and in public places. 32 pp. (1996. DOJ) **520F. Free.**

Are There Any Public Lands for Sale? Describes the federal program to sell excess undeveloped public land and why there is no more available for homesteading. 12 pp. (1997. DOI) **110F. $1.00.**

Federal Information Center. Lists where to call when you have a question about the federal government. 1 pp. (1998. GSA) **521F. Free.**

A Guide to Disability Rights Laws. Describes your rights regarding fair housing, public accommodations, telecommunications, education, and employment. 14 pp. (1996. DOJ) **522F. Free.**

Guide to Federal Government Sales. Learn more about how to buy homes, cars and other property from 17 federal sales programs. 19 pp. (1998. GSA) **111F. $2.00.**

How You Can Buy Used Federal Personal Property. Describes used equipment and industrial items sold by the government, how they are sold, and where to call for more information. 5 pp. (1998. GSA) **322F. 50¢.**

National Sellers List. The government sells real estate and personal property that has been forfeited to federal law enforcement agencies. Here's a list of dealers who sell items, their addresses and phone numbers. 8 pp. (1998. DOJ) **323F. 50¢.**

U.S. Real Property Sales List. Lists government real estate properties for sale that are sold by auction or sealed bid. Tells how to get more information on specific properties. 5 pp. (Bimonthly. GSA) **523F. Free.**

Your Right to Federal Records. Use the Freedom of Information Act (FOIA) and the Privacy Act to obtain records from the federal government. Answers questions and has a sample request letter. 26 pp. (1996. DOJ/GSA) **324F. 50¢.**

Your Social Security Number. Explains why we have social security numbers, when and how to get one, and how to protect its privacy. 2 pp. (1996. SSA) **524F. Free.**

Benefits

Basic Facts on Social Security. Explains the different kinds of Social Security benefits, who receives them, and how they're financed. 17 pp. (1998. SSA) **525F. Free.**

Federal Benefits for Veterans and Dependents. Explains disability compensation, pension, health care, education and housing loans, and other benefit programs for veterans and their families. 95 pp. (1998. VA) **112F. $3.75.**

Subject Bibliographies (SB) Series

Issued irregularly as a numbered series, the Subject Bibliographies are arranged by topic, series, or agency. While the *Sales Product Catalog* (below) covers the more than 12,000 different products available for sale, these publications are listed in more than 150 free subject catalogs. The first of these individual pamphlets, titled *Home Gardening of Fruits and Vegetables,* was issued in 1975, replacing a series of "Price Lists" on various subjects, all of which were discontinued except *Price List 36* (Periodicals), which became *U.S. Government Subscriptions.* Many entries are annotated and updated when prices change or new products are created. There is a Subject Bibliography Index, which lists the titles and numbers of the individual bibliographies alphabetically. Figure 2.4 shows a page from Subject Bibliography 314, *Electronic Information Products.*

The Internet Sales Connection

All of the current awareness catalogs listed above are available on, or linked to, the GPO's Web site. One category missing from the list above is arguably the most useful of the online services and is accessible only via GPO Access.

Sales Product Catalog

The predecessor to the *Sales Product Catalog* (SPC) was the *Publications Reference File* (PRF), a microfiche catalog of all publications currently in stock for sale by the SuDocs, which was also made available to depository libraries in a bimonthly fiche edition with monthly supplements and a biweekly magnetic tape service. This series was in effect from 1976 until 1997, when it was replaced by the SPC and made available online via GPO Access. The SPC is updated daily and contains all the information previously found on the PRF. Entries have a six-digit Stock Keeping Unit (SKU) number, replacing the old twelve-digit Stock Number for ordering accuracy. In addition to SKUs, each SPC entry can be accessed by International Standard Book Numbers (ISBN); SuDocs classification numbers; and alphabetically by authors, subjects, titles, agency series and report numbers, and keywords and phrases. The SPC also includes citations to forthcoming government information products as well as to titles that have recently been superseded or have gone out of print. The origin of this major change is an Integrated Processing

System (IPS), developed over many years, which replaces "mainframe legacy systems dating back to 1970, with off-the-shelf, but significantly modified, integrated software."[17]

Figure 2.4. Page from *Electronic Information Products*.

Page 10   ELECTRONIC INFORMATION PRODUCTS

	Stock Number	Price
Joint Electronic Library, Volume 3, Number 1, May 1995: Approved Joint Publications; Selected Service Publications; Research Papers. CD-ROM. 1995. Includes: Joint Publications; Selected Service Publications; Terminology; Military Indexes; Military Related Papers, Articles and Studies; and Users Information. Software: re:Search. System requirements: IBM compatible 286 PC; EGA for image viewing; laser printer for image printing.	008-000-00665-2	$15.00
Licensed Operating Reactors (NUREG-0020) on Diskette. SUBSCRIPTION. LIST ID LOR95. Issued monthly. Provides data on the operation of nuclear units. Contains highlights and statistics for commercial operating units, detailed information on each unit and an appendix for miscellaneous information such as spent fuel storage capabilities. Software: Report Generator. File Format: dBase. Available on one 3.5 inch low density diskette. Subscription price: Domestic - $73.00 a year (first-class); Foreign - $91.25 a year. Single copy price: Domestic - $14.00 a copy; Foreign - $17.50 a copy. File Code 1F.	752-039-00000-3	73.00
Longitudinal Study of Aging, 1984-1990, Number 1. CD-ROM. 1993. Contains three files: Longitudinal Study of Aging (LSOA) Interview and National Death Index Data; Medicare Hospital Record, Part A; and Other Medicare Use Record, Parts A and B. Software: SETS (Statistical Export and Tabulation System) Version 2.1. System requirements: IBM compatible 286 PC; 640K RAM; 7 MB free hard disk space; MS-DOS 3.1; Microsoft CD-ROM extensions, version 2.0; CD-ROM reader.	017-022-01230-8	16.00
National Biennial RCRA Hazardous Waste Report, 1991: List of Large Quantity Generators. DISKETTE. 1994. Contains a list of large quantity generators of hazardous waste, as identified by EPA's Biennial Report. The Biennial Report is a census of hazardous waste generators and managers that are regulated by the Resource Conservation and Recovery Act (RCRA). List includes 24,426 large quantity generators. Software: WordPerfect 5.2. System requirements: IBM compatible PC; 3 MB free hard disk space. 3.5 inch computer diskette.	055-000-00480-3	15.00
National Criminal Justice Reference Service Document Data Base. CD-ROM. 1994. Contains bibliographic information on over 130,000 items for the period 1972-1994. Software: CD-Answer. System requirements: For DOS: IBM compatible PC; 512K memory; DOS 3.0; CD-ROM drive. For Windows: IBM compatible PC; 2 MB RAM; 20 MB hard drive; VGA monitor, Microsoft Windows 3.1; Microsoft CD extensions; CD-ROM drive.	027-000-01361-9	28.00

Other Online Sales Products

From the GPO home page, click the icon "Online Bookstore" and you come to several headings, each of which can be searched for various products. For example, you can both search and order titles from the SPC. "New Product Announcements" takes you to a page titled "New Products and Services Announcements," which provides access to selected Superintendent of Documents sales product releases, such as the federal budget, GPO "best sellers" by month and for the federal fiscal year, tax products on CD-ROM, and a host of other salient documents. A heading "Government Information Products for Sale by Topic" is roughly the equivalent of the semiannual *United States Government Information.* That site links to Subject Bibliographies, and the online Subject Bibliography Index ("Publications by Topic") is a more detailed version of the tangible Subject Bibliographies (SB) series. "Catalog of Available Subscriptions" morphs into "Subscriptions by Topic and Agency," an online version of *U.S. Government Subscriptions.* "The Consumer Information Center (Pueblo, CO)" transports you to the *Consumer Information Catalog,* which has a number of navigational buttons, including browsing or searching by specific subject. "Locations of U.S. Government Bookstores," noted above, improves in specificity on the information found in the several print products.

As best I can tell, two sites have no tangible edition. "CD-ROMs Available for Purchase" takes you to a site named "CD-ROM Titles Available from the Superintendent of Documents," which lists more than 100 titles alphabetically with ordering information. "United States Fax Watch" sends you to a page where a listing of documents and instructions on ordering by fax is provided. There are other features on Fax Watch, including information about subscribing to the *Federal Register* and *Code of Federal Regulations,* over 200 subject listings of products, and more. However, United States Fax Watch, which was initiated in March 1995, is a promotional information service that does not accept orders for sales items or provide the texts of government publications.

All this means that you can sit at your computer and view and/or order any SuDocs in-print publication in various formats depending on your needs. The one negative, in my judgment, is having to learn two different titles for essentially the same information, a tangible item and its online twin. One must be constantly aware that agencies make continual changes in the organization and esthetics of their home pages and their internal pages; GPO is no exception to this tinkering and has changed the wording and structure of its home page and subsidiary pages more than once. URLs change also, of course; as of early 1999 the address for the above "Online Bookstore" categories was **http://www.access.gpo.gov/su_docs/sale.html**.

CATALOGING ISSUES AND ACTIVITIES

Cataloging procedures have been affected no less by electronic formats, especially the Internet, than other policies that are part of the responsibility of the SuDocs office. Because policy and practice in every aspect of government information evolve as GPO, the documents library community, and users adapt to the electronic information environment, any issue or activity stated here is, of course, subject to change and revision. And while traditional cataloging is necessary to the numerous print, microfiche, and CD-ROM publications, the various technologies for maintaining effective Web addresses related to *Monthly Catalog* records loom ever more significant as the migration of government information to the Internet continues apace. In addition, a commercial firm, Marcive (San Antonio, Texas), offers GPO records for online catalogs, a Shipping List Service through which subscribers receive laser-printed labels, Marcive Web DOCS, and other enhanced search features.

If I may mix arachnoid and canine metaphors, the Web is the tail that wags the GPO dog. The following discussion is excerpted and paraphrased from articles in the literature and official statements in *Administrative Notes,* the monthly newsletter issued by the Library Programs Service in print and on the Web (**http://www.access. gpo.gov/su_docs/dpos/adnotes.html**). For those who love acronyms, the following account is like Godiva chocolate to a sweet tooth.

Cataloging Electronic Titles

The Cataloging Branch of the Library Programs Service follows Cooperative ONline SERials (CONSER) guidelines, endorsed by the ALA/GODORT Cataloging Committee, that allows LPS to update tangible product records to indicate that an electronic version is also available. LPS also uses the existing bibliographic record to tie the tangible and electronic products together. Cataloging procedures are summarized in this *Administrative Notes* account:

- LPS applies CONSER and ALA/GODORT (American Library Association/Government Documents Round Table) approved policies for choosing a "single record" option and applies ALA/GODORT approved collection level records policies, as appropriate, because they provide reasonable access to electronic products in a manner that is consistent with available personnel. LPS does not have sufficient personnel to produce original cataloging records for each format that may be associated with a particular title.

- When electronic products are cataloged as physical forms (paper, microfiche, CD-ROMs, etc.) before they become available electronically, LPS upgrades existing bibliographic records by adding an electronic note (often, "Also available via the Internet" in the 530 field) and, where appropriate, a PURL (Persistent Uniform Resource Locator) to the 856 field for linked electronic access. More about PURLs below.

- When no suitable record for a physical format version of an electronic product is available for upgrading, LPS produces an "electronic only" record as the means of providing access. In some instances, records representing works that existed only in electronic form and were cataloged initially as "electronic only" are upgraded by the addition of physical description data to reflect subsequent publishing of paper and other editions. Thus, a record for a work cataloged as "electronic only" may itself be upgraded to reflect the availability of later physical form editions.

- Multiple titles of works related by subjects that appear at "dynamic Web sites" (characterized by the addition or deletion of titles and/or URLs generated "on the fly" as a result of a user's search) are often represented by "collection level" records. This policy is consistent with *AACR2* (*Anglo-American Cataloging Rules*, 2d edition, rev.), and its use was authorized by the ALA GODORT Cataloging Committee. This policy was initiated in 1998 and provides users with reasonable access to works, through OPACs (Online Public Access Catalogs), as they are actually accessible at agency Web sites.[18]

CONSER, OCLC, and PURLs

CONSER advocates the use of the 856 field of OCLC (Online Computer Library Center) to provide direct access to electronic works. The hot-linked 856 field saves users the trouble of producing a print-out or copying an address and then typing an address into a browser. Approval of this policy, and CONSER's "single record" option (above), are supportive of LPS Internet-related cataloging operations. However, these policies alone are insufficient to provide cost-effective electronic access to the Internet, so OCLC's free Persistent Uniform Resource Locators (PURLs) software furnishes institutions with a seamless redirect function in which users click on a PURL in the 856 field of a bibliographic record and are routed through a server that connects the PURL to the most active URL at a Web site or archive. Moreover, PURLs servers are easier to maintain than frequently changing URLs (Uniform Resource Locators) in bibliographic records.

With this instrument, librarians need not change URL addresses in GPO-produced records within their local OPACs. The PURL system is not perfect, however. For one thing, it is labor-intensive, requiring additional LPS personnel. In the future it is hoped that improvements in PURL software will make it easier to provide improved support for access. For explanations and examples of PURLs, see **http://purl.oclc. org**.

WorldCat

OCLC, a nonprofit computer service and research organization whose network includes more than 30,000 libraries in sixty-five countries and territories, helps libraries locate, acquire, catalog, access, and lend library materials. OCLC FirstSearch is an online reference service that provides searching and subject access to more than seventy databases, including WorldCat, the planet's largest and most comprehensive bibliographic utility. WorldCat is searchable using FirstSearch, EPIC, and other services. On January 1, 1999 OCLC and WLN (Western Library Network) merged. For additional information, visit **http://www. oclc.org/wln**.

GPO joined OCLC in 1976 to streamline production of its new and improved version of the *Monthly Catalog* (MOCAT), the first issue of which was launched July 1976 to coincide with the celebration of the American Bicentennial. Although not as splendid as the clipper ships with their grand, billowing sails gliding proudly into New York harbor, the MOCAT's connection with OCLC has had far-reaching consequences. For decades the GPO used its own system for cataloging publications, involving the use of a locally produced cataloging manual and a locally maintained subject thesaurus. By joining OCLC, GPO was obliged to abandon its old cataloging practices and abide by AACR2 rules and Library of Congress subject headings (LCSH). GPO catalogers were given intensive training in Library of Congress cataloging rules, and in 1980 GPO became a member of CONSER and began cooperating with major libraries in the United States and Canada to maintain an authoritative and current file of serial records on OCLC.

WorldCat can be searched by subject, author, title, accession number, SuDocs classification notation, place (for example, Washington, D.C.), publisher (issuing agency), series/report number, or ISBN/ISSN. Virtually every publication that has been announced in the MOCAT since July 1976 is searchable on WorldCat.

Monthly Catalog on FBB

In late 1998 the *Monthly Catalog of United States Government Publications* (MOCAT) became available on the Federal Bulletin Board (FBB) in the SPCMOCAT directory, with the continuous stream of unedited USMARC records arranged by OCLC number. If you want to download an FTP file of every record created, produced, or updated during that month on OCLC by GPO catalogers, visit the FBB site at **http://fedbbs.access.gpo.gov.** To search for individual records, LPS recommends that you continue to use the MOCAT product in one of its other media: paper, CD-ROM, or the Internet via GPO Access.

The Future of Internet Cataloging

One writer, Dena Holiman Hutto, identifies several areas that require improvements to effect a "cohesive bibliographic control system for government information" in the twenty-first century:

- Revise bibliographic standards; for example, limit or discontinue details such as collation and descriptive notes, Library of Congress Subject Headings (LCSH); load MARC-compatible information into OPACs if full cataloging is not available from government information providers.

- Expand availability of "loadable bibliographic tapes" by keeping current with the products of "Automation vendors [who] are offering innovative services for the growing outsourcing market for copy cataloging."

- Substitute an eight-digit number, such as an ISSN or ISBN, for the SuDocs class notation with its clunky alphanumeric spacing and punctuation, in "linking individual records found in different databases to one another."

- Expand the scope of cataloging; "There is a need for finding aids that can direct users of traditional library collections to the World Wide Web when Internet resources are appropriate."[19]

There is, of course, much more to GPO cataloging than this brief overview; complete LPS cataloging policies are available on the FDLP Administration page at **http://www.access.gpo.gov/dpos/fdlppubs. html**.

SUPERINTENDENT OF DOCUMENTS CLASSIFICATION SYSTEM

The Superintendent of Documents Classification System, known by its short title "SuDocs class system," was developed in the Library of the Government Printing Office between 1895 and 1903, by Ms. Adelaide R. Hasse. Based on the principle of provenance, or issuing agency, the classification is an alphanumeric record whereby the publications of any government entity are grouped under like notation. It is not a subject classification system like the Library of Congress or Dewey decimal systems commonly used in libraries. It is more akin to methods used in archival administration to organize documents in record groups.

Because the scheme is based on the current organizational status (and often the name as well) of an agency, it changes with government reorganization. The result is that printed publications of some issuing agencies are located in as many as eight different places in a segregated collection of federal documents that uses the system. For example, publications of the Children's Bureau, established in 1912, can be found at C 19, L 5, FS 3.200, FS 14.100, HE 21.100, HE 1.450, and HE 23.1200.

A complete SuDocs classification notation consists of three major elements: author symbol, series designation, and book number. The combination of author symbol and series designation (typically found before the colon) is called the class stem. The book number gives the publication its unique classification identification so that no two publications have, or should have, the same book number.

The author symbol consists of a letter or letters and a number. For example, TD 7 designates the Federal Transit Administration, an agency within the Department of Transportation. "Author" is somewhat misleading, as the symbol designates the issuing agency, which may or may not also be the government author. The system does not necessarily show "authorship" in the sense of an individual or corporate body responsible for the intellectual content of a document. Many congressional committee reports and committee prints, for example, are authored by the Congressional Research Service, an agency within the Library of Congress; but they are issued by the committee, and the SuDocs notation is assigned to the publications of that committee. However, when the publication is cataloged under AACR2, the main entry will show Congressional Research Service, or even an individual, as the author. There are, moreover, publications in which the intellectual author and the issuing agency are one and the same.

The series designation follows the author symbol after the period. A number is assigned to each agency series, and this number is followed by a colon. The following numbers are reserved for the most common series issued by government agencies:

.1:   Annual reports

.2:   General publications

.3:   Bulletins

.4:   Circulars

.5:   Laws

.6:   Regulations, rules, and instructions

.7:   Press releases

.8:   Handbooks, manuals, guides

.9:   Bibliographies and lists of publications

.10:   Directories

.11:   Maps and charts

.12:   Posters

.13:   Forms

.14:   Addresses, lectures, etc.

Numbers 1 through 4 were assigned between 1895 and 1903, when the system was established. Numbers 5 through 8 were assigned in the 1950s. And numbers 9 through 14 were designated in 1985. Older classes will deviate from the current practice of using numbers 5 through 8 and 9 through 14. Thus, depending on the date when the publication was cataloged and classified, the form designations either apply or are inapplicable. New titles and series are assigned an arbitrary number if they do not represent any of the form categories above. However, new series that are closely related to existing series may be extended by the use of a shilling mark or slash (also called diagonal, dash, separatrix, forward slant, solidus). A theoretical example that attaches related classes is as follows:

.4:   Circulars

.4/a: Separates from Circulars (numbered)

.4/b: Separates from Circulars (unnumbered)

.4/2: Administrative Circulars

.4/3: Technical Circulars[20]

The system is structured to designate only the first two levels of any agency hierarchy. However, modifications have been made to the scheme to permit designation of agencies at the third and fourth levels, using 100s and 1000s, respectively. For example, D 101 designates the Department of the Army (second level) in the Department of Defense (D 1) and D 103 designates the Army Corps of Engineers (third level) in the Department of the Army. Accordingly, D 103.1:999 is the Annual Report of the Army Corps of Engineers for 1999. An example of the uses of 100s and 1000s is found in the Public Health Service, HE 20 (second level) in the Department of Health and Human Services (HE 1). Publications of the Indian Health Service are assigned an HE 20.302 (third level) notation and publications of the National Institutes of Health (NIH) are designated an HE 20.3000 (fourth level). Within the NIH there are a number of research institutes. Thus the quarterly *Psycho-pharmacology Bulletin* has a class stem of HE 20.8109 and its provenance is the National Institute of Mental Health, a unit within the National Institutes of Health, Public Health Service, Department of Health and Human Services. "Multiples of ten" arrangements are also found in the issuances of several agencies within the Commerce Department (C 1), such as the National Oceanic and Atmospheric Administration (C 55), the National Weather Service (C 55.100), National Marine Fisheries Service (C 55.300), and so forth.

The unique individual book number follows the colon. One-time monographs designated in the "General Publications" forms schedule typically are assigned a number based on the first letter of the keyword in the title followed by the venerable two-figure author table created by

Charles A. Cutter. Thus, *James Madison and the Search for Nation-hood,* issued by the Library of Congress, was designated LC 1.2:M 26. Periodicals are identified by issue number, volume and issue number, or season and year, as the case may be. Most government publications are serials (periodicals, annuals, and so forth); therefore, various combinations of numbers and/or letters following the colon serve to identify the uniqueness of the publication.

Special methods of identification have been applied to several categories of government information, including publications of boards, committees, and commissions; Congress and its committees; presidential and vice-presidential publications; committees and commissions established by the president; multilateral international organizations in which the United States participates; Braille versions of documents; and publications in electronic formats. Things can get a wee bit complicated. A report of the temporary Commission to Promote Investment in America's Infrastructure titled *Financing the Future* was assigned the notation Y 3.2: IN 8/F 28, the class stem being the designation set aside for the reports and publications of commissions, committees, and boards.

Classifying Electronic Products

The first CD-ROM to be classified and sent to selective depository libraries was a 1988 hybrid product called Census Test Disc No. 2. It was designated as follows:

C 3.275:	T 28/CD no. 2	The disk itself.
C 3.275:	T 28/Soft	Software for performing simple data retrieval on a floppy disk.
C 3.275:	T 28/Doc.	A print product—the technical documentation providing information on the file format.

The disk, no longer useful except for historical comparisons, contains agricultural data for counties from the 1982 census of agriculture and retail trade statistics by ZIP code from the 1982 census of retail trade. Since that time the number of CD-ROMs has rapidly grown, and disks containing numeric information from many agencies are now common-place. The Census Bureau leads all agencies in the quantity of information issued on CD-ROM, but many other agencies have jumped on the electronic bandwagon. "CD-ROM Titles Available from the Superintendent of Documents," listed on GPO Access and noted above, numbers over 100; and there are many more electronic products sent to depository libraries that are not sales items.

In addition to the classification of CD-ROMs specifically, "Electronic Products" as a miscellaneous category has been assigned a notation. Examples include the Bureau of Labor Statistics (L 2.134) and the Bureau of Land Management (I 53.58). Because the SuDocs notation is expandable (unlike the procrustean Dewey Decimal System), there is always going to be a notation available for non-print products. Classifying online resources enables documents librarians and users to relate electronic products to tangible products in depository collections, if a tangible edition exists. *Administrative Notes Technical Supplement* (ANTS), a companion to *Administrative Notes* (AN) that began in January 31, 1994, announces (1) publications that have migrated to the Internet while leaving their print or microfiche equivalents intact; (2) products that, when migrating, have abandoned the tangible version and are available only in an electronic format (whether Internet, CD-ROM, diskette, and so forth); and (3) new products available only on the Internet. For example, the *United States Government Manual* is available in print and on GPO Access. The *NIH Guide Supplement for Grants and Contracts* is no longer issued in paper; thus the classification notation has been canceled and the information can be retrieved only from the National Institutes of Health Internet site. And the *Appalachian Reporter,* a new product announced in early 1999, is available only from the Appalachian Regional Commission's Web site. More than 120 microfiche publications were discontinued in 1997 alone because, according to LPS, "reliable electronic alternatives" were available.[21] Attesting to the pace of migration, almost every issue of the "Update to the List of Classes" section of ANTS runs many pages. Figure 2.5, page 40, shows a page from ANTS indicating revisions in the *List of Classes.*

Classifying Fugitive Publications

Tangible government information products that are not cataloged and classified by LPS are called "fugitive," or sometimes "renegade," publications. It is estimated that at least 50 percent of all publications generated by government entities fail to be included in the Federal Depository Library Program,[22] and this perennial problem is addressed in more detail in chapter 3. However, a method for classifying publications that, having bypassed the LPS classifiers, find their way into libraries "builds on the class stem for General Publications and entails dashing or slashing the numbers 2 through 9 onto the appropriate class stem." This method is most effective when used with publications "for which there is no class listed in the *List of Classes*." LPS points out that "each library should feel completely free in assigning these numbers."[23] Done with care, this technique should pose no problem. The only inexpiable sin in the SuDocs classification scheme is assigning the same complete notation to more than one publication. The larger issue of fugitive documents concerns public access and the contravention of the purpose of the FDLP.

Figure 2.5. Update to the *List of Classes*.

Update to the List of Classes			
December 1998		Miscellaneous	1998-12
CLASS	ITEM	TITLE	STATUS
A 17.27/2:	0095-C-01	Animal Welfare Information Center Newsletter	Change title to: Animal Welfare Information Center Bulletin with vol. 9, no. 1-2, fall 1998
C 3.138/3:	0147-B	Monthly Retail Trade	Change format to (EL). No longer issued in paper. URL: http://www.census.gov/svsd/www/monret.html
D 101.3/6-2:	0323-A	Manprint Quarterly	Change format to (EL). URL: http://www.manprint.army.mil. No longer available in paper format to depository libraries.
HE 22.18:	0512-A-10	Health Care Financing Review	Cancel class. Now see: HE 22.512: Now published by the Health Care Financing Administration, Office of Strategic Planning
HE 22.512:	0512-A-10	Health Care Financing Review	New class. Previously classed: HE 22.18: Now published by the Health Care Financing Administration, Office of Strategic Planning
LC 1.18:	0785-C	Library of Congress Information Bulletin	Change frequency to monthly
NAS 1.42:	0830-V	NASA'S University Program, Grants and Research Contracts	Discontinued by publisher. Cancel class and item no.
NS 1.3:	0834-F-08	NSF Bulletin	Change title to: E-Bulletin with the Sept. 1, 1998 edition. Change format to (EL). URL: http://www.nsf.gov/od/lpa/news/publicat/bulletin/bulletin.htm
PM 1.13:	0293-D	The Federal Labor-Management and Employee Relations Consultant	Ceased with issue 98-5, June 15, 1998. Cancel class and item no.
T 1.45/3:	0925-G-06	Contingent Foreign Liabilities of the U.S. Government	Ceased in 1994. Cancel class.
TD 7.19/2:	0982-H-13	A Directory of Urban Public Transportation Service	Discontinued by publisher. Cancel class.
TD 8.26:	0982-D-29	Automotive Fuel Economy Program, Annual Report to Congress	Change format to: (EL). URL: http://www.nhtsa.dot.gov:80/cars/problems/studies/fuelecon/index.html

Guides to the SuDocs Classification System

Sources that furnish, inter alia, information about and guides to the SuDocs classification system are available at the FDLP Administration Publications page of GPO Access, including the above-mentioned *List of Classes*; AN; ANTS; and WEBTech Notes, which contains the main components of ANTS, updated weekly and cumulated since 1991; *GPO Classification Manual: A Practical Guide to the Superintendent of Documents Classification System* (1993), a detailed manual that in print is issued in looseleaf binder; and a shorter, simplified guide titled *An Explanation of the Superintendent of Documents Classification System*. Begun in 1963, this last has gone through several editions and revisions and is quite adequate for a basic understanding of the scheme.

Despite some inherent problems associated with all provenance classification plans, the federal system has for more than a century proven durable and helpful in organizing a paper collection of documents separately housed from the main library holdings in Dewey, Library of Congress, or another non-provenance system. However, its usefulness in designating government information on the Internet is less certain.

GIVING PRINT ITS DUE

If I seem to make too much of the enthusiasm the Government Printing Office evinces in carrying out the congressional mandate "toward maximum use of electronic information dissemination technologies by all departments, agencies, and other entities of the Government with respect to the Depository Library Program and information dissemination generally,"[24] permit me to quote some kind words for the neglected medium of print. From the 1998 "Introduction" to the Notable Documents issue of the *Journal of Government Information* we find this affirmation of the uses of the paper format not only for federal but also for state, local, and international intergovernmental products:

> It may be surprising just how many useful print materials continue to be produced in this modern age of electronic publishing. While the Notable Documents issue of JGI highlights an increasing number of notable government web sites in its entries, the great majority of the nearly 600 selections chosen by our column editors are still in print format. . . . In this issue, there are over 500 items that you can hold in your

hand, throw in your briefcase, read on the train, or do anything else the paper format allows. In many ways, we are in an ideal period in which government information is disseminated in a variety of formats that offer citizens tremendous possibilities for the fast and flexible retrieval of information.[25]

NOTES

1. *100 GPO Years, 1861–1961: A History of United States Public Printing* (Washington: Government Printing Office, 1961), pp. 35–36.

2. Ibid., p. 15.

3. Ibid., pp. 31–33.

4. *Documents to the People* 7: 195 (September 1975).

5. For a more detailed account of GPO and non-GPO printing activities, see Joe Morehead and Mary Fetzer, *Introduction to United States Government Information Sources,* 4th ed. (Englewood, CO: Libraries Unlimited, 1992), pp. 7–11.

6. *Administrative Notes* 19: 12 (November 15, 1998).

7. *Administrative Notes* 20: 5 (March 15, 1999).

8. *GPO Newsletter* 22: 1 (June/July 1998); *Administrative Notes* 20: 6 (March 15, 1999).

9. James L. Harrison, Fourteenth Public Printer of the United States, "Foreword," in Robert E. Kling, Jr., *The Government Printing Office* (New York: Praeger, 1970), p. v.

10. Comptroller General of the United States, *Government Printing— Treatment of Prompt Payment Discounts* (B-276509), August 28, 1998, pp. 2–3.

11. *Administrative Notes* 20: 6 (March 15, 1999).

12. *GPO Newsletter* 22: 1 (February/March 1998).

13. U.S. General Accounting Office, *Government Printing: GPO Faces Management Challenges* (GAO/T-GGO-98-180), July 29, 1998, p. 2.

14. *Administrative Notes* 20: 10 (March 15, 1999).

15. Ibid., p. 6.

16. *Administrative Notes* 20: 3 (February 25, 1999).

17. *Administrative Notes* 18: 3–4 (November 25, 1997).

18. *Administrative Notes* 19: 2–3 (November 15, 1998); *Administrative Notes* 20: 13–16 (February 25, 1999).

19. Dena Holiman Hutto, "Old Solutions in a New Age: Cataloging and the Future of Access to Government Information," *Journal of Government Information* 23: 339–42 (1996).

20. Library Programs Service, *An Explanation of the Superintendent of Documents Classification System* (Washington: Government Printing Office, 1990), p. 2.

21. *Administrative Notes* 18: 6–8 (October 15, 1997).

22. *Administrative Notes* 18: 14 (June 15, 1997).

23. *Administrative Notes* 5: 2 (January 1, 1984).

24. Legislative Branch Appropriations Act of 1996, PL 104-53, 109 Stat. 533, § 210 (2).

25. *Journal of Government Information* 35: 531 (November/December 1998).

CHAPTER THREE

THE FEDERAL DEPOSITORY LIBRARY PROGRAM

Where is the wisdom we have lost in knowledge?
Where is the knowledge we have lost in information?
—T. S. Eliot

INTRODUCTION

The purpose of the Federal Depository Library Program (FDLP) is set forth in general terms in the legislative history of the Depository Library Act of 1962 (82 Stat. 1282) as follows:

> The depository library system is a long established cooperative program between the federal government and designated major libraries throughout the United States under which certain classes of Government publications are supplied free of cost to those libraries for the purpose of making such publications readily accessible to the American public.[1]

While the program extends beyond the fifty states to include the Canal Zone, Guam, Micronesia, Puerto Rico, and the Virgin Islands, and includes small, local libraries as well as major institutions, the above statement is based on language in the 1962 act (below), codified as 44 U.S.C. § 1911, that "Depository libraries shall make Government publications available for the free use of the general public." The legislative history also highlights a key feature of the system: It is a cooperative program between the federal establishment and the nation's library community. Free distribution and government-library cooperation form the essential elements of the program. Although depository libraries receive government information products in several formats free of charge, they also incur considerable expense in providing staff and facilities to process, maintain, and provide access services to the collection.

Still, depository libraries obtain, without charge, many publications they would want to purchase anyway for their clientele, and the savings in acquisitions costs generally outweigh the expenses involved in the administration of the program.

Today, under the provisions of Title 44, *United States Code* (Public Printing and Documents), Chapter 19 (Depository Library Program), Sections 1901–1916, the government provides information free of charge to designated federal depository libraries in private or public institutions, which in turn must make them available to any member of the public who wishes to use them. Only the highest state appellate court libraries are exempt from this public access provision (44 U.S.C. § 1915). However, instances of libraries with depository collections denying access have been reported;[2] and in at least two situations, the issue reached the courts. In *Commonwealth of Pennsylvania v. Downing* (1986), the state Supreme Court of Pennsylvania, reversing a lower court decision, held that the Temple University Law School Library, a designated depository collection in a private school, was within its right not to allow ingress by an unauthorized person. The court stated that "the private nature of the Law School library is not changed by virtue of the fact that the law library has sought and received status as a federal depository library."[3] In *Carroll v. Temple University* (1995), a federal district court upheld the same library's right to turn away a visitor because "Temple's [law school library] policy is to permit members of the public with valid identification to view public documents between the hours of 9:00 A.M. and 5:00 P.M., Monday through Friday, and the plaintiff claimed that he went to [the law library] about 6:30 P.M."[4] This restrictive time policy violates the provisions of 44 U.S.C. § 1911 and Superintendent of Documents guidelines governing public access. In both actions, the uncouth behavior and vague intentions of the plaintiffs seeking admittance clearly did not help their case; nevertheless, these court decisions, which were not appealed, are dispiriting indeed.

With the passage of the Government Printing Office Electronic Information Access Enhancement Act of 1993 (44 U.S.C. § 4010 et seq.), discussed in chapter 2, the scope of the FDLP was expanded to include no-fee access to a large and ever-growing number of electronic government information products.

A BRIEF HISTORY OF THE FDLP

To begin with, we are here discussing the Title 44 depository system because we need to distinguish it from other federal depository arrangements authorized under other acts and administrative procedures, such as those libraries designated as Census (chapter 9) and Patent and Trademark (chapter 10) depositories. The FDLP had its origins in special acts of the first twelve Congresses, which provided for the printing of a sufficient number of copies of the House and Senate *Journals* for distribution to the executive branch and each house of the state and territorial legislatures. An act of 1813 authorized one copy of each chamber's journal to be sent to selected university and state libraries and to historical societies. Legislation enacted during the 1850s established the framework of the present system: A Superintendent of Public Printing (which became the Public Printer of the United States) was appointed within the Interior Department, the Secretary of the Interior was authorized to designate depository libraries, representatives were authorized to designate one depository from their own districts, and senators were assigned one depository in their state. An 1860 act transferred the Government Printing Office (GPO) to the legislative branch, and an act of 1869 created a line for a Superintendent of Public Documents within the Interior Department.

The Printing Act of 1895

Major changes in the depository library program were made by the landmark Printing Act of 1895 (28 Stat. 601), which, among other things, consolidated existing laws on the printing, binding, and distribution of public documents; transferred the position of Superintendent of Public Documents to the GPO and dropped the word "Public" from the title; significantly increased the categories of materials eligible for distribution to depository libraries; and in Section 74 of the act first enunciated the free access or use clause: "[A]ll government publications delivered to designated depositories or other libraries shall be for public use without charge."

The Depository Library Act of 1962

Between 1895 and 1962, various amendments to the 1895 act expanded public access by increasing the types of institutions eligible for depository status and the categories of materials disseminated. The Depository Library Act of 1962, in addition to consolidating earlier provisions of law, made several important revisions in the system. It increased from one to two the number of designations that could be authorized by each representative, delegate, and senator. It added to the system additional libraries from independent agencies and from each major bureau, office, or division within executive departments. It expanded the categories of depository materials by authorizing the distribution of non-GPO publications. It authorized the establishment of a maximum of two regional depositories in each state, which would allow selective depositories to discard materials after holding them for five years.[5]

This last provision was welcomed by librarians. One of the major complaints of depository libraries prior to 1962 was that they were required to retain permanently all depository publications. The 1962 law reduced the mandatory retention period to five years and required regional depositories to accept all materials, hold them permanently (with some exceptions), and "within the region served [to] provide interlibrary loan, reference service, and assistance for depository libraries in the disposal of unwanted Government publications." There were, as of 1998, fifty-three regional depository libraries (and 1,312 selective libraries), because some states have two regionals while a few states are without a regional. States without regionals are served by regional depository libraries in contiguous or nearby states. The duties and responsibilities of regional libraries are set forth in 44 U.S.C. § 1912.

THE FDLP TODAY

As noted above, the present Title 44 system is a twofold structure consisting of a small number of regionals and more than 1,300 selective institutions. As the word suggests, selective depositories may choose from among the thousands of categories (called items) available those that will meet the needs of their clientele. Regionals, on the other hand, automatically receive every item available for distribution. Items do not reflect the number or ratio of publications to categories. For example, libraries selecting item 577 will receive one copy per year of the annual *United States Government Manual*. However, choosing item 770 will ensure receipt of twelve copies of the *Monthly Labor Review*. Other items cover series with an indeterminate number of individual issues; for example, public laws, treaties and agreements, Supreme Court reports, and bills and resolutions. It is important to remember that all this largess comes with one big string attached: The collection is the property of the federal government, held by librarians to manage for the benefit of the public.

Just about everything you may want to know about the Federal Depository Library Program (laws, manuals, guides, instructions, directories, shipping lists, items, and so forth) can be found from the GPO Access Home Page (**http://www.access.gpo.gov/su_docs/index.html**). As of March 1999, the procedure was to click on "Library Services" and then "Depository Libraries" and/or "FDLP Administration." From then on it is simply a matter of scrolling and clicking. Alternately, you can access a site coded and designed by Thomas J. Tyler, University of Denver Library, titled "Basic Depository Library Documents: The Unauthorized HTML Editions." This address, which contains some enhancements such as GPO-Marc Internet resources, also covers just about everything you ever wanted to know about the administration and management of a depository collection (**http://du.edu/~ttyler/bdldhome.htm**). Whichever site you choose, the information that follows can be found at either location.

Categories and Designations

Academic libraries account for about one-half of the total number of Title 44 depository libraries. Public libraries are a distant second, with 20 percent of the total. Libraries of accredited law schools have 11 percent of the whole, followed in single digits by community college libraries, federal agency institutions, the highest state appellate court libraries, and special libraries, with libraries of federal agencies and military service academies accounting for the smallest numbers.

Authority for the nomination of a new depository library is found at 44 U.S.C. § 1905 and amplified in the *Designation Handbook for Federal Depository Libraries,* in print or online. This guide covers procedures for every type of designated institution, including sample letters and forms, a depository checklist, and supporting technical publications.

A designated library has the right to voluntarily relinquish its depository status at any time by sending a letter to the Superintendent of Documents providing an explanation and an effective date. The withdrawing institution works with the regional depository to determine the disposition of the collection. Conversely, depository status can be terminated by the Superintendent of Documents under 44 U.S.C. § 1909 if an institution fails to meet the requirements set forth in the inspection. Libraries have voluntarily surrendered depository status because their publications were seldom used, because they lacked a professional staff to maintain service, or because participation became a financial burden.[6] A list of libraries that have dropped from or been awarded depository status is announced periodically in a section of *Administrative Notes Technical Supplement* entitled "Update to Federal Depository Library Directory." Figure 3.1, page 50, is an example of this list.

Figure 3.1. "Update to Federal Depository Library Directory," *Administrative Notes Technical Supplement,* **vol. 6, no. 1.**

ADMINISTRATIVE NOTES
Technical Supplement

U.S. Government Printing Office		Library Programs Service
Vol. 6, no. 1	GP 3.16/3-3:6/1	January 31, 1999

Update to Federal Depository Library Directory
January 1999   **1999-01**

LIBRARY NO.	ENTRY	STATUS
0112C	University of Miami School of Law Library 1311 Miller Dr. Coral Gables, FL 33124-0247	Dropped
0249B	Towson University Albert S. Cook Library 8000 York Rd. Towson, MD 21252-0001	Dropped
0512B	Penn State New Kensington Elisabeth S. Blissell Library 3550 Seventh St. Road Rt. 780 Upper Burrell, PA 15068-1765	Added
0629B	Department of the Navy Office of Judge Advocate Washington Navy Yard 1322 Patterson Ave. SE Suite 30 Washington, DC 20374-5066	Dropped

Federal Depository Library Directory

Updated on GPO Access on the first Friday of the month and formerly published annually in paper copy as a Committee Print, the *Federal Depository Library Directory* contains information on all Title 44 depository libraries. The PAMALA Search Results screens include links to the full item selection profile record and, if applicable, a hot-linked e-mail address and a Web site URL. Very thorough directory information is provided, including the type of library, designation (representative, senatorial, and so forth), size, and year of designation. The Tyler/BDLD version includes all the standard directory information based on the current edition of GPO's Profiles Database plus the number of items selected and percentage of selection.

Inspection Program

Title 44, Section 1909, states: "The Superintendent of Documents shall make firsthand investigation of conditions for which need is indicated and include the results of investigations in his annual report." The SuDocs relied upon the Biennial Survey (see below) in lieu of visitations until the mid-1970s, when full-time inspectors were hired and systematic, formal inspections were initiated. Depository libraries are inspected about once every five or six years, in chronological order by date of last inspection. Typically, the inspection occupies nearly a full workday. During the last half hour of the process, the inspector meets privately with the library director or that person's representative. In addition to the documents librarian, key clerical staff are available during the inspection visit.

The inspection should not be viewed as a punitive activity. Its primary goal is to ensure that depository libraries fulfill their responsibilities as outlined in 44 U.S.C. § 1909 and in the *Instructions to Depository Libraries* (regulations issued by the LPS that all depositories are required to follow). Areas of strength and weakness are identified. The Inspection Report rates the depository in several categories: collection development, bibliographic control, maintenance, human resources, physical facilities, public service, cooperative efforts, and regional services (to be filled out by regional depositories, including partners in shared regionals).

Severe deficiencies can result in a depository being placed on probation and subsequently reinspected. Occasionally, a recidivous library is shorn of its designation, but this occurs infrequently. Ideally, the inspection affords inspectors an opportunity to remind the library administration of the unique benefits depository status confers upon public access to federal government information.

In 1994 the Library Programs Service (LPS) proposed a self-study questionnaire for depository libraries, which was endorsed by the Depository Library Council to the Public Printer in October of that year. The self-study is viewed as a strategic assessment document that will walk the documents staff through issues such as collection development policy, compliance with the Americans with Disabilities Act (ADA), public access computer workstations, and so forth, which need careful consideration. Depositories are required to conduct this mandatory self-evaluation that, in some cases, may replace an on-site inspection. Each calendar quarter, LPS will request self-studies from a group of libraries in chronological order from the date of last inspection and then determine whether an on-site inspection is warranted based on the self-study, follow-up questions, consultation with the regional library, and specific criteria including recent staff changes, results of prior inspections, and, if applicable, any complaints from depository library users.[7] For guidance, the text of the self-study is found in *Federal Depository Library Manual, Supplement 3,* which is available in print or on the FDPL Web site (**http://www.access.gpo.gov/su_docs/dpos/selfstud. html**). In the *Proceedings of the 7th Annual Federal Depository Library Conference* (April 20–23, 1998), it was reported that inspectors would visit those libraries that meet at least one of four criteria: (1) the library did not meet depository standards, (2) the library had never been inspected, (3) the library requested a site visit from an inspector, or (4) the library reported exemplary services or accomplishments, including a new building.[8] This information is available on the FDLP Administration page of GPO Access.

Biennial Survey

Participation in a biennial survey is required by 44 U.S.C. § 1909 and, according to a 1993 ukase from LPS, is a condition for remaining in the Federal Depository Library Program.[9] The survey provides the LPS with important information used to administer the program and provide an updated profile for inclusion in the Federal Depository Library Directory. In 1995 the survey included, for the first time, questions on GPO Access, the Federal Bulletin Board (FBB), accessibility of CD-ROM products, and computer workstations with Internet access. The 1997 survey, which was mailed to depository libraries in October 1997 and due December 1, 1997, was answered online for the first time, using a Web address set up for that purpose on the FDLP Administration page. Every biennial survey has some new questions, in recent years involving new developments in technology, and old queries such as number of users, *Monthly Catalog* access, staff training, and the like.

Depository Library Council

The purpose of the Depository Library Council to the Public Printer, which was established in 1972 and held its first meeting in February 1973, is to provide advice on policy matters dealing with the FDLP to the Public Printer, Superintendent of Documents, and appropriate members of the GPO staff. Specifically, it focuses on practical options for the efficient management and operation of the program. Membership consists of fifteen individuals who are invited by the Public Printer to serve three-year terms, at least half of whom shall work in depository libraries and have experience as a documents librarian.

Because the council is just an advisory body, the Public Printer is not bound by its recommendations and resolutions.

The council holds open meetings, announced in the *Federal Register,* twice a year; and its summary reports, which include the text of all council recommendations, are published in *Administrative Notes.* Its Web pages furnish information on its Charter, a brief history, a list of selected council accomplishments, a mission statement, current list of members, and a bibliography of its several reports and publications.

Disposition Guidelines

Section 1912 of Title 44 permits selective depositories to dispose of government publications that they have retained for five years after first offering them to other depository libraries within their area, then to other libraries. The five-year period is from the date of receipt, not the document's publication date. Approval must be made by the library's regional depository. Discard lists are reviewed by the regional and it gets the first chance to pick off any discards to plug a gap in its holdings. Materials not needed by the regional are offered to other selective depositories in the state or states covered by the regional. Finally, documents left over are offered to non-depository institutions for public access. Remaining items of an historical nature should be offered through the national Needs and Offers List **(http://docs.sewanee. edu/nando/nando.html)**. Finally, any other leftover publications may be destroyed or sold as secondhand books or waste paper. If the latter, the proceeds must be sent to the SuDocs with a letter of explanation. The disposal by the documents librarian of some 29,000 depository publications without authorization from the regional or the GPO resulted in an angry letter from the Public Printer, which was published on the first page of the July 1987 issue of *Administrative Notes.*

Certain publications by their nature and function may be discarded before the five-year retention period. A *Superseded List* carries those titles that may be discarded without the regional's participation. This list is updated periodically on the FDLP Web page and is an irregular feature of ANTS. Materials that can be disposed of are logical candidates for discarding. They include duplicates, issues of a publication that cumulates, looseleaf pages of a subscription service upon receipt of revised pages, materials with a time-expiration date such as Civil Service examination announcements, and earlier editions of a document when a new edition is issued. This last requires good judgment. A research institution may wish to retain earlier editions of a publication for comparative scholarship purposes.

Depository copies of microfiche may be discarded after being retained for five years without submitting lists to the regional, which will continue to obtain replacement copies of missing fiche and provide copies to selectives through interlibrary loan. Exceptions to this policy include large or significant microfiche runs, such as the Department of Energy Contractor Reports and Publications series.

Listservs and askLPS

GOVDOC-L, the general listserv for documents librarians, was established on January 16, 1990. A useful account of its origins and purposes was written by Diane K. Kovacs, who notes that GOVDOC-L serves several purposes, principal among them "the provision of timely and accurate information and access to a pool of experienced colleagues." The listserv "provides a forum through which scholars from all fields can discuss government documents access."[10]

A specialized listserv, DocTech-L, is devoted to questions concerning the technical processing of government information: federal, state, and United Nations. It is not a place for reference questions or conference announcements. Questions concerning everything from shipping list problems to types of stickers are welcome. For more information, check out their Web site at **http://www.usu.edu/~library/about/doctech/html**.

A somewhat different source of securing information from the "horse's mouth," as it were, is through askLPS, an official Web-based inquiry and notification system mounted on the FDLP Administration pages of GPO Access. With a link to WEBTech Notes, which updates AN and ANTS, askLPS has inquiry forms for questions that are routed to the appropriate LPS staff person; an e-mail reply will be sent as soon as possible. Answers that have broad interest to the FDLP community will be posted and cumulated on the askLPS FAQs & News page of this useful site.

FDLP Partnerships

FDLP Partnerships are arrangements between GPO and one or more depository libraries or other service institutions to work jointly on projects that expand or enhance the capabilities of the program. There are two types of partnerships: (1) Content Partnerships that host remote Internet sites for official FDLP electronic collections; and (2) Service Partnerships, wherein partners engage in service activities that enhance the FDLP. An example of the latter is an agreement between GPO and the Louisiana State University (LSU) Libraries, which are maintaining a list of federal agency Internet sites based on linking agency entries in the *United States Government Manual* to the Internet sites maintained by those agencies. (See Laurie Andriot, *The Internet Blue Pages,* **http://www.fedweb.com**, for comparison.) The LSU site is available by link from the GPO Access page. Documents Data Miner (DDM), a partnership of Wichita State University, is another example of a synergistic alliance (see below). LPS encourages libraries to participate in the FDLP Partnership Program by contacting the Electronic Transition Staff by phone or e-mail (ets@gpo.gov).[11]

Expunge This Doc!

On occasion publications are sent to depository libraries by mistake. In those instances, the Superintendent of Documents sends a letter to depository libraries that have received the unauthorized publication by virtue of item selection; subsequently, the letter is published in *Administrative Notes*. Examples of titles sent in error are technical documents from agencies like the United States Geological Survey that contain faulty data and those publications that contain classified information. Examples of the latter include the Marshals Service's *USMS Protective Detail Glossary of Terms* and the Alcohol, Tobacco and Firearms Bureau's *The Animal Liberation Front in the 90's.* These announcements come with stern instructions either to withdraw these publications from the collection and destroy them by any means that will prevent disclosure of their contents, return them to the issuing agency, or in the case of the Animal Liberation Front (a terrorist group), secure the publication for a "Secret Service agent who will collect it."[12] These recalls are authorized under the provisions of 44 U.S.C. § 1902, which states in part that government publications "required for official use only [or] for strictly administrative or operational purposes" are exempt from distribution to depository libraries. For an informative article on publications inadvertently disseminated since 1981, which agencies have asked depository libraries to destroy or return, see Saragail Runyon Lynch, "GPO Recalls of Depository Documents: A Review," *Journal of Government Information* 22: 23–31 (1995). But isn't it only a matter of time until the text of a classified document is published on an agency's Web page and thereby becomes unreturnable in cyberspace?

Fugitive Documents

In chapter 2, I addressed the issue of classifying fugitive government publications, those which for one reason or another are not cataloged by LPS and entered into bibliographic databases such as the *Monthly Catalog* or WorldCat. The larger issue is one of public access to government information. In 1997, the Senate Rules Committee estimated that more than 50 percent of all tangible government information products are not being made available to the FDLP. Publications that belong to the program but that bypass the LPS are known as fugitive documents. The Rules Committee identified four factors that have contributed to this problem:

- electronic dissemination of information via agency Web sites without notifying the FDLP;

- decreasing compliance with statutory requirements for agencies to print through GPO or to provide copies of non-GPO publications to the FDLP; that is, violations of the various sections of 44 U.S.C. Chapter 19 that I have cited above;

- an increasing trend for agencies to establish exclusive arrangements with private-sector entities that place copyright or copyright-like restrictions on the products involved in such agreements. Under loose interpretations of copyright statutes, government agencies may allow an independent contractor or grantee to secure copyright in works prepared in whole or in part with the use of government funds. In those instances, the publications would be exempt from the depository collection.

- increasing use by agencies of language in 44 U.S.C. § 1903 that permits publications to be excluded if they are so-called cooperative publications that must necessarily be sold to be self-sustaining.

In a 1997 issue of *Administrative Notes* in which this list was published, LPS cited some egregious examples of failure to comply with statutory requirements. Offending agencies included the Department of Transportation, the Central Intelligence Agency, the National Technical Information Service (the main culprit), the Bureau of Export Administration, the National Cancer Institute, and other entities.[13] That fugitive documents are nothing new was cited by Stephen C. Weiss in an article in *Documents to the People:* "Fugitive U.S. government information has existed to some extent since the first Continental Congress."[14]

SELECTED TOOLS OF THE TRADE

The following resources are employed for the benefit of both participating depository libraries and the Library Programs Service. All are available on the GPO Access Web site or links therefrom.

List of Classes

The full title of this august series is *List of Classes of United States Government Publications Available for Selection by Depository Libraries,* a good reason why it is known by its short title. Published semiannually in superseded print editions, it is arranged by SuDocs classification class stem, referencing the series title, format, and depository item number. Paper and microfiche products are coded (P) and (MF). Electronic products have four codes as follows:

(E)   Electronic Products (miscellaneous)

(EL)   Online Electronic Format

(CD)   CD-ROM

(FL)   Floppy Diskette (or Diskettes)

The format "EL" and the status fields can be searched using the WEBTech Notes database that is available on the FDLP Administration Web site.

Entries marked with an asterisk (*) are new item additions and/or additional class items added since the last issue. After the entries there is a "List of Items and Class Stems" arranged by Item Number. Appendix I is an "Alphabetic Listing of Government Authors" and Appendix II is a list of discontinued classes. Figure 3.2, page 58, shows a page from the *List of Classes.*

Shipping Lists

The Depository Shipping List is used primarily as an invoice to a complete shipment of publications contained in a standard depository shipping box. Shipping Lists have been used since August 1, 1951, and each has been numbered, although the numbering system has changed over the years. The shipping list contains columns for the item number, SuDocs classification notation, and title. At the end of the title entries

Figure 3.2. Page from *List of Classes*.

EDUCATION DEPARTMENT—CONTINUED
National Center for Educational Statistics—
Continued

ED 1.122/2:	Statistics of Public Libraries (quadrennial) (P) 0460-B-02
ED 1.122/3:	Library Statistics of Colleges and Universities (triennial) (P) 0460-A-15
ED 1.123:	Participation in Adult Education (triennial) (P) 0461-A-18
ED 1.125:	FRSS (Fast Response Survey System) Reports (numbered) (irregular) (P) 0460-B-03
ED 1.126:	NCES Bulletins (MF) 0461-A-22
ED 1.127:	Survey of College Graduates, ED(NCES) Form 2385 (annual) (P) 0460-B-04
ED 1.129:	Directory of Library Networks and Cooperative Library Organizations (quinquennial) (MF) 0461-A-19
ED 1.130:	Directories (MF) 0461-A-20
ED 1.132/2:	Trends in Bachelors and Higher Degrees (annual) (MF) 0455-F-04
ED 1.133:	SPEEDE/ExPRESS Newsletter (quarterly) (P) 0461-A-23

Special Education and Rehabilitative Services Office

ED 1.202:	General Publications 0529
ED 1.208:	Handbooks, Manuals, Guides 0529-B
ED 1.209:	Bibliographies and Lists of Publications (P) 0506-C-05
ED 1.209/2:	Catalog of Captioned General Interest Videos and Films (MF) 0506-C-05
ED 1.209/2-2:	Catalog of Educational Captioned Films/ Videos for the Deaf (annual) (MF) 0506-C-05
ED 1.210:	Annual Report of the Rehabilitation Services Administration to the President and the Congress on Federal Activities Related to the Administration of the Rehabilitation Act of 1973 (MF) 0529-D
ED 1.211:	American Rehabilitation (quarterly) 0506-C-04
ED 1.213:	OSERS (Office of Special Education and Rehabilitative Services) News in Print (quarterly) (P) 0506-C-07
ED 1.214:	Application for New Grants Under Certain Direct Grant Programs (annual) (MF) 0529-D-01
ED 1.215:	NIDRR Program Directory (annual) (MF) (EL) 0529-D-02
ED 1.215/2:	Disability Statistics Report (series) (P) 0529-D-03
ED 1.215/3:	Disability Forum Report (series) (P) 0529-D-04
* ED 1.215/4:	Disability Statistics Abstract (EL) 0529-D-03

Educational Research and Improvement Office

ED 1.302:	General Publications 0461-D-05
ED 1.303/2:	OERI Bulletin (quarterly) (P) 0455-G-11
ED 1.303/4:	The Link (P)/(EL) 0455-G-11
ED 1.308:	Handbooks, Manuals, Guides 0455-G-04
ED 1.308/2:	Educational Research Consumer Guide (series) (P) 0455-G-04
ED 1.310:	Resources in Education (monthly) (P) 0466-A

ED 1.310/2:	Education Documents Announced in RIE (Resources in Education) (MF) 0466-A-03
ED 1.310/3:	Thesaurus of ERIC Descriptors (MF) 0466-A-01
ED 1.310/4:	Current Index to Journals in Education (monthly) (MF) 0466-A-02
ED 1.317:	Bibliographies and Lists of Publications (P) 0455-G-06
ED 1.317/2:	Recent Department of Education Publications in ERIC (quarterly) (P) 0455-G-06
ED 1.317/3:	Perspectives in Reading Research (P) 0455-G-06
ED 1.317/4:	Advances in Education Research (irregular) (P) 0455-G-06
ED 1.322:	Research in Brief (P) 0455-G-11
ED 1.322/2:	Issue Brief (series) (P) 0455-G-11
ED 1.322/3:	Education Research Report (series) 0455-G-11
ED 1.323:	The Best of ERIC (Educational Resources Information Center) (P) 0466-A-04
ED 1.324:	Request for Proposal (P) 0461-D-05
ED 1.326:	Digest of Education Statistics (P) 0461-D-09
ED 1.327:	Youth Indicators, Trends in the Well-Being of American Youth (annual) (P) 0461-D-05
ED 1.328:	Survey Report (series) (MF) 0455-G-09
ED 1.328/2:	Analysis Report (series) (MF) 0455-G-09
ED 1.328/3:	E.D. Tabs (series) (MF) 0455-G-09
ED 1.328/4:	Statistics in Brief (series) (P) 0455-G-11
ED 1.328/5:	Statistical Analysis Report (series) (MF) 0455-G-09
ED 1.328/6:	Research and Development Report (series) (MF) 0455-G-09
ED 1.328/7:	Technical Report (series) (P) 0455-G-11
ED 1.328/8:	Federal Support for Education (Fiscal Year) (P) 0455-G-11
* ED 1.328/9:	Methodology Report (series) (MF) 0455-G-14
ED 1.328/10:	Technical/Methodology Report (series) (P) 0455-G-17
ED 1.328/11:	Descriptive Report (MF) 0455-G-18
ED 1.329:	Dropout Rates in the United States (annual) (MF) 0461-D-05
ED 1.330:	Directories 0461-G
ED 1.330/2:	Directory of ERIC Resource Collections (annual) (P) 0461-G-01
ED 1.331:	The ERIC Review (quarterly) (P) 0455-G-11
ED 1.331/2:	ERIC Digest (P) 0455-G-11
ED 1.332:	Schools and Staffing Survey (CD-ROM) 0455-N-01
ED 1.333:	National Postsecondary Student Aid Study (NPSAS) (CD-ROM) 0455-N-02
ED 1.334:	High School and Beyond (CD-ROM) 0455-N-03
ED 1.334/2:	Electronic Products (misc.) (E) 0455-N-04
ED 1.334/3:	Public Library Data (Diskettes) 0455-N-05
ED 1.334/4:	Intergrated Postsecondary Education Data System (annual) (CD-ROM) 0455-N-06
ED 1.334/5:	National Household Education Survey (biennial) (CD-ROM) 0455-N-07
ED 1.334/6:	School District Data Book (CD-ROM) 0455-N-08
ED 1.335:	NAEPfacts (P) 0455-G-11

are the series number and sales information, if applicable. There are four categories of lists: paper (P), microfiche (M), electronic (E), and separates (S). This last consists of products mailed from contractors and not sent to libraries in regular shipment boxes because they are too large for the standard boxes or because they may need special handling. Separates include maps, charts, posters, and prepackaged and over-sized publications.

An enhanced shipping list service is another of the FDLP Partner-ships offered to depository libraries through a cooperative agreement between the State University at Buffalo, New York, and the GPO. This service automatically checks your inclusion list against shipping lists and prints Call Number labels for your library. The Buffalo server is available at both **http://ublib.buffalo.edu/libraries/units/cts/acq/gpo** and via the Federal Bulletin Board (**http://fedbbs.access.gpo.gov**) by clicking on Federal Depository Library Information. Claims for miss-ing items on any shipping list must be postmarked within sixty calendar days of receipt of the shipment.

Items and Item Lister

In former times, depository libraries received a pad of "Amend-ment of Selections" green postcards and printed instructions. But in late May 1998, a packet of item selection update materials was mailed to de-pository libraries. Each library's packet contained a letter, a sheet con-taining an additional password for agency electronic resources, and instructions for the Fiscal Year (FY) Annual Selection Update Cycle and for completing a survey of depository URL sites. Although items can be dropped at any time, they may be added only during the update cycle, which takes place from June 1 to July 31. At the time, LPS announced that it would no longer accept green cards for making changes.

An "Item Lister" on the FDLP Administration page of GPO Access reflects the item selection information as of the most recent update to the GPO's Depository Distribution Information System (DDIS). More-over, the complete Item Lister file for all depository libraries is on the Federal Bulletin Board, under the heading UNIONL, an abbreviation, of course, for Union List (**http://fedbbs.access,gpo.gov/libs/unionl. htm**). The Tyler/BDLD Web site has an enhanced item selection suite consisting, for example, of item selection percentages for depository li-braries and other features.

Inactive or Discontinued Items

In its print format, the *Inactive or Discontinued Items from the 1950 Revision of the Classified List* is arranged by item number with reference to series title, class stems, and provenance. It is available not only in print but also via GPO Access and the Tyler/BDLD: University of Denver Web site. The latter is based on the current text file edition from the FBB. Figure 3.3 shows a page from the print version of the 1950 revision.

Documents Data Miner

A partnership of Wichita State University, the National Institute of Aviation Research, and FDLP, the Documents Data Miner (DDM) provides access to various administrative forms. For instance, files from the FBB downloaded into DDM's search engine include the *List of Classes,* item number selection profiles for depository libraries, the *Inactive or Discontinued Items,* and the *Federal Depository Library Directory.* The DDM is available via GPO Access or directly from Wichita State University at **kronos.niar.twsu.edu/govdocs**.

DOCUMENTS EXPEDITING PROJECT (Doc Ex)

Although the FDLP is the major vehicle for acquiring federal government products, other means of procuring tangible materials are many and varied. When I want a government publication to be able to annotate it, I seek out the issuing agency or my representative or senator. In addition, I am on the mailing list of several agencies that maintain registers for free distribution of their newsletters, annual reports, and publications lists. Jobbers such as Bernan provide publications for a fee. Outright gifts, microfiche, and paper copy purchases from commercial vendors and other means still thrive. And now, of course, the vast storehouse known as the Internet is the place to download and print out scads of information. Remember that there are some 29,000 libraries and almost 300 million persons in the United States that do not enjoy depository status.

Enter the Documents Expediting Project, called by its diminutive Doc Ex. Begun in 1946 and operating out of the Exchange and Gift Division, Library of Congress, since 1968, Doc Ex was originally designed to procure and distribute war documents and other publications not available through the GPO. Through the years, Doc Ex also became the primary distributor of congressional committee prints (see chapter 5)

Figure 3.3. Page from *Inactive or Discontinued Items from the 1950 Revision of Classified List*.

INACTIVE OR DISCONTINUED ITEMS FROM THE
1950 REVISION OF CLASSIFIED LIST

Office of the Assistant Public Printer (Superintendent of Documents),
U.S. Government Printing Office, Washington, D.C. 20402

(CLASSIFICATION NUMBER: GP 3.24/2:996)

NOTE.—Entries marked with an asterisk (*) are new item additions added since the last issue.

Item Number	
0005	Agriculture Monographs A 1.78:(Agriculture Department)
0006-A	Directories A 1.89/3:(Agriculture Department)
0006-B	Information and Technical Assistance Delivered by the Department of Agriculture in Fiscal Year, Annual Report to Congress (MF) A 1.1/2:(Agriculture Department)
0006-D	Rural Development Goals, Annual Report of Secretary of Agriculture to Congress (MF) A 1.85/2:(Agriculture Department)
0006-E	Location of New Federal Offices and Other Facilities, Annual Report (MF) A 1.111:(Agriculture Department)
0006-F	Agriculture and the Environment (annual) (MF) A 1.127:(Agriculture Department)
0007	Bibliographical Bulletins A 1.60:(Agriculture Department)
0008	Circulars A 1.4/2:(Agriculture Department)
0011-A	Household Food Comsumption Survey Reports A 1.86:(Agriculture Department)
0011-E	Financial and Technical Assistance Provided by the Department of Agriculture and the Department of Housing and Urban Development for Nonmetropolitan Planning Districts, Annual Report to Congress (MF) A 1.113:(Agriculture Department)
0013	Management Improvement A 1.74:(Agriculture Department)
0013-D	Rural Development Program Committee Annual Report A 1.85:(Agriculture Department)
0013-E	National Fire Prevention Week (annual) A 1.92:(Agriculture Department)
0013-F	Reports of Technical Study Groups on Soviet Agriculture A 1.94:(Agriculture Department)
0013-H	National Farm Safety Week (annual leaflet) A 1.96:(Agriculture Department)
0013-I	Periodic Reports of Agricultural Economics (annual) A 1.99:(Agriculture Department)
*0013-J	AgRISTARS (Agriculture and Resources Inventory Surveys Through Aerospace Remote Sensing) Annual Report (MF) A 1.132:(Agriculture Department)
0013-L	News (Press Releases) (irregular) (P) A 1.133:(Agriculture Department)

Item Number	
0013-M	News, Daily Summary (daily) (P) A 1.133/2:(Agriculture Department)
0013-N	News, Feature (irregular) (P) A 1.133/3:(Agriculture Department)
0014-B	Science Study Aids A 1.104:(Agriculture Department)
0014-C	Land Use Notes (irregular) (P) A 1.128:(Agriculture Department)
*0018	The Journal of Agricultural Economic Research (quarterly) (MF) A 93.26:(Economic Research Service,Agriculture Department)
0018-B	Agricultural Outlook Charts (annual publication) A 36.50:(Agriculture Department)
*0018-C-01	SRS series (MF) A 92.34:(National Agricultural Statistics Service,Agriculture Department)
0018-C-02	Sugar Market Statistics (quarterly) (MF) A 92.41:(National Agricultural Statistics Service,Agriculture Department)
0018-D	Acreage-Marketing Guides A 88.26/4:(Agricultural Marketing Service,Agriculture Department)
0019	Farmline (MF) A 93.33/2:(Economic Research Service,Agriculture Department)
0019-A-41	Fresh Fruit and Vegetable Carlot Shipments by States, Commodities, Counties and Stations (annual) (AMS-41) A 88.40:41/DATE(Agricultural Marketing Service,Agriculture Department)
0020	Annual Report A 36.1:(Agricultural Economics Bureau,Agriculture Department)
0020-A	Consumer Purchases of Fruits and Juices by Regions and Retail Outlets A 88.12/4-2:(Agricultural Marketing Service,Agriculture Department)
0021	Crops and Markets A 88.24/3:(Agriculture Department)
0021-A	Demand & Price Situation A 93.9/2:(Economic Research Service,Agriculture Department)
0021-B	Dairy Outlook and Situation (DS-nos., 5 times a year) A 105.17/2:(Economic Research Service,Agriculture Department) Dairy Situation and Outlook Yearbook (annual) (MF) A 93.13/2-2:(Economic Research Service,Agriculture Department)

until the LPS began to include them more consistently through the FDLP. Today, Doc Ex distributes non-depository publications to more than 100 library subscribers, including a separate subscription service for the Central Intelligence Agency's (CIA) Reference Aids series. It is also an excellent source of replacements for missing issues of periodicals.[15]

CONCLUSION

Predictions that the depository library system would not survive the twentieth century have once again illustrated the point that Cassandras are often as wrong as Pollyannas. There is reason to be cautiously optimistic so long as the legislatively mandated migration toward a largely electronic depository library system does not proceed like the thundering herds of wildebeest across the Serengeti plains. In a seminal report to the Congress titled *Study to Identify Measures Necessary for a Successful Transition to a More Electronic Federal Depository Library Program,* dated June 1996, migration was defined as meaning "both (1) the periodic refreshing or transfer of Government information products from one medium to another in order to minimize loss of information due to physical deterioration of storage media and (2) the reformatting of information to avoid technological obsolescence due to software or platform dependence." Call me a latter-day Luddite, but I doubt that information in electronic formats will migrate to print anytime soon. Don't get me wrong. I enjoy pulling useful information off the Internet while sitting in the comfort of my home office, especially at that time of year when a trip to the library would entail leasing one of the Iditarod trail sled-dog teams. But there's a reassuring quality, a substantiality, about the heft and opacity of a book. In the current professional jargon, it is indeed tangible.

Whether for good or ill, the migration to the Internet is inexorable, inevitable, and a one-way street. One of the five principles for federal government information set forth in the *Study* is "The government has an obligation to preserve its information. And one of the seven goals warrants the continued transfer to NARA [the National Archives and Records Administration] of information disseminated to depository libraries by GPO, as well as the initiation of transfer to NARA of electronic information held by GPO for depository library access."[16] This should be an urgent priority. We believe that print on acid-free paper, with proper moisture and temperature controls, will last 500 years. We also are confident that microfilm properly cared for has a 500-year life. But the rate of digital obsolescence keeps accelerating, and the serious search for a long-term strategy for storage has just begun. Digital storage media such as magnetic tape and CD-ROMs have ten-year life spans. What we do with digital documents is refresh them every time there's a change in technology, or every eighteen months, whichever comes first. This is an expensive approach! We need a digital equivalent to microfilm, a 500-year solution.[17]

The United States Public Printer got it right when, in remarks before a House of Representatives committee on August 1, 1995, he averred:

> Mr. Chairman, whatever its faults, ink-on-paper today is still the most egalitarian of information formats. It is accessible, transportable, and economical. It is still recognized as the official medium for Government documents. It still has the best chance of preservation for future generations. And it still is sought by vast numbers of Americans who use Government information for a wide variety of purposes, including the most basic of all: holding the Government accountable for its actions.[18]

NOTES

1. 87-2: S.Rpt. 1587 (1962), p. 3.
2. Lynn Foster, "Access to Academic Law Library Services," *Law Library Journal* 84: 741–58 (1992).
3. *Commonwealth of Pennsylvania v. Downing*, 511 A.2d 792, 795.
4. This opinion was not reported in *Federal Supplement*. See *Carroll v. Temple University*, 1995 U.S. Dist. LEXIS 7410.
5. For a succinct outline of "Historical Highlights" of the FDLP, see *Administrative Notes* 19: 20–22 (February 15, 1998).
6. Peter Hernon et al., *GPO's Depository Library Program: A Descriptive Analysis* (Norwood, NJ: Ablex, 1985), p. 136.
7. *Federal Depository Library Manual, Supplement 3*, pp. 1–2.
8. Gail Snider and Stephen Henson, "Writing the Depository Self-Study," *Proceedings of the 7th Annual Federal Depository Library Conference*, April 20–23, 1998, p. 1.
9. *Administrative Notes* 14: 1 (October 15, 1993).
10. Diane K. Kovacs, "GovDoc-L: An Online Intellectual Community of Documents Librarians and Other Individuals Concerned with Access to Government Information," *Government Publications Review* 17: 413–14 (September/October 1990).

11. *Administrative Notes* 18: 9–10 (June 15, 1997).

12. *Administrative Notes* 13: 2 (December 31, 1992); see also *Administrative Notes* 19: 7 (October 15, 1998).

13. *Administrative Notes* 18: 14–19 (June 15, 1997).

14. Stephen C. Weiss, "Fugitive U.S. Government Publications in Perspective," *Documents to the People* 24: 239 (December 1996), note 4.

15. For additional information, e-mail David Bloxsom, Chief, Documents Expediting Project (dbloxsom@mail.loc.gov).

16. *Study to Identify Measures Necessary for a Successful Transition to a More Electronic Federal Depository Library Program* (Washington: Government Printing Office, June 1996), pp. v, 5, 7.

17. Stewart Brand, "Escaping the Digital Dark Age," *Library Journal,* February 1, 1999, p. 46.

18. *Administrative Notes* 16: 2 (September 1, 1995).

CHAPTER FOUR

GENERAL FINDING AIDS AND SELECTED REFERENCE SOURCES

> Knowledge is of two kinds. We know a subject ourselves, or we know where we find information upon it.
>
> —Samuel Johnson

INTRODUCTION

The bibliographic apparatus for U.S. government information is complex and unwieldy, a reflection of the materials it attempts to encompass. Lists, guides, bibliographies, and indexes in print and microfiche; maps and charts; audiovisuals; and electronic formats often exhibit a pattern that is irregular and confusing. Even those purporting to be exhaustive fall short of the bibliographic ideal. The dramatic increase in the dissemination of information online exacerbates the already difficult problem of information management, as users are confronted with a vast array of systems to access government materials. Indeed, as one learns more of the problems associated with the control and retrieval of government information, the inadequacies of the apparatus appear to increase. One is reminded of the eponymous protagonist of Tennyson's *Ulysses* who, in the famous poem, viewed experience's vistas with some despair. Mastering all the search engines of public documents is like gazing upon

> an arch wherethro'
> Gleams that untravell'd world whose margin fades
> For ever and for ever when I move.

65

This chapter selectively surveys some of the more prominent retrospective and current sources that create a structure for this mass of federal government information. No theme, however fey, antic, arcane, or ostensibly inapposite, ever remains far from the omnivorous curiosity of government; this phenomenon is a major reason the bibliographic ideal is unattainable.

RETROSPECTIVE SOURCES

Many worthy publications assist researchers in their quest for U.S. government information. Among the notable retrospective guides, especially useful for large collections, are:

- J. H. Powell, *The Books of a New Nation: United States Government Publications, 1774–1814* (Philadelphia: University of Pennsylvania Press, 1957).

- LeRoy Merritt, *The United States Government as Publisher* (Chicago: University of Chicago Press, 1943).

- Anne M. Boyd, *United States Government Publications,* 3d ed. rev. by Rae E. Rips (New York: H. W. Wilson, 1949).

- Laurence F. Schmeckebier and Roy B. Eastin, *Government Publications and Their Use,* 2d rev. ed. (Washington: Brookings, 1969). This classic work is particularly useful for its detailed descriptions of the idiosyncrasies that characterize some of the pre-1969 bibliographic tools still in use.

- James Bennett Childs, *Government Publications: A Guide to Bibliographic Tools* (Washington: Government Printing Office, 1942).

- Vladimir M. Palic, *Government Publications: A Guide to Bibliographic Tools* (Washington: Library of Congress, 1975). This work covers official publications worldwide. A compilation of catalogs, checklists, indexes, accession lists, and bibliographies issued by federal agencies is found on pages 11–80. This guide was combined with another work by Palic and republished in one volume as *Government Publications: A Guide to Bibliographic Tools Incorporating Government Organization Manuals: A Bibliography* (New York: Pergamon Press, 1977).

- Everett Brown, *Manual of Government Publications* (New York: Appleton-Century-Crofts, 1950).

- Yuri Nakata, *From Press to People: Collecting and Using U.S. Government Publications* (Chicago: American Library Association, 1979).[1]

PRINT RESOURCES

Ironically, as the amount of government information in print has decreased, owing to misguided congressional and executive attempts to abridge government access in this form as cost-saving measures, there has been no decrease in the number and variety of printed guides to the literature reporting and commenting on the federal publishing enterprise. Omnibus guides to reference sources inevitably list many government publications and works about them. There are the standard classics such as Robert Balay's *Guide to Reference Books* and its *Supplements* and Bohdan S. Wynar's *American Reference Books Annual.* Guides to the literature of a specific discipline frequently cite government reference sources. In addition, official issuances such as the *National Union Catalog* and *New Serial Titles* should not be overlooked when searching for government information. Following is a selection of resources published since 1994 that contain federal government information for expert and tyro alike.

- Gayle J. Hardy and Judith Schiek Robinson, *Subject Guide to U.S. Government Reference Sources,* 2d ed. (Englewood, CO: Libraries Unlimited, 1996). Important reference materials are featured, including print and electronic formats.

- Edward Herman, *Locating United States Government Information,* 2d ed. (Buffalo, NY: William S. Hein, 1997). The author first published this monograph in 1983. The second edition, like the first, is a practical guide in workbook format, incorporating illustrations from indexes and abstracts, including questions and answers.[2] A 1999 *Internet Supplement* updates the basic volume.

- Peter Hernon, John A. Shuler, and Robert E. Dugan, *U.S. Government on the Web: Getting the Information You Need* (Englewood, CO: Libraries Unlimited, 1999). A successful attempt to bring order out of the unpredictable vagaries of federal Web sites, this book furnishes options for conducting a search by the use of search engines, by provenance, by browsing "one-stop shopping sites," by type of resource (e.g., maps, statistics), or by selected subjects. Moreover, between editions the information will be updated frequently via the publisher's home page (**http://www.lu.com**).

- Frank W. Hoffmann and Richard J. Wood, *Guide to Popular U.S. Government Publications, 1995–1996,* 5th ed. (Englewood, CO: Libraries Unlimited, 1998). The fifth edition of this guide continues the policy of providing a subject arrangement to the 1,500 most popular titles of both free and inexpensive federal publications of interest to the layperson. A broad range of document types is included: monographs, periodicals, posters, pamphlets, and so forth. Entries give complete bibliographic information, including annotations, for titles published between 1995 and 1996.

- Judith Schiek Robinson, *Tapping the Government Grapevine: The User-Friendly Guide to U.S. Government Sources,* 3d ed. (Phoenix, AZ: Oryx Press, 1998). A breezy, informal style, many mirthful sidebars, and meticulous attention to the minutiae of Internet protocols inform this well-regarded work. Included are a chapter on foreign and international documents and a very brief section on state government sources of information. Like Herman's text, *Tapping* has Q & A.

- Jean L. Sears and Marilyn K. Moody, *Using Government Information Sources: Print and Electronic,* 2d ed. (Phoenix, AZ: Oryx Press, 1994). This is a single-volume, extensive revision of the authors' 1985/1986 two-volume work. The focus is on a wide variety of information sources in print and electronic formats, with new chapters on astronomy and space, state and local government statistics, and judicial reports. Appendixes include directory information, including electronic bulletin board numbers, for federal agencies and selected nongovernmental organizations.

- Jerrold Zwirn, comp., *Accessing U.S. Government Information: Subject Guide to Jurisdiction of the Executive and Legislative Branches* (Westport, CT: Greenwood, 1996). A revised and expanded edition of an earlier effort, this is issued as part of Greenwood's Bibliographies and Indexes in Law and Political Science series. Designed as a ready reference source, it links entities in the executive and legislative branches with their respective jurisdictions and responsibilities.

GENERAL GUIDES

- Greg Notess, *Government Information on the Internet,* 2d ed. (Lanham, MD: Bernan Press, 1998). This fine work contains more than 1,500 Web sites, the majority of them federal government agencies. Also included are sites for state governments, international intergovernmental organizations (IGOs), and more than fifty national governments from Andorra to the Vatican. Each entry includes the title, sponsoring agency, primary URL, alternative access if applicable (telnet, ftp, gopher), subject heading(s), and a detailed and accurate descriptive and evaluative annotation of the site's main features. Rounding out the work are indexes referencing the entry numbers and organized by primary and alternative access URLs, SuDocs numbers, titles, issuing agencies, acronyms, and subjects. So long as it is updated annually, Notess remains the best print guide for worldwide coverage of Internet sites for entities of the several categories of governments.

- Laurie Andriot, *Internet Blue Pages: The Guide to Federal Government Web Sites, 1999 Edition* (Medford, NJ: CyberAge Books, 1998). A daughter of the late, legendary John Andriot, whose many monographic series on federal government agencies and titles grace numerous library reference areas, continues in her father's tradition of service to documents librarians. Using the *United States Government Manual* as a guide, the author visited as many federal Web sites as were available in 1998, providing the name of each agency, its Web address, an annotation, and links if applicable. Included are numbered entries for Congress, the judiciary, the executive branch with its departments and agencies, "Independent and Quasi-Official Agencies," and two entries under "Other Government Sites." Finding aids consist of an alphabetical list of agencies, with their URLs, and a subject index. One very useful feature of Andriot's compilation lies outside the print edition. Laurie Andriot has established her own Web site (**www.fedweb.com**). By using the entry number of the site, the user will be linked to that location. This in part solves the problem of the shifting Internet sands, and Andriot welcomes e-mail if one finds that a site has been moved or a new site has materialized (landriot@fedweb.com).

- A similar source is the "U.S. Government Agencies Directory," developed and maintained by the Louisiana State University Library Program. This site provides access to many agencies listed in the *United States Government Manual* by links to the agencies' Internet sites. You can perform a keyword search of federal agencies as well as link to the *Manual*'s online edition via GPO Access. Not every level of organization is indexed. Some organizations (for example, the Navy Department) have numerous subunits and provide good indexes from their home pages. Therefore, if an institution is not represented here, try the parent organization. No annotations are provided, but a direct link to the *Manual*'s online edition via GPO Access will give you valuable information about the entity's mission and related topics. The LSU site can be located through GPO Access or directly at **http://www.lib.lsu.edu/gov/fedgov.html**.

INTERNET SITES

At the outset of the fin-de-siècle decade, there existed a minuscule number of World Wide Web (WWW) sites capable of dispatching software spiders to canvass the Internet and carry back government information to be integrated into capacious indexes. Although gaining in number and sophistication as the decade approached the millennium, many of these Internet search companies still index by witchcraft and wizardry, not by established principles of the trade. Most users simply want to enter a word or phrase and wait for their favorite browser to sprinkle its technological pixie dust, but that technique (which is no technique at all) often brings up great numbers of unwanted locations. There are general purpose search engines that everyone with a computer and Internet access is aware of: search-and-metasearch directories such as Altavista, Ask Jeeves, Excite, HotBot, Infoseek, Lycos, Metacrawler, SavvySearch, WebCrawler, and Yahoo! Indeed, there is a nationwide list of Internet Service Providers (**http://thelist.internet.com**) to keep track of the growing number of engines. Companies such as Yahoo!, Excite, and Lycos are hot properties on the Internet (and on the stock exchanges) because they operate Web sites known as "portals." Portals grew out of the "search engine" concept, a service that allows the user to find Web sites simply by typing in some key words or phrases. They expanded to deliver a suite of online services such as free e-mail, news, chat rooms, and personalized functions such as stock quotes, local weather, sports, and even local lottery numbers. These sites get much of their revenue from advertising. Examples of top portals in terms of numbers of visitors, in addition to Lycos, Excite, and Yahoo!, include AOL.com, MSN.com, Geocities.com, and Netscape.com. Virtually all of these general sites have links to government information Web sites and can be limited to searching the .gov and .mil top-level domains. To fine tune these instrumentalities, the documents community often relies upon government general purpose search engines. Some of the better-known finding aids in this category, all worthy of being bookmarked, are:

- The Federal Web Locator (**http://www.law.vil.edu/Fedagency/fedwebloc.html**). Sponsor: Villanova University Center for Information Law and Policy;

- Fedworld (**http://www.fedworld.gov**). Sponsor: National Technical Information Service;

- GovBot Database of Government Web Sites (**http://eden.cs.umass.edu/Govbot**). Sponsor: Center for Intelligent Information Retrieval;

- Government InfoMine (**http://lib-www.ucr.edu/govsearch/html**). Sponsor: University of California, Riverside Library;

- The Great American Web Site: The Citizen's Guide to U.S. Government Resources on the World Wide Web (**http://unclesam.com**). Sponsor: Inside Information;

- United States Government Information (**http://wwwnhc.nhmccd.cc.tx.us/public/lrc.gov/gov.html**). Sponsor: North Harris College, Houston, Texas. This fine site has numerous "quick links" to just about every aspect of government information, and has been duly acknowledged by the reliable Argus Clearinghouse ratings service.

- Yahoo! Government (**http://yahoo.com/government**). Sponsor: Yahoo!Inc. This last is typical of the range of information and is illustrative of a fairly reliable search directory. In the federal legislative branch alone there are more than twenty buttons providing links to most of the primary and secondary source materials a researcher could profitably explore.

Praiseworthy indeed are the creative efforts of libraries like North Harris, which have agreed to serve as GPO Gateways and partnerships or have struck out on their own. For instance, the Government Documents

Department Web site of the University of Memphis library has a database called "Migrating Government Publications" covering monographs and serials that have left their home in print (often never to return to that format) and migrated to the Internet (**http://www.lib.memphis.edu/ gpo/mig.htm**).

The United States General Accounting Office (GAO)'s *World Wide Web Sites Reported by Federal Organizations* (GAO/GGD97-86S), June 1997, contains approximately 4,300 WWW sites reported to the GAO by federal entities and is available on the Internet via GPO Access or directly at **http://www.gao.gov/cgi/bin/getrpt/ GGD97-86s**. In a companion report, GAO notes that "a WWW site can . . . be broadly defined as the entire WWW presence for an organization. Under this definition, for example, NOAA [the National Oceanic and Atmospheric Administration, an agency within the Commerce Department] would have one WWW site at Internet address 'http://www.noaa.gov.' Furthermore, a WWW site can be defined as a distinct computer that hosts the WWW pages. Using this definition, NOAA would have 85 WWW sites because 85 different computers actually host its WWW presence. Using [the latter] definition, NOAA reported having 383 WWW sites, that is, 383 distinct activities or services on the WWW being maintained within NOAA."[3]

There are many other services, some of which may continue to thrive while others may fall into desuetude. Alas, Internet sites wax and wane with respect to accuracy of addresses and, perhaps of greatest importance, frequency of updating. The alert information professional continually scans the screens of GOVDOC-L, *Administrative Notes,* and other relevant resources including, of course, the Internet itself, simply to keep up with what's hot and what's not. For example, a Web site that includes reviews of search engine performance and furnishes basic information about how the engines work and how they compare may be visited at **http://www.searchenginewatch.com**. Or simply go to a search directory and search for "search engine."

AGENCY HISTORIES

The late John L. Andriot began publishing guides to federal statistics and to major U.S. government series in the 1950s. Of his several efforts, his *Guide to U.S. Government Publications* is the most prominent and consistently updated. His family seems to have inherited Papa's knack for generating helpful resources. *Guide to U.S. Government Publications* (McLean, VA: Documents Index), now edited by Donna Andriot, is an annual that furnishes a listing in SuDocs class number order of series currently being issued by the various government agencies. Each entry contains a brief note on the agency's creation and history. One helpful feature is an "Agency Class Chronology" in which, for example, one can easily trace the transition from Education Department (I 16) to Education Bureau (FS 5, HE 5, HE 19.10) back to Education Department (ED 1). The guide is indexed by both agency and title.

PROFESSIONAL LITERATURE

The literature of librarianship is replete with numerous articles and studies about government information. Many of the journals regularly feature columns, bibliographic roundups, annual updates, reviews, general commentary, news notes, and specialized articles on topics of interest to the profession. For example, a "Notable Documents List," which contains state and international documents as well as federal publications, is published annually in an issue of *Library Journal*. For a full range of secondary source materials, indexing/abstracting services such as *Library Literature, Information Science Abstracts,* and *Resources in Education* and *Current Index to Journals in Education* (which together make up the ERIC database) should be consulted.

Professional journals devoted entirely to the publications and activities of governments at all levels include the *Journal of Government Information* (JGI), formerly titled *Government Publications Review; Government Information Quarterly* (GIQ); and *Documents to the People* (DttP). The first two are research-oriented, scholarly periodicals, the last is the professional news magazine of the Government Documents Round Table (GODORT) of the American Library Association. Individual issues of GIQ contain an editorial, reviews, and articles analyzing information policies and practices. JGI is published six times a year and has a "Notable Documents" issue at the end of each year. It also features in one issue a bibliography of primary and secondary source materials titled "Recent Literature on Government Information." *Documents to the People* has a similar feature in one of its quarterly issues titled "DttP Bibliography on Documents Librarianship and Government Information." All three periodicals cover government information at all levels and publish the kinds of articles that advance one's scope and knowledge of government information and its effects.

Because of the growth of materials in electronic formats, coverage of government information in journals such as *Database, CD-ROM Librarian, CD-ROM Professional, Computers in Libraries, Internet Research, The Internet Connection: Your Guide to Government*

Resources, Library Hi Tech, and *Library Software Review* has proliferated; and these journals, among others, should be accessed as well.

DIRECTORIES

Directories connect the user with other people or collections, can get one started when floundering in new territory, and can provide contacts of a last resort where difficult queries are involved. An indispensable source is the *Directory of Government Documents Collections & Librarians,* 7th ed. The 1997 edition, as in past editions, is copyrighted by the American Library Association (Government Documents Round Table) but is published by Congressional Information Service, a private company located in Bethesda, Maryland. It profiles thousands of institutions with substantial holdings of federal, state, local, international, and foreign government publications. The main entries (Section I) for each library appear in geo-alphabetical order by state, city, and institution and, if necessary, by library within an institution. Each entry includes copious amounts of useful information, including the library's e-mail address and Web site, if available. Nine other sections include, inter alia, state document authorities, the lead agency in each state for the State Data Centers (see Chapter 9), library school instructors of government information, and a library's areas of exceptional subject strength for state and local documents and documents of international organizations.

A good example of a specialized directory is William R. Evinger, ed., *Directory of Federal Libraries,* 3d ed. (Phoenix, AZ: Oryx Press, 1998). More than 2,500 federal libraries and information centers are included, from large institutions such as the National Library of Medicine and the National Technical Information Service (NTIS) to very small libraries with one or two employees. Arrangement is by federal agency and then alphabetically by name. Standard directory information is furnished, as well as the types of service for those institutions serving the public. Indexes are by subject, geography, and type of library.

Joyce A. McCray Pearson and Pamela M. Tull's *U.S. Government Directories, 1982–1995* (Englewood, CO: Libraries Unlimited, 1998) is a subject approach to directories and related publications with directory-type information, including those published in print, on microform and CD-ROM, and in computer files. Grouped into twelve chapters, the entries are arranged by issuing agency. Supplied is complete bibliographic information for each entry. There are separate author/title and subject indexes. Pearson and Tull's work continues Donna Rae Larson's two-volume *Guide to U.S. Government Directories* (Phoenix,

AZ: Oryx Press, 1981–1985), in which volume 1 covers the period 1970–1980 and volume 2, 1980–1984.

CITATION MANUALS

There is no single, uniform way to cite all federal government materials. Citations should, however, contain sufficient bibliographic information to lead the reader to the source, and similar material should be consistent in format. There are a multitude of citation manuals and many of them are quite good. Three, however, merit special mention. The authoritative source for the legal community is *The Bluebook: A Uniform System of Citation,* 16th ed. (Cambridge, MA: Harvard Law Review Association, 1996). Previous editions of this venerable source were published as *A Uniform System of Citation* with the word "Bluebook" as an unwritten popular name. The work has been traditionally bound in a blue cover, and a new edition is issued about every five years.

Complementing *The Bluebook* is Mary M. Prince's *Bieber's Dictionary of Legal Citations: Reference Guide for Attorneys, Legal Secretaries, Paralegals and Law Students,* 5th ed. (Buffalo, NY: William S. Hein, 1997), which furnishes citation examples in accordance with the rules appearing in the sixteenth edition of *The Bluebook.* Chapter 8 explores the issues surrounding legal citation formats.

Diane L. Garner and Diane H. Smith's *The Complete Guide to Citing Government Information Sources: A Manual for Writers and Librarians,* rev. ed. (Bethesda, MD: Congressional Information Service, 1993) is an updated version of their 1984 manual. It includes all governments and all forms, including electronic citing, and is to the government documents librarian what *The Bluebook* is to the law librarian.

BIBLIOGRAPHIES

A bibliography of government bibliographies may itself be a commercially published source; conversely, governmentally published bibliographies may cite privately published sources. A retrospective guide is the *Annotated Bibliography of Bibliographies on Selected Government Publications and Supplementary Guides to the Superintendent of Documents Classification System.* Alexander C. Body first published this work in 1967, and five supplements were issued by Body through 1977. Beginning with the sixth supplement in 1980, the bibliography was supplemented by Gabor Kovacs. The eleventh edition (1990) was compiled by Mary L. Alm (Greeley, CO). This work has always been distinguished by its lengthy and meticulously thorough annotations. There is a cumulative microfiche index to the various editions.

Several other bibliographic guides cover discrete periods of time. One is the seven-volume *Cumulative Subject Guide to U.S. Government Bibliographies 1924–1973,* compiled by Edna Kanely (Arlington, VA and Inverness, Scotland: Carrollton Press, 1976–1977), which extracts and arranges by subject the 112 pages of bibliographies found under each heading in the fifteen-volume *Cumulative Subject Index to the Monthly Catalog . . . 1900–1971,* as well as all entries from the *Monthly Catalog* in which the phrase "with bibliography" or "with list of references" appeared. The Kanely set identifies 40,000 bibliographies in all. Some libraries may own *U.S. Government Bibliography Masterfile 1924–1973,* a corresponding microfiche package that Carrollton Press originally compiled.

Other guides include Roberta A. Scull's *A Bibliography of United States Government Bibliographies, Vol. 1: 1968–1973* (Ann Arbor, MI: Pierian Press, 1974), which was updated in a second volume covering 1974–1976 and subsequently updated through 1979 in *Reference Services Review.* The set covers over 2,600 bibliographies grouped within broad subject categories, with both subject and title indexes. Most entries are annotated and include full bibliographic information. Noted in chapter 2, GPO's own *Subject Bibliography Index* lists (but does not index) more than 180 individual subject bibliographies that users can request from the Superintendent of Documents. These brief guides, usually two to eight pages long, cover topics from Accounting and Auditing to Youth. The *Index* assists customers in selecting the subject bibliography that is most closely related to their needs. Both the *Subject Bibliography Index* and the individual subject bibliographies are free of charge and are available in print or in an electronic edition on GPO Access or on the Federal Bulletin Board (FBB).

ACRONYMS

Guide to Federal Government Acronyms (Phoenix, AZ: Oryx Press, 1989), edited by William R. Evinger, includes almost 20,000 abbreviations, acronyms, and initialisms found in federal government entities, programs, projects, statutes, agency products and services, automated information systems, and other sources. The preface notes that some agencies, such as EPA, NASA, NOAA, NUREG, and the Army Department, "are more thoroughly covered due to the existence of acronym compilations available for those agencies." Although many of these ubiquitous subspecies of the language are duplicated in other works, including the massive *Acronyms, Initialisms, and Abbreviations Dictionary* (Farmington, MI: Gale Group, formerly Gale Research), the major advantage of Evinger's guide is its scope and specialized attention to the multitude of acronyms and related word-condensation forms spawned by the activities and entities of the federal establishment. The first section gives the short form followed by its title and, in most cases, the federal department or agency associated with the abbreviation. In the second section the user can proceed from the full name or title to the acronym. Examples include SPACETRACK (National Space Surveillance Control Center) and Amtrak (National Railroad Passenger Corporation). Selected lists of acronyms are found in Robinson's *Tapping the Government Grapevine* (previously mentioned) and in the *United States Government Manual.*

INFORMATION MANAGEMENT

Written by seasoned practitioners, *Management of Government Information Resources in Libraries* (Englewood, CO: Libraries Unlimited, 1993) consists of a series of essays covering specific management issues such as cataloging, staff training, and acquisitions. Edited by Diane H. Smith, the collection is designed as a practical manual for those learning about or currently managing government information. It includes state and international documents as well as U.S. government materials and discusses the use of new technologies, policy issues, and financial considerations.

AUDIOVISUAL MATERIALS

Audiovisual (AV) materials are not considered "publications" under the provisions of chapter 19, Title 44, *United States Code,* and are not distributed to depository libraries. Rarely are they listed individually by title in the *Monthly Catalog,* sales catalogs, or standard bibliographic sources for government information; moreover, some of the catalogs are not depository items. The National Audiovisual Center (NAC), a unit within the National Archives and Records Administration (NARA), acts as a clearinghouse to collect copies of federally produced audiovisual products and to make them available to other agencies and the public for sale or rent. Agencies are not required to deposit their AV materials with NAC; thus, the collection housed at NAC is not comprehensive. However, the NAC provides information on the availability of federal AV materials from agencies and other sources if the materials are not in the NAC collections. NAC's home page, via NTIS, is easy to use and shows more than 9,000 audiovisual and media productions grouped into more than 600 individual subject headings. Subject areas include training in occupational safety and health, fire services, law enforcement, and foreign languages. Educational materials include areas such as history, health, agriculture, and natural resources. Just select the title you want to order at **http://www.ntis.gov/nac/nac.htm**. Moreover, from the FedWorld Web site (**http://www.fedworld.gov/search.htm**), you can select as a metadatabase the NAC collection consisting of more than 1,600 descriptions of U.S. government audiovisual products.

In general there are two types of audiovisual catalogs: those that list or announce AV materials produced by the agency and those that list collections of AV materials in a library media center as a guide to authorized users of those facilities. An example of the former is *National Science Foundation Films,* which lists films produced by the Foundation. An example of the latter (and more common of the two) is the Army National Training Center's *Audiovisual Catalog: Photo Devices, Graphics, Audiovisuals,* which lists materials available for loan only to authorized military personnel of the Training and Audiovisual Support Center, Fort Irwin, California. Audiovisual catalogs are indexed in the *Monthly Catalog,* but, as noted, the individual products are not. Two free catalogs offering AV materials are available from NTIS: the *Catalog of Multimedia Training Products* (PR-1001CGB) and the *Catalog of Educational Multimedia Products* (PR-1047CGB). These can be viewed or downloaded from NTIS's Web site (**http://www.ntis. gov/catalogs.htm**).

The Library of Congress publishes two serials that provide bibliographic coverage of AV materials. The *National Union Catalog: Audiovisual Materials* contains information on motion pictures, filmstrips, transparency and slide sets, and video recordings. The *Catalog of Copyright Entries, Fourth Series* includes motion pictures and filmstrips in part 4 and sound recordings in part 7.

The *Catalog of Audiovisual Productions,* issued by the Department of Defense, was published in looseleaf format in four volumes: *Army Productions, Navy and Marine Corps Productions, Air Force and Miscellaneous DoD Productions,* and *DoD Productions Cleared for Public Release.* The National Library of Medicine (NLM) has an online database called AVLINE (AudioVisuals onLINE) that gives full bibliographic descriptions of over 21,000 AV and other non-print teaching materials in clinical medicine cataloged by NLM (**http://www.nlm. nih.gov**). AVLINE is also available in magnetic tape. In addition, NLM issues *Health Sciences Audiovisuals Catalog* on microfiche and the

National Library of Medicine Audiovisuals Catalog, which lists serials and monographs produced both publicly and privately.

CATALOGS, INDEXES, AND CHECKLISTS

Current bibliographic efforts at GPO are remarkably reliable and accurate in their own right, but especially so when compared to the endeavors of the government during the nineteenth and early twentieth centuries. Although the need for a catalog of official U.S. publications was first publicly discussed in 1845, Congress waited until 1883 before charging Benjamin Perley Poore with the unenviable task of locating and cataloging all federal government publications produced since the beginning of the republic. We have indeed come a long way since Poore compared his task to that of "Christopher Columbus when he steered westward on his voyage of discovery, confident that a new world existed, but having no knowledge of its distance or the direction in which it lay. No one could estimate how many publications were to be cataloged, where they were to be found, how long it would take to perform the work, or what would be the probable cost."[4]

The official sources that follow in this section include Poore's activity as well as four other key bibliographical tools produced under the aegis of the federal government that continue to remain in use in large research libraries. As federal documents are rarely copyrighted, reprints of these catalogs usually can be obtained from commercial publishers. Sources are listed chronologically, with the dates that appear after the popular name heading intended to assist the searcher by indicating scope of coverage. Although all the sources below include federal publications from each branch of the government, access to pre-twentieth-century executive branch, or departmental, documents can be difficult when relying solely upon official sources. Those official sources intended to index only congressional reports and documents are discussed in a later section of this chapter.

Poore (1774–1881)

More than 100 years had passed since the birth of the nation when Benjamin Perley Poore, Clerk of the Senate's Committee on Printing, and his fourteen equally inexperienced helpers, undertook the monumental bibliographic task of compiling all federal government publications: executive, legislative, and judicial. After scouring the contents of the major federal libraries, as well as other appropriate public and private libraries, they were able to identify 63,063 documents. The result was Poore's *Descriptive Catalogue of the Government Publications of the United States, September 5, 1774–March 4, 1881,* issued as Senate Miscellaneous Document 67, 48th Congress, Second Session (Serial Volume 2268).

Alas, this chronological list lacks an effective index, is riddled with errors, omits many early documents, and is particularly weak in its coverage of departmental (executive) documents. Nonetheless, for many documents librarians unable to afford an expensive commercial index, Poore's *Descriptive Catalogue* is the mainstay for identifying early federal government publications. Because Poore did not furnish serial volume numbers for congressional documents, the *Checklist* or *Tables and Index* (see below) may need to be used in conjunction with the *Descriptive Catalogue.*

Ames (1881–1893)

In his capacity as Superintendent of Documents, Dr. John Griffith Ames began an official enumeration of documents in 1881, at the point where Poore's *Descriptive Catalogue* left off. Ames's *Comprehensive Index to the Publications of the United States Government, 1881–1893* was issued in two volumes as House Document 754, 58th Congress, second session (Serial Volumes 4745 and 4746). Although coverage of departmental publications still showed some neglect, the *Comprehensive Index* was a manifest improvement over Poore's endeavor. Arrangement is alphabetical by subject (keyword in the title) with a personal name index. Serial volume numbers are given in tables under the subject heading "Congressional Documents." An excellent account of Ames's several contributions to public document reform is found in an essay by Bell and Richardson.[5]

Checklist (1789–1909)

Not only did Ames produce the *Comprehensive Index,* he also developed the concept of serial set numbering and was responsible for the issuance of the *Checklist of United States Public Documents, 1789–1909.* The *Checklist* reproduced the shelflist of the Public Documents Library. It is arranged by classification number in three sections: congressional edition by serial number, departmental edition by SuDocs classification notation, and miscellaneous publications of Congress. The inclusion of departmental publications marks a significant improvement over the *Descriptive Catalogue* and the *Comprehensive Index.* It is useful for examining the scope of a particular agency's publishing from the time of its establishment through 1909, as well as the evolution of editions of a particular document. Unfortunately, the projected index volume—which would have provided author, subject, and title access to the documents—was never published, thereby making it difficult for the neophyte documents searcher to use the *Checklist.*

Document Catalog (1893–1940)

The Printing Act of 1895 mandated that "the Superintendent of Documents shall, at the close of each regular session of Congress, prepare and publish a comprehensive index of public documents beginning with the 53rd Congress." The resulting biennial work is praiseworthy for its bibliographic thoroughness and accuracy. Such high standards of cataloging no doubt contributed to the fact that production of the *Document Catalog* was continually behind schedule. Finally, in 1947, as the cost of compiling and printing the retrospective work grew ever more burdensome, the Superintendent of Documents recommended to the Joint Committee on Printing that it be discontinued after being brought up to 1940.

The official title of this analytical dictionary catalog, with entries for personal and governmental author, subject, and, frequently, title, is *Catalogue of the Public Documents of the [Fifty-third—Seventy-sixth] Congress and of All Departments of the Government of the United States.* Proclamations and executive orders are indexed, as are articles in periodicals that were issued regularly. A list of government offices appears at the end of each catalog to serve as a guide to government organization. Beginning with the 56th Congress, the serial volume number is also included in brackets to permit easy access to the bound volumes of the Congressional Serial Set. The *Document Catalog* is a splendid source, the most accurate and the most comprehensive official bibliography for the period 1893–1940.

Monthly Catalog (1895–)

For the above period, the *Document Catalog* reigns supreme. The *Monthly Catalog of United States Government Publications,* however, is the most comprehensive ongoing source for federal publications, including both depository and non-depository materials. Because it fulfills so many functions in libraries, including reference, cataloging, and acquisitions, it is indispensable.

Known simply as the *Monthly Catalog,* or MOCAT, this source also had its origin in the Printing Act of 1895. It began as little more than an in-print list, designed to remedy the haphazard system of distribution and sales of public documents. It was only after the *Document Catalog* ceased publication that the *Monthly Catalog* was required by law to expand its coverage and improve its bibliographic accuracy. From 1940 until the advent of the *Publications Reference File* (now on GPO Access as the *Sales Product Catalog*), the *Monthly Catalog* served as the single official source of publications, fulfilling both statutory requirements of the 1895 law: that there be a "comprehensive index" and a "Monthly [sales] Catalog." It is the flagship publication of its provenance, the Office of the Superintendent of Documents.

The MOCAT Today: Print and CD-ROM

Since it was first issued in 1895, the *Monthly Catalog* has changed its name seven times and has undergone numerous other modifications, some minor and others major, the most extensive occurring with the July 1976 issue on the occasion of the U.S. bicentennial celebrations. Prior to July 1976, the *Monthly Catalog* was arranged alphabetically, either by department or by issuing agency, with the exception of the publications of the Congress, which were subdivided both by form and by issuing entity. Entries were short and barely adequate, and monthly and annual indexes of marginal quality were organized in an interfiled author-title-subject format. Decennial indexes (1941–1950 and 1951–1960), quinquennial cumulations (1961–1965 and 1966–1970), and a cumulation covering the period 1971 through June 1976 made searching somewhat easier. These indexes were slow to appear in print, however, thereby making the search process tedious. Because most libraries with segregated documents collections used the MOCAT as a substitute for their card catalog, users needed to consult multiple volumes (both monthlies and annuals) to locate a specific publication if the date was unknown or to develop a bibliography of documents on a particular subject. Commercial products discussed elsewhere in this chapter have eased the retrospective search considerably.

Relatively simple and unsophisticated, the earlier *Monthly Catalog's* format was as familiar to users as the playing of Henryk Wieniawski's violin concerto at classical music festivals. That relative stability was shattered with the appearance of the July 1976 issue. Not only was there a visible change in its size and appearance, but also, for the first time, the *Monthly Catalog* used Library of Congress subject headings, followed Anglo-American Cataloging Rules, incorporated MARC format, and participated in the OCLC cataloging network. There followed over a period of years the creation of multiple, separate indexes (author, title, title/keyword, subject [LCSH]), series/report number, contract number, stock number, and SuDocs number (in the semiannual and annual cumulations). Accompanying this expanded print edition was a microfiche version, which was discontinued after the December 1995 issue. Since 1976 several commercial publishers have purchased GPO's machine-readable tapes from the Library of Congress's Cataloging Distribution Service and issued their own CD-ROM versions of the upgraded product.

The Library Programs Service, on Survey Shipping List 96-00007-E dated November 3, 1995, announced that the official edition of the MOCAT on CD-ROM was scheduled for release January 1996. It didn't happen until that summer, but the first disk included the cumulative data sets from January and a special issue that had been appearing in print, called the *Periodicals Supplement*. The CD-ROM incorporated most of the features of the expanded, post-July 1976 paper version, but the revised print edition consisted of entries even more emaciated than the pre-July 1976 MOCAT. In its present curtailed form, the print version contains abbreviated descriptions of the records on the CD-ROM and but one index, an alphabetical list of truncated titles arranged by keywords selected from the publication titles. To be fair, the "new" print edition includes the same number of entries announced on the official CD-ROM (and its commercial versions); but the lone title-keyword index significantly limits access, and the skimpy, information-starved entries do a disservice to small libraries that may not wish to spend more than $200 for the compact disk version. The present formats have replaced microfiche and print editions that existed from July 1976 to December 1995. Both the paperback and CD-ROM editions are listed in *U.S. Government Subscriptions* as SuDocs sales publications. Selective depository libraries may choose either the abridged print or the CD-ROM but not both, whereas regionals receive both versions.

The CD-ROM version of the post-January 1996 MOCAT continues the same complete bibliographic records and separate, additional indexes. Other features of the MOCAT include documents sales information, ordering information, deposit accounts, standing order service, book dealer discounts, international customers, and a directory for ordering assistance; an order form; a list of government bookstores; a list of current regional depository libraries; a list of special materials such as errata, change notices, transmittals, and so forth; corrections for previous issues; an alphabetical list of government authors; and a sample entry, shown here as Figure 4.1, page 84.

Figure 4.1. Sample entry from *Monthly Catalog*.

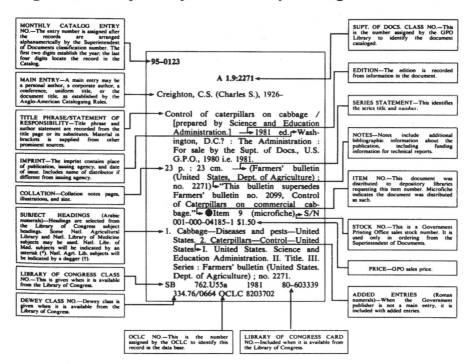

The CD-ROM MOCAT cumulates entries monthly so that an annual cumulation is reflected in the December issue. Moreover, each monthly issue includes a file called the "Periodical Supplement," exactly the same as the annual printed *Periodicals Supplement.* In short, the version of the MOCAT that began with the July 1976 issue has been transmuted from print to compact disk while an abridged print edition reverts to a pre-1976 level of attenuation—back to the future, as it were.

Periodicals Supplement to the MOCAT

The *Periodicals Supplement,* a special issue of the *Monthly Catalog,* has a peculiar history in its print version. It was published annually, usually as the first catalog issued during the year, beginning with Entry Number 1. From 1977 to 1984 the annual was called the *Serials Supplement,* which replaced a comparable listing that was published in the February issue of the pre-July 1976 MOCAT. In 1985 it assumed its present name. With the January 1996 issue, the *Periodicals Supplement* became a file of each monthly issue of the CD-ROM *Monthly Catalog,* a vast improvement in timeliness over the annual issues. In 1996 and 1997 the *Supplement* was only available on the official

MOCAT CD-ROM. However, in 1998 the print annual was reborn and depository libraries subscribing to Item 557-D-1 could receive their copy in that format again. Meanwhile, the *Supplement* continued to be available in cumulative form on the compact disk.

Entries in both formats are arranged in the same manner. The index contains collective records for serial publications that are issued three or more times each year. Bibliographic records for serials issued twice a year or less are announced in the issues of the MOCAT. The preliminary pages include useful information about sales publications, ordering information, and so forth. The bibliographic entries represent current serial titles, updated annually in lists named "Title Changes From Previous Periodicals Supplement" and "Discontinued Periodicals From Previous Periodicals Supplements." SuDocs classification changes are identified in the "Classification Changes" list. Access is by all the indexes noted for the MOCAT above except the contract number index.

It is important to distinguish the sales program's *U.S. Government Subscriptions,* discussed in chapter 2, from the *Periodicals Supplement.* The former lists only those periodicals and subscription services for sale by the Superintendent of Documents. The latter includes all sales titles and in addition contains periodicals not available through SuDocs sales. Figure 4.2, page 86, shows a sample entry from the *Periodicals Supplement.* Note the "Indexed by" feature in the sample entry, a most useful addition to the bibliographic record inasmuch as determining what government periodicals are indexed in which of the many indexing services is not an exact science.

The MOCAT on the Internet

As if to compensate for the diluted print edition, the MOCAT is available on the Internet via the GPO Access Web site. This product consists of bibliographic records published in the MOCAT since January 1994, but this database is updated daily with preliminary cataloging records that are edited and published in future issues of the MOCAT. At the page titled "Search Databases Online Via GPO Access" **(http://www.access.gpo.gov/su_docs/db2.html)** you will espy "Catalog of U.S. Government Publications (MOCAT)," the name given to the Internet version of this ubiquitous index. Select this heading and you are greeted by a veritable pedagogy of helpful hints; search terms and strategies; fields to be searched; and search results, including relevance rankings; location of the document in depository libraries; and MARC tags.

Figure 4.2. Sample entry from *Periodicals Supplement*.

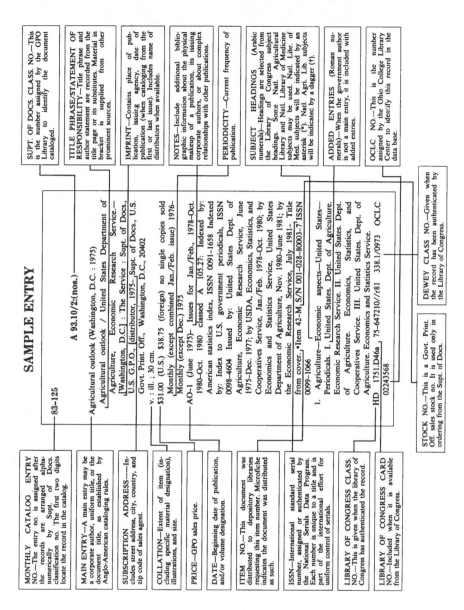

Search terms are abundant and include subjects; names of authors, editors, or organizations; words in a title or series; geographic terms such as the name of a state; format terms such as computer file, database, microfiche, or videorecording; identifying numbers; and dates. There is a roundup of the usual protocols: phrases enclosed by quotation marks, operators in capital letters, truncation identified with an asterisk, precise word order if searching by provenance, and so forth. It is likely that well before the end of the first decade of the twenty-first century, the universality and sophistication of speech recognition systems will render these user-unfriendly commands as extinct as the Cambrian fossils of the Burgess Shale.

The full name for the Web-based MOCAT, *Catalog of United States Government Publications,* is an obvious accommodation, since the word "monthly" is not applicable. The search results reveal a summary record that includes title, date, issuing entity, SuDocs class notation, stock number (if applicable), depository item number, and format. Records are presented in relevance ranked order, based on the occurrence of the search terms in the title and other factors, the most relevant titles having the rank of 1000. Below each entry on the "Rank" line are three items to select: Locate Libraries, TEXT, and HTML. The first is a nice touch. The user can select the depository library or libraries receiving that title, by state or area code, to create an instant, customized union list. Selecting TEXT renders the full cataloging record; selecting HTML offers the same record with a hyperlink to an electronic document. Finally, as noted in chapter 2, MOCAT records are also available on the Federal Bulletin Board at **http://www.fedbbs.access.gpo.gov**. However, to search for individual records, it is best to continue to use the MOCAT on the World Wide Web or on CD-ROM.

INDEXES TO THE UNITED STATES CONGRESSIONAL SERIAL SET

A detailed discussion of the contents and organization of the serial set is assayed in chapter 5. It is my purpose to introduce here the several finding aids to this eminent series from its inception. The serial set was established in 1817 to provide a uniform system of congressional publishing. A serial number, or accession number, is assigned to the spine of each bound volume, with the first volume assigned the number 1 in 1817 continuing through the latest serial numbering. The serial number itself is a locational device intended for convenience in shelving.

Specialized government-produced indexes to the serial set include the titles listed below in chronological order. Because serial numbering did not begin until the 15th Congress, the publications of the first four-teen congresses (1789–1817) were assigned a special series of num-bers, 01 to 038, known as the *American State Papers,* "which contain reprints of the publications of the first 14 congresses, as well as those of some later congresses. The only other congressional publications not given serial numbers are the reports on private bills for the 3d session of the 58th Congress (1904–05) and the two sessions of the 59th Con-gress (1905–07)."[6] It is important to remember that these sources are of use in accessing executive as well as congressional publications because many such departmental publications required by law to be transmitted to Congress were subsequently ordered to be issued in a "Congressional edition." This publishing practice is noted in greater detail in chapter 5.

Greely (1789–1817)

Adolphus Washington Greely was a soldier, scientist, and Arctic ex-plorer who supervised a compilation of congressional publications for the early congresses. His *Public Documents of the First Fourteen Congresses, 1789–1817—Papers Relating to Early Congressional Documents,* issued as Senate Document 428, 56th Congress, first ses-sion, overlaps somewhat with Poore, although Greely made no attempt to include departmental publications as such. The arrangement is chronological by congress, followed by a name index. A supplement was published in volume 1 of the 1903 Annual Report of the American Historical Association.

Tables and Index (1817–1893)

Continuing Greely's work, the *Tables of and Annotated Index to the Congressional Series of United States Public Documents* lists publications of the 15th to the 52nd Congresses, 1817–1893. The first section of the book, the "Tables," replicates the first section of the *Checklist* (pp. 5–169) and gives congressional series information, with notes on contents and on omission or duplication in the Congressional Serial Set. The second section, the "Index," which the *Checklist* lacks, is a helpful reference by subject and name, with the accompanying serial number of the bound congressional set. However, because the *Tables and Index* includes little more than half of the congressional reports and documents issued during the period covered, the researcher must turn to the commercially produced *CIS US Serial Set Index, 1789–1969* for comprehensive coverage.

Document Index (1895-1933)

The Printing Act of 1895 also required the Superintendent of Documents to "prepare and print in one volume a consolidated index of congressional documents." The resulting *Index to the Reports and Documents of the [Fifty-fourth–Seventy-second] Congress, with Numerical Lists and Schedule of Volumes, 1895–1933* is an alphabetical subject (or inverted title) listing for congressional reports and documents contained in the serial set. Libraries that have the *Document Catalog* will rarely need to use the *Document Index* unless the researcher has only the number of the publication.

Numerical Lists and Schedule of Volumes (1933-1980)

The *Numerical Lists and Schedule of Volumes* continues those sections of the *Document Index* identifying the congressional reports and documents in numbered sequence (the "Lists") and showing the arrangement of the reports and documents by serial set numbered volumes (the "Schedule"). There is no subject access. With the demise of the *Document Catalog,* the *Numerical Lists* assumed a more important role in accessing the serial set volumes. Because of its importance in this respect, the *Numerical Lists* is considered in more detail in chapter 5.

Monthly Catalog—Congressional Serial Set Supplements

Beginning with the 97th Congress (1981–1982) the *Numerical Lists* was renamed, reformatted, and issued as a special edition of the *Monthly Catalog* utilizing the same expansive format and indexing as the MOCAT. The title given for that Congress was *Monthly Catalog— U.S. Congressional Serial Set Supplement, 97th Congress, 1981–1982.* A title change occurred with the next Congress, and this supplement was renamed *United States Congressional Serial Set Catalog: Numerical Lists and Schedule of Volumes, 98th Congress: 1983–1984, Entries and Indexes.* Subsequent biennial issues have retained this name. Entries for the reports and documents are arranged by SuDocs classification number and are given the same full bibliographic information as previously appeared in various issues of the MOCAT. These supplements are indexed by author, title, subject, series/ report, and bill number. They are for sale by the Superintendent of Documents and available to depository libraries either in paper or on microfiche. Unfortunately, these supplements experienced a time lag of three or more years, and it is presumed that they have been mercifully abandoned.

Perhaps because of the lack of timeliness of these biennial supplements, the LPS has published periodically a "Schedule of Serial Set Volumes" for several congresses (not the "Numerical Lists") in *Administrative Notes,* but this information is not published in a timely fashion. Discontinuing the easy-to-use *Numerical Lists* was, in my judgment, a mistake on the part of the LPS. Adding to the woes of serial set users, the Congress, in a misguided effort to effect savings, directed the GPO to discontinue distribution of the bound Serial Set volumes except those sent to regional depository libraries and one library in each state without a regional. The ukase became effective with the 105th Congress (1997–1998).[7]

CIS US Serial Set Index, 1789–1969

This monumental undertaking permits researchers to bypass the earlier, flawed bibliographic guides described above and provides access through 1969. From 1970, coverage of serial set publications, as well as other congressional materials, is made available by *CIS/Index.* The *CIS US Serial Set Index* is the definitive retrospective reference work, providing access to over 11 million pages of information. The indexes consist of fourteen parts. Parts I–XII consist of three volumes each, with a uniform indexing format. Access is by subjects and keywords, private relief and related actions (private legislation affecting persons or organizations), numerical lists of report and document numbers, and a schedule of serial volumes. Part XIII is an index by reported bill number in four volumes. Part XIV is an index and carto-bibliography of maps. The full text is available by subscribing to the *CIS US Serial Set on Microfiche.*

PERIODICAL INDEXES

Federal government periodicals are underrated and underutilized. They offer current information of reference and research value, reflect public policy trends, contain timely reviews, have many other useful features, and themselves serve as indexing and abstracting sources (for example, *Index Medicus, Resources in Education*). Despite these virtues, the indexing of federal periodicals has been generally haphazard.

Although indexing services such as *Readers' Guide to Periodical Literature* and its related "Wilson" indexes, *PAIS International, LEXIS-NEXIS Academic Universe, Air University Library Index to Military Periodicals, InfoTrac,* and others index government periodicals selectively (and often minimally), systematic indexing of federal periodicals is a recent phenomenon. Two sources that represented major breakthroughs in the 1970s were the *Index to U.S. Government Periodicals* (IUSGP) and *American Statistics Index* (referred to in detail in chapter 9).

IUSGP (Chicago: Infodata International) was published quarterly and gave author and subject access to about 170 federal government journals, many of which were not depository items. The index was also available online and on CD-ROM. During the late 1980s, publication problems developed, and IUSGP fell behind as much as four years. The service was discontinued at the end of 1987 with volumes available from 1970.

Fortunately, the index was replaced with Congressional Information Service's *U.S. Government Periodicals Index* (USGPI), the first quarterly issue covering the period October–December 1993. Including articles in about 180 journals, USGPI's Index by Subjects and Names furnishes access by subject, personal and government authors, and names of companies and institutions that are the subjects of articles. The depth of indexing far exceeds that of its predecessor. The subscription service includes the quarterly paperbound issues plus a clothbound annual cumulation. The index is also available on CD-ROM, consisting of four cumulative disks per year; online; and on magnetic tape. Moreover, individual articles announced in USGPI are available on demand in paper copy. Because IUSGP's publication schedule ended with its 1987 volume, CIS provides retrospective coverage from 1988 to the year preceding the current issues. Figure 4.3, page 92, shows a sample entry from USGPI.

Government Journals in Electronic Formats

Fee-based, selected federal journals in electronic formats are published by Information Access Company (IAC), now part of the Gale Group; Congressional Information Service; and EBSCO. An excellent Web site for free access to federal periodicals is maintained by Auburn University's Ralph Brown Draughon Library. Organized alphabetically by title, the scope notes indicate whether published in HTML, PDF, or TXT; SuDocs class numbers; sources that index them (ASI, USGPI, *Readers' Guide*); whether distributed to depository libraries in an online version; title changes; even the occasional brief abstract (**http://www.lib.auburn.edu/madd/docs.htm**).

Figure 4.3. Sample entry from USGPI.

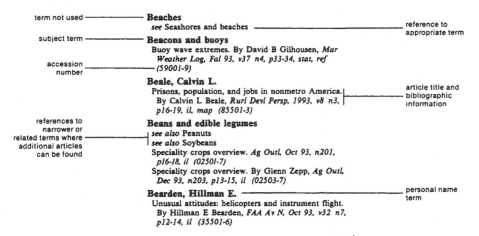

Copyright © 1995 Congressional Information Service, Inc. Used by permission. All other reproduction is strictly prohibited without the express written consent of CIS.

COMMERCIAL SOURCES ENHANCING USE OF MOCAT

That the federal government itself does not always provide the best indexing for its own publications comes as no surprise to frequent users of government information. As a remedy to the limitations of the government's own indexes, most specifically the earlier issues of the *Monthly Catalog,* a number of commercial sources have arisen to enhance the utility of the MOCAT. Performing a general subject search or a search on a specific topic, date unknown, was a tedious undertaking before the advent of the *Cumulative Subject Index to the Monthly Catalog of United States Government Publications 1900–1971,* a fifteen-volume, single-alphabet index published by Carrollton Press (Washington, DC). The *Cumulative Subject Index,* compiled by Edna A. Kanely and William Buchanan, conveniently merged the indexing from forty-eight annual indexes, the 1941–1950 and 1951–1960 decennial indexes, and one six-month index. It also added original indexing for thirty issues of the MOCAT that were never indexed by subject.

Classes Added Reprint Edition of the Monthly Catalog of U.S. Government Publications, 1895–1924, compiled by Mary Elizabeth Poole and also published by Carrollton Press, added SuDocs classification numbers, which were absent from the original edition, to this thirty-year run of the MOCAT. Further enhancing access to the historical period is *Cumulative Index to Hickcox's Monthly Catalog of U.S.*

Government Publications, 1885–1894, compiled by Edna A. Kanely. Her three-volume decennial index offers cumulative subject and author entries to Hickcox's ten annual catalogs, which were compiled and published privately by John H. Hickcox.[8] In addition, Mary Elizabeth Poole compiled and Carrollton Press published a six-volume "Classes Added" *Reprint Edition of Hickcox's Monthly Catalog of U.S. Government Publications, 1895–1899.*

Personal Author Indexes

Although personal authorship is not as pervasive a concept in relation to government publications as it is to privately published materials, personal authors are sometimes known or cited, especially in scientific and technical works. Pierian Press (Ann Arbor, MI) pioneered personal author indexing with the *Cumulative Personal Author Indexes to the Monthly Catalog, 1941–1975.* Edited by Edward Przebienda, the volumes include two decennial and three quinquennial indexes consisting of alphabetical lists of all personal names that have appeared in the entries of the *Monthly Catalog* for those years. The names supplied include virtually every relationship of author to cited publication—editor, compiler, translator, researcher, lecturer, illustrator, joint author(s)—including a systematic author approach to Joint Publications Research Service (JPRS) translations.

These indexes are invaluable because from September 1946 to December 1962 personal authors were omitted from the MOCAT indexes, including the two decennial cumulative indexes (1941–1950 and 1951–1960). In other years, the *Monthly Catalog* indexed first author only. The *Document Catalog* includes personal authors, and since July 1976 the *Monthly Catalog* has been thoroughly indexing authorial relationships.

The Readex Collection

Another commercial venture in support of improved *Monthly Catalog* access is the full-text edition of entries filmed by Readex, the Academic & Research Library Division of NewsBank, Inc. (New Canaan, CT). In 1953, when Readex Microprint Corporation was a separate company, it began filming and selling the text of MOCAT non-depository titles and in 1956 began offering the depository series of *Monthly Catalog* titles. The SuDocs notation and MOCAT entry number are displayed in the upper left corner of the microfiche title stripes. From the program's inception through the 1980 edition, the text was published in a microprint format. Beginning with 1981,

Readex switched to microfiche, bowing to numerous complaints about the microprint product from users and librarians alike.

The *U.S. Government Documents and Publications Collection* can be acquired in three ways. One can order the "comprehensive collection" (1981 to date), issued monthly and organized in the library's choice of either SuDocs number or MOCAT entry number order. The "profiled collection" allows libraries to purchase only those agencies or subject areas of interest. A "documents-on-demand" service permits purchase of either microfiche or photocopies of individual documents. Whatever the type of subscription, a checklist that functions as a shipping list accompanies each box shipped to libraries.

Other Non-Print Products

The decision in the mid-1970s to make the *Monthly Catalog* available in machine-readable form made it possible to format the bibliographic data in novel ways. Over the years to the present the avenues of non-print access were, and are, by subscription to the GPO tapes, on the "official" MOCAT CD-ROM, online through vendors, by purchase or lease of a commercial CD-ROM edition, and on GPO's Web-based *Catalog*. For a short time, the *Monthly Catalog* was also offered by private publishers in an automated, cumulative microform (COM) version. Although having the advantage of continuous cumulation, these products had many disadvantages. Subscriptions (microfilm plus equipment) were costly, few librarians were able to support the purchase of more than one reader, queues to use the reader were not uncommon, and equipment was frequently inadequate (for example, the readers were not ordinarily equipped with printers). Only Readex has been able to retain its sales capability in a microfiche version because of its full-text feature.

Time alone will register the impact of a free CD-ROM *Monthly Catalog* available to 1,400 depository libraries. The various commercial editions have been far more attractive to users than the print or microfiche editions, and that justified the cost of buying the products. Eventually, however, Internet access to an official "daily" MOCAT will likely win the affections of users. Meanwhile, several vendors retail the catalog on CD-ROM, including Auto-Graphics, Information Access Company, Marcive, and SilverPlatter. This is a highly competitive industry, and commercial firms enter and exit this market with alacrity. Similarly, reviews of competing electronic sources become rapidly dated as vendors react to competitors, use and user studies, and subscriber comments, and refine their products. About the only certain statement is that the

Monthly Catalog, in its several official and commercial editions, is now or was available in print, on magnetic tape, online with commercial vendors, on compact disk, on microfiche, and on GPO Access.

POPULAR NAME CATALOG

A valuable source prepared by the Library of Congress is *Popular Names of U.S. Government Reports: A Catalog,* now in its fourth edition (1984). The list includes selective reports cited by their commonly used name as well as by the official titles used in library catalogs and bibliographies. Coverage dates back to the nineteenth century and includes not only reports of advisory bodies but also selected congressional committee reports, committee prints, and hearings that have come to be known by the name of the chairperson or chief investigative officer. Although the media often refer to newsworthy reports by their popular names, indexing tools like the *Monthly Catalog* usually have not supplied the popular name in the bibliographic record.

The *Catalog* is updated from time to time in the periodical literature. Marjorie C. Bengtson's "Popular Names of U.S. Government Reports: A Supplement," *Illinois Libraries* 69: 472–77 (September 1987); Marjorie C. Bengtson's "Popular Names of U.S. Government Reports: Second Supplement," *Illinois Libraries* 75: 161–65 (April 1993); and Jeffrey Graf and Louise Malcomb's "Identifying Unidentified U.S. Government Reports," *Journal of Government Information* 21: 105–28 (March/April 1994) have contributed praiseworthy additions, but a new edition of *Popular Names* is obviously overdue.

ACCESSING
OLDER PRIMARY SOURCES

Several related commercial projects merit attention in that they supplement official tools for accessing older materials. The shelflist of the old Public Documents Library of the Government Printing Office, which in 1972 became part of the Printed Archives Branch of the National Archives and Records Administration (NARA), was microfilmed; and a dual-media edition of 118 microfilm reels and 5 paper copy indexes, called *Checklist of United States Public Documents, 1789–1976,* was marketed by the U.S. Historical Documents Institute, a Washington, DC, based publisher. *Checklist '76,* as it is commonly called, contains some 1.3 million bibliographic entries for over 2 million publications and represents all the information found in the official 1909 *Checklist,* the *Document Catalog,* and the *Monthly Catalog,* as well as shelflist entries that were never listed in any catalog either because supply of the publication was limited and the issuing agency did not want it advertised or because of security classification.

A spin-off of *Checklist '76* was the useful *Cumulative Title Index to United States Public Documents, 1789–1976,* compiled by Daniel Lester, Marilyn Lester, and Sandra Faull. This sixteen-volume hardcover listing of all titles in the above microfilm set gives, in addition to title, the SuDocs classification, date, and corresponding microfilm reel section, wherein the full description can be found in *Checklist '76.* Excluded are publications that are part of the U.S. Congressional Serial Set, because such publications were not classified in the SuDocs system at that time.

Upgrading the GPO Shelflist

Two projects that relate to the 1909 *Checklist* and *Checklist '76* are noteworthy. A small but utilitarian supplement to the early *Checklist* is Mary Elizabeth Poole's *1909 Checklist, Correlation Index* (Millwood, NY: Kraus-Thomson, 1976), which offers a quick method for determining the SuDocs number for a departmental edition when the user already knows the serial number of the equivalent congressional document.

The second project is vastly more ambitious. The Congressional Information Service (CIS) published, in a six-part series, the *CIS Index to U.S. Executive Branch Documents, 1789–1909.* Based upon the listings in the 1909 *Checklist,* CIS created the index, which, as noted above, was planned by the government as a second volume but never published. Part 1 includes the Departments of Commerce and Labor, and Treasury; Part 2, the War Department; Part 3, the Departments of the Interior, Justice, Labor, the Interstate Commerce Commission (ICC), and the Library of Congress. Part 4 comprises the Agriculture Department; American Republics Bureau; District of Columbia, Civil Service, and Fish Commissions; Geographic Board; Government Printing Office; and General Supply Committee. Part 5 covers the Navy Department. Part 6 encompasses the State and Post Office Departments, National Academy of Sciences, National Home for Disabled Volunteer Soldiers, President of the United States, and Smithsonian Institution. In addition, a supplement to this endeavor covers additional items, primarily from Parts 1 and 2, identified in the 1909 *Checklist,* that were located in library searches after the initial publication of Parts 1 through 6. Filmed on more than 47,000 microfiche, CIS offers access in twenty-six volumes of bibliographies and indexes. Typical of CIS's dual-media products, a companion *U.S. Executive Branch Documents, 1789–1909,* on *Microfiche* comprises all titles listed in the 1909 *Checklist* except those included in the *CIS US Serial Set Index* or other Congressional Information Service indexes. A "Reference Bibliography" allows users to identify and evaluate a document before retrieving it from the companion microfiche or in hard copy if the library has retrospective holdings. Moreover, CIS is in the process of creating MARC records for the 1789–1909 segment of this work, which will provide direct access from the user's online catalog to individual microforms.

The microfilm edition of the former Public Documents Library's shelflist, noted above, is the source for the company's next major retrospective endeavor: *CIS Index to U.S. Executive Branch Documents, 1910–1932*. Part 1 of this continuing work comprises the Treasury Department, Smithsonian Institution, Tariff Commission, Veterans Administration, Veterans Bureau, and Vocational Education Board; Part 2, the Commerce Department; Part 3, the War Department (excluding the Philippine Islands) and the War Trade Board; and Part 4, the Departments of Justice, Interior, and Labor, the Interstate Commerce Commission, and other agencies. Parts 5, 6, and 7 are scheduled to appear at the rate of one part per year and are scheduled for completion by the year 2002. Indexes are by subject and name, Superintendent of Documents class numbers, agency report numbers where applicable, and titles. As in the first series, a microfiche collection will furnish the full text of these valuable historical documents.

Congressional Information Service has other products and services that represent a formidable contribution to the bibliographic and textual control and retrieval of federal documents. These sources are examined in forthcoming chapters.

SUMMARY

This chapter offers a selection of guides to federal government materials. Other lists, indexes, and finding aids are discussed in the chapters that follow. New products or updated editions of existing sources will appear at a steady rate, increasingly in electronic formats. Owing to technological advances and a better appreciation of organizing information, bibliographic control has been enriched since the heroic but incomplete efforts of individuals such as Poore and Ames. Yet as we strive to master the means of expanding the scope and enhancing the quality control of government information, the result seems only to reveal the need for more and better systems. Indeed, the sheer amount of information continually threatens to overwhelm traditional structures that seek to contain it and render it manageable. As for information on the Internet, Clifford Lynch, writing in *Scientific American,* states,

> the Web . . . still lacks standards that would facilitate automated indexing. As a result, documents on the Web are not structured so that programs can reliably extract the routine information that a human indexer might find through a cursory inspection. . . . As the Net matures, the decision to opt for a given information collection will depend mostly on users. For which uses will it then come to resemble a library, with a structured approach to building collections? And for whom will it remain anarchic, with access supplied by automated systems?. . . Thus, social and economic issues, rather than technological ones, will exert the greatest influence in shaping the future of information retrieval on the Internet.[9]

Unfortunately, while there have been piecemeal efforts by librarians here and there, according to the Executive Director of the OCLC Institute, "It is clear to virtually all who use the Internet that chaos reigns there. What impact is the library profession having on this chaos? I would say that it is almost unnoticeable."[10]

NOTES

1. See Bill Katz, *Cuneiform to Computer: A History of Reference Sources* (Lanham, MD: Scarecrow Press, 1998), pp. 368–70.

2. Edward Herman, *Locating United States Government Information: A Guide to Sources,* 2d ed. (Buffalo, NY: William S. Hein, 1997), p. vi.

3. U.S. General Accounting Office, *Internet and Electronic Dial-Up Bulletin Boards: Information Reported by Federal Organizations* (GAO/GGD-97-86, June 1997), p. 7.

4. Benjamin Perley Poore, *Descriptive Catalogue of the Government Publications of the United States, September 5, 1774–March 4, 1881,* Senate Miscellaneous Document 67, 48th Cong., 2d Sess., 1885, p. iii.

5. Christina D. Bell and John V. Richardson, "Unselfish Work: John G. Ames and Public Documents Reform, 1874–1895," *Libraries & Culture* 23: 152–71 (Spring 1988).

6. Laurence F. Schmeckebier and Roy B. Eastin, *Government Publications and Their Use, Second Revised Edition* (Washington: Brookings, 1969), p. 162.

7. *Administrative Notes* 19: 21 (January 25, 1998).

8. See Nancy F. Stimson and Wendy Y. Nobunaga, "Life and Times of John H. D. Hickcox: Government Publications History Revisited," *Journal of Government Information* 22: 403–12 (September/October 1995).

9. Clifford Lynch, "Searching the Internet," *Scientific American* 276: 53, 56 (March 1997). Lynch is director of library automation at the Office of the President, University of California, Berkeley.

10. Norman Oder, "Cataloging the Net: Can We Do It?" *Library Journal,* October 1, 1998, p. 47.

CHAPTER FIVE

LEGISLATIVE BRANCH INFORMATION SOURCES

> With all its defects, delays and inconveniences, men have discovered no technique for long preserving free government except that the executive be under the law, and that the law be made by parliamentary deliberations.
>
> —United States Supreme
> Court Justice Robert H. Jackson

> A problem that strikes one in the study of history, regardless of period, is why man makes a poorer performance of government than of almost any other human activity.
>
> —Historian Barbara Tuchman

INTRODUCTION

The framers of the Constitution had no major doubts about Congress as primus inter pares. Congress antedates both the presidency and the judicial branch. The 1st Congress made the arrangements for counting the ballets of the first electoral college and for inaugurating George Washington and John Adams as the first executive officers. The office of Attorney General and the Departments of War, Foreign Affairs, and Treasury were established by acts of the 1st Congress. Moreover, this first assembly established the judicial system of the United States and enacted bills on tariffs, appropriations, patents and copyrights, the punishments of crimes, uniform militia, succession to the presidency, reduction of the public debt, rates of foreign exchange, naturalization, harbors, the establishment of hospitals, and the progress of the useful arts. The crown jewel in the diadem of the 1st Congress was the submission of the first ten amendments to the Constitution, the Bill of Rights.

The word "congress" was taken from the Articles of Confederation, whereas the words "house of representatives" and "senate" emerged from the Constitutional Convention of 1787. In addition to the committees of Congress, from which emanate most of the significant information available to the public, Congress established agencies designed to support congressional operations. These include the Architect of the Capitol, United States Botanic Garden, Library of Congress (in which the Congressional Research Service resides), Government Printing Office, General Accounting Office, and Congressional Budget Office.

This chapter is concerned with, among other things, the intrinsic publications that Congress as a lawmaking body generates. In the nineteenth and twentieth centuries, the number of introduced bills and joint resolutions exceeded the number approved in each Congress by a ratio of 5 to 1 or greater. The tables found in the authoritative "Final Edition" of the *Calendars of the United States House of Representatives and History of Legislation* show a significant decrease in the ratio of introduced measures that survive the committee process. When a committee declines to report a bill, that measure is said to "die in committee." Before he became the nation's twenty-eighth president, the scholarly Woodrow Wilson, writing in 1885, waxed metaphorical about the fate of bills in committees: "As a rule, a bill committed [referred to committee] is a bill doomed. When it goes from the Clerk's desk to a committee room, it crosses a parliamentary bridge of sighs to dim dungeons of silence whence it will never return."[1] Whatever the ratio of introduced measures to committee reports to law or veto over the decades, the process has remained, in broad outline, relatively stable, although the details and strategies may vary from bill to bill. Underlying all congressional activities is the interrelationship of procedure and politics.

THE LEGISLATIVE PROCESS

A knowledge of the process by which a bill becomes a law is a prerequisite to an understanding of the publications generated in that process. Useful commercial guides published by CQ Press, a division of Congressional Quarterly, Inc. (Washington, DC) include Roger H. Davidson and Walter J. Oleszek's *Congress and Its Members,* 6th ed. (1997); Lawrence C. Dodd and Bruce I. Oppenheimer's *Congress Reconsidered,* 6th ed. (1997), and Walter J. Oleszek's *Congressional Procedures and the Policy Process,* 4th ed. (1995). From Congressional Quarterly Books (Washington, DC) comes Fenton S. Martin and Robert U. Goehlert's *How to Research Congress* (1996). Congressional

Quarterly, Inc. has long been a highly regarded publisher not only of congressional monographs but also of books dealing with the presidency, the federal courts, elections, public policy and administration, and related categories. A commendable Internet site is sponsored by the North Harris College Library, Houston, Texas. Its page, "The Legal Process," shows the steps involved in the passage of bill to law and what happens next. This section is divided into three columns, providing the name of the print version with the publications' SuDocs class stem notations; the action in the Congress; and the Internet version of the same sources, with a jump cite to those Web locations. The process, of course, does not end with the enactment of a bill into law, and so the columns extend beyond congressional action to the drafting of regulations that appear in the *Federal Register* and the *Code of Federal Regulations*, and judicial review by the courts if and when they are called upon to interpret putatively ambiguous statutes or regulations (**http://wwwnhc.nhmccd.cc.tx.us/public/lrc/gov**). The entire process, summarized and condensed in the Harris site, is discussed in this chapter and in the next two chapters. The best-known official publication is the venerable *How Our Laws Are Made,* first published in 1953 and frequently revised and updated. It is available in pamphlet form and via the THOMAS Web site or directly at **http://thomas.loc.gov/home/ lawsmade.toc.html**. Many of the illustrations used in this chapter are taken from the Bicentennial Edition of this work, which is issued as a House document. A companion publication, *Enactment of a Law: Procedural Steps in the Legislative Process,* is revised less frequently. Issued as a Senate document, it illustrates the progress of legislation originating in the Senate. A chart showing the stages is shown in Figure 5.1, page 104. Taken from *Our American Government* (102-2: H.doc. 192), the chart traces the passage of legislation in both houses of Congress and illustrates the process from introduction to enactment or veto.

Figure 5.1. How a bill becomes a law.

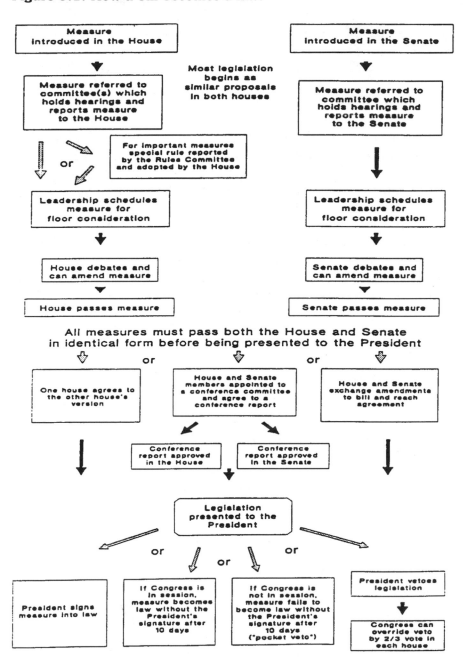

Introduction of Legislation

Legislation may originate in many ways: from the president and his staff; in the executive branch departments or agencies; by special interest groups such as labor unions, chambers of commerce, and professional societies; and even by individuals. Legislative ideas may come from senators and representatives, of course. These initiatives arise from campaign pledges, pressure by constituents, or, after the member has taken office, from experience gained concerning the need for changes to or repeal of existing laws.

Whatever its origin, only a member of Congress can introduce legislation. Bills and resolutions are the forms of legislation, and they may be introduced in either chamber. As noted, most introduced measures never become law. Those that do not complete the legislative process automatically die at the end of a two-year Congress and must be introduced anew in a subsequent Congress.

Introduced measures fall into four categories: bills, joint resolutions, concurrent resolutions, and simple resolutions. Joint resolutions are considered in a category with bills because they must be passed by both chambers and signed by the president into law or vetoed. Concurrent and simple resolutions must be passed by one or both houses, but they are generally used either for procedural purposes or to express the "sense" of the body and do not require presidential approval. All are numbered sequentially throughout a Congress.

Bills (H.R.; S.)

The term "bill" is used for most legislative proposals that involve the appropriations of monies. Bills may originate in either chamber, except for measures raising revenue, which, according to Article I, Section 7, of the Constitution, shall originate in the House. It is also customary, but not required, that general appropriations measures originate in the House. Bills are assigned a number in the order in which they are introduced during the two-year congressional term. The number is retained throughout the parliamentary stages with one exception. If a bill has been amended extensively in committee, the panel may decide to report a new bill incorporating these amendments, which is called a "clean bill" and is assigned a new bill number.

Joint Resolutions (H.J.Res.; S.J.Res.)

There is little practical difference between a bill and a joint resolution, and the two forms have been used interchangeably. However, joint resolutions are traditionally the vehicle for constitutional amendments, most of which do not survive committee scrutiny. The vast majority of these amendments are introduced regularly as a matter of political expediency, although some are initiated with sincere conviction, such as a constitutional amendment to balance the budget, to declare flag desecration a crime, to prohibit abortion, and to end school busing. With inexorable consistency, at least one member introduces in every Congress an amendment to repeal the Sixteenth Amendment (federal income tax). Amendments to the Constitution, after introduction, are sent to the respective House or Senate Judiciary Committees, where they almost always suffer the fate described by Woodrow Wilson. To survive they require a two-thirds affirmative vote in each chamber followed by approval of three-fourths of the state legislatures. When Michigan, the thirty-eighth state, ratified the "congressional pay amendment" on May 7, 1992, many members of Congress had forgotten about it. The amendment had begun its bicentennial odyssey when Maryland ratified it on December 19, 1789; and ended its interminable journey when the United States Archivist certified the procedure as valid and promulgated the ritual of ratification in 27 *Federal Register* 21188, May 18, 1992, when it became the Twenty-seventh Amendment to the Constitution. In the process of amending the Constitution, the president has no formal role.[2]

The joint resolution used to be the instrument for initiating commemorative legislation, by which the Congress authorized and requested the president to designate a celebratory day, week, month, or year by issuing a proclamation. The legislative aspect of this formality was abolished by the House in the 104th Congress, but proclamations are still promulgated and are discussed in chapter 6.

Figures 5.2 and 5.3, pages 107 and 108, show a House introduced print and the introduced print of a Senate companion bill, a bill that is similar or identical to a bill introduced in the other chamber. Figure 5.4, page 109, shows a constitutional amendment introduced as a House joint resolution.

(Text continues on page 110.)

Figure 5.2. House-introduced print.

101st CONGRESS
1st Session

H. R. 1722

To amend the Natural Gas Policy Act of 1978 to eliminate wellhead price controls on the first sale of natural gas, and to make technical and conforming amendments to such Act.

IN THE HOUSE OF REPRESENTATIVES

APRIL 6, 1989

Mr. SHARP (for himself, Mr. MOORHEAD, Mr. TAUZIN, Mr. DANNEMEYER, Mr. LELAND, Mr. FIELDS, Mr. SYNAR, Mr. OXLEY, Mr. RICHARDSON, Mr. NIELSON of Utah, Mr. BRYANT, Mr. BILIRAKIS, Mr. HALL of Texas, Mr. BARTON of Texas, Mr. WALGREN, Mr. CALLAHAN, Mr. SWIFT, Mr. BATES, Mr. COOPER, Mr. BRUCE, Mr. THOMAS A. LUKEN, Mr. WHITTAKER, Mr. SLATTERY, Mr. BLILEY, Mr. WYDEN, Mr. SCHAEFER, Mr. McMILLAN of North Carolina, Mr. WAXMAN, Mr. LENT, and Mr. DINGELL) introduced the following bill; which was referred to the Committee on Energy and Commerce

---

A BILL

To amend the Natural Gas Policy Act of 1978 to eliminate wellhead price controls on the first sale of natural gas, and to make technical and conforming amendments to such Act.

1   *Be it enacted by the Senate and House of Representa-*

2   *tives of the United States of America in Congress assembled,*

3   **SECTION 1. SHORT TITLE.**

4   This Act may be cited as the "Natural Gas Decontrol

5   Act of 1989".

*   *   *   *   *   *   *

(Sample copy of first page and end of last page of this 3-page introduced bill)

*   *   *   *   *   *   *

21   (b) PERMANENT ELIMINATION OF WELLHEAD PRICE

22   CONTROLS.—Title I of the Natural Gas Act of 1978 (15

23   U.S.C. 3311–3333) is repealed, effective on January 1,

24   1993.

Figure 5.3. Senate-introduced print.

101ST CONGRESS
1ST SESSION

S. 783

To amend the Natural Gas Policy Act of 1978 to eliminate wellhead price and nonprice controls on the first sale of natural gas, and to make technical and conforming amendments to such Act.

IN THE SENATE OF THE UNITED STATES

APRIL 13 (legislative day, JANUARY 3), 1989

Mr. JOHNSTON (for himself, Mr. McCLURE, Mr. NICKLES, Mr. FORD, Mr. BINGAMAN, Mr. WALLOP, Mr. BREAUX, Mr. WIRTH, Mr. BOREN, Mr. SIMPSON, Mr. GARN, Mr. COATS, and Mr. GRAMM) introduced the following bill; which was read twice and referred to the Committee on Energy and Natural Resources.

A BILL

To amend the Natural Gas Policy Act of 1978 to eliminate wellhead price and nonprice controls on the first sale of natural gas, and to make technical and conforming amendments to such Act.

1   *Be it enacted by the Senate and House of Representa-*

2 *tives of the United States of America in Congress assembled,*

3 **SECTION 1. SHORT TITLE.**

4   This Act may be referred to as the "Natural Gas Well-

5 head Decontrol Act of 1989".

Figure 5.4. House joint resolution.

97TH CONGRESS
1ST SESSION

H. J. RES. 16

Proposing an amendment to the Constitution of the United States relative to freedom from forced assignment to schools or jobs because of race, creed, or color.

IN THE HOUSE OF REPRESENTATIVES

JANUARY 5, 1981

Mr. ASHBROOK introduced the following joint resolution; which was referred to the Committee on the Judiciary

---

JOINT RESOLUTION

Proposing an amendment to the Constitution of the United States relative to freedom from forced assignment to schools or jobs because of race, creed, or color.

1   *Resolved by the Senate and House of Representatives of*

2 *the United States of America in Congress assembled (two-*

3 *thirds of each House concurring therein),* That the following

4 article is proposed as an amendment to the Constitution of

5 the United States, which shall be valid to all intents and

6 purposes as part of the Constitution when ratified by the leg-

7 islatures of three-fourths of the several States:

Concurrent Resolutions (H.Con.Res.; S.Con.Res.)

The term "concurrent" does not necessarily mean simultaneous introduction and consideration in both chambers. Concurrent resolutions are not normally legislative in character and do not require the president's signature. They may be introduced in either chamber and are used to express an opinion, purpose, fact, principle, or "sense" of the Congress. Figure 5.5 shows an example of a House concurrent resolution.

Resolutions (H.Res.; S.Res.)

Known as "simple" resolutions, these govern the action of the body in which they originate and are for the concern only of the chamber passing them. They are typically used to initiate administrative or housekeeping procedures, such as adoption of rules, assignment of committee members, or making a declaration of affirmation or rejection on some issue or formality. Nevertheless, resolutions may consist of solemn matters; House Resolution 611, December 15, 1998, submitted by Representative Henry J. Hyde (R-IL), chairman of the House Judiciary Committee, consisted of four Articles of Impeachment against William Jefferson Clinton. Figure 5.6, page 112, is an example of a House resolution.

Availability of Bills and Resolutions

The full text of bills and resolutions is available in electronic format via commercial online services and on the Internet. Examples of the former include WESTLAW, LEXIS-NEXIS, CQ Washington Alert, Legi-Slate, and CIS Congressional Universe. All of these providers include, as well as bills and resolutions, access to the text of the other documents generated in the legislative process. A comparative analysis of the last three concluded that whereas CQ Washington Alert and Legi-Slate "offer superior bill tracking for pending legislation," Congressional Universe "provides superior bibliography for historical research."[3] A "Hot Bills" feature, whereby users can view the text of legislative proposals making news, is available on CIS Congressional Universe, THOMAS, and Legi-Slate. State Net (Sacramento, CA) is best known for its state legislative and regulatory information, but it has bill tracking and bill text for the Congress.

Figure 5.5. House concurrent resolution.

House Concurrent Resolution

97TH CONGRESS
1ST SESSION

H. CON. RES. 131

To express the sorrow of the Congress upon the death of former world heavyweight boxing champion Joe Louis.

IN THE HOUSE OF REPRESENTATIVES

MAY 12, 1981

Mr. SAVAGE submitted the following concurrent resolution; which was referred to the Committee on Post Office and Civil Service

---

CONCURRENT RESOLUTION

To express the sorrow of the Congress upon the death of former world heavyweight boxing champion Joe Louis.

Whereas Joe Louis, who was born the son of a black sharecropper, overcame the barriers of racial bigotry to become the longest reigning world heavyweight boxing champion in history;

Whereas Joe Louis was a man of exceptional talent, pride, and determination, both inside and outside of the boxing ring;

Whereas the life and career of Joe Louis continue to serve as inspirations for people of all races throughout the world and as models of courage and achievement for all Americans; and

Figure 5.6. House resolution.

House Resolution

97TH CONGRESS
1ST SESSION

H. RES. 16

To reaffirm the use of our national motto on currency.

IN THE HOUSE OF REPRESENTATIVES

JANUARY 5, 1981

Mr. GUYER submitted the following resolution; which was referred to the
Committee on Banking, Finance and Urban Affairs

RESOLUTION

To reaffirm the use of our national motto on currency.

1   *Resolved*, That it is the sense of the House that the

2   national motto, "In God We Trust", shall be reaffirmed and

3   shall continue to be engraved and printed on our currency.

The two best-known official providers of bill information are THOMAS and GPO Access. THOMAS, subtitled "In the Spirit of Thomas Jefferson," is a service of the Library of Congress (**http://thomas. loc.gov**) and was inaugurated January 5, 1995. Newt Gingrich deserves credit for the creation of THOMAS. The former Speaker of the House, who resigned in 1998, conceived of the database as a "process of putting every bill, every report, every conference report on the Internet so that every citizen has the same instantaneous access as the highest paid lobbyist in Washington, D.C."[4] Bill summary and status, as well as full text, are searchable by bill number or word/phrase. Resolutions are included because "bill" is used as a broad term to subsume the other form. GPO Access was inaugurated six months before THOMAS, and there is much duplication of congressional information with the latter. Here bills and resolutions can be searched in much the same way as on THOMAS; coverage of bills for both Web sites exists from the present back through several previous congresses. From the Senate home page (**http//www.senate.gov**) one can conduct a bill search by number or keyword. Numerous free, nongovernmental Web sites also have links to congressional bills and resolutions; Yahoo!Government is but one of many. But the user should definitely bookmark THOMAS and GPO Access for easily accessed official congressional documents.

Senate and House bills and resolutions are also available to depository libraries on microfiche, but the amendments are not in bill number sequence. Before 1979, bills, resolutions, and amendments were sent to depository libraries in paper copy. The microfiche-only distribution policy was adopted beginning with the 96th Congress as a cost-savings measure. This was a penny-wise, pound-foolish decision; bills and resolutions in all their parliamentary stages and with all their amendments shipped to depositories in paper copy did not occupy that much file-cabinet space to present a shelving burden. Public bills, resolutions, and amendments are also sales items and are announced in *U.S. Government Subscriptions.*

Bills in all their original, amended, and revised versions are available, correctly sequenced, in *CIS/Congressional Bills, Resolutions & Laws,* in a retrospective and current edition. Because CIS waits until the end of a Congress before filming, the bills and resolutions in their parliamentary stages, including amendments, are arranged by number behind the introduced print, thus avoiding the scattering effect of the LPS's microfiche edition.

Bill Digests

Formerly sent to depository libraries in several cumulative issues during a session and then only annually, the *Digest of Public General Bills and Resolutions,* provenance of the Congressional Research Service (CRS) of the Library of Congress since 1936, ended its print edition with the Final Issue, 101st Congress, Second Session. Its unique feature was the provision of digests or summaries of every public measure, with legislative history information included. Useful indexes by sponsors, co-sponsors, identical bills, short titles, and subjects enabled you to access its main contents. It is now online via THOMAS, Legi-Slate, CIS Congressional Universe, and CQ Washington Alert.

Parliamentary Stages

The first printing of a bill is known as the introduced print, but when legislation is reported out of committee, there is a reported print (Figure 5.7) bearing a calendar number and report number. "Engrossed bills" are printed on blue paper. When passed by one chamber and sent to the other body, the bill becomes known as a referred (Act) print (Figures 5.8, page 116, and 5.9, page 117). When reported out of a Senate committee, the bill is called a Senate reported print and carries a calendar and report number for that chamber (Figure 5.10, page 118). A bill that contains an error is designated a "star print"; the corrected bill has a small star in its lower left corner. A detailed description of these parliamentary stages, with illustrations, is found in the current edition of *How Our Laws Are Made* and in a number of commercial publications.

Committee Action

After introduction, a bill is referred to the appropriate committee of the House or Senate. Within a committee, a bill is normally referred directly to a subcommittee. Internal committee reforms of the 1970s, 1980s, and 1990s increased the power of the subcommittees and reduced that of the committee chairpersons, who may no longer "pocket," or kill, a bill by refusing to act on it promptly.

(Text continues on page 119.)

Figure 5.7. Reported print.

Union Calendar No. 17

101ST CONGRESS
1ST SESSION

H. R. 1722

[Report No. 101–29]

To amend the Natural Gas Policy Act of 1978 to eliminate wellhead price
controls on the first sale of natural gas, and to make technical and conforming amendments to such Act.

IN THE HOUSE OF REPRESENTATIVES

APRIL 6, 1989

Mr. SHARP (for himself, Mr. MOORHEAD, Mr. TAUZIN, Mr. DANNEMEYER, Mr.
LELAND, Mr. FIELDS, Mr. SYNAR, Mr. OXLEY, Mr. RICHARDSON, Mr.
NIELSON of Utah, Mr. BRYANT, Mr. BILIRAKIS, Mr. HALL of Texas, Mr.
BARTON of Texas, Mr. WALGREN, Mr. CALLAHAN, Mr. SWIFT, Mr. BATES,
Mr. COOPER, Mr. BRUCE, Mr. THOMAS A. LUKEN, Mr. WHITTAKER, Mr.
SLATTERY, Mr. BLILEY, Mr. WYDEN, Mr. SCHAEFER, Mr. McMILLAN of
North Carolina, Mr. WAXMAN, Mr. LENT, and Mr. DINGELL) introduced the
following bill; which was referred to the Committee on Energy and
Commerce

APRIL 17, 1989

Additional sponsors: Mr. ARCHER, Mr. BARTLETT, Mr. SMITH of Texas, Mr.
COMBEST, Mr. DeLAY, and Mr. ARMEY

APRIL 17, 1989

Committed to the Committee of the Whole House on the State of the Union and
ordered to be printed

A BILL

To amend the Natural Gas Policy Act of 1978 to eliminate
   wellhead price controls on the first sale of natural gas, and
   to make technical and conforming amendments to such Act.

1   *Be it enacted by the Senate and House of Representa-*

2 *tives of the United States of America in Congress assembled,*

*   *   *   *   *   *   *

(Sample copy of beginning and end of this 4-page reported bill)

*   *   *   *   *   *   *

6   (b) PERMANENT ELIMINATION OF WELLHEAD PRICE

7 CONTROLS.—Title I of the Natural Gas Act of 1978 (15

8 U.S.C. 3311–3333) is repealed, effective on January 1,

9 1993.

Figure 5.8. Engrossed bill.

101ST CONGRESS
1ST SESSION

H. R. 1722

AN ACT

To amend the Natural Gas Policy Act of 1978 to eliminate wellhead price and nonprice controls on the first sale of natural gas, and to make technical and conforming amendments to such Act.

1   *Be it enacted by the Senate and House of Representa-*

2   *tives of the United States of America in Congress assembled,*

3   **SECTION 1. SHORT TITLE.**

4   This Act may be cited as the "Natural Gas Wellhead

5   Decontrol Act of 1989".

*   *   *   *   *   *   *

(Sample copy of part of first page and last page of this 8-page bill)

*   *   *   *   *   *   *

1   (A) by striking "AUTHORITY TO PRESCRIBE

2   LOWER" and inserting in lieu thereof "AUTHOR-

3   ITY TO PRESCRIBE"; and

4   (B) by striking "which does not exceed the

5   applicable maximum lawful price, if any, under

6   title I of this Act".

Passed the House of Representatives April 17, 1989.

Attest: DONNALD K. ANDERSON,

Clerk.

Figure 5.9. Referred (Act) print.

101ST CONGRESS
1ST SESSION

H.R. 1722

IN THE SENATE OF THE UNITED STATES

APRIL 18 (legislative day, JANUARY 3), 1989

Received; read twice and referred to the Committee on Energy and Natural Resources

AN ACT

To amend the Natural Gas Policy Act of 1978 to eliminate wellhead price and nonprice controls on the first sale of natural gas, and to make technical and conforming amendments to such Act.

1   *Be it enacted by the Senate and House of Representa-*

2   *tives of the United States of America in Congress assembled,*

3   SECTION 1. SHORT TITLE.

4   This Act may be cited as the "Natural Gas Wellhead

5   Decontrol Act of 1989".

*   *   *   *   *   *   *

(Sample copy of part of first page and last page of this 8-page bill)

*   *   *   *   *   *   *

1   (A) by striking "AUTHORITY TO PRESCRIBE

2   LOWER" and inserting in lieu thereof "AUTHOR-

3   ITY TO PRESCRIBE"; and

4   (B) by striking "which does not exceed the

5   applicable maximum lawful price, if any, under

6   title I of this Act".

Passed the House of Representatives April 17, 1989.

Attest: DONNALD K. ANDERSON,

Clerk.

Figure 5.10. Senate reported print.

Calendar No. 77

101st CONGRESS
1st SESSION

H. R. 1722

[Report No. 101–39]

IN THE SENATE OF THE UNITED STATES

APRIL 18 (legislative day, JANUARY 3), 1989
Received; read twice and referred to the Committee on Energy and Natural
Resources

MAY 31 (legislative day, JANUARY 3), 1989
Reported by Mr. JOHNSTON, with amendments
[Omit the part struck through and insert the part printed in italic]

AN ACT

To amend the Natural Gas Policy Act of 1978 to eliminate
wellhead price and nonprice controls on the first sale of
natural gas, and to make technical and conforming amendments to such Act.

1   *Be it enacted by the Senate and House of Representa-*

2   *tives of the United States of America in Congress assembled,*

3   SECTION 1. SHORT TITLE.

4   This Act may be cited as the "Natural Gas Wellhead

5   Decontrol Act of 1989".

*   *   *   *   *   *   *

(Sample copy of first page and end of last page of this 8-page bill)

*   *   *   *   *   *   *

5   (A) by striking "AUTHORITY TO PRESCRIBE

6   LOWER" and inserting in lieu thereof "AUTHOR-

7   ITY TO PRESCRIBE"; and

8   (B) by striking "which does not exceed the

9   applicable maximum lawful price, if any, under

10   title I of this Act".

Passed the House of Representatives April 17, 1989.

Attest: DONNALD K. ANDERSON,

Clerk.

Hearings

If a bill warrants consideration, the subcommittee will usually schedule public hearings. After hearings are held, the subcommittee engages in the "marking-up" process, a section-by-section analysis of the measure, at which time major or minor revisions may take place. As noted, if the bill is extensively revised, it will be rewritten and reintroduced as a "clean bill" with a new bill number. Although hearings pursuant to legislation are perhaps the most familiar category, they are held by committees and subcommittees for other purposes. Hearings may be exploratory, providing testimony and data about general topics. Evaluative hearings furnish information about the economy and efficiency of program operations. Appropriations hearings proffer testimony and information about department or agency operations, oversight activities, and comparative fiscal information. Investigatory hearings explore the need for legislation, inform public opinion, or consider the many scandals that beset the nation's capital.

Today, hearings are routinely televised by C-SPAN and other cable channels, public television, and the major networks. The first reported instance of a televised congressional hearing "occurred in 1948 when the Senate Armed Services Committee allowed coverage of its March 30 and April 2 hearings on universal military training." In that same year, the House Committee on Un-American Activities (HUAC) "allowed telecasting of its hearings regarding claims of communist infiltration of the U.S. Government." Popularly known as the Hiss-Chambers hearings, the televised portion "of these hearings lasted for twenty-one days, running from late July through early September 1948."[5] From the Kefauver Committee hearings on organized crime, to Watergate (Nixon), to the 1998 Clinton impeachment hearings, each held by the House Judiciary Committee a quarter of a century apart, this kind of committee activity represents a powerful and visible forum.

Electronic Sources of Hearings

WESTLAW, LEXIS-NEXIS, GPO Access, THOMAS, Washington Alert, Legi-Slate, and CIS Congressional Universe furnish the full text of hearings. But it must be emphasized that none of these sources has retrospective hearings much before the 1990s. It must also be recognized that hearings may be selective in quantity (THOMAS, for example) or selective in coverage for individual hearings. Concerning the latter, only GPO Access publishes all the elements of a hearing, including all the materials at the end of the verbal testimony, such as written statements, statistics, and articles from journals or newspapers. Finally, it should be noted that these sites change constantly and their contents and links must be reviewed regularly. This caveat is applicable to all congressional sources discussed in this chapter and, for that matter, all electronic products and services.

Retrospective Hearings

The Congressional Information Service (CIS), located in Bethesda, Maryland, makes available *CIS US Congressional Committee Hearings Index,* providing bibliographic access to more than 40,000 titles from the 1830s through 1969. The full text of these hearings is available on microfiche. CIS also produces a series titled *CIS Unpublished US Congressional Committee Hearings* for both House and Senate from the early nineteenth century to the 1970s. Indexes by subjects and organizations, personal names, titles, and bill numbers offer access to the bibliographic listings that reference the full text on microfiche.

From 1970 to the present, *CIS/Index* indexes and abstracts hearings and offers the full text on microfiche. This index, the first product developed by the Congressional Information Service, contains abstracts and indexes for other congressional publications, which are discussed below. The complete line of CIS titles may be accessed at CIS's home page **(http://www.cispubs.com)**.

Committee Prints

Committee Prints are publications prepared for the use of committees and their staffs. They are frequently written by the Congressional Research Service; they may also be researched and composed by independent consultants or by the committee staff members. Prints consist of a wide variety of material, from legislative histories to bibliographies. Studies on topics of public policy, investigative reports, confidential staff reports and memoranda, analyses of similar bills on a topic, and excerpts from hearings constitute some of the information that one may find in committee prints. They are indexed and abstracted in *CIS/Index* and the retrospective *CIS US Congressional Committee Prints Index* (1830–1969). Although more committee prints have been made available to depository libraries in recent years, the series is not automatically distributed. Under the "administrative or operational" exemption provision of 44 U.S.C. § 1902, a committee chairperson is not obliged to authorize all committee prints for distribution or sale. However, be patient, for someday, your prints will come. The Documents Expediting Project of the Library of Congress has been able to obtain a number of prints and send them to its subscribers, and there is the microfiche text for the current and retrospective CIS products noted above. Moreover, CIS Congressional Universe has the full text of selected committee prints online from 1995 to the present.

Many committee prints contain valuable information. Two disparate documents will suffice as illustrative: the "Plum Book" and the "Green Book." A publication that garners a great deal of media attention after a presidential election is the quadrennial *United States Government Policy and Supporting Positions,* issued alternately every four years by a House Committee and a Senate Committee. Known as the "Plum Book," this print contains data on several thousand civil service leadership and support positions in the legislative and executive branches that are subject to noncompetitive appointments, a polite way of describing patronage jobs. Not all of them may be plummy. Listings include the mighty (department heads) and the humble (chauffeurs and housekeepers). For the 104th Congress, Second Session, the Plum Book was available via GPO Access (**http://www.access.gpo.gov/plumbook**).

The House Ways and Means Committee issues an important numbered print called *Overview of Entitlement Programs,* which includes descriptions of Social Security, railroad retirement, child support, foster care, Medicare, and other programs. Popularly known as the "Green Book," *Overview* is a heavily used title in libraries.

An often overlooked source that indexes, abstracts, and has a subject approach to selected committee prints and hearings is *PAIS International,* a nonprofit educational corporation headquartered at the New York Public Library. *PAIS International* is online with DIALOG, OCLC, and InfoTrac Searchbank. CD-ROM versions of *PAIS International* are available from SilverPlatter and EBSCO Publishing Company. *PAIS Select* is a full-text subset of *PAIS International* containing selected English-language journal articles, including a few federal government periodicals. As Shakespeare might have said, Good night, sweet prints.

Committee Reports

Committee reports on bills and resolutions describe the purpose and scope of the measure and the reasons for recommending approval of the measure to the full chamber. Few bills are reported unfavorably; in some instances, however, a committee may report a measure "without recommendation," which has the chilling effect of an unfavorable report. When a committee declines to report a bill, that measure is effectively killed. House and Senate reports are assigned a report number and include the bill or resolution number. For example, House Report 105-830 (the 830th report of the 105th Congress) on the impeachment of President Clinton, pursuant to House Resolution 611, was favorably reported out of the House Judiciary Committee. Issued initially in slip (pamphlet) form, committee reports are later gathered into the bound volumes of the United States Congressional Serial Set. Figure 5.11 shows an example of a House committee report; Figure 5.12, page 124, shows an example of a Senate committee report.

Reports are indexed and abstracted in *CIS/Index* from 1970 to the present. The *CIS US Serial Set Index, 1789–1969* includes citations to reports on both public and private legislation as well as other materials that constitute the historical serial set. Part XIII of this set is an *Index by Reported Bill Numbers,* which shows in chronological order the Congress in which the bill or resolution was introduced, the bill or resolution number, the title and number of the relevant report, and the serial set volume number where the text of the report can be located. The companion CIS microfiche contains the full text of reports from 1789 through 1969. The West Group's *United States Code Congressional and Administrative News* (USCCAN) gives the full text of selected committee reports along with complete listings of senators, representatives, and committees.

For electronic access there is an abundance of duplication. GPO Access, THOMAS, CIS Congressional Universe, CQ Washington Alert, WESTLAW, LEXIS-NEXIS, and Legi-Slate all offer the text of reports online, but retrospective coverage is limited to a relatively few years. Committee recorded votes are accessible through CQ Washington Alert, Legi-Slate, WESTLAW, and LEXIS-NEXIS.

Floor Action

After a bill is reported, it is placed on a calendar and may be called to the floor of the originating chamber for consideration. Action on pro forma legislation is typically characterized by no debate and passage by voice vote. Amendments are permitted on the floor of both houses and consist of parliamentary motions to insert, strike out and insert, strike out, and substitute. A strategy sometimes practiced is the introduction on the floor of a "rider," a provision not germane to the subject matter of the bill. The *Congressional Record* is the official vehicle through which floor action—consideration (debate) and passage of legislation— is recorded.

Figure 5.11. House committee report.

<table>
<tr><td>101st Congress
1st Session</td><td>HOUSE OF REPRESENTATIVES</td><td>Report
101–29</td></tr>
</table>

NATURAL GAS DECONTROL ACT OF 1989

April 17, 1989.—Committed to the Committee of the Whole House on the State of the Union and ordered to be printed

Mr. Dingell, from the Committee on Energy and Commerce, submitted the following

REPORT

together with

DISSENTING VIEWS

[To accompany H.R. 1722]

[Including cost estimate of the Congressional Budget Office]

The Committee on Energy and Commerce, to whom was referred the bill (H.R. 1722) to amend the Natural Gas Policy Act of 1978 to eliminate wellhead price controls on the first sale of natural gas, and to make technical and conforming amendments to such Act, having considered the same, report favorably thereon without amendment and recommend that the bill do pass.

CONTENTS

Figure 5.12. Senate committee report.

Calendar No. 77

101st Congress *1st Session*	SENATE	Report 101-39

NATURAL GAS WELLHEAD DECONTROL ACT OF 1989

May 31 (legislative day, January 3), 1989.—Ordered to be printed

---

Mr. Johnston, from the Committee on Energy and Natural
Resources, submitted the following

REPORT

together with

MINORITY VIEWS

[To accompany H.R. 1722]

The Committee on Energy and Natural Resources, to which was referred the Act (H.R. 1722) to amend the Natural Gas Policy Act of 1978 to eliminate wellhead price and nonprice controls on the first sale of natural gas, and to make technical and conforming amendments to such Act, having considered the same, reports favorably thereon with amendments and recommends that the Act, as amended, do pass.

The amendments are as follows:

1. On page 2, line 6, strike "(2), (3), and (4)," and insert "(2), and (3),".

2. On page 3, strike lines 10 through 15.

Purpose of the Measure

The purpose of H.R. 1722 is to promote competition for natural gas at the wellhead in order to ensure consumers an adequate and reliable supply of natural gas at the lowest reasonable price. H.R. 1722 does so by amending the Natural Gas Policy Act of 1978 (NGPA) to repeal on January 1, 1993, all remaining price and nonprice controls on the first sale (generally, the wellhead or producing field sale) of natural gas.

In certain circumstances, H.R. 1722 also decontrols first sale transactions earlier than January 1, 1993. The bill would decontrol

Congressional Record

In the early days of the republic there was little interest in transcribing the deliberations of the House and Senate. Thomas Lloyd of New York recorded many of the debates in the 1st Congress in shorthand and published them in a commercial edition called *The Congressional Register.* Indeed, from 1789 to 1873, there was no official record of debates, and commercial ventures were haphazard and often biased. Their "accuracy and comprehensiveness" were "limited by such factors as the column space available in newspapers, the political leanings of the editors and reporters, the ability of a reporter to actually hear the debates when his assigned seat may have been far from the speakers, and the inadequacy of existing longhand and shorthand methods for recording the debates." That the textual record is so abysmal is not surprising. No precedent existed; the "English Parliament did not report its debates, though the House of Lords and House of Commons did keep journals of their proceedings, as did colonial American assemblies."[6] It should be noted that the only specific reference to a government publication in the Constitution is found in Article I, Section 5, Clause 3, which states that "Each House shall keep a Journal of its Proceedings, and from time to time publish the same." Accordingly, the proceedings (not the transcription of debates) are recorded in the *House Journal* and *Senate Journal,* which are issued annually and discussed later in this chapter.

For the proceedings and debates, the first formal sustained effort was called the *Annals of Congress* (1789–1824). Compiled by Joseph Gales and William Seaton "over a period of 22 years, from 1834–1856," this retrospective effort relied upon "old press accounts and other published sources . . . and only included summaries of House and Senate activities and debates deemed most important by its compilers." Neither chamber was fully covered, the Senate less so. In fact, it was not until 1802 that the Senate "voted to admit reporters to the floor."

The *Register of Debates* (1824–1837) "was contemporaneously published and so actually was printed before the Annals . . . appeared in print." Like the *Annals,* the *Register* was not a "verbatim account but rather a compilation of summaries of the debates. . . . Since the speeches were not recorded verbatim, Members of Congress were welcomed by Gales and Seaton to revise their speeches before they were printed."[7] The *Congressional Globe* (1833–1873) competed with the *Register* from 1833 to 1837 and continued "after the Register's demise until the birth" of the present *Congressional Record* on March 5,

1873. By the mid-nineteenth century the *Globe* had succeeded in becoming a "more verbatim account of Congressional debates" owing to "improvements in shorthand" and a "new Congressional willingness to pay the salaries of the [official floor] reporters and to purchase copies of the reports."[8]

The National Digital Library Program of the Library of Congress makes available via its own Web site (**http://lcweb2.loc.gov**) or a GPO Access page (**http://www.access.gpo.gov/su_docs/dpos/coredocs.html**) the full text of certain historical documents. Examples include *A Century of Lawmaking for a New Nation: U.S. Congressional Documents and Journal, Annals of Congress,* and the *Journal of William Maclay, 1789–1791.* Other primary sources in this collection include *The Debates in the Several State Conventions on the Adoption of the Federal Constitution,* compiled by Jonathan Elliot and covering the period of the First Federal Congress in March 1789, and *The Records of the Federal Convention of 1787,* by Max Farrand, considered the single best source for discussions of the Constitutional Convention. These texts are only part of an ambitious project titled *Core Documents of Democracy,* an electronic collection being made available via GPO Access for the purpose of informing the public about information vital to the democratic process.

The Congressional Record Today

The daily *Congressional Record* is available for sale by the Superintendent of Documents in paper or microfiche and free to depository libraries in either paperback or microfiche editions. The quotidian CR has four sections: the proceedings and debates of the House and Senate, arrangement of which may alternate with issues; the Extensions of Remarks; and the Daily Digest, a summary of proceedings for that day in each house and before each of their committees and subcommittees. Each section is paged continuously and separately during a session, and each page in each section has a letter prefix as follows: S (Senate), H (House), E (Extensions of Remarks), and D (Daily Digest).

A permanent edition of the CR is available on microfiche to selective depository libraries, but since 1985 only regional depositories can receive the bound version. Due to revision and rearrangement, the pagination of the final bound edition differs from that of the daily edition. Congressional Information Service films the bound edition of the *Record* from 1873 (43rd Congress) and makes it available for purchase; CIS has also filmed its predecessors as separate collections and these are available on fiche as individual series or as a complete set.

The practice of revision of speeches began, as noted above, with the *Register of Debates* and continues today. Members are permitted to insert "speeches" into the *Record* that were not actually delivered on the floor, but only since March 1, 1978, have both House and Senate distinguished "non-speeches" from remarks actually delivered in the chambers by the use of a bullet (•) symbol. After perceived disaffection with the way the bullet was being applied, the House launched a review of the use of the bullet and whether it had been helpful in distinguishing between spoken and "non-spoken" floor remarks. The result of the review was to eliminate the symbol from the House portion of the *Record*, pursuant to House Resolution 230, to become effective September 1, 1985, on a trial basis for the remainder of the 99th Congress, First Session. Oddly, the change called for non-speeches to be printed in bold-face, presenting a clear visual contrast with the typeface used for speeches delivered in person and for other proceedings. But some critics noted that perhaps the untutored reader might get the impression that the more visually compelling type constituted the real declamations and its paler cousin the faux speeches. For whatever reason or reasons, beginning with the 99th Congress, Second Session, a less prominent but still darker monotonal type without serifs was used for non-speeches, and the actual debates and other matter constituting the proceedings continued to be printed in the serif style. The serif/sans-serif distinction is given at the bottom of the first page of each day's House Proceedings. Meanwhile, the Senate continues happily to employ the bullet device for its own oxymoronic unspoken speeches. But because the same type is employed for both spoken and unspoken comments in the upper chamber, the visual impact is muted.

Under the rules, members also have the right to revise and edit their remarks before they are published in the daily CR and again before the bound *Record* goes to press. Studies have shown that the editing privilege is not abused; the great majority of revisions concern the correction of stylistic or grammatical infelicities and are thus within the bounds of propriety, but there have been violations. Perhaps cognizant of the temptation to change the substance of remarks uttered in the heat of verbal battle, the House of Representatives in January 1995 declared that the CR "shall be a substantially verbatim account of remarks made during the proceedings of the House, subject only to technical, grammatical, and typographical corrections authorized by the Member making the remarks involved."[9] The irony of this addition to Clause 9(a) of Rule XIV of the *House Manual* is that it is essentially the language of 44 U.S.C. § 901, which states that the CR "shall be substantially a verbatim report of proceedings," the adverb presumably implying technical corrections.

Televising the Debates: C-SPAN

On March 19, 1979, then Representative Al Gore (D-TN) read a one-minute speech welcoming TV cameras into the House, and with that short introduction the marriage of television and open debate was consummated. On June 2, 1986, then Senate Majority Leader Robert Dole (R-KS) stood on the floor of the Senate and, with the TV cameras grinding away, wryly remarked, "I think that today we catch up with the 20th century." It had taken the Senate over seven years to catch up to the House, never mind the century. Both chambers had faced strong opposition to the televising of floor proceedings. They would not allow the major networks or public television to do the job; rather, they purchased their own equipment, at no small cost to the taxpayer, so that they could exercise control over where the camera roams. C-SPAN (Cable-Satellite Public Affairs Network), a nonprofit cooperative of the cable-television industry, was created in 1977 to deliver public-affairs programming from the nation's capital to a national cable-TV audience, and the network's debut in 1979 coincided with the inauguration of live telecasts from the House floor.[10]

Today, C-SPAN I covers the House and C-SPAN II the Senate. Both channels have expanded their programming far beyond their original basic coverage of floor activities and now operate twenty-four hours a day with committee hearings, public policy conferences, viewer call-in programs, White House press briefings, Book TV and the peerless "Booknotes" consisting of author interviews, addresses by public officials and private pundits, political party conventions, panel discussions sponsored by executive agencies, National Press Club luncheon addresses, office seekers on the hustings, the Clinton impeachment opéra bouffe, and so forth. C-SPAN also carries Russian television news and selective debates in the British House of Commons, where, honed by centuries of practice, invective has been raised to an art form rendering by comparison our congressional deliberations, if anything, demure and jejune.

Of course, the camera renders a wholly faithful transcription of floor proceedings, the audiotapes preserving forever the melancholy evidence that many of the legislators possess less than Demosthenean eloquence. One venue, however, permits House members to deliver speeches to a virtually empty chamber after regular legislative hours. These are called "special orders" and are assigned on a rotating basis by the House leadership. Turn your TV remote to C-SPAN I in the late evening and you might see representatives honing their rhetorical skills. If the cameras remain fixed on the speaker, a viewer might get the erroneous impression that the member was addressing a rapt audience of his or her peers. Special order speeches, too, give members an opportunity to transcend the limitations of time imposed in regular floor debate. If, for example, members are allowed five minutes to debate a piece of legislation, they can ask that the remainder of their remarks be "extended"; this request is automatically granted by that day's presiding officer and published in the daily CR in the Extensions of Remarks section. Still, members of the House who want to declaim further can seek the special order route.

Other C-SPAN products and services include C-SPAN in the Classroom, study guides that help teachers use C-SPAN programming to enhance classroom learning; thrice-yearly two-day seminars held in Washington for college professors who are interested in learning how to integrate C-SPAN programming into their teaching or research; periodic mailings that contain programming information of special interest to educators; a toll-free educators hotline; online services at C-SPAN's Web site (**http:www.c-span.org**); and access to videotapes of various C-SPAN telecasts. An example of a useful videocassette is "How a Bill Becomes a Law: The Clean Air Act." Supplied by the Purdue University Public Affairs Video Archives under an agreement with C-SPAN, the video consists of thirteen excerpts of about eight minutes each taken from C-SPAN live, selected to illustrate steps by which the Clean Air Act amendments of 1990 (S.1630) were enacted into law (PL 101-549, 104 Stat. 2399, 42 U.S.C. § 7407(d) et seq.). Although the video does not cover all aspects of the legislative process, it epitomizes the twists and turns in the political dialectic by which this bill was enacted into law. Included in the thirteen segments are background hearings, President Bush's proposal, news conferences, floor amendments and debate, roll call, the conference committee, final House passage, and presidential signing.

Electronic Sources

The full text of the CR is available via GPO Access, THOMAS, CIS Congressional Universe, Legi-Slate, WESTLAW, LEXIS-NEXIS, and CQ Washington Alert. Each database has a different beginning year, which will change as retrospective editions are entered into their systems. Several CD-ROM publishers offer versions of the *Record*. Use the current edition of annual publications such as *CD-ROMs in Print,* edited by Amy R. Suchowski (Farmington Hills, MI: Gale Group) and *Directory of Law-Related CD-ROMs,* edited by Arlene Eis (Teaneck, NJ: Infosources). This market is, like all competing electronic products, volatile and subject to abrupt change.

CR Finding Aids

The daily *Record* has a fortnightly index composed of two parts: an index by subject and individual name to the proceedings and debates, including material in the Extensions of Remarks; and a History of Bills and Resolutions. The history is arranged by chamber and, within chamber, by bill and resolution number. In the print edition of the CR, bills and resolutions cumulate every two weeks, so that the most recent index can be used to trace current legislation with page references to the measure's introduction, referral to committee, consideration and passage, and enactment or veto. However, with free text, full-text searching available via the electronic sources noted above, the biweekly index may be bypassed. For instance, the "History of Bills" database on GPO Access permits searching by public law number as well as by keywords, sponsor(s), and bill or resolution number.

Voting Records

The *Congressional Record* publishes recorded votes and tallies of voice votes and that information can be found via THOMAS and GPO Access. Individual floor votes can be accessed through C-SPAN, CIS Congressional Universe, Legi-Slate, CQ Washington Alert, LEXIS-NEXIS, and WESTLAW. *CQ Weekly* (formerly named *CQ Weekly Report*), a product of Congressional Quarterly, Inc. (Washington, DC), is available in electronic format via CQ Washington Alert and in print and contains House and Senate recorded voting charts with annotations covering each motion, names of members, and party affiliation, including a notation as to whether the senator or representative is an ND (Northern Democrat) or an SD (Southern Democrat). The numbered voting charts are taken from the CR but are reformatted in such a way that they are easier to use than the comparable information in the original source. Moreover, unlike newspapers and general news magazines, *CQ Weekly* contains precise citations to all the intrinsic publications generated in the legislative process, allowing the researcher to access the primary source materials directly. *CQ Almanac* is a voluminous hardbound annual, a distillation and reorganization of the information reported in *CQ Weekly*. Well over 1,000 pages, it is organized by major policy areas and indexed by subject and bill number. It has retained the voting charts from its weekly companion product and retained the virtues of citation specificity found in *CQ Weekly*. Moreover, Congressional Quarterly, Inc. publishes *Congressional Role Call,* an annual examination of the key votes taken on the major issues of the session. Voting records are also available via the Library of Congress Internet resource page (**http://lcweb.loc.gov**).

Action in the Other Chamber

When the House passes a bill, an enrolling clerk in that chamber prepares an "engrossed bill" containing all the amendments agreed to; it is delivered to the Senate, referred to the appropriate committee, re-printed and called an "Act Print" (see Figure 5.9). With minor exceptions, the bill then follows the same process as described for the House: subcommittee action, hearings if necessary, a committee report, floor action, and vote (see Figure 5.1). Bills introduced in the Senate follow the reverse process.

The Conference Committee

Differing versions of a measure must be resolved before the bill can be sent to the president. The formal machinery for reconciling differences, if the bill has any degree of complexity, is the conference committee, a strategy adopted by the 1st Congress and used ever since. Conference committees have been referred to as the "Third House of Congress." Conferees, called "managers," are appointed from each body; their task is to effect a compromise satisfactory to both chambers. When the managers reach agreement, a conference report is prepared. Beginning with the 92d Congress in 1971, the conference report was required to be printed in both houses, but that unnecessary duplication can be waived.

Conference reports, like House and Senate committee reports, are sent in pamphlet form to depository libraries in paper copy or on microfiche. Later they are incorporated into the bound volumes of the Congressional Serial Set for regional libraries and microfiche for the selective depositories. Reports on public bills are also announced for sale in *U.S. Government Subscriptions.*

Like the regular committee reports generated in each chamber, conference reports are available online with THOMAS, GPO Access, CQ Washington Alert, Legi-Slate, and CIS Congressional Universe, and are indexed and abstracted in *CIS/Index.* Figure 5.13, page 132, shows a conference report issued by the House of Representatives.

Figure 5.13. Conference report.

101st Congress *1st Session*	HOUSE OF REPRESENTATIVES	Report 101–100

NATURAL GAS WELLHEAD DECONTROL ACT OF 1989

JUNE 22, 1989.—Ordered to be printed

Mr. DINGELL, from the committee of conference,
submitted the following

CONFERENCE REPORT

[To accompany H.R. 1722]

The committee of conference on the disagreeing votes of the two Houses on the amendments of the Senate to the bill (H.R. 1722) to amend the Natural Gas Policy Act of 1978 to eliminate wellhead price and nonprice controls on the first sale of natural gas, and to make technical and conforming amendments to such Act, having met, after full and free conference, have agreed to recommend and do recommend to their respective Houses as follows:

That the Senate recede from its amendment numbered 1.

That the House recede from its disagreement to the amendment of the Senate numbered 2, and agree to the same with amendments as follows:

*   *   *   *   *   *   *

(Sample copy of part of first page and page 2 of conference report)

*   *   *   *   *   *   *

And the Senate agree to the same.

JOHN D. DINGELL,
PHILIP R. SHARP,
BILLY TAUZIN,
NORMAN F. LENT,
CARLOS MOORHEAD,
Managers on the Part of the House.

J. BENNETT JOHNSTON,
DALE BUMPERS,
WENDELL H. FORD,
JAMES A. McCLURE,
PETE DOMENICI,
Managers on the Part of the Senate.

Presidential Action

The president may be the last, or next to last, actor in the legislative process. After approval by both Houses, a copy of the bill is enrolled for presentation to the president. Prepared by the enrolling clerk of the chamber in which the bill originated and signed by the Speaker of the House and the President of the Senate pro tempore, it is sent to the chief executive for veto or signature into law. Article I, Section 2, Clause 7, of the Constitution mandates the procedures that may follow signature or veto. If the president approves the bill, he signs it and usually stamps the bill "approved" and the date, although the Constitution requires only the president's signature. If the president does not return the bill with objections within ten days, excluding Sundays, it becomes law as if the president had signed it. Figure 5.14, page 134, is an example of this procedure; see the "Note" near the bottom of the figure. The Office of the Federal Register has a boilerplate comment, which appears after the text of the measure and before the "Legislative History." Conversely, if Congress adjourns, thus preventing return of the measure, it does not become law. This is called a "pocket veto." If the president vetoes in the usual way by sending his objections to Congress, a two-thirds vote of both chambers is necessary to override, a congressional task as difficult as it is rare. When it occurs over the president's objections, however, it becomes the law of the land. Figure 5.15, page 135, shows a bill vetoed by the president but overridden by both House and Senate.

Presidential veto messages are published either as House or Senate documents depending upon the bill's origin. *Presidential Vetoes, 1789–* have been published as Senate documents and thus become part of the Congressional Serial Set. They cumulate periodically, with a time lag of a few years, list vetoes from the 1st Congress, and can be accessed by subject and name indexes, with citations to the *Congressional Record*. Congressional voting records on presidential vetoes are available in the same print and online services mentioned above.

(Text continues on page 136.)

Figure 5.14. Law passed without presidential signature.

PUBLIC LAW 101-131—OCT. 28, 1989   103 STAT. 777

Public Law 101-131
101st Congress

An Act

To amend section 700 of title 18, United States Code, to protect the physical integrity of the flag.

Oct. 28, 1989
[H.R. 2978]

Be it enacted by the Senate and House of Representatives of the United States of America in Congress assembled,

Flag Protection
Act of 1989.
18 USC 700 note.

SECTION 1. SHORT TITLE.

This Act may be cited as the "Flag Protection Act of 1989".

SEC. 2. CRIMINAL PENALTIES WITH RESPECT TO THE PHYSICAL INTEGRITY OF THE UNITED STATES FLAG.

(a) IN GENERAL.—Subsection (a) of section 700 of title 18, United States Code, is amended to read as follows:

"(a)(1) Whoever knowingly mutilates, defaces, physically defiles, burns, maintains on the floor or ground, or tramples upon any flag of the United States shall be fined under this title or imprisoned for not more than one year, or both.

"(2) This subsection does not prohibit any conduct consisting of the disposal of a flag when it has become worn or soiled.".

(b) DEFINITION.—Section 700(b) of title 18, United States Code, is amended to read as follows:

"(b) As used in this section, the term 'flag of the United States' means any flag of the United States, or any part thereof, made of any substance, of any size, in a form that is commonly displayed.".

SEC. 3. EXPEDITED REVIEW OF CONSTITUTIONAL ISSUES.

Section 700 of title 18, United States Code, is amended by adding at the end the following:

"(d)(1) An appeal may be taken directly to the Supreme Court of the United States from any interlocutory or final judgment, decree, or order issued by a United States district court ruling upon the constitutionality of subsection (a).

"(2) The Supreme Court shall, if it has not previously ruled on the question, accept jurisdiction over the appeal and advance on the docket and expedite to the greatest extent possible."

[Note by the Office of the Federal Register: The foregoing Act, having been presented to the President of the United States on Monday, October 16, 1989, and not having been returned by him to the House of Congress in which it originated within the time prescribed by the Constitution of the United States, has become law without his signature on October 28, 1989.]

LEGISLATIVE HISTORY—H.R. 2978 (S. 607) (S. 1338):

HOUSE REPORTS: No. 101-231 (Comm. on the Judiciary).
SENATE REPORTS: No. 101-152 accompanying S. 1338 (Comm. on the Judiciary).
CONGRESSIONAL RECORD, Vol. 135 (1989):
    Mar. 16, S. 607 considered and passed Senate.
    Sept. 12, H.R. 2978 considered and passed House.
    Oct. 4, 5, considered and passed Senate, amended.
    Oct. 12, House concurred in Senate amendments.
WEEKLY COMPILATION OF PRESIDENTIAL DOCUMENTS, Vol. 25 (1989):
    Oct. 26, Presidential statement.

Figure 5.15. Congressional veto override.

Public Law 100–259
March 22, 1988
100th Congress, S. 557

JIM WRIGHT
Speaker of the House of Representatives.

HARRY M. REID

Acting President of the Senate pro tempore.

IN THE SENATE OF THE UNITED STATES,

March 22 (legislative day, March 21), 1988.

The Senate having proceeded to reconsider the bill (S. 557) entitled "An Act to restore the broad scope of coverage and to clarify the application of title IX of the Education Amendments of 1972, section 504 of the Rehabilitation Act of 1973, the Age Discrimination Act of 1975, and title VI of the Civil Rights Act of 1964", returned by the President of the United States with his objections, to the Senate, in which it originated, it was

Resolved, That the said bill pass, two-thirds of the Senators present having voted in the affirmative.

Attest: WALTER J. STEWART
Secretary.

I certify that this Act originated in the Senate.

WALTER J. STEWART
Secretary.

IN THE HOUSE OF REPRESENTATIVES, U.S.,

March 22, 1988.

The House of Representatives having proceeded to reconsider the bill (S. 557) entitled "An Act to restore the broad scope of coverage and to clarify the application of title IX of the Education Amendments of 1972, section 504 of the Rehabilitation Act of 1973, the Age Discrimination Act of 1975, and title VI of the Civil Rights Act of 1964", returned by the President of the United States with his objections, to the Senate, in which it originated, and passed by the Senate on reconsideration of the same, it was

Resolved, That the said bill pass, two-thirds of the House of Representatives agreeing to pass the same.

Attest:

DONNALD K. ANDERSON
Clerk.

The Brief Existence of the Line-Item Veto

On April 9, 1996, President Clinton signed into law the Line Item Veto Act (PL 104-130, 110 Stat. 1200, 2 U.S.C. § 681), thus giving a president, for the first time in the nation's history, a limited power to cut pork-barrel expenditures, a modified line-item veto with several built-in loopholes, and an eight-year sunset provision. The law became effective January 1, 1997, but the very next day several congressional opponents of the new law filed a constitutional challenge in federal district court, which on February 12, 1998, declared the act unconstitutional. With relative speed (escargots move faster than most federal court appeals) the case reached the U.S. Supreme Court, which held, in a 6 to 3 decision rendered June 25, 1998, that the Line Item Veto Act violates the constitutional requirement that legislation be passed by both houses and presented in its entirety to the president for signature.[11] Meanwhile, the president had used the new power eighty-two times in eighteen months. Under the act he was able to sign appropriations bills and then cancel spending for specific projects, narrowly targeted tax breaks, or reduce new or expanded entitlement programs.

Justices Antonin Scalia, Sandra Day O'Connor, and Stephen G. Breyer dissented, all declaring that the line-item veto should have been declared constitutional. Said Scalia, "There is not a dime's worth of difference between Congress authorizing the president to cancel a spending item, and Congress's authorizing money to be spent on a particular item at the president's discretion. And the latter has been done since the founding of the nation."[12] Ironically, Bill Clinton had line-item veto authority as governor of Arkansas, as do forty-two other state governors. The power seems to work well at the state level, reducing pork-barrel projects tucked into spending bills that may be wasteful but are not sufficient, in and of themselves, to provoke a veto of the entire measure.

PUBLICATION OF LAWS

When a bill becomes a law, it is sent to the Office of the Federal Register for publication. Technically speaking, upon enactment the legislative process ends, but this oversimplifies a dialectic involving administrative entities and the federal judiciary. Questions of "legislative intent" may arise, and the several documents intrinsic to the legislative process may be examined to determine the "meaning" of a provision of a statute and/or the "intent" of the Congress. Before considering these interrelationships, however, it may be useful to examine the publishing of the law in its various states and formats.

Slip Laws

The first appearance of a law is in "slip" (meaning pamphlet) form. Official slip laws are announced for sale in *U.S. Government Subscriptions* and are sent to depository libraries, but commercial editions are used for timely convenience and editorial enhancements. Slip laws are identified by Congress and a sequential number, for example, Pub. L 106-1, Pub. L 106-2, etc.; Priv. L 106-1, etc. (PL is a standard abbreviation for Public Law). *United States Law Week* (USLW), published by the Bureau of National Affairs (BNA), a Washington, DC-based company, includes the text of selected public laws, as well as supreme court and selected lower federal court cases, and a topical index. USLW and a daily edition are also online. USCCAN, noted above, includes the full text of all public laws. The *United States Code Service Advance Service,* published by LEXIS Law Publishing, has the text of recent public laws. Reproductions of slip laws are also published selectively in the several looseleaf services (see chapter 8), depending on the subject of the enactment.

Electronic editions of slip laws are furnished by WESTLAW, LEXIS-NEXIS, GPO Access, THOMAS, Legi-Slate, CQ Washington Alert, CIS Congressional Universe, and USLW-Daily Edition. Assigned a public law number, the slip law concludes with a "Legislative History" that includes citations to the basic publications generated in the legislative process, including any presidential statements made upon approval of the legislation. Figure 5.16, page 138, shows a public law in slip form.

United States Statutes at Large

A chronological arrangement of the slip laws in bound sessional volume is published as the *United States Statutes at Large* (Stat.). The volumes, which experience a distinct time lag, include in numerical order in discrete series public laws, private laws (discussed below), joint resolutions, concurrent resolutions (but not "simple" resolutions, which are published in the *Congressional Record*), and some presidential materials (see chapter 6). The *Statutes at Large* has a subject index, an individual (name) index for access to private laws, and, since 1991, a popular name index. When a sessional volume of the *Statutes at Large* is received in depository libraries, the equivalent slip laws for that session may be discarded or given to other libraries. As noted, Congressional Information Service publishes *CIS/Congressional Bills, Resolutions, & Laws* and a separate series that furnishes users with the text of the *Statutes at Large* on microfiche.

Figure 5.16. Public (slip) law.

PUBLIC LAW 101-60—JULY 26, 1989   103 STAT. 157

Public Law 101-60
101st Congress

An Act

To amend the Natural Gas Policy Act of 1978 to eliminate wellhead price and nonprice controls on the first sale of natural gas, and to make technical and conforming amendments to such Act.

July 26, 1989
[H.R. 1722]

Be it enacted by the Senate and House of Representatives of the United States of America in Congress assembled,

Natural Gas
Wellhead
Decontrol
Act of 1989.
15 USC 3301
note.

SECTION 1. SHORT TITLE.

This Act may be cited as the "Natural Gas Wellhead Decontrol Act of 1989".

SEC. 2. DEREGULATION OF FIRST SALES OF NATURAL GAS.

(a) INTERIM ELIMINATION OF CERTAIN MAXIMUM LAWFUL PRICES.—Section 121 of the Natural Gas Policy Act of 1978 (15 U.S.C. 3331) is amended by adding at the end the following new subsection:

"(f) ADDITIONAL DECONTROL.—The provisions of subtitle A respecting the maximum lawful price for a first sale of natural gas shall cease to apply to natural gas described in paragraphs (1), (2), (3), and (4), as follows:

"(1) EXPIRED, TERMINATED, OR POST-ENACTMENT CONTRACTS.—In the case of natural gas to which no first sale contract applies on the date of enactment of the Natural Gas Wellhead Decontrol Act of 1989, subtitle A shall not apply to any first sale of such natural gas delivered on or after the first day after such date of enactment.

"(2) EXPIRING OR TERMINATING CONTRACTS.—In the case of natural gas to which a first sale contract applies on the date of enactment of the Natural Gas Wellhead Decontrol Act of 1989, but to which such contract ceases to apply after such date of enactment, subtitle A shall not apply to any first sale of such natural gas delivered after such contract ceases to apply.

"(3) CERTAIN RENEGOTIATED CONTRACTS.—In the case of natural gas to which a first sale contract applies on the date of enactment of the Natural Gas Wellhead Decontrol Act of 1989, where the parties have expressly agreed in writing after March 23, 1989, that all or part of the gas sold under such contract shall not be subject to any maximum lawful price under subtitle A after a specified date, subtitle A shall not apply to any first sale of the natural gas subject to such express agreement delivered on or after the date so specified, except that subtitle A shall not cease to apply to any such natural gas pursuant to this paragraph before the date of enactment of the Natural Gas Wellhead Decontrol Act of 1989.

"(4) NEWLY SPUDDED WELLS.—In the case of natural gas produced from a well the surface drilling of which began after the date of enactment of the Natural Gas Wellhead Decontrol Act of 1989, subtitle A shall not apply to any first sale of such natural gas delivered on or after May 15, 1991.

Approved July 26, 1989.

LEGISLATIVE HISTORY—H.R. 1722 (S. 783):

HOUSE REPORTS: No. 101-29 (Comm. on Energy and Commerce) and No. 101-100 (Comm. of Conference).
SENATE REPORTS: No. 101-38 accompanying S. 783 (Comm. on Energy and Natural Resources) and No. 101-39 (Comm. on Energy and Natural Resources).
CONGRESSIONAL RECORD, Vol. 135 (1989):
    Apr. 17, considered and passed House.
    June 8, 9, 13, 14, considered and passed Senate, amended.
    June 15, House disagreed to Senate amendments.
    June 22, Senate agreed to conference report.
    July 12, House agreed to conference report.
WEEKLY COMPILATION OF PRESIDENTIAL DOCUMENTS, Vol. 25 (1989):
    July 26, Presidential statement.

United States Code

The official *United States Code* (U.S.C.) consists of a consolidation and codification of the general and permanent laws. Arranged under titles, the U.S.C. gives subject or topical access, collates the initial laws with subject amendments, and excludes statutory provisions that over time have been repealed or superseded. It is published every six years in a new edition, with cumulative annual supplements. Provenance of the Office of the Law Revision Counsel, House of Representatives, the bound volumes are available to depository libraries in hard copy and the annual supplements on CD-ROM. The official U.S.C. is available via GPO Access. The *Code* can also be searched, using the same protocols, on CIS Congressional Universe and LEXIS-NEXIS Academic Universe.

Revised Statutes

The *United States Code,* like Schubert's symphony No. 8 in B minor, is an unfinished work. It was not published until 1926, but it has a muddled past. Before the U.S.C., the first codification was called the *Revised Statutes of the United States* (1875). This endeavor became "positive law," that is, existing law created by legally valid procedures. Alas, the 1875 effort was fraught with inaccuracies, so a second edition was authorized in 1878. This edition, however, was never enacted into positive law by the Congress. Hence, the Law Revision Counsel, mentioned above, is charged by statute to revise the U.S.C. title by title in accordance with 1 U.S.C. § 204.

In other words, "Titles, once enacted and their direct amendments are 'legal evidence of the law' . . . but those titles of the United States Code which have never been enacted as a whole are merely prima facie evidence of the law."[13] As of 1999, roughly one-half of the titles of the *United States Code* (including Title 44) have been enacted into positive law. A list of titles enacted into positive law is found in the official *United States Code* and in its commercial editions.

Commercial Editions

Commercial editions include the *United States Code Annotated* (U.S.C.A.), published by the West Group, and the *United States Code Service* (U.S.C.S.), a product of LEXIS Law Publishing. These contain "bells and whistles," value-added editorial enhancements that facilitate research, notably digests of cases that have construed provisions of the code, sophisticated indexing, cross-references, and historical notes.

Both sets include the United States Constitution. In U.S.C.A. it consists of several unnumbered volumes, with an index in the last of the unnumbered volumes. The U.S.C.S. has fewer volumes; both sets contain cross-references to their own sister publications and carry the editorial enhancements noted above. Moreover, for both annotated editions, the Federal Rules of Criminal Procedure are found in the Appendix to Title 18 and the Federal Rules of Civil Procedure in the Appendix to Title 28.

An important difference between the two is the way positive law is indicated. For those titles not enacted into positive law, U.S.C.S. uses the words that appear in the *Statutes at Large,* whereas U.S.C.A. makes no such distinction. "Unless the Code title has been reenacted into positive law, citation of statutory material in legal writing is to the original statutes with parallel references to the Code." However, the work of the codifiers is so well done that the "Code has largely supplanted the statutes which are the real authority."[14] The other differences between these major services are relatively minor.

Shepard's and KeyCite

Shepard's United States Citations: Statute Edition traces the history and treatment of cases citing the United States Constitution, the *United States Code* (and its commercial editions), the *Statutes at Large,* the United States treaty series, and the court rules of the United States Supreme Court. *Shepard's Federal Citations* provides citations to cases in *Federal Supplement, Federal Rules Decisions, Court of Claims Reports, Federal Claims Reporter, Federal Cases,* and the three series of *Federal Reporter.* In addition to the print edition, Shepardizing is available on CD-ROM and on the Internet as a subscription product (**http://www.shepards.com**). It is also available at the LEXIS-NEXIS Xchange home page (**http://www.lexis.com/xchange**), also a Web-based subscription service providing access to the several Shepard's units. KeyCite, which replaced Insta-Cite (see chapter 8), is available as a WESTLAW database and offers the same information as Shepard's with the same daily update capabilities.

Popular Names Indexes

Popular names of laws are found online and in print in the *United States Code,* USCCAN, U.S.C.A., and U.S.C.S. *Shepard's Acts and Cases by Popular Names, Federal and State,* as the title suggests, lists federal acts by their popular names citing either the public law number, the *Statutes at Large,* or the *United States Code.* This comprehensive source includes familiar names such as the Sherman

Antitrust Act (15 U.S.C. § 1) and obscure laws such as the Oh! Grab Me Act (Embargo 1807; December 22, 1807, 2 Stat. 451), "the popular name for the unpopular Embargo Act of 1807, which forbade U.S. ships to sail with cargoes to foreign ports" during the time when Thomas Jefferson was president and George Clinton was vice president.[15] Drop the "h" (as London cockneys are wont to do) and you have a proper palindrome.

Electronic Sources of Public Laws

The full text of statutes is available via CQ Washington Alert, Legi-Slate, WESTLAW, LEXIS-NEXIS, and CIS Congressional Universe. The official edition of the *United States Code* is available on GPO Access, while the U.S.C.S. is on LEXIS-NEXIS and the U.S.C.A. on WESTLAW. Other vendors include CQ Washington Alert, Legi-Slate, and CIS Congressional Universe. Moreover, you can search the U.S.C. through the Internet Law Library of the House of Representatives (**http://www.house.gov/laws.html**). A button on LEXIS-NEXIS Academic Universe conveys you to the U.S. Constitution, the *United States Code,* and court rules. FedLaw EasySearch (Phoenix, AZ: Oryx Press) maintains the *Statutes at Large* and the *United States Code* on CD-ROM. If you do not want to access these sites, there are any number of law-related Web locations, such as the peerless FindLaw Internet Legal Resources, that link to the federal laws (see chapter 8).

PRIVATE LEGISLATION

The framers of the U.S. Constitution adopted the concept of private legislation from the British Parliament, but the practice dates at least from Roman times. Based on the principle of equity, the introduction of a private bill is intended to exempt "specific individuals, groups, or localities from the application of a [public] law that was not intended to apply to them."[16] House Parliamentarian Asher C. Hinds proposed this definition: "A private bill is a bill for the relief of one or several specified persons, corporations, institutions, etc., and is distinguished from a public bill, which relates to public matters and deals with individuals only by classes." He added this caveat: "The line of distinction between public and private bills is so difficult to be defined in many cases that it must rest on the opinion of the Speaker and the details of the bill."[17] Despite this difficulty, when a private bill becomes law, it is routinely assigned a separate slip law number and grouped in a separate section of the *Statutes at Large.*

The number of private bills over the last century has decreased dramatically, with a corresponding attrition in the number of private laws enacted. This reduction has been achieved through case law and by a series of "public laws delegating to executive agencies the authority to act on cases previously handled by Congress."[18] However, the Congress remains involved in private legislation. Two main categories predominate: claims, and immigration and naturalization matters. The former category includes moral and legal obligations of the federal government and is anchored in Article I, Section 8, Clause 1, of the Constitution. The latter is based on the fact that public laws on the admission of aliens into this country do not cover all hardship cases. Granting relief includes not only a specific individual but a group or class of persons (for example, relief of certain naval officers; relief of farmers in storm and flood areas), municipalities (for example, relief of Glendale, California) and even states (for example, relief of New York), and enterprises (for example, relief of the whaling industry).

Legislative Procedure

The steps by which a private bill becomes a private law are similar in their general lineaments to those of a public measure. Individuals or institutions initiate the process directly or through an intermediary such as an attorney or a lobbyist, by contacting the representative or senator in the appropriate jurisdiction. In virtually all instances, the introduced measure is referred to the House or Senate Judiciary Committee, which in turn delegates the bill to the relevant subcommittee or to the individual sponsoring member. If the bill is reported favorably out of committee, it is placed on the Senate's Calendar of Business or the Private Calendar of the House, where floor action takes place on certain predetermined days of the month. Figure 5.17 shows a House reported print of a private bill, and Figure 5.18, page 144, shows a House Judiciary Committee report accompanying a private bill.

Floor action on favorable committee reports typically is routine. But before final passage, the House and Senate may refer a claim "involving determination of facts" to the United States Court of Federal Claims for guidance. Presidential approval or veto completes the process. Of those private measures that the claims court determines to have merit, the judiciary committees report favorably, and the plenary chambers pass, very few are vetoed by a president.[19] Figure 5.19 (page 145) shows a private law, which is later incorporated into the *United States Statutes at Large*.

Figure 5.17. House reported print on private bill.

Private Calendar No. 47

100TH CONGRESS
2D SESSION

H. R. 3439

[Report No. 100–552]

For the relief of Marisela, Felix, and William [Doe].

IN THE HOUSE OF REPRESENTATIVES

OCTOBER 6, 1987

Mr. FUSTER introduced the following bill; which was referred to the Committee on the Judiciary

MARCH 31, 1988

Committed to the Committee of the Whole House and ordered to be printed

---

A BILL

For the relief of Marisela, Felix, and William [Doe].

1   *Be it enacted by the Senate and House of Representa-*

2 *tives of the United States of America in Congress assembled,*

3 That Marisela, Felix, and William [Doe], the children of

4 Manual [Doe], a Secret Service agent who was killed in a

5 fire while on duty in the Dupont Plaza Hotel in Puerto Rico,

6 shall for the purposes of section 6(c) of the Act of Sep-

7 tember 30, 1950 (20 U.S.C. 241(c)), be considered to be chil-

8 dren residing with a parent employed by the United States

9 and thus be eligible to receive free public education arranged

10 by the Secretary of Education under such section.

Figure 5.18. Committee report on private bill.

100TH CONGRESS 2d Session	HOUSE OF REPRESENTATIVES	REPORT 100–552

MARISELA, FELIX, AND WILLIAM [DOE]

MARCH 31, 1988.—Committed to the Committee of the Whole House and ordered to be printed

Mr. FRANK, from the Committee on the Judiciary, submitted the following

REPORT

[To accompany H.R. 3439]

The Committee on the Judiciary, to whom was referred the bill (H.R. 3439), for the relief of Marisela, Felix, and William [Doe], having considered the same, report favorably thereon without amendment and recommend that the bill do pass.

PURPOSE

H.R. 3439 authorizes the Secretary of Defense to allow the children of a secret service agent killed while on duty to attend school at a military facility in Puerto Rico.

BACKGROUND

On December 31, 1986, Special Agent Manual [Doe], who was assigned to the San Juan Office of the U.S. Secret Service, was killed in the line of duty at the Dupont Plaza Hotel fire in San Juan. At the time of his death, Mr. [Doe] was conducting an investigation in the manager's office when fire and explosions broke out. The fire quickly engulfed the lower level of the hotel, and Special Agent [Doe] died of smoke inhalation. He was killed in the line of duty and was survived by a wife and three children.

Following his death, the family was notified by the Defense Department that his three children were no longer eligible to attend the Antilles Consolidated Military School System due to the fact that the children were no longer dependents of a federally employed person in Puerto Rico.

*　　*　　*　　*　　*　　*　　*

(Sample copy of part of first and second pages of this 4-page House report)

*　　*　　*　　*　　*　　*

COMMITTEE ACTION

The Committee on the Judiciary on March 15, favorably reported by voice vote H.R. 3439 to the House. The Committee concluded that the children of Special Agent Manual [Doe] should be authorized to continue attending school in a military facility operated by the Department of Defense. Therefore, the Committee recommends that the House favorably consider H.R. 3439.

Figure 5.19. Private law.

PRIVATE LAW 100–11—MAY 5, 1988

Private Law 100–11
100th Congress

An Act

For the relief of Marisela, Felix, and William [Doe].

May 5, 1988
[H.R. 3439]

Be it enacted by the Senate and House of Representatives of the United States of America in Congress assembled, That Marisela, Felix, and William [Doe], the children of Manual [Doe], a Secret Service agent who was killed in a fire while on duty in the Dupont Plaza Hotel in Puerto Rico, shall for the purposes of section 6(c) of the Act of September 30, 1950 (20 U.S.C. 241(c)), be considered to be children residing with a parent employed by the United States and thus be eligible to receive free public education arranged by the Secretary of Education under such section.

Manual [Doe].

Approved May 5, 1988.

Sources of Information

Bibliographic aids include the "Private Calendar" section of the *Calendars of the House of Representatives and History of Legislation* (short title *House Calendars*); the *Monthly Catalog* since July 1976; the *Congressional Record*; *Journal of the House of Representatives of the United States* (short title *House Journal*); and the *Journal of the Senate of the United States of America* (short title *Senate Journal*). Reported private bills bear an individual report number and are later incorporated into the Congressional Serial Set. The *Numerical Lists and Schedule of Volumes* and its MOCAT supplements noted in chapter 4 bridge the gap between the numerical designation of individual reports on private bills and their subsequent appearance in numbered serial set volumes. The *CIS US Serial Set Index, 1789–1969* is the definitive source for locating citations to reports on private bills for that period. *CIS/Index* in its four-year cumulative and its annual indexes contains the private report numbers but no abstracts are given in its monthly and annual issues.

Depository libraries receive the text of private bills on microfiche and committee reports in paper or on fiche. Private bills used to be available for sale from the Superintendent of Documents, but are no longer. Reports on private bills and private laws are not a SuDocs sales category. The full text of private laws are published in the sessional volumes of the *Statutes at Large;* because they are not of a permanent or general nature, they are not published in the *United States Code*. The

"Individual Index" in each sessional volume has an alphabetical list of individuals and institutions that have been the recipient of private legislation.

For recent Congresses, electronic sources include the MOCAT on CD-ROM and via GPO Access, THOMAS, WESTLAW, and LEXIS-NEXIS. As I have mentioned before, these sites offer coverage of current and retrospective documents for specific categories of information. This coverage changes regularly if not incessantly, and the user should consult the database before making assumptions rather than relying on this text or any other secondary source.[20]

THE UNITED STATES CONGRESSIONAL SERIAL SET

The United States Congressional Serial Set has been known by different short or popular names including the serial number set, congressional edition, congressional set, congressional series, and sheep, or sheep-bound, set (owing to its distinctive sheepskin binding). Today it is known as the congressional serial set or simply the serial set. Throughout its illustrious history it has included a wide variety of titles and series. Thorough accounts of the historical set are presented in Schmeckebier and Eastin;[21] in the "User Guide" section found in the several volumes of the *CIS US Serial Set Index, 1776–1969;* and on the Superintendent of Document's home page, GPO Access, complete with a "virtual tour" showing the binding process (**http://www.access.gpo.gov/su_docs/ dpos/sset.html**).

The serial numbering system was developed by Dr. John G. Ames (see chapter 4) in the late nineteenth century. Not part of Ames numbering scheme were reprints of records covering the first fourteen congresses and some later sessions and published by Gales and Seaton between 1832 and 1861. Known as the *American State Papers,* they are considered part of the set and were numbered 01 to 038 when shelved in the old Public Documents Division, which housed a collection that was called a "Library."[22]

Some significant changes occurred in the format and distribution of the serial set beginning with the 96th Congress; and their subsequent availability on the Internet via THOMAS, GPO Access, and commercial electronic producers gives us a record of the series as it exists today. The current set consists of three categories of congressional publications issued in six discrete parts: House reports, Senate reports, House documents, Senate documents, Senate treaty documents, and Senate executive reports.

House and Senate Reports

House and Senate Reports on public and private measures have been described in this chapter in some detail. Pursuant to legislation, they constitute the majority of the report series. In addition, "special reports" include investigative activities of committees, summaries of committee oversight functions, study of matters relating to public policy, and the like. From the 84th through the 95th Congresses, House and Senate reports on public and private bills were bound separately in serial set volumes entitled "Miscellaneous Reports on Public Bills." Beginning with the 88th Congress, Second Session, special reports were also bound separately. With the 96th Congress, all House and Senate materials are bound in numerical sequence because of the exigencies of issuing the serial set in a microfiche format (discussed infra).

House and Senate Documents

Throughout this text, the word "documents" has been used largely in a generic sense, synonymous with "publications," "materials," or "sources." For serial set publications, however, the word assumes a specificity not encountered elsewhere.

The kinds of materials ordered to be published as House or Senate documents are many and varied. Prior to the 96th Congress, documents labeled "miscellaneous" were bound in serial volumes bearing the same base serial number, with individual volumes designated by a numerical suffix (for example, 13145-1, 13145-2, 13145-3). In these volumes one finds, among other things, presidential messages, including vetoes; memorial addresses; reports on rescissions and deferrals of budget authority; budget estimates and amendments; and the president's Annual State of the Union Address. Other titles issued in the House and Senate document series include annual reports of federal departments and agencies and standard works of reference and research value such as *How Our Laws Are Made, Biographical Directory of the United States Congress, Senate Ethics Manual, Constitution of the United States, Analysis and Interpretation* and its biennial supplements, and the *Budget of the United States Government.*

A category users may be unfamiliar with includes the annual or fiscal audits of federally chartered corporations. This group comprises well-known entities such as the National Railroad Passenger Corporation (Amtrak) and the Tennessee Valley Authority and other incorporated societies and associations such as the Boy Scouts and Girl Scouts of America; Little League Baseball, Incorporated; Daughters of the American Revolution; Paralyzed Veterans of America; American Gold

Star Mothers, Incorporated; National Federation of Music Clubs; National Safety Council; Navy Wives Club of America, Incorporated; Daughters of Union Veterans of the Civil War; and so forth. Each of these entities was incorporated by statute. For example, the annual report of the Girl Scouts is required to be printed as a House document by Act of April 16, 1951 (65 Stat. 32). Federally chartered corporations are required under 36 U.S.C. §§ 1102–1103 to present the corporation's assets and liabilities and reasonable detail on the corporation's income and expenses, obtain an annual financial audit by an independent public accountant, and submit the auditor's report and the corporation's financial statements to the Congress not later than six months following the close of the corporation's fiscal year. A typical procedure is for the Accounting and Information Management Division of the General Accounting Office (GAO) to review the audit for compliance with the financing reporting requirements of the law as requested by the appropriate congressional committee exercising oversight. These corporations are listed in an annual pamphlet titled *Reports to Be Made to Congress,* itself issued as a House document.

The latitude that inheres in the documents series results in something that falls short of bibliographic consistency. For example, committee prints have been published as House or Senate documents and in the *Congressional Record* ("all the news that fits, we print"). Some "special reports" in the House and Senate reports series could just have easily been issued as "documents." Nevertheless, the series is replete with gems for the persevering researcher. Figure 5.20 shows the title page of a publication in the House documents series.

Senate Treaty Documents

Senate treaty documents, formerly called Senate executive documents, were issued in a letter series. In 1977 this series was made available to depository libraries, and it became part of the serial set beginning with the 96th Congress (1979). Before this availability, the Documents Expediting Project of the Library of Congress was the principal source for obtaining treaty documents. With the 97th Congress, the title change became effective and the treaty documents became a numbered series throughout a Congress.

Senate treaty documents consist of messages from the president to the Senate Foreign Relations Committee transmitting the text of the treaty itself before Senate mark-up and advice and consent. Treaty documents are examined in greater detail in chapter 6.

Figure 5.20. Title page of House document.

100th Congress, 1st Session - - - - - - - - - House Document 100–23

DISABLED AMERICAN VETERANS
65th NATIONAL CONVENTION

COMMUNICATION

FROM

THE NATIONAL ADJUTANT,
DISABLED AMERICAN VETERANS

TRANSMITTING

THE REPORT OF THE PROCEEDINGS OF THE ORGANIZATIONS
65TH NATIONAL CONVENTION, INCLUDING A REPORT OF RE-
CEIPTS AND EXPENDITURES AS OF DECEMBER 31, 1985, PURSU-
ANT TO TITLE 44, UNITED STATES CODE, SECTION 1332, AND
SECTION 3 OF PUBLIC LAW 88–504

JANUARY 21, 1987.—Referred to the Committee on Veterans' Affairs and
ordered to be printed, with illustrations

U.S. GOVERNMENT PRINTING OFFICE
65–458 O   WASHINGTON : 1987

Senate Executive Reports

Like treaty documents, Senate executive reports were first made available to depository institutions in 1977 and became part of the serial set beginning in 1979. They, too, are a numbered series and serve two purposes: (1) when issued by the Senate Foreign Relations Committee, they recommend to the full Senate that a treaty proposed by the president (in a Senate treaty document) be approved; and (2) when issued by any Senate committee with the appropriate oversight function, they recommend confirmation of nominations of high officials in the executive and judiciary. For executive reports on nominations, there is no prior "executive document" series, but nominations are noted in the *Weekly Compilation of Presidential Documents,* the *Public Papers of the Presidents,* the *Congressional Record,* and the *Senate Journal.* Treaty documents and executive reports can be accessed bibliographically in *CIS/Index* and in the *Monthly Catalog,* and Congressional Information Service has a definitive set of retrospective documents and reports. Executive reports, like treaty documents, are discussed in more detail in the context of treaties and agreements in chapter 6.

Numerical Lists and Schedule of Volumes

As noted in chapter 4, the *Numerical Lists* was a convenient, user-friendly guide to the bound volumes of the serial set. In existence from 1933 to 1980, it connected the numerical designation of individual reports and documents to the numerical designation of their subsequent republication in the bound serial set volumes. The *Lists* were issued sessionally and were the provenance of the Office of Superintendent of Documents. The title of the publication identifies its two-part organization. The first part, the "Numerical Lists," arranges the categories by individual number, title, and serial volume designation. The second part, the "Schedule of Volumes," shows the same categories grouped by inclusive numbers within a volume, referencing the serial volume number. Users will discover that the "Schedule of Volumes" section before the 96th Congress reflects the grouping of like reports and documents in the bound serial volumes and, of course, did not include treaty documents and executive reports. Moreover, the bound set in its entirety as indicated in the "Schedule of Volumes" was sent only to the Senate and House libraries, the Library of Congress, the National Archives, and the Office of Superintendent of Documents.

Also noted in chapter 4, beginning with the 97th Congress, the *Numerical Lists* was replaced by special editions of the *Monthly Catalog,* cumbersome volumes covering a two-year Congress in which entries are organized by SuDocs classification notation and contain full bibliographic information like the entries in the regular MOCAT. The amount of bibliographic information for *every* report and document did not compensate for the egregious delay in producing these special editions. Of some help but no real substitute for the original are periodic issuances of only the "Schedule of Volumes" part of the *Numerical Lists,* first in *Administrative Notes* and later in *Administrative Notes*

Technical Supplement. Figure 5.21 and Figure 5.22 (page 152), show, respectively, a page from the "Numerical Lists" and a page from the "Schedule of Volumes."

Figure 5.21. Page from "Numerical Lists."

NUMERICAL LISTS

No.	HOUSE REPORTS	Vol.; serial
537.	Earnings test for social security beneficiaries. 2 pts ____	15; 13302
538.	Reduce unemployment compensation by retirement benefits ____	15; 13302
539.	Unemployment compensation, employees of National Oceanic and Atmospheric Administration. 3 pts____	15; 13302
540.	Civil Service authorization act of 1979 _____	15; 13302
541.	2d concurrent resolution on budget, fiscal 1980 ____	15; 13302
542.	Appropriations for Department of Housing and Urban Development ____	15; 13302
543.	Designate birthday of Martin Luther King, Jr., as legal holiday ____	15; 13302
544.	Amend act of Dec. 22, 1974, 88 Stat. 1712____	15; 13302
545.	Tax administration provisions revision act of 1979 ____	15; 13302
546.	Department of Defense authorization act, fiscal 1980 ___	15; 13302
547.	Consideration of H.J. Res. 430 ____	15; 13302
548.	Civil suits for violations of civil rights ____	15; 13302
549.	Amend District of Columbia redevelopment act of 1945__	15; 13302
550.	Extend borrowing authority for District of Columbia ___	15; 13302
551.	Conveyance to Little Sisters of the Poor ____	15; 13302
552.	Low-income energy assistance supplemental appropriation. 2 pts ____	15; 13302
553.	Appropriations for Agriculture, Rural Development, and related agencies programs, fiscal 1980____	15; 13302
554.	Consideration of H.R. 4904 ____	15; 13302
555.	Consideration of H.R. 5192 ____	15; 13302
556.	Maritime appropriation authorization act, fiscal 1980 ___	15; 13302
557.	Indiana Dunes National Lakeshore ____	15; 13302
558.	Report by Permanent Select Committee on Intelligence pursuant to sec. 108(b), Foreign intelligence surveillance act ____	15; 13302
559.	Revitalize passenger ship industry ____	15; 13302
560.	Relief of Ohio Wesleyan University, Delaware, Ohio____	15; 13302
561.	Relief of St. Paul's Episcopal Church, Riverside, Conn. 2 pts ____	15; 13302
562.	Temporary duty suspension on certain alloy steels used for making chipper knives____	15; 13302
563.	Temporary reduction of duty on strontium nitrate ____	15; 13302
564.	Temporary suspension of duty on fluorspar____	15; 13302
565.	Temporary duty reduction on titanium sponge ____	15; 13302
566.	Tariff classification of cold finished steel bars ____	15; 13302
567.	Temporary suspension of duty on pillow blanks of latex foam rubber____	15; 13302
568.	Child health assurance act of 1979____	15; 13302
569.	Miscellaneous tariff schedules amendments____	15; 13302
570.	Establish Legionville National Historic Site in Pennsylvania ____	15; 13302
571.	Consideration of H.R. 4985 ____	15; 13302
572.	Term of Federal Reserve Board Chairman____	15; 13302
573.	Further expenses of investigations, etc., by Permanent Select Committee on Intelligence ____	15; 13302
574.	National Archives film-vault fire, Suitland, Maryland, Dec. 7, 1978 ____	15; 13302
575.	Express sense of Congress with respect to Baltic States and Soviet claims of citizenship over U.S. citizens __	15; 13302
576.	Consideration of H.R. 2603 ____	15; 13302
577.	Consideration of H.R. 2608 ____	15; 13302
578.	Consideration of H.R. 3994 ____	15; 13302
579.	Consideration of H.R. 2063 ____	15; 13302

Figure 5.22. Page from "Schedule of Volumes."

SCHEDULE OF VOLUMES

SENATE EXECUTIVE DOCUMENTS—SENATE REPORTS SENATE EXECUTIVE REPORTS—HOUSE DOCUMENTS	Serial no.	Date of receipt
SENATE EXECUTIVE DOCUMENTS		
Letters A–II: Senate executive documents	13235	
SENATE REPORTS		
Vol. 1. Nos. 1–47: Senate miscellaneous reports _	13236	
Vol. 2. Nos. 48–65: Senate miscellaneous reports_	13237	
Vol. 3. Nos. 66–104: Senate miscellaneous reports	13238	
Vol. 4. Nos. 105–155: Senate miscellaneous reports _ _ _ _ _ _ _ _ _ _ _ _ _ _ _ _	13239	
Vol. 5. Nos. 156–195: Senate miscellaneous reports _ _ _ _ _ _ _ _ _ _ _ _ _ _ _	13240	
Vol. 6. Nos. 196–237: Senate miscellaneous reports _ _ _ _ _ _ _ _ _ _ _ _ _ _ _	13241	
Vol. 7. Nos. 238–250: Senate miscellaneous reports _ _ _ _ _ _ _ _ _ _ _ _ _ _ _	13242	
Vol. 8. Nos. 251–299: Senate miscellaneous reports _ _ _ _ _ _ _ _ _ _ _ _ _ _ _	13243	
Vol. 9. Nos. 300–330: Senate miscellaneous reports _ _ _ _ _ _ _ _ _ _ _ _ _ _ _	13244	
Vol. 10. Nos. 331–374: Senate miscellaneous reports _ _ _ _ _ _ _ _ _ _ _ _ _ _ _	13245	
Vol. 11. Nos. 375–394: Senate miscellaneous reports _ _ _ _ _ _ _ _ _ _ _ _ _ _ _	13246	
Vol. 12. Nos. 395–423: Senate miscellaneous reports _ _ _ _ _ _ _ _ _ _ _ _ _ _ _	13247	
Vol. 13. Nos. 424–471: Senate miscellaneous reports _ _ _ _ _ _ _ _ _ _ _ _ _ _ _	13248	
Vol. 14. Nos. 472–547: Senate miscellaneous reports _ _ _ _ _ _ _ _ _ _ _ _ _ _ _	13249	
SENATE EXECUTIVE REPORTS		
Nos. 1–26: Senate executive reports _ _ _ _	13250	
HOUSE DOCUMENTS		
Vol. 1. Nos. 1–15: Miscellaneous documents _ _ _	13251	
Vol. 2. Nos. 16–20: Examinations of rivers and harbors _ _ _ _ _ _ _ _ _ _ _ _ _ _ _ _ _	13252	
Vol. 3. Nos. 21–23: Examinations of rivers and harbors _ _ _ _ _ _ _ _ _ _ _ _ _ _ _ _	13253	
Vol. 4. Nos. 24–26: Examinations of rivers and harbors _ _ _ _ _ _ _ _ _ _ _ _ _ _ _ _	13254	
Vol. 5. Nos. 27–39: Miscellaneous documents_ _ _	13255	

Distribution of Serial Set Is Abridged

Starting with the 96th Congress, all congressional materials listed in the "Schedule of Volumes" were sent to depository libraries that subscribed to the appropriate depository items. However, the House report on Legislative Branch Appropriations for fiscal year 1997 (H.rp. 104-657) required the Government Printing Office, effective with the 105th Congress (1997), to limit distribution of the number of bound serial set volumes to only the regional depositories and one depository library in those states that do not have a regional. Slip copies of the series continue to be sent to selective (and regional) depositories that subscribe to the appropriate items. The more than 1,300 selective depositories were given notice that if they wished to purchase the bound volumes, they would have to shell out some $15,400 per Congress.[23]

Assigned Serial Set Numbers Not Used

Virginia Saunders and August Imholtz of Congressional Information Service compiled a collection management aid titled *U.S. Congressional Serial Set: Assigned Serial Numbers Not Used.* The compilation is published in print in the November 30, 1998, issue of *Administrative Notes Technical Supplement* and is also available via GPO Access. The list is organized in parallel tables by serial volume number, title, and status. For example, serial set number 7143/reserved for H.doc. 2132, 64th Congress, 2d Session, Army Register 1917/ was not issued.

Departmental and Congressional "Editions"

As indicated above, the House and Senate document series include a number of publications from sources outside the Congress. Congressional policy was never consistent regarding this practice. In some nineteenth-century Congresses, executive materials made up more than half of the serial set. These publications, although they originated in the executive, were required by statute to be sent to Congress. They included, in addition to the annual reports of the agencies and the federal budget noted above, several serial publications such as the *Geological Survey Bulletins,* a few periodicals, and reports and bulletins issued by the Bureau of Labor Statistics and the Smithsonian Institution. Notification of these kinds of non-congressional materials was given in every sessional issue of the *Numerical Lists.* In the "Schedule of Volumes" section preceding the titles of these "departmental editions," there is this explanatory statement:

Note.—The documents listed below originated in executive departments and agencies. They were or will be furnished to depository libraries and international exchanges at the time of printing in that format used by the departments and agencies. They will not be furnished as Congressional documents nor in the volumes as indicated hereby.

That last sentence is the crucial one. The result was that two editions of the same publication were often printed: the "departmental" edition and the "congressional" edition. But depository libraries received those titles only in the "departmental" edition with the SuDocs classification notation and only if the library subscribed to the appropriate depository item number. This practice resulted in apparent gaps in the serial set, unless a cross-reference was made to the departmental edition. Typically, the only difference between the two editions was the title page, one reflecting the department or agency provenance, the other (kept in the House or Senate libraries) showing the individual serial number (for example, 101st CONGRESS/2d Session {House of Representatives} Document/No. 101-139). The occasional exception, however, can be found. A General Accounting Office study titled *Audit of the Rural Telephone Bank* was issued as 96-2: H. Doc 297 but in its departmental edition was titled *Examination of the Rural Telephone Bank's Financial Statements* and classified in the SuDocs author symbol (GA). The main entries in the *Monthly Catalog* give bibliographic information for serial set publications and include the availability of other editions. The number of such duplicate printings was gradually reduced to decrease costs. Cost was further diminished by eliminating the so-called posterity edition (one with red, green, and black ink labels, stamped with imitation gold); the traditional, less elaborate edition is sent to depository libraries and all other authorized recipients of the serial set. Today the set contains few executive branch documents. That it is not so cluttered with executive branch issuances is a positive development; the executive is thoroughly represented in its numerous departmental and agency provenances.

Certain serial set volumes are important reference sources. Because of their size, they are not issued in slip form but are sent directly in bound volumes with a serial volume number on the spine. They are, however, assigned an individual House or Senate report or document number for bibliographic consistency. They include investigative studies such as the Iran-Contra reports in the Reagan Administration and the report of independent counsel Kenneth W. Starr to the House of Representatives and other impeachment-related materials in the Clinton

Administration; the *Constitution of the United States, Analysis and Interpretation* and its supplements; the quarterly *Report of the Clerk of the House of Representatives;* financial disclosure reports of members of both chambers; appropriations and budget estimates statements, and so forth. These bound volumes are exempt from the congressional mandate to limit the hard copy serial set to regional depository libraries. The "Starr Report" (105-2: H.doc. 310), for example, was distributed to all federal depository libraries under item number 1004-E, which is set aside for the Joint Committee on Printing "ALL LIBRARIES" designation (SuDocs class notation Y 4.P 93/1-10); but the class number under which it was shipped (Y 1.1/7:) signifies House Documents in paper copy. Librarians should consider the option of moving useful reference sources from their numerical sequence in the serial set shelves to the reference collection in the classification system used by the library, or at least have a cross-reference to these sources in a file easily accessible by librarians and users alike.

The Serial Set on Microfiche

A major change adopted in 1979 was the filming and distribution of the serial set in a microfiche edition. In December of that year, depository libraries were offered the choice of microfiche or paper copy distribution. Those libraries opting for the microfiche are furnished with polymer dividers imprinted with the SuDocs classification system indicating the serial volume number and the numbers of the reports and documents included in that volume. Accordingly, the initial sequence of materials issued becomes, in fact, the "bound" serial volume. Libraries choosing to continue paper copies receive the series as it was always issued, in slip form and in bound volumes up to 1996, when the edict to limit the set in bound format became effective. Commercial firms like Congressional Information Service and Readex offer the text of these materials on microfiche; but the advent of Internet and commercial online access to these reports and documents does not equalize the loss of bound printed volumes that preserve these valuable sources for researchers.

Serial Set Classification

Before the 96th Congress, the serial set was simply designated, without a SuDocs classification symbol. Thus, for example, a committee report for legislation extending the Library Services and Construction Act was designated 95-1: H.rp. 97. Today that report would be designated and classified; for example, Y 1.1/8: 106-97. The present class notation was designed to encompass both paper copy and microfiche distribution and improve bibliographic control. As with all other classified publications, the serial set alphanumeric notation is published in the latest issue of the *List of Classes of United States Government Publications Available for Selection by Depository Libraries* in paper or electronic formats. The following table shows the classification of the serial set and its distribution to depository libraries in print (P) or microfiche (MF).

SERIAL SET CLASSIFICATION

SuDocs Class Number	Category	Format Depository	Item Number
Y 1.1/2: (Serial Volume Number)	Serial Set (H & S Docs, S.Treaty Docs)	MF	0996-B
Y 1.1/2: (Serial Volume Number)	Serial Set (H & S Docs, S. Treaty Docs)	P	0996-C
Y 1.1/2: (Serial Volume Number)	Serial Set (H & S Rpts, S. Exec. Rpts)	MF	1008-D
Y 1.1/2: (Serial Volume Number)	Serial Set (H & S Rpts, S. Exec. Rpts)	P	1008-E
Y 1.1/3: (Cong.-no.)	Senate Documents	P	0996-A
Y 1.1/3: (Cong.-no.)	Senate Documents	MF	0996-B
Y 1.1/4: (Cong.-no.)	Senate Treaty Docs.	P	0996-A
Y 1.1/4: (Cong.-no.)	Senate Treaty Docs.	MF	0996-B
Y 1.1/5: (Cong.-no.)	Senate Reports	P	1008-C
Y 1.1/5: (Cong.-no.)	Senate Reports	MF	1008-D
Y 1.1/6: (Cong.-no.)	Senate Exec. Rpts	P	1008-C
Y 1.1/6: (Cong.-no.)	Senate Exec. Rpts	MF	1008-D
Y 1.1/7: (Cong.-no.)	House Documents	P	0996-A
Y 1.1/7: (Cong.-no.)	House Documents	MF	0996-B
Y 1.1/8: (Cong.-no.)	House Reports	P	1008-C
Y 1.1/8: (Cong.-no.)	House Reports	MF	1008-D

In addition, Y 1.1/9 (Item 1008-D-01) is used for the polymer dividers that "convert" the reports and documents into a microfiche version of the bound serial set. The notation Y 1.1/10 (Item 1008-D-02), effective with the 105th Congress, specifies the title page and/or table of contents, printed on acid-free paper, for libraries that want to bind the slip reports and documents to create serial set volumes and avoid spending over $15,000 for the bound set.

Studies have shown that the earlier serial set is underutilized in some academic libraries.[24] This is a pity; the congressional series is an historical resource for a number of disciplines not confined to politics and government. Although the diminution of documents from the executive branch has reduced the quantity of serial volumes in recent years, the set is still a trove of significant information on the workings of the Congress and the role of the president in that office's shared duties with the legislative branch.

OTHER REPORTS REQUIRED BY CONGRESS

The relatively few titles generated by agencies in the executive branch and reprinted in the serial set do not indicate the scope of congressional oversight of executive activities. Every year, Congress requires submission of thousands of reports prepared by the other branches, primarily the executive departments and agencies, but even some by the judiciary, and, as noted above, federally chartered institutions. Pursuant to House of Representative rules, the Clerk of the House is required to publish annually as a House Document *Reports to Be Made to Congress,* which, as noted above, lists the type of report, statutory authority, and date or time when the report is to be submitted. These reports, referred to collectively as Executive Communications (ECs), are received by the Clerk of the House and by the Secretary of the Senate, who assign sequential numbers to them and publish a notice of transmittal in the *Congressional Record.* Therefore, the *Reports to Be Made to Congress* does not provide exhaustive coverage of this oversight activity.

Congressional Information Service's *Reports Required by Congress: CIS Guide to Executive Communications* furnishes comprehensive access from January 1994 to all numbered ECs that appear in the *Congressional Record* in three cumulative quarterly issues plus a clothbound annual. Because neither chamber coordinates the transmittal and numbering process with the other, identical reports may be received by both House and Senate. In cases of duplication, the CIS editors eliminate the Senate communication. These publications are generally not printed by GPO or indexed in official sources. About 30 percent of ECs are indexed in *CIS/Index, American Statistics Index,* and the *American Foreign Policy Index*. However, *Reports Required by Congress* has full subject indexing for these materials and includes a citation to their accession number in the CIS service in which they are microfilmed, but they have not been filmed again for this collection.

The main entry section for each issue, called "List of Documents," is followed by indexes by subjects, EC numbers, and statutory authorities. *Reports Required by Congress* has a companion microfiche collection of the text of the executive communications. Figure 5.23 shows a page from the "List of Documents."

Figure 5.23. Page from *Reports Required by Congress*.

94-A-0001 *'RRC*
Joint Report to Congress on the FAA-NASA Subsonic Noise Reduction Technology Program.
Dec. 1993. vii+16 p. 49 U.S.C. app. 1353 note. House E.C. 2197.
[Federal Aviation Administration; National Aeronautics and Space Administration; Aircraft noise; Technological innovations]

94-A-0002 *'ASI 94 9264-5*
Farm Credit Administration 1992 annual report, report from the Chairman, Farm Credit Administration.
1/25/94. Annual. 12 U.S.C. 1141 b(3). House E.C. 2198.
To: House Committee on Agriculture
[Farm Credit Administration]

94-A-0003 *'AFPI 94 7000-9.46*
Foreign assistance allocations to be made available by the executive branch from FY94 funding levels, report from the Assistant Secretary, Legislative Affairs, Department of State.
1/25/94. 22 U.S.C. 2413 (a). House E.C. 2199.
To: House Committee on Appropriations
[Department of State; Foreign assistance]

94-A-0004 *'CIS 94 H180-1*
Notification making available appropriations in budget authority for DOT to provide immediate assistance to southern California for roads and bridges damaged by the earthquake, and for outstanding Midwest flood costs, communication from the President.
1/25/94. 31 U.S.C. 1107. House E.C. 2200.
To: House Committee on Appropriations
[Presidential communications and messages; Department of Transportation; Disaster relief; California; Highways; Earthquakes; Mississippi River; Floods; Balanced Budget and Emergency Deficit Control Act]

94-A-0005 *'CIS 94 H180-2*
Notification making available appropriations for SBA to provide disaster loans to victims of Los Angeles earthquake and Midwest floods, and to enable SBA to respond rapidly to assist victims of upcoming spring flood and summer hurricane seasons, communication from the President.

1/25/94. 31 U.S.C. 1107. House E.C. 2201.
To: House Committee on Appropriations
[Presidential communications and messages; Small Business Administration; Loans; Disaster relief; Los Angeles, Calif.; Earthquakes; Floods; Hurricanes; Balanced Budget and Emergency Deficit Control Act]

94-A-0006 *'CIS 94 H180-6*
Notification making available appropriations for SBA and FEMA disaster relief programs, notification under the Balanced Budget and Emergency Deficit Control Act of 1985, communication from the President.
1/25/94. House E.C. 2202.
To: House Committee on Appropriations
[Presidential communications and messages; Small Business Administration; Federal Emergency Management Agency; Disaster relief; Earthquakes; California; Balanced Budget and Emergency Deficit Control Act]

94-A-0007 *'CIS 94 H180-7*
Notification making available appropriations for DOT under the Balanced Budget and Emergency Deficit Control Act of 1985, communication from the President.
1/25/94. House E.C. 2203.
To: House Committee on Appropriations
[Presidential communications and messages; Department of Transportation; Balanced Budget and Emergency Deficit Control Act]

94-A-0008 *'CIS 94 H180-8*
Notification making available appropriations for DOD under the Balanced Budget and Emergency Deficit Control Act of 1985, communication from the President.
1/25/94. House E.C. 2204.
To: House Committee on Appropriations
[Presidential communications and messages; Department of Defense; Balanced Budget and Emergency Deficit Control Act]

94-A-0009 *'CIS 94 H180-5*
Review of the President's third special impoundment message from fiscal year 1994, report from the Comptroller General, GAO.
1/25/94. 2 U.S.C. 685. House E.C. 2205.
To: House Committee on Appropriations
[General Accounting Office; Impoundment of appropriated funds]

94-A-0010 *'ASI 94 25922-2*
Appropriation expenditures during the period April 1, 1993, through September 30, 1993, report from the Architect of the Capitol.
1/25/94. Semiannual. 40 U.S.C. 16 b. House E.C. 2206.
To: House Committee on Appropriations
[Architect of the Capitol]

94-A-0011 *'RRC pending*
Anti-Deficiency Act violation in the Department of Navy, report from the Comptroller, DOD.
1/25/94. 31 U.S.C. 1517 (b). House E.C. 2207.
To: House Committee on Appropriations
[Department of Defense; Anti-Deficiency Act; Department of Navy]

94-A-0012 *'RRC pending*
Anti-Deficiency Act violation in the Department of Air Force, report from the Comptroller, DOD.
1/25/94. 31 U.S.C. 1517 (b). House E.C. 2208.
To: House Committee on Appropriations
[Department of Defense; Anti-Deficiency Act; Department of Air Force]

94-A-0013 *'AFPI pending*
Presidential determination on assistance program for the independent states of the former Soviet Union, copy from the Assistant Secretary, Legislative Affairs, Department of State.
1/25/94. P.L. 101-508, sec. 13101 (a). House E.C. 2209.
To: House Committee on Appropriations
[Department of State; Foreign assistance; Commonwealth of Independent States; Eastern Europe; Estonia; Latvia; Lithuania]

94-A-0014 *'RRC*
OMB Final Sequestration Report to the President and Congress for Fiscal Year 1994.
Dec. 10, 1993. Annual. iii+14 p. ll. P.L. 101-508, sec. 13101 (a). House E.C. 2210.
To: House Committee on Appropriations
[Office of Management and Budget; Sequestration of appropriated funds; Government spending; Public debt; Balanced Budget and Emergency Deficit Control Act; Statistical data: government]

LEGISLATIVE HISTORIES
AND LEGISLATIVE INTENT

> Statutes are the courts' daily bread. The way in
> which courts go about reading those statutes in
> the federal system is therefore of particular im-
> portance to our jurisprudence.
>
> —Judge Kenneth W. Starr

Legislative histories comprise citations to and the text of those internal documents generated in the legislative process, including any
comments by the president upon signing or vetoing the legislation.
Once a bill or resolution has been introduced and referred to the appropriate committee, its legislative history has begun. Therefore, all
sources, in print and electronic formats, which have bill tracking and
current status systems, eo ipso furnish legislative history information.
Current measures and retrospective laws, by definition, leave a paper
(or electronic) trail of documentation in their often arduous journey, like
salmon swimming upstream to spawn.

Some of these texts have been consulted by the courts in an attempt to determine "legislative intent" if the meaning or purpose of a
statute is ambiguous because of imprecise language or political shenanigans. At one time or another, the courts have cited the remarks in the
Congressional Record of the chief sponsor of a measure that has become law. In more recent decades, committee reports were considered
the most reliable source for finding legislative intent because they
allegedly represent the "considered and collective understanding of
those Congressmen involved in drafting and studying proposed legislation."[25] But jurists have questioned that assumption; indeed, discussion
about the appropriate role legislative history plays in statutory interpretation goes back to medieval England, and in the United States has oscil-
lated between reliance upon and disdain of legislative history as an aid to
construction.

Ever since he came to the Supreme Court in 1986, Associate Justice Antonin Scalia has waged an often passionate war of words against
the use of legislative histories to interpret statutes. Advocating a return
to the "Plain Meaning Rule," which is followed today in England and
was embraced by the United States Supreme Court through most of the
nineteenth century, Scalia and other prominent jurists have railed
against reliance upon legislative history and for a literalist view of the
law. Here is a typical Scalia statement in a 1993 Supreme Court concurring opinion:

> The greatest defect of legislative history is its illegitimacy. We
> are governed by laws, not by the intention of legislators. . . .
> [N]ot the least of the defects of legislative history is its indeter-
> minacy. If one were to search for an interpretive technique
> that, on the whole, was more likely to confuse than to clarify,
> one could hardly find a more promising candidate than legis-
> lative history.[26]

Even committee reports, much favored by proponents of the use of
legislative history, are disparaged by the literalists. Scalia and like-
minded judges and justices would argue that "Because reports are prepared by committee staff and not necessarily even read by committee
members, let alone by the vast majority of voting members not on the
recommending committee," they are ineffective instruments for ascertaining intent.[27]

"While the propriety of using legislative history . . . is an issue en-
gendering great controversy . . . it is incontrovertible that the Supreme
Court [as well as other federal and state courts] does, in fact, find such
history useful in the interpretation of statutes, and uses it as a basis for
case resolution."[28]

If the courts have difficulty construing the intent of legislation Congress enacted a year, a decade or a generation ago, consider the problems they face when trying to determine "original intent." In a
concurring opinion, Supreme Court Justice Robert H. Jackson, reflecting upon the extent of presidential authority implicit in the Constitution,
said:

> Just what our forefathers did envision, or would have envi-
> sioned had they foreseen modern conditions, must be divined
> from materials almost as enigmatic as the dreams Joseph was
> called upon to interpret for Pharaoh. A century and a half of
> partisan debate and scholarly speculation yields no net result
> but only supplies more or less apt quotations from respected
> sources on each side of the question. They largely cancel each
> other.[29]

The matter of "intent" has become an esoteric exercise for scholars
spinning commentary in law review journals that comes perilously close
to sophistry. Fortunately, the sources that comprise federal legislative
histories are relatively easy to collect and collate, and it is an undertaking
that documents and law librarians are frequently asked to perform.

Selective Information Sources

The sources cited at the end of each slip law (see Figure 5.16) constitute a minimal legislative history: the bill; House and Senate reports, including a conference report if appropriate; dates of consideration and passage in the *Congressional Record;* and any presidential statements made upon signing (or veto) published in the *Weekly Compilation of Presidential Documents* (WCPD). Beyond that, legislative histories may include related bills, bills on the subject that failed passage in previous congresses, hearings, committee prints, and secondary sources such as journal articles and monographs.

The several print, microfiche, and electronic sources for bills, reports, hearings, committee prints, and the debates and votes have been discussed previously in this chapter. The WCPD and other presidential sources are examined in chapter 6. A number of official and commercial finding aids contain citations to the several congressional materials that may constitute a legislative history. What follows is a selective listing.

Commercial Sources

A useful starting point is *Sources of Compiled Legislative Histories: A Bibliography of Government Documents, Periodical Articles, and Books, 1st Congress*—compiled by Nancy P. Johnson. Published for the American Association of Law Libraries by Fred B. Rothman (Littleton, CO) and issued in looseleaf binder for updating, the basic volume with periodic supplements covers selective compilations of legislative histories from the 1st Congress. The contents include citations to looseleaf, microfiche, and electronic sources and services; collections dealing with specific subjects arranged by topic; and parallel tables. The tables are helpful; if you know the public law number, references are made to the bill number, *Statutes at Large* citation, title of act, law review articles that discuss the statute, and the like.

CIS/Annual from 1970 through 1983 includes legislative history citations as a section of the "Abstracts" volume. Beginning in 1984, detailed legislative history citations are published in a separate volume titled *CIS Annual: Legislative Histories of U.S. Public Laws.* Accompanied by a full-text microfiche service, the print format is large and user-friendly and includes citations to all pertinent documents for every law enacted during a session of Congress. *United States Code Congressional and Administrative News* (USCCAN) contains a "Table of Legislative History and Index" arranged by public law number referencing the date approved, *Statutes at Large* citation, bill number, House and Senate report numbers, abbreviations for the names of the House and Senate committees reporting, dates of consideration and passage in the CR, and citations for presidential signing statements. *CCH Congressional Index* contains "Status of House Bills" and "Status of Senate Bills" divisions that show the current status of legislation. Published weekly, these entries cumulate providing an ongoing, current legislative history that can be used as a retrospective finding aid for bills that eventually become law.

CCH Incorporated (formerly Commerce Clearing House) published a service, now discontinued, called *Public Laws—Legislative Histories on Microfiche,* which covered the period 1979–1988. Another abandoned series is Congressional Information Service's *Basic Legislative History Service* and *Comprehensive Legislative History Service.* Selected microfiche histories of these series were made available for the years 1909 through 1952.

Fee-based electronic sources include WESTLAW, LEXIS-NEXIS, CQ Washington Alert, CIS Congressional Universe, and Legi-Slate. Selective legislative histories on "selected high-profile federal laws" since about 1972 have been compiled by the Washington, DC, law firm of Arnold & Porter and are available on WESTLAW.[30]

Government Sources

The fortnightly *Congressional Record Index* contains, as noted above, a cumulative "History of Bills and Resolutions" section. Moreover, the annual cumulation of the "Daily Digest" division of the CR features a "History of Bills Enacted into Public Law" arranged by slip law number. The weekly *Calendars of the House of Representatives and History of Legislation (House Calendars),* which include Senate action, has a section titled "Numerical Order of Bills and Resolutions Which Have Passed Either or Both Houses, and Bills Now Pending on the Calendars." This section contains by chamber, and within chamber by form of measure, the current status and legislative history of all actions on each bill. A "Status of Major Bills" table is arranged by bill number with reference to title, committee report numbers, reported dates, dates of passage in both chambers, conference report dates, and public law numbers. Moreover, tables of "Bills in Conference" and "Bills Through Conference" furnish number and date, brief title of measure, names of House and Senate conferees (managers), and conference report numbers with dates. The several "calendars" of the House are arranged by date, with bill or report number, sponsor and committee, title of measure, and calendar number. Unlike the Senate, which has a *Calendar of Business,* the House has a Union Calendar, House Calendar,

Private Calendar, Corrections Calendar, and Calendar of Motions to Discharge Committees. The functions of these calendars are discussed in the current edition of *How Our Laws Are Made.*

The *House Calendars* cumulate bill status information. At the end of a Congress, the *Final Edition* should be permanently retained. It becomes a most valuable retrospective source for the information noted above as well as for its numerous tables and summary pages of bills and resolutions introduced, committee reports, public and private laws, presidential vetoes, vetoes overridden, constitutional amendments submitted to the states for ratification, and comparative statistics for previous Congresses. In ascertaining current legislative progress, the *House Calendars* can be most profitably used after a bill has been reported out of committee. These calendars are seachable via GPO Access.

The *Senate Calendar of Business* is far less useful for tracking legislation because it does not cumulate and has no index. However, it has a "Bills in Conference" section arranged by date sent to conference, with bill number, brief title, Senate and House conferees, Senate report number, and current status. A separate table, "Status of Appropriations Bills," is arranged by bill number with brief title and legislative history to date. The Senate home page, noted above, contains this information.

The *United States Statutes at Large* from 1963 through 1974 contain a "Guide to Legislative History of Bills Enacted into Public Law," which gives tabular data by public law number referencing date, volume, and page of the *Statutes,* bill number, House and Senate report number and name of committee, and CR dates of consideration and passage. Although this table was discontinued, USCCAN and other sources mentioned above supply this information. In 1975 the slip laws began to make available citations to legislative history and, of course, these public laws appear in the bound volumes of the *Statutes at Large.*

Voluminous legislative histories are issued on a selective basis by House or Senate committees. Usually prepared by the Congressional Research Service and issued as committee prints, they are indexed in the *Monthly Catalog* and in *CIS/Index.* Citations to these legislative histories are given in Nancy Johnson's *Sources of Compiled Legislative Histories,* and researchers fortunate enough to locate a "ready made" legislative history on a law germane to their interests will find an abundance of useful texts and commentary.

Since its creation in 1921, the General Accounting Office (GAO) has compiled and maintained an extensive file of legislative histories of public laws to assist the agency and its divisions in their duties. REMAC/Information on Demand, Inc., a private company located in McLean, Virginia, sells the full text of the legislative histories compiled by GAO on microfiche or in paper format. Included in this package are bills in all their parliamentary editions, including amendments; committee reports; debates and general remarks from the *Congressional Record,* hearings, and related congressional materials, and, if applicable, the history of related measures. Subscribers can purchase the retrospective files from the 67th Congress (1921), individual collections for a Congress, specific laws and associated amendments to enacted legislation, or compilations on particular subjects or impacted federal agencies. Moreover, "on-demand" orders can be placed for specific laws or portions of materials relating to the legislative process, such as debates, hearings, or reports.

Other official sources for legislative history citations include the annual *House Journal* and *Senate Journal* and, to a limited extent, the *Journal of the Executive Proceedings of the Senate of the United States of America,* which is more useful for information on nominations and treaties. Official electronic sources are THOMAS, GPO Access, and LOCIS, the Library of Congress Information System (**http://lcweb.loc.gov**).

SELECTIVE CONGRESSIONAL INFORMATION

Publications in print and electronic formats issued by the Congress and its committees and by commercial publishers not discussed in the preceding pages supply supporting documentation for the legislative process. A selective account of these several sources follows.

House and Senate *Journals*

The House and Senate *Journals* have the distinction of being the only publications explicitly stated in the United States Constitution. Article I, Section 5, Clause 3 states that "Each House shall keep a Journal of its Proceedings, and from time to time publish the same, excepting such Parts as may in their judgments require Secrecy; and the Yeas and Nays of the Members of either House on any question shall, at the Desire of one fifth of those Present, be entered on the Journal." Because the predecessors of the *Congressional Record* were published privately and were neither complete nor free from bias, the proceedings and voting records of members up to 1873 are most accurately reflected in the *Journals.* "One of the interesting features of the *Journals* is the similarity of the modern edition to that of the first. Over the years, the *Journals* have remained fairly consistent in content and quality of material."[31] Indeed, even when the *Congressional Record* began, in 1873, to be printed by the GPO, the *Journals* continued to "constitute the true proceedings of each house and contain no speeches or extraneous material."[32]

The House and Senate *Journals* are issued in print format at the end of a session. Their contents include the proceedings, rules, questions of orders, motions, actions taken, voting information, memorials and petitions received, the text of communications from the president, and, like the *Congressional Record,* a "History of Bills and Resolutions," including private measures, arranged by bill number, and within number by date. The *Journals* are available in hard copy or on microfiche to depository libraries, and *CIS Congressional Journals on Microfiche, 1789–1978* permits libraries to fill the gaps in their collections. And a link from the Library of Congress home page delivers the researcher to the early *Journals* (1789–).

House and Senate *Manuals*

Short titles have their advantages. The full title of the *House Rules and Manual* is *Constitution, Jefferson's Manual, and Rules of the House of Representatives of the United States.* The full title of the *Senate Manual* is *Senate Manual, Containing the Standing Rules, Orders, Laws and Resolutions Affecting the Business of the United States Senate, Articles of Confederation and the Constitution of the United States.* Both are published biennially as a House and Senate document respectively; as part of the serial set, they are available to depository libraries and available via GPO Access. Both volumes contain previous codes under which Congress functioned and from which it continues to derive precedents. The powers of committees are outlined, and the rules set forth may be changed only by elaborate chamber actions specified in the manuals. That explains the complex parliamentary maneuvers debated during the Senate's trial of William Jefferson Clinton.

While current rules are handed down by the House Rules Committee and the Senate Committee on Rules and Administration, adopted at the beginning of a new Congress, analyses of House and Senate precedents fill several volumes written by former and current parliamentarians of the chambers. The early precedents of the House, dating from the 1st Congress, are found in Asher C. Hinds's precedents, followed by Clarence Cannon and Lewis Deschler. Senate procedure by Floyd Riddick is published as Senate document 97-2 (1981). Because of their technical knowledge of the specialized and arcane rules of procedure, the parliamentarians traditionally hold their offices regardless of changes in political control of the two chambers. The role of these precedents is discussed in Section 12 of *How Our Laws Are Made* and bibliographically noted in the Appendix to that work.

Memorial Addresses

Eulogies delivered in the House or Senate upon the death of a current or former member are available to depository libraries that subscribe to Item 1005. They once were published in bound volumes with a black cover but now are issued on microfiche only. When presidents, vice-presidents, or presidential appointees who have held high office in the executive or judiciary are memorialized, the compilation of tributes is issued in the serial set as House or Senate documents. Memorial publications in the case of persons who have enjoyed careers in both the Congress and other government positions may be found in both series because issuing patterns have not always been consistent. Clarification of the distinction between the "departmental" and the "congressional" editions of memorial addresses was provided in *Administrative Notes* 12: 1 (June 15, 1991).

Constitution of the United States

> The proposed Constitution is . . . neither a national nor a federal Constitution but a composition of both. In its foundation it is federal, not national. In the sources from which the ordinary powers of the government are drawn, it is partly federal and partly national. In the operation of these powers, it is national, not federal; in the extent of them . . . it is federal, not national; and finally, in the authoritative mode of introducing amendments, it is neither wholly federal nor wholly national.
>
> —James Madison, *The Federalist* No. 39

Prepared by the Congressional Research Service of the Library of Congress, a new edition of *The Constitution of the United States of America, Analysis and Interpretation* every ten years, with biennial supplements between editions, is required by PL 91-589, 84 Stat. 1585, 2 U.S.C. § 168, to be issued as Senate documents. Sometimes known as the *Constitution Annotated,* the work offers commentary on every article, section, and clause of the basic instrument, as well as the amendments, with citations to numerous Supreme Court decisions construing these provisions. The basic volume and the two-year supplements contain useful reference tables that include proposed amendments not ratified by the states, acts of Congress held unconstitutional in whole or in part by the High Court, state and municipal laws held unconstitutional, Supreme Court decisions overruled by subsequent decisions, a table of cases, and an index. The 1992 edition was issued as 103-1:S.doc.6 but was sent to depository libraries as serial volume 14152. Upon notification of shipment of serial volume 14152 to all depository libraries, the Library Programs Service noted: "As in the past, this volume was bound with room at the back for the insertion of 'pocket parts.' The ¾" area in the back of the volume that looks as if pages have been cut out was left this way intentionally. When supplements or updates are produced for the Constitution, they can easily be placed in this new volume without causing damage to the binding."[33] Researchers can avoid the print Constitution entirely if they wish because it is one of the databases available through GPO Access. In the 1992 basic volume and its 1996 supplement (104-1: S.doc. 14), no amendments were listed as pending before the states, a table that had appeared in previous decennial editions.

An eighty-one-page pamphlet titled "The Constitution of the United States as Amended" was issued in 1987. The text is not annotated but contains footnotes on ratification dates and on clauses superseded or affected by constitutional amendments. Prepared under the direction of the House Judiciary Committee, this booklet (100-1:H.doc.94) is a good starting point for the novice student of government.

Directories

The *Biographical Directory of the United States Congress* in print format has undergone several cumulative editions. The edition covering the period 1774–1989, issued as Senate Document 100-34 (serial volume 13849) and timed to celebrate the bicentennial of the Congress, was the first to employ the services of professional historians to review existing entries and bring the current work "into line with . . . historical scholarship and accepted standards of accuracy and consistency." Accordingly, this version is more accurate than previous editions, although the editors recognize that the "volume is and will always be a work in progress."[34]

Now the public can search an updated and expanded version of this reference source on the Internet (**http://bioguide.congress.gov**) including the membership of the most current Congress. This site is maintained under the direction of the Secretary of the Senate and the Clerk of the House. In addition to the biographical entries, the Secretary and the Clerk have included information regarding the disposition of members' papers, bibliographical information previously published in the House's *Guide to Research Papers of Former Members* and information prepared by the Senate Historical Office for the Senate. A commercial version, *Biographical Directory of the American Congress, 1774–1997,* 1st edition (Mt. Vernon, VA: Staff Directories, Ltd., 1996), has, in addition to the standard biographical information, some added data, but the price ($295) may discourage the ordinary, fiscally challenged library. Also, the title change from *United States* to *American* is a typical ploy of commercial firms that take a public domain publication and duplicate its main contents.

The *Official Congressional Directory* is issued biennially. Its main entries update the print edition of the *Biographical Directory* for biographical sketches of current members. In addition, it contains several reference features, including maps of congressional districts; rules governing radio and television correspondents' galleries; lists of key officials in executive departments and agencies, independent agencies, boards, commissions, and advisory organizations; names of those impeached and tried in the Senate; names and addresses of foreign diplomatic representatives and foreign consular offices in the United States; tables of statistics; and much more ready reference information. The 1997–1998 edition (105th Congress) included, for the first time, Web sites and e-mail addresses. The directory is available in print and on GPO Access.

The *Congressional Staff Directory* (Mount Vernon, VA: Staff Directories, Ltd.) is completely revised and published three times a year; it duplicates much of the information found in the *Official Congressional Directory* as well as expanding the biographies to include the staffers of members and other useful data. The company's other products include *Staff Directories on CD-ROM,* which contains information on the executive and judicial branches as well as the Congress; diskettes such as *Member Data Disk, Member Mailing List on Disk, CDbyZIP;* and so forth. Bernan Press (Lanham, MD) offers *The New Members of Congress Almanac, 106th Congress* and *The Almanac of the Unelected, 1999* covering the key staff members of Congress.

The *Congressional Pictorial Directory* is available via GPO Access for the 105th and 106th Congresses. A self-serving document, the purpose of this biennial book is to show the governed what their leaders look like in posed photographs. Included are pictures of the president and vice-president; senate and house leadership; senate and house officers and officials (for example, chaplain, sergeant at arms); Capitol officials; members by state; delegates from the Virgin Islands, Guam, American Samoa, and District of Columbia; the resident commissioner of Puerto Rico; and, of course, all the senators and representatives, alphabetically. The pages retrieved from the online *Pictorial Directory* can be viewed in Adobe Acrobat Portable Document Format (PDF); the directory is also available in a print edition through the Superintendent of Documents sales service and free on depository distribution.

The House of Representatives and the Senate home pages, noted above, have many links to directory information about members: committee and member sites, leadership pages, information searchable by state or member names, chamber operations, and the like. To say that there is no shortage of congressional directories of one kind or another is almost an understatement.

Financial Disclosure

All lobbyists are required by statute to tell the government who hired them, how much money they spend, their areas of special interest, and whether they worked in certain government positions in a previous two-year period. The Center for Responsive Politics, a non-partisan, nonprofit research group based in Washington, DC specializes in the study of Congress and particularly in the role that money plays in congressional elections and voting. Elected officials are required to file personal financial disclosure reports every year, based on the principle that information concerning possible conflicts of interest should be available to the public.

This information, and much more, is available from the Center's Web site (**http://www.crp.org**), a source that tracks campaign contributions and much more. At the several links of the site one can find out how much money senators and representatives have received and who the donors were. A useful feature of this site is a "Do-It-Yourself Congressional Investigation Kit," by which you pick an interest area and see who got money, how much they got, and then how they voted on an issue related to the lobby's interest. Other free Web sites, such as **http//www.tray.com/fecinfo**, also track spending; and you can, of course, access campaign-contribution data directly from the Federal Election Commission (FEC). An independent agency established by section 309 of the Federal Election Campaign Act of 1971, as amended (2 U.S.C. § 437c), the Commission is responsible for, among other things, ensuring public disclosure of the campaign finance activities reported by political committees supporting federal candidates. Its Web site is at **http://www.fec.gov**.

Major Studies and Issue Briefs

Major Studies and Issues Briefs of the Congressional Research Service (Bethesda, MD: University Publications of America) consists of a compilation of valuable CRS studies ranging from business law to nuclear weapons proliferation, autism to Vietnam, and covering the period 1916 to date. The CRS, sometimes called the "personal librarian" of members and their committee staffs, does in-depth research providing essential background information for congressional investigations and legislative proposals. The major studies are monographs while the shorter papers are called issue briefs. Retrospective files are available on microfilm as are current annual studies and briefs accompanied by a printed guide. Beginning with the 1991 series, a quarterly index and microfiche service was produced, the index providing access by subjects, CRS report number, and title. Moreover, an annual and a retrospective Congressional Research Service Index on CD-ROM permit access by subject, author, CRS report number, title, or in any word in the abstract provided for each title. A detailed *Reference Manual* in hard cover is issued with the disk. As of 1998 CRS was prohibited from disseminating its work directly to the public, but some senators and representatives mount selected CRS studies and briefs on their Web sites. The chairperson and ranking minority member of the Senate Rules and Administration Committee have urged senators to "post CRS products on your Web site," and legislation is in the pipeline to require CRS to put on the Internet all unclassified information it generates.[35]

Congressional Quarterly, Inc.

Congressional Quarterly, Inc. (Washington, DC) enjoys a deserved reputation for the quality of its many publications and its online service CQ Washington Alert. Selective examples that afford access to government activities in general and congressional actions in particular follow.

CQ Weekly (formerly *CQ Weekly Report*), noted above, contains essays on major legislation and related activities of the legislative branch, as well as information of a public policy nature on the executive and judiciary, and voting records. *CQ Almanac,* as presented above, is a distillation and reorganization of the information in *CQ Weekly.* Both are excellent guides for current status of legislation and retrospective legislative histories.

Other Congressional Quarterly sources usually found in research libraries include, in their various editions, *Guide to Congress, Congress A to Z, Congress and the Nation, Congress and Its Members,*

Committees in Congress, Congressional Procedures and the Policy Process, The Congressional Yearbook, and more. The "CQ Library" Web site (**http://resources.cq.com**) allows subscribers to access the current issues of *CQ Weekly* and *The CQ Researcher.*

SUMMARY

The length of this chapter reflects the complexity of Congress as an institution, the intricacy of its procedures, and the sheer amount and kinds of information generated by or on behalf of its official duties. Numerous jokes about the Congress have found their way into books and anthologies. Mark Twain famously observed that "It could probably be shown by facts and figures that there is no distinctly native American criminal class except Congress." Ridiculing Congress "is as American as apple pie."[36] To be sure, there have been, are, and will always be knaves and fools representing the people, probably in direct proportion to the rascals and buffoons being governed. But there have been valorous members too, like Henry Clay, John C. Calhoun, and Daniel Webster. The framers of the Constitution knew that if "angels were to govern men, neither external nor internal controls on government would be necessary," and in "republican government the legislative authority necessarily predominates."[37] "Democracy," in a statement attributed to Thomas Jefferson, "is cumbersome, slow and inefficient, but in due time, the voice of the people will be heard and their latent wisdom will prevail." Or, if you prefer a less sanguine aphorism, Winston Churchill, in a 1947 speech in the House of Commons, said

> Many forms of government have been tried, and will be tried in this world of sin and woe. No one pretends that democracy is perfect or all-wise. Indeed, it has been said that democracy is the worst form of Government except all those other forms that have been tried from time to time.[38]

NOTES

1. *Guide to the Congress of the United States: Origin, History and Precedent* (Washington: Congressional Quarterly Service, 1971), p. 41.

2. For a detailed account of this unusual occurrence, see Joe Morehead, "Back to the Future: James Madison's Twenty-Seventh Amendment," *The Serials Librarian* 24: 39–51 (1993).

3. John Spencer Walters, "U.S. Congressional Floor Versus Committee Information: How the Vendors Compare," *Journal of Government Information* 24: 378 (1997).

4. John T. Cocklin, "FedWorld, THOMAS, and CBDNET: United States Federal Government Information Dissemination in the 1990s," *Journal of Government Information* 25: 403 (1998).

5. Ronald Garay, *Congressional Television: A Legislative History* (Westport, CT: Greenwood, 1984), pp. 36–37.

6. Peggy Garvin, "Before the Record," *Law Library Lights* 32: 1 (January/February 1989).

7. Ibid., p. 4.

8. Ibid. See also Robert E. Kling, Jr., *The Government Printing Office* (New York: Praeger, 1970), pp. 98–109.

9. *The Washington Post,* January 9, 1995, p. A15.

10. Joe Morehead, "Ariadne's Thread: The United States Congress Celebrates Its Bicentennial—Part One," *The Serials Librarian* 18: 88–89 (1990).

11. *City of New York v. Clinton,* 1998 U.S. Dist. LEXIS 1295 (February 12, 1998), *aff'd, Clinton v. City of New York,* No. 97–1374 (June 25, 1998).

12. Helen Dewar and Joan Biskupic, "Line-Item Veto Struck Down," *The Washington Post,* June 26, 1998, p. A1.

13. Michael J. Lynch, "The U.S. Code, the Statutes at Large, and Some Peculiarities of Codification," *Legal Reference Services Quarterly* 16: 70 (1997).

14. Miles O. Price et al., *Effective Legal Research,* 4th ed. (Boston: Little, Brown, 1979), p. 41. See, for example, Public Law 86-682, 74 Stat. 578, which reenacted Title 39, The Postal Service, into positive law.

15. My thanks to the West Group's *Password,* May–June 1998, p. 12, for this delightful tidbit.

16. *Guide to the Congress of the United States*, p. 329.

17. Asher C. Hinds, *Hinds' Precedents of the House of Representatives of the United States,* vol. 4 (Washington: Government Printing Office, 1907), p. 247.

18. *Guide to the Congress of the United States*, p. 329.

19. *Congressional Quarterly's Guide to the Congress,* 2d ed. (Washington: Congressional Quarterly Service, 1976), p. 307.

20. A handy summary of bibliographic and textual primary and secondary sources for private legislation is found in *Legal Reference Services Quarterly* 16: 83–85, 90 n.13 (1998).

21. Laurence F. Schmeckebier and Roy B. Eastin, *Government Publications and Their Use,* 2d rev. ed. (Washington: Brookings, 1969), passim.

22. The "library" was a collection developed in the Public Documents Division because of the requirement under the Printing Act of 1895 to prepare the *Document Catalog* and the *Monthly Catalog.* It was closed to the public.

23. *Administrative Notes* 18: 9 (February 15, 1997).

24. Suzanne deLong, "What Is the United States Serial Set?" *Journal of Government Information* 23: 123 (1996).

25. George A. Costello, "Reliance on Legislative History in Interpreting Statutes," *CRS Review* 11: 30 (January/February 1990).

26. *Conroy v. Aniskoff,* 61 USLW 4301, 4303 (1993).

27. Costello, "Reliance on Legislative History in Interpreting Statutes," p. 11.

28. Bernard D. Reams, comp., *Federal Legislative Histories: An Annotated Bibliography and Index to Officially Published Sources* (Westport, CT: Greenwood, 1994).

29. *Youngstown Sheet and Tube Company v. Sawyer,* 343 U.S. 579, 72 S.Ct. 863, 870 (1952).

30. *Password,* November 1997, p. 5.

31. Walter Stubbs, "Finding Congressional Journals in the U.S. Serial Set," *Journal of Government Information* 24: 39 (1997). A useful list (pp. 41–45) enables researchers to easily locate the House and Senate *Journals* in the volumes of the historical serial set.

32. Robert E. Kling, Jr., *The Government Printing Office* (New York: Praeger, 1970), p. 101 note.

33. *Administrative Notes* 18: 3 (February 15, 1997).

34. *Biographical Directory of the United States Congress, 1774–1989* (Washington: Government Printing Office, 1989), p. 7.

35. *American Libraries,* August 1998, p. 13.

36. "Congress Turns 200: A Special Section of the Bicentennial," *Roll Call: The Newspaper of Congress,* vol. 34, section 3 (February 27–March 5, 1989), p. 1.

37. "The Federalist No. 51" (Madison), in *The Federalist Papers* (New York: New American Library, 1961), p. 322.

38. Cited in Suzy Platt, ed., *Respectfully Quoted: A Dictionary of Quotations Requested from the Congressional Research Service* (Washington: Library of Congress, 1989), pp. 82, 85.

CHAPTER SIX

THE PRESIDENCY

> The presidency is not merely an administrative office. . . . It is preeminently a place of moral leadership. All our great Presidents were leaders of thought at times when certain historic ideas in the life of the nation had to be clarified.
>
> —Franklin D. Roosevelt

INTRODUCTION

Article II, Section 1, of the Constitution states that the "executive power shall be vested in a President of the United States of America." The pertinent sections of Article II for our purposes include those powers and responsibilities that the president shares with the Congress, specifically the Senate. These include the making of treaties and agreements; the nomination of officials to serve in high positions in the executive departments and agencies, including the independent agencies; and the transmission of the budget to the Congress. In all of these activities, significant government publications are generated. The content, indexing, bibliographic control, and availability in print and electronic formats of these and other important documents constitute the focus of this chapter.

THE WHITE HOUSE COMPLEX

The staff of the president, located in the White House Office, maintains communication with the Congress, its individual members and their staffs, the heads of executive agencies, the press and other information media, and the general public. Information regarding the activities of the president is furnished to the print and broadcast media through press releases and briefings and through the Internet. Publications of the "President of the United States" have been assigned Superintendent of Documents author symbol "PR [no.]." The number indicates the chronology of the persons who have held the office; for example, Ronald Reagan (PR 40), George Bush (PR 41), William J. Clinton (PR 42), and so forth.[1] Issued under the "PR" class are several annual reports of the president, most of which are prepared by other executive agencies. One of the more important publications is the *Economic Report of the President* (discussed below). Also assigned a PR author symbol is the *Federal Advisory Committee Annual Report of the President;* the PR [no.].8 class stems are used to designate special committees and commissions appointed by the president, with a Cutter symbol following the colon to indicate the name of the body. For example, PR 40.8:S1 was the notation assigned to the report of the Presidential Commission on the Space Shuttle *Challenger* Accident.

In addition, several publications issued by the Office of the Federal Register constitute a rich source of information on presidential actions. Presidential materials are also found in House and Senate documents, the *Congressional Record,* and the House and Senate *Journals,* when they represent messages or communications transmitted to the Congress by the president.

EXECUTIVE ORDERS AND PROCLAMATIONS

At the beginning of the daily *Federal Register* (FR) is a section titled "Presidential Documents," when an issue contains such materials. The most common forms of unclassified executive authority are executive orders (EOs) and proclamations (Proc.). EOs and proclamations are the formal mechanism through which the president prescribes the conduct of business in the executive branch. Scholars and government officials widely regard executive orders and proclamations as "presidential legislation": a form of executive lawmaking used in instances in which the Constitution or Congress directly or indirectly permits or mandates the president to take action.[2]

According to Schmeckebier and Eastin, executive orders generally relate to the conduct of government business or to the organization of government agencies. They have "never been defined by law or regulation"; thus, "in a general sense every act of the President authorizing or directing that an act be performed is an executive order."[3] Authority for executive orders and proclamations is claimed by a president in virtue of his office, in his role as commander in chief of the armed forces, under the implicit or explicit powers granted by the Constitution, or, most commonly, pursuant to existing legislation.

Almost all current executive orders have the force of law, and some proclamations have significant legal force and effect. The latter concern matters such as tariff and trade schedules, extending copyright protection to other nations' inventors, and executive clemency. Presidents by tradition have used proclamations to exercise their pardoning power under Article II, Section 2 of the Constitution. Gerald Ford's pardon of Richard Nixon was first published in the *Federal Register* as Proc. 4311, September 8, 1974 (3 CFR 1971–1975 Comp., p. 385). On December 24, 1992, George Bush's "Grant of Executive Clemency" exonerated Caspar Weinberger and others "for their conduct related to the Iran-Contra affair" (Proc. 6518; 3 CFR 1992 Comp., pp. 265–67). It is also customary to announce "hortatory" occasions such as celebratory or commemorative days, weeks, months, and years, in the form of proclamations. Thus Executive Order 12968 is titled "Access to Classified Information," whereas Proclamation 6810 is titled "Captive Nations Week." Until the start of the 104th Congress, new or non-recurring proclamations went the route of the public law. The House or Senate authorized and requested the president to declare a certain day, week, month, or year as something to be commemorated. It had a little legislative history all its own, even though in the vast majority of cases it was a pro forma exercise. Introduced as a House or Senate Joint Resolution, it was considered and passed by both chambers, amended on rare occasions by one body, referred back to the other body for concurrence, signed by the president, and given a public law number. Later the president dutifully proclaimed it. Thus, for instance, Benign Essential Blepharospasm Awareness Week, Public Law 100-118 (S.J. Res. 135), was promulgated as Proc. 5721 (October 5, 1987). Proclamations of this nature are mainly boilerplate. This wasteful and costly procedure, known as "commemorative legislation," was abolished in 1995.

In 1907 the Department of State began numbering executive orders that it had on file and later received. Since March 14, 1936, all executive orders "except such as have no general applicability and legal effect" have been published in the *Federal Register*. Congressional Information Service published a multivolume research guide titled *CIS Index to Presidential Executive Orders & Proclamations,* with a companion microfiche text collection, *CIS Presidential Executive Orders & Proclamations on Microfiche.* The information in this retrospective collection, in two parts, covers over 75,000 presidential documents issued between 1789 and 1983. Presidential directives in earlier times have been known by names such as administrative orders, military orders, general orders, presidential regulations, and presidential ordinances.[4]

Perhaps the most infamous executive order was EO 9066 (7 FR 1407, February 19, 1942; 3 CFR 1938–1943 Comp., pp. 1092–93), which authorized the removal of over 100,000 persons of Japanese ancestry and hundreds of non-naturalized Italian-Americans from their homes to be placed in internment facilities in California and a network of camps in other Western states for the duration of World War II. Among the children of Nisei who were incarcerated are Lance Ito, judge in the criminal trial of O. J. Simpson; and Kristi Yamaguchi, figure skating gold medalist in the 1992 winter Olympics. Because there was no official executive ukase rescinding EO 9066, President Gerald R. Ford used the occasion of the nation's bicentennial to issue Proclamation 4417 (February 19, 1976; 3 CFR 1976 Comp., p. 9) reaffirming "that all the authority conferred by Executive Order No. 9066 terminated upon the issuance of Proclamation No. 2714 which formally proclaimed the cessation of the hostilities of World War II on December 31, 1946."[5] Figure 6.1 and Figure 6.2, page 180, show an executive order and a proclamation as promulgated in the *Federal Register*.

Presidential rulings other than EOs and proclamations published in the *Federal Register* and in Title 3, *Code of Federal Regulations* (CFR), include memoranda designating matters such as assignments for officials of agencies; presidential findings and determinations, resolving that certain provisions of law are or are not in the national interest; letters, such as instructions to department heads or chiefs of diplomatic missions; and reorganization plans. The last are instruments by which the president proposes changes in the structure of agencies below the departmental or independent agency level and are discussed later in this chapter. A president may also issue classified edicts such as National Security Decision Directives (NSDDs), which, by definition, are absent from the pages of the FR and Title 3, CFR.

The full text of Executive Orders and Proclamations is available online through CQ Washington Alert, Legi-Slate, WESTLAW, LEXIS-NEXIS, CIS Congressional Universe, and DIALOG. Internet sites include GPO Access and the White House Virtual Library (**http://www.whitehouse.gov**), a site that also includes press briefings, radio addresses, and "historic national documents." Several commercial firms issue the FR and CFR on CD-ROM, among them Solutions Software Corporation; Counterpoint Publishing, Inc.; Oryx Press; The Dialog Corporation; FastSearch Corporation; and Management Concepts, Inc. It is advisable to consult the current edition of *CD-ROMS in Print* (Farmington Hills, MI: Gale Group) for updating these publishers. A discussion of the contents of the other parts of the *Federal Register* and other titles of the *Code of Federal Regulations* is assayed in chapter 7.

Figure 6.1. Executive order.

Federal Register / Vol. 63, No. 192 / Monday, October 5, 1998 / Presidential Documents   53273

Presidential Documents

Executive Order 13103 of September 30, 1998

Computer Software Piracy

The United States Government is the world's largest purchaser of computer-related services and equipment, purchasing more than $20 billion annually. At a time when a critical component in discussions with our international trading partners concerns their efforts to combat piracy of computer software and other intellectual property, it is incumbent on the United States to ensure that its own practices as a purchaser and user of computer software are beyond reproach. Accordingly, by the authority vested in me as President by the Constitution and the laws of the United States of America, it is hereby ordered as follows:

Section 1. *Policy.* It shall be the policy of the United States Government that each executive agency shall work diligently to prevent and combat computer software piracy in order to give effect to copyrights associated with computer software by observing the relevant provisions of international agreements in effect in the United States, including applicable provisions of the World Trade Organization Agreement on Trade-Related Aspects of Intellectual Property Rights, the Berne Convention for the Protection of Literary and Artistic Works, and relevant provisions of Federal law, including the Copyright Act.

(a) Each agency shall adopt procedures to ensure that the agency does not acquire, reproduce, distribute, or transmit computer software in violation of applicable copyright laws.

(b) Each agency shall establish procedures to ensure that the agency has present on its computers and uses only computer software not in violation of applicable copyright laws. These procedures may include:

(1) preparing agency inventories of the software present on its computers;

(2) determining what computer software the agency has the authorization to use; and

(3) developing and maintaining adequate recordkeeping systems.

(c) Contractors and recipients of Federal financial assistance, including recipients of grants and loan guarantee assistance, should have appropriate systems and controls in place to ensure that Federal funds are not used to acquire, operate, or maintain computer software in violation of applicable copyright laws. If agencies become aware that contractors or recipients are using Federal funds to acquire, operate, or maintain computer software in violation of copyright laws and determine that such actions of the contractors or recipients may affect the integrity of the agency's contracting and Federal financial assistance processes, agencies shall take such measures, including the use of certifications or written assurances, as the agency head deems appropriate and consistent with the requirements of law.

(d) Executive agencies shall cooperate fully in implementing this order and shall share information as appropriate that may be useful in combating the use of computer software in violation of applicable copyright laws.

Sec. 2. *Responsibilities of Agency Heads.* In connection with the acquisition and use of computer software, the head of each executive agency shall:

(a) ensure agency compliance with copyright laws protecting computer software and with the provisions of this order to ensure that only authorized computer software is acquired for and used on the agency's computers;

Figure 6.2. Proclamation.

53271

Federal Register
Vol. 63, No. 192
Monday, October 5, 1998

Presidential Documents

Title 3—

The President

Proclamation 7129 of September 30, 1998

National Domestic Violence Awareness Month, 1998

By the President of the United States of America

A Proclamation

Domestic violence is a leading cause of injury to American women, and teenage girls between the ages of 16 and 19 experience one of the highest rates of such violence. A woman is battered every 15 seconds in the United States, and 30 percent of female murder victims are killed by current or former partners. Equally disturbing is the impact of domestic violence on children. Witnessing such violence has a devastating emotional effect on children, and between 50 and 70 percent of men who abuse their female partners abuse their children as well. From inner cities to rural communities, domestic violence affects individuals of every age, culture, class, gender, race, and religion.

Combatting the violence that threatens many of our Nation's families is among my highest priorities as President. Through the Violence Against Women Act (VAWA), included in the historic Crime Bill I signed into law, we have more than tripled funding for programs that combat domestic violence and sexual abuse—investing over half a billion dollars since 1994. The Violence Against Women Office at the Department of Justice, which coordinates the Federal Government's implementation of the Act, is leading a comprehensive national effort to combine tough Federal laws with assistance to State and local programs designed to fight domestic violence and aid its victims. With VAWA grants, communities across our country have been able to hire more prosecutors and improve domestic violence training among police officers, prosecutors, and health and social service professionals.

My Administration has also worked to enact other important legislation that sends the clear message that family violence is a serious crime. The Interstate Stalking Punishment and Prevention Act of 1996 stiffens the penalties against perpetrators who pursue women across State lines to stalk, threaten, or abuse them; and an extension of the Brady Law prohibits anyone convicted of a domestic violence offense from owning a firearm. Since 1996, the 24-hour National Domestic Violence Hotline (1–800–799–SAFE) we established has provided immediate crisis intervention, counseling, and referrals for those in need, responding to as many as 10,000 calls each month.

In observing the month of October as National Domestic Violence Awareness Month, we also recognize the dedicated efforts of professionals and volunteers who take up this cause every day, offering protection, guidance, encouragement, and compassion to the survivors of family violence. We reaffirm our pledge to strengthen our collective national response to crimes of domestic violence. Most important, we strengthen our commitment to raise public awareness of the frequency of domestic violence, recognize the signs of such violence, and intervene before it escalates. If we are ever to erase the pain of these heinous crimes, we must help victims become survivors and, once and for all, end the scourge of violence in America's homes.

TITLE 3, CFR

Title 3 of the *Code of Federal Regulations* (CFR) is called *The President* and contains the full text of documents signed by the chief executive during a calendar year. Periodic cumulations of Title 3 include 1936–1938, 1939–1942, 1943–1948, 1949–1953, 1954–1958, 1959–1963, 1964–1965, 1966–1970, and 1971–1975. The Title 3 series began with Proclamation 2161 (March 19, 1936) and Executive Order 7316 (March 13, 1936).

An annual issue of Title 3 typically contains executive orders and proclamations in separate numbered sequence; other presidential documents, noted above, arranged by date; and regulations of the Executive Office of the President. Various tables and finding aids are also included, as is an index at the end of the issues. For user convenience, *Title 3, 1936–1965—Consolidated Indexes* and *Title 3, 1936–1965— Consolidated Tables* are available. The former consists of a consolidated subject index covering the period; the latter contains tables and other finding aids to facilitate searching presidential documents during this period.

Duplication of the text of EOs and proclamations in several places constitutes a windfall for the researcher. These directives can be found not only in the FR and Title 3, CFR, but also in the *Congressional Record, Weekly Compilation of Presidential Documents, Public Papers of the Presidents,* the West Group's *United States Code Congressional and Administrative News* (USCCAN) Advance Pamphlets, and the Advance Service pamphlets of LEXIS Law Publishing's *United States Code Service.* In addition, the text of proclamations is published in the *United States Statutes at Large.*

WEEKLY COMPILATION OF PRESIDENTIAL DOCUMENTS

The *Weekly Compilation of Presidential Documents* (WCPD) began on August 2, 1965, and is the single most accessible collection of presidential activities in the public record. It includes the text of proclamations and executive orders; addresses and remarks; communications to Congress; letters, messages, telegrams, and news conferences; reorganization plans; resignations; swearing-in ceremonies; retirements; and a checklist of White House Office press releases. In addition, it cites laws approved by the president and lists nominations sent to the Senate. Beginning with the January 9, 1995 (v. 31, no. 1), WCPD indexes no longer cumulate in each issue; they are issued quarterly and distributed separately. Presidential documents are available online with WESTLAW and LEXIS-NEXIS. Published each Monday, the WCPD contains the various presidential actions for the previous week The Internet edition has been available on the GPO Access Web site since January 6, 1997.

PUBLIC PAPERS OF THE PRESIDENTS

In response to a recommendation of the National Historical Publications Commission, an annual series of *Public Papers of the Presidents* was begun with the 1957 volume covering the fifth year of the Eisenhower Administration. Provision was also made for retrospective collections, and volumes were subsequently published for the earlier years of the presidency of Dwight Eisenhower (1953–1956), and the years of Harry Truman (1945–1952), and Herbert Hoover (1929–1933). Compilations for President Franklin D. Roosevelt and earlier chief executives have been published commercially. Kraus International has issued *The Cumulative Indexes to the Public Papers of the Presidents of the United States* (1977–1983). A CD-ROM product, *The Presidential Papers: Washington–Taft* (Provo, UT: CDex Information Group, 1995), is based upon but goes beyond James D. Richardson's multivolume work, *A Compilation of the Messages and Papers of the Presidents, 1789–1897*.[6]

Prior to the 1977 volume, the *Public Papers* was an edited version of WCPD. Beginning with the Carter Administration, the 1977 volumes of the *Public Papers* were expanded to include virtually all materials published in the WCPD. However, beginning with 1989, the first year of the administration of George H. W. Bush, executive orders and proclamations are not republished. As if to make amends for this regrettable decision, a table cites to the *Federal Register* where these documents were first published. Current volumes in this series arrange presidential materials in chronological order within each week. Text notes, footnotes, and cross-references are furnished by the editors for purposes of identification and clarity. The information is indexed by subject entries and by categories reflecting the type of presidential activity or document.

CODIFICATION OF PRESIDENTIAL PROCLAMATIONS AND EXECUTIVE ORDERS

In 1997 the paper version of this important publication went out of print.[7] Begun in 1979, the *Codification of Presidential Proclamations and Executive Orders* was updated periodically and is arranged in titles like the CFR. The last print edition covers the period April 13, 1945–January 20, 1989, spanning the administrations of Harry S. Truman through Ronald W. Reagan. As a retrospective and ongoing cumulation, the *Codification* is still the best source to use in researching proclamations and EOs for the period indicated because it makes available in one volume the text of all EOs and proclamations, with amendments, in effect as of January 20, 1989. If an executive order or proclamation relates to more than one subject area, the most appropriate title/chapter is chosen. Moreover, the *Codification* includes a comprehensive index and "Disposition Tables." The latter lists, by number, EOs and proclamations referencing all amendments regardless of current status, with a "disposition" column that indicates documents that were revoked, superseded, temporary, or hortatory. Fortunately, the individual issues of Title 3 have a table titled "Presidential Documents Affected by Documents Published During [year],"which shows executive orders, proclamations, and public land orders (under the provisions of Title 43, CFR) that were amended, superseded, or revoked by subsequent actions, but you now have to search Title 3 year by year from early 1989 to date.

The Internet version of the *Codification* covers the same period (**http://www.nara.gov/fedreg/codhome.html**), but has an added feature, a link to a list of executive orders (but not the text) covering the period January 21, 1961, to the present. These are arranged according to presidential administration and are organized by EO number, title, date of signing by the president, citation to *Federal Register* page and date, amendments if any, and current status, if applicable. At least this information permits the user to access the full text, and it may be just a matter of time before the online edition of the *Codification* is updated so that we do not have to search issues of the FR or Title 3 for the period after January 20, 1989. Figure 6.3, page 184, shows a page from the "Disposition Tables" section of the *Codification*.

Shepard's Code of Federal Regulations Citations cites to the CFR, including proclamations, executive orders, and reorganization plans published in Title 3. The citing sources include federal and state cases reported in units of the *National Reporter System,* A.L.R. "Annotations," and selected legal periodicals.

Figure 6.3. "Disposition Tables" from *Codification*.

Proclamations

Number	Amendments	Disposition
4457		Hortatory.
4458		Hortatory.
4459		Hortatory.
4460		Hortatory.
4461		Hortatory.
4462		Hortatory.
4463	Amended by Proc. 4466	Tariff.
4464		Hortatory.
4465		Hortatory.
4466		Tariff.
4467		Hortatory.
4468		Hortatory.
4469		Tariff.
4470		Hortatory.
4471		Hortatory.
4472		Hortatory.
4473		Hortatory.
4474		Hortatory.
4475		Hortatory.
4476		Hortatory.
4477		Tariff.
4478	Amended by Proc. 4480	Tariff.
4479		Hortatory.
4480		Tariff.
4481		Hortatory.
4482		Tariff.

EXECUTIVE ORDERS

Number	Amendments	Disposition
8684	Amended by EO 11673	Revoked by EO 11886.
9066		Terminated by Proc. 2714; termination confirmed by Proc. 4417.
9586	Amended by EO 10336, 11085, 11515.	Codified at Chapter III.
9698		See note at Chapter XXII.
9708	Amended by EO 10532, 11070	Codified at Chapter XLII.
9751	Amended by EO 10083, 10864	See note at EO 9698, Chapter XXII.
9823		See note at EO 9698, Chapter XXII.
9863		See note at EO 9698, Chapter XXII.
9911		See note at EO 9698, Chapter XXII.
9972		See note at EO 9698, Chapter XXII.
10000	Amended by EO 10261, 10623, 10636, 10903, 11938.	Codified at Chapter XXII.
10016		Revoked by EO 10903.
10025	Amended by EO 10983	See note at EO 9698, Chapter XXII.
10086		See note at EO 9698, Chapter XXII.
10096	Amended by EO 10695, 10930	Codified at Chapter XXXVII.
10122	Amended by EO 10400, 11733	Codified at Chapter XXXII.
10228		See note at EO 9698, Chapter XXII.
10242	Amended by EO 10773, 11051. See EO 11725.	Codified at Chapter XXXII.
10261		Revoked by EO 10903.

EXECUTIVE OFFICE OF THE PRESIDENT

Under authority of the Reorganization Act of 1939 (53 Stat. 561, 5 U.S.C. §§ 133–133r, 133t note), various agencies were transferred to the Executive Office of the President by Reorganization Plans 1 and 2 of 1939, effective July 1, 1939. EO 8248 (September 8, 1939) established the divisions of the Executive Office and defined their functions. Subsequently, presidents have used EOs, reorganization plans, and legislative initiatives to reorganize the Executive Office in an attempt to further the goals of their administrations. In terms of public policy, some of these agencies within the Executive Office exercise substantial power and influence.

Office of Management and Budget

The Office of Management and Budget (OMB) was originally established as the Bureau of the Budget by an Act of June 10, 1921 (42 Stat. 20). Pursuant to Reorganization Plan 2 of 1970 and EO 11541, July 1, 1970, the agency was transferred to the Executive Office of the President and given its present name. OMB wields great influence in formulating federal information policies. Its various edicts in this area are revised and refined over time, typically in the form of numbered bulletins and circulars, and published in the *Federal Register*. OMB can be accessed on the Internet via the White House home page.

The Budget of the United States Government

Some economists have said that budgeting is the fundamental act of governance: choosing how much, and on what, to spend. The federal budget is arguably the nation's most important public document and conspicuously its most contentious political document. In effect, the president's budget analyzes and compiles separate presentations for hundreds of budget accounts, covering all fiscal activities for the federal establishment, including such "off-budget" accounts as the Social Security Trust Funds and the Postal Service Fund. The budget contains a wealth of information presented in a daunting array of schedules, tables, graphs, and narrative summaries. Its comprehensiveness is its main strength and most obvious weakness: its sheer size and complexity.

Broadly viewed, it represents a continual process involving analysis and discussion among the president, the Director of OMB, the Comptroller General, the Board of Governors of the Federal Reserve System, the General Accounting Office, the Congressional Budget Office, the

House and Senate Appropriations Committees, and the several committees of Congress that must authorize and appropriate monies for the programmatic activities of the entire federal establishment. It is the origin of the old maxim, "The president proposes, the Congress disposes."

In the past the budget has been issued either as a series of related but separately published documents or as a single document with several parts. For fiscal year 1999 the budget consisted of the following separate documents, all of which were available through GPO Access, in print and on CD-ROM to depository libraries and by subscription.

- *Budget of the United States Government* contains the budget message of the president and presents the president's budget proposals.

- *Budget of the United States Government—Appendix* comprises detailed budget estimates by agencies and contains more detailed financial information on individual accounts than is found in the other budget documents. It is the most useful of these source documents.

- *Analytical Perspectives* contains analyses that are designed to highlight specified program areas or give other significant presentations of budget data that place the budget in perspective.

- *Historical Tables* furnishes data on budget receipts, outlays, surpluses or deficits, federal debt, and federal employment covering an extended time period (for example, fiscal year 1940 through fiscal year 2003).

- *A Citizen's Guide to the Federal Budget* contains a brief summary of the budget and the budget process for the general public, serving the purpose of the former *United States Budget in Brief.*

- *Budget System and Concepts* consists of an explanation of the terms used to formulate the president's budget proposal.

- *Mid-Session Review* was released May 28, 1998, and consists of revised estimates of the budget receipts, outlays, and budget authority for fiscal years 1998 through 2003 and other summary information required by law.

- *Sequestration Update Report to the President and Congress* consists of the current status of enforcement mechanisms under the Budget Enforcement Act (BEA) and enacted legislation reported on under the BEA by OMB as of August 15, 1998.

In addition, the U.S. Budget Web site contains a number of supporting documents available for downloading such as *Budget Information for States,* providing state-by-state estimated data for FY 1999 for the major federal formula grant programs to state and local governments, and the *Public Budget Database User's Guide,* which contains account-level data on receipts, outlays, and budget authority in spreadsheet format.

For those who do not want to navigate this huge bayou of data, the General Accounting Office prepared a 112-page *Compendium of Budget Accounts, Fiscal Year 1999* that offers users a convenient way to sort through the fiscal structure of the federal government and to determine the level of budgetary resources—used, estimated, or requested by fiscal year—for individual accounts.[8]

The "Black Budget"

Article I, Section 9, Clause 7, of the U.S. Constitution states in part that "a regular statement and account of the receipts and expenditures of all public money shall be published from time to time"; this is, of course, part of the budget process in which monies are authorized and appropriated by Congress. Despite that constitutional requirement, the intelligence agencies of the United States are allowed to spend money in secret without any public accounting.

Everyone is familiar with the shenanigans of the Central Intelligence Agency (CIA), but in addition to that entity, twelve other intelligence units exist within the federal establishment: the National Security Agency, which specializes in electronic reconnaissance and code breaking; the highly secret National Reconnaissance Office, which runs the U.S. satellite surveillance program; the Defense Intelligence Agency (DIA); the four intelligence arms of the Navy, Air Force, Army, and Marines; the Federal Bureau of Investigation (FBI) and Drug Enforcement Administration within the Justice Department; and the intelligence branches of the Departments of State, Energy, and Treasury. Altogether these entities are believed to spend about $30 billion a year, and these covert billions are called the nation's "black budget."

These expenditures are concealed within the *Budget of the United States Government—Appendix,* primarily in the Department of Defense (DoD) segment of that document, in a variety of ways. For instance, blank spaces appear where dollar figures normally belong; code words shield the identity of secret programs; covert projects are buried within allotments for seemingly unclassified items; and meaningless descriptions, such as "special activities," may shield large sums in line items. Thus, if you access the entry for the CIA in the *Budget—Appendix,* all you will find is the Central Intelligence Agency Retirement and Disability System Fund, for which $202 million was allotted in FY 1999. But the actual budget of the CIA, which appears to be something of an open secret, is more than $3 billion. Many members of Congress have expressed an interest in declassifying the aggregate data presented in the black budget; indeed, the Director of the CIA in 1997 indicated "that he could support making the total budget figure public as long as it does not lead to disclosure of the amount spent on specific activities."[9] The publications and the declassified documents available on the CIA's Web page (**http://www.odci.gov/cia**) are addressed in detail in chapter 11.

Economic Report of the President

The Council of Economic Advisers was established to furnish economic analysis and advice to the chief executive. It assists in the preparation of the annual *Economic Report of the President,* the major part of which includes its annual report. The Council also assists in the preparation of the monthly *Economic Indicators,* the provenance of the Joint Economic Committee of the Congress. This periodical has relevant economic information on prices, wages, production, business activity, purchasing power, credit, money, and federal finance. Both the annual and the periodical are available in full text on GPO Access and to depository libraries and sales subscription.

Catalog of Federal Domestic Assistance

The *Catalog of Federal Domestic Assistance* (CFDA) is one of the brighter constellations in the federal empyrean. Issued in looseleaf format, the *Catalog* is a compendium of financial and nonfinancial federal programs, projects, services, and activities administered by government agencies that provide assistance or benefits to the public. CFDA entries describe the type of assistance available and the eligibility requirements for assistance to state and local governments, public and private institutions, and specialized groups and individuals. Entries are classified by type of assistance, such as formula grants, direct payments, loans, scholarships and fellowships, exchange programs such as Fulbright-Hays, and other forms. One should update either source in the Notices section of the *Federal Register.*

The *Catalog* is available in a variety of formats. It is a sales item, announced in *U.S. Government Subscriptions;* it is available in paper copy to depository libraries; and it is available on machine-readable magnetic tape, high-density floppy diskettes, CD-ROM, and the Internet (**http://www.gsa.gov/fdac**).

Government Assistance Almanac

As librarians and users know, the *Catalog* is not the easiest source from which to extract relevant information. A commercial publication, the *Government Assistance Almanac,* edited by J. Robert Dumouchel (Detroit, MI: Omnigraphics), is an annual compilation that covers every program described in the CFDA. Part I is a guide to make it easier for the seeker to navigate the maze of requirements to secure the federal largess. Part II is a detailed description of more than 1,300 programs. Part III contains summary tables revealing the funding levels of all programs for the previous four years. Part IV provides contact information for the federal entities that administer the programs. The indexes make searching user-friendly, with extensive cross-references.

North American Industry Classification System

Another important publication that is the provenance of the Executive Office of the President became available in 1998 and is titled the *North American Industry Classification System* (NAICS)—*United States, 1997,* a 1,250-page manual that replaces the *Standard Industrial Classification* (SIC) *Manual* and permits business marketers to classify customers and prospects by industry type. Its purposes as set forth in the *Federal Register* are "(1) to facilitate the collection, tabulation, presentation, and analysis of data relating to establishments, and (2) to promote uniformity and comparability in the presentation of statistical data describing the economy." It is widely used by "State agencies, trade associations, private businesses, and other organizations."[10]

The NAICS comprises 350 new industries, including the growing service sector and technological industries. The manual contains definitions for each industry, tables showing correspondence between 1997 NAICS and the 1987 SIC codes, an alphabetical list of more than 18,000 businesses and their corresponding NAICS codes, a special section on what small businesses need to know about NAICS, and a comprehensive index. With this system, government and business analysts can make direct comparisons of industrial production statistics collected and published in the three North American Free Trade Agreement (NAFTA) countries: the United States, Mexico, and Canada. Moreover, NAICS allows increased comparability with the International Standard Industrial Classification System (ISIC, Revision 3), developed and maintained by the United Nations. However, the 1987 *Standard Industrial Classification Manual* should be retained, "as many of the non-statistical areas [such as administrative, taxes, and so forth] will not switch to the system for several years."[11]

The NAICS manual is available for sale through the Superintendent of Documents and on CD-ROM from the National Technical Information Service (NTIS) and was sent to depository libraries in 1998 (PREX 2.6/2:IN27/997). You can access the list of NAICS codes and the correspondence tables between NAICS and SIC, and other files can be downloaded from the NAICS Web site (**http://www.census.gov/epdc/ www/naics.html**) or indirectly through the Census Bureau home page.

O*NET: THE OCCUPATIONAL INFORMATION NETWORK

O*NET, issued by the Employment and Training Administration (ETA), Department of Labor, is a comprehensive database system for collecting, organizing, describing, and disseminating information on job characteristics and worker attributes. It replaces the venerable *Dictionary of Occupational Titles* (DOT), which was the definitive source for occupational information. O*NET products are reproduced by the Government Printing Office (GPO), which has mounted Web sites for downloading and ordering products using an online interactive order form. The CD-ROM edition of O*NET and the *Data Dictionary and User's Guide* in paper format were sent to depository libraries as separates in late December 1998. Detailed instructions on downloading O*NET 98 data are published in *Administrative Notes* 20: 5–6 (January 15, 1999).

For guidance in using O*NET online, access the O*NET home page (**http://www.doleta.gov/programs/onet**), which has navigational buttons to pages for individuals looking for work, employers searching for qualified workers, and the latest on ETA programs and initiatives. This Internet service is superior to the old DOT schedules. During the transition period, an alphabetical index (but not the full text) to the revised fourth edition of the *Dictionary of Occupational Titles* remained available on the Internet (**http://www.immigrationusa.com/ dot_index.html**).

O*NET Products

*O*NET 98 Viewer* is a software application developed to help users access the information in the O*NET 98 database. It contains almost 500 descriptors covering skills, knowledge, abilities, generalized work activities, interest, work values, and occupational-specific tasks. This product is available on CD-ROM, diskettes, and Internet download. Accompanying this package is an *O*NET 98 Viewer User's Guide,* available on CD-ROM, in a print version, and Internet download. The O*NET 98 database itself links twenty-three individual tables that comprise four categories: data tables, the data dictionary, occupation-related tables, and files that link O*NET codes and titles to other classification systems (CD-ROM, diskettes, Internet). The *O*NET Data Dictionary* (CD-ROM, print, Internet) is the primary source of documentation for the database, providing the definition, location, and coding for each variable in the database. These products are available for sale; in addition, selected O*NET 98 products are free: Select the "Download O*NET 98" bar on the Web site.

OCCUPATIONAL COMPENSATION SURVEY

The *Occupational Compensation Survey,* provenance of the Bureau of Labor Statistics (BLS), Department of Labor, contains far more specific data than those found in the *Standard Occupational Classification Manual* (SOC), a publication that is being revised in light of O*NET. Titles and numeric codes, however, are taken from the SOC and used in the occupational descriptions, which can be accessed on the Survey's Internet page (**http://www.bls.gov/ocs**).

OCCUPATIONAL OUTLOOK HANDBOOK

Issued biennially by the BLS, this estimable tome was first published in 1949. It covers several hundred occupations but makes available a great deal of information that the DOT, by the nature of its mandate, did not contain. In the *Handbook* one finds for an occupation or profession information about the nature of the work, working conditions, places of employment, training, educational requirements, advancement possibilities, earnings, related occupations, and that all-important category, the projected job outlook. To help job seekers, employment planners, and guidance counselors keep abreast of current occupational and employment trends between editions of the *Handbook,* the BLS issues the *Occupational Outlook Quarterly,* which consists of articles and statistics on selected vocations. Both the *Handbook* and the *Quarterly* are sales and depository items, and the *Handbook* can be accessed from the BLS home page or directly (**http://stats.bls.gov/ocohome.html**), where it can be searched by keyword, by using the index, or by selecting from an occupational cluster.

PRESIDENTIAL ADVISORY COMMITTEES AND COMMISSIONS

In 1794 an advisory body was established by President George Washington, who appointed trusted men in the private sector to report on an unlawful uprising by rebel farmers in two counties in Pennsylvania, a brouhaha that came to be known as the Whiskey Insurrection. They failed in their negotiations with the seditionists, and their recommendations led to the president's ordering the militia to march and subdue the rebellion. Washington describes this action in his sixth annual address to the nation in 1794, and he is given credit for convening the government's first advisory committee.

Government probably came into being through the effort of committees. After Washington's precedent, advisory bodies were commonly established to assist the president, the departments and agencies, and the independent agencies, on matters of greater or lesser moment. Indeed, there appears to be an overwhelming tendency to appoint a committee or commission whenever a problem or an emergency occurs that at the time seems difficult or politically unpalatable to resolve. It is no coincidence that as government has increased in size and responsibilities, the number of advisory bodies has grown.

Ideally, the advisory committee effects a significant contribution by the governed to the government; it affords a means by which the best talent and experience available in business, labor, and the professions can be made accessible. By definition, however, advisory committees have no independent enforcement or quasi-legislative authority, and presidents and other officers within the executive branch often fail to make use of a committee's findings. In fact, creation of a committee has been used to delay, stall, or thwart solution or resolution of a problem. Incidents that create headlines often result in the creation of a presidential commission to study the problem, but when the final report is issued, a president is frequently obliged, for political or other reasons, to ignore, pigeonhole, or even denounce the findings. President Richard Nixon, for example, repudiated the recommendations of the Commission on Obscenity and Pornography and the Commission on Marihuana and Drug Abuse before their publication.

Blue-ribbon panels such as the Warren Commission on the Assassination of John F. Kennedy get all the media attention, but these ad hoc bodies are rare compared to the hundreds of standing advisory committees. Some of these meet only once a year (and many committees meet even less frequently) and have names like the Iditarod National Historic Trail Advisory Council. Throughout most of the nation's history, the functions and management of these entities have been haphazard. After many congressional studies and reports and several presidential executive orders, the Federal Advisory Committee Act of 1972 (FACA), codified at 5 U.S.C. App., established a centralized management system and brought some order to the process of establishing and terminating advisory bodies. The General Services Administration (GSA), an independent entity, devised guidelines for the implementation of FACA; and Executive Order 12838, February 10, 1993, placed a ceiling on the number of "discretionary advisory committees" (those created under agency authority or authorized by Congress). The GSA is responsible, under FACA, for ensuring that the sponsoring agencies are following the requirements of the Act and supporting GSA regulations.

The best source for information on the workings of FACA and advisory committees and commissions is the *Annual Report of the President on Federal Advisory Committees,* which is submitted to the president by the GSA. The main section is an alphabetical listing of advisory committees by sponsoring department or agency with an identification number assigned by the GSA; the authority type, whether required by statute or executive order (non-discretionary) or authorized by statute or under general agency authority (discretionary); a recommendation to terminate, merge with another advisory entity, or continue in force; the number of meetings annually; and the cost for the fiscal year of the report. The total number of committees has decreased between FY 1988 and FY 1997. Figures for the latter fiscal year show a total of 963 committees, of which 491 are discretionary, with a total cost of $178 million and the number of members at 36,586.[12]

Frequently, the news media will use the name of the chairperson of an advisory committee, and it becomes known to the public by that popular title. For example, the Tower Commission Report that investigated the "Iran-Contra" scandal was officially titled *Report of the President's Special Review Board.* A president may authorize, amend, or terminate an advisory body by promulgating an executive order citing

FACA as authority. The Serial and Government Publications Division of the Library of Congress issued a useful publication titled *Popular Names of U.S. Government Reports: A Catalog.* This compilation, now in its fourth edition, suffers a time lag and is not comprehensive. It has been updated in the periodical literature as noted in chapter 4. In addition to these articles, two monographs supplement and augment the *Popular Names Catalog.* T. R. Wolanin's *Presidential Advisory Commissions: Truman to Nixon* (Madison, WI: University of Wisconsin Press, 1975) includes these advisory bodies through 1972. Steven D. Zink's *Guide to the Presidential Advisory Commissions, 1973–84* (Alexandria, VA: Chadwyck-Healey, 1987) contains detailed information on seventy-four commissions and committees during this period. Replete with accurate information and citations to the genesis, termination, composition, functions, and summary of each panel's activities, including its popular name and appropriate directory information, Zink's compilation includes an annotated bibliography of reports published pursuant to the mandate of the committee or commission. Moreover, Zink supplies citations to privately published reports as well as to the Government Printing Office (GPO) edition.

The *Encyclopedia of Governmental Advisory Organizations* (Farmington Hills, MI: Gale Group) is the most comprehensive guide to permanent, continuing, terminated, and authorized but never funded advisory bodies reporting not only to the president but also to Congress and to executive departments and agencies. The typical edition edited by Donna Batten contains more than 6,000 entries and is organized into general subject chapters, from agriculture to transportation. Entry information includes addresses, contact persons' names, telephone and fax numbers, history and authority, programmatic mandates, publications and reports, meetings, and popular names. Appendixes include a directory of committee management officers and the full text of the 1972 Federal Advisory Committee Act, as amended. Five indexes provide access to the entries by staff or contact name, publication and report titles, a list of committees established by presidential administration, committees associated with federal departments or agencies, and organization name by keyword. The *Encyclopedia* is updated by periodic supplements titled *New Governmental Advisory Organizations.*

Although their recommendations are not binding, advisory committees have been extensively used by the federal government. As noted, it is not unusual for a president, Congress, or a department or agency to ignore the recommendations of an advisory committee. Nevertheless, advisory bodies have played an important role in prompting presidential actions or congressional initiatives. Their proliferation and occasional persuasive authority led a House Government Operations Committee to call them the "fifth arm of the Federal establishment,"[13] albeit not as influential as the constitutionally created three branches and the independent regulatory entities.

PRESIDENTIAL LIBRARIES

The Presidential Library System comprises nine presidential libraries and one Presidential Project. These nationwide facilities are monitored by the Office of Presidential Libraries within the National Archives and Records Administration (NARA). Unlike traditional libraries, these institutions are repositories for preserving and making available the papers, records, and other historical materials of presidents since Herbert Hoover. Each presidential library contains a museum and offers an active series of public programs.

Before the advent of the System, presidential papers were often dispersed after the close of each administration. Although many pre-Hoover documents are now housed in the Library of Congress, others are split among libraries, historical societies, and private collections. Unfortunately, many presidential materials have been lost or destroyed.

The Presidential Library System formally began in 1939, when Franklin D. Roosevelt donated his personal and presidential papers to the National Archives; friends of Roosevelt formed a nonprofit corporation to raise funds for the construction of the library and museum building. Completed in 1946, the Roosevelt Library proved so successful that in 1955 the Presidential Libraries Act was passed, enabling other presidents to donate their materials to the government.

The 1955 Act was based on the premise that a president's papers are his personal property, a concept that goes back to George Washington's administration. As a result of the Watergate scandal, the Presidential Records Act of 1978 as amended (92 Stat. 2423, 44 U.S.C. § 2201 et seq.) replaced this concept with the principle that the presidential records that document the constitutional, statutory, and ceremonial duties of the president are the property of the federal government, but the Act allowed presidents to continue to establish libraries in locations of their choice.

The nine libraries and one project maintain more than 250 million pages of textual material; 5 million photographs; 13.5 million feet of motion picture film; 68,000 hours of disk, audiotape, and videotape recordings; and 280,000 museum objects. Other important holdings include the personal papers and historical materials donated by individuals associated with the president. These may include cabinet officials, envoys to foreign governments, political party associates, and the president's family and personal friends. Another category of materials comprises papers accumulated by presidents before and after their tenure in office. Examples include Franklin Roosevelt's term as governor of New York and Dwight Eisenhower's long military career.

Presidential libraries are located at West Branch, Iowa (Hoover), Hyde Park, New York (Roosevelt), Independence, Missouri (Truman), Abilene, Kansas (Eisenhower), Boston, Massachusetts (Kennedy), Ann Arbor, Michigan (Ford), Atlanta, Georgia (Carter), Simi Valley, California (Reagan), and College Station, Texas (Bush). The Gerald R. Ford Museum is located in Grand Rapids, Michigan.

The single Project is the Nixon Presidential Materials Staff, located at the National Archives in College Park, Maryland. It is open to the public for research, where scholars and the media are able to access the Watergate tapes and other Nixoniana. However, the Richard M. Nixon Library and Birthplace is located in Yorba Linda, California, where one can access public policy materials of a less inflammatory nature. The above information, and much more, can be read at the NARA Web site (http://www.nara.gov) with a link to "Presidential Libraries."

TREATIES AND AGREEMENTS

Nowhere in the constitutional mandate is the "shared powers, separation of functions" concept more evident than in the forging of treaties and other international compacts. Article II, Section 2, of the Constitution states that the president "shall have power, by and with the advice and consent of the Senate, to make treaties, provided two thirds of the Senators present concur." The making of treaties involves a series of steps that generally include negotiation, signing, approval by the Senate, ratification by the president, deposit or exchange of ratification with the other party or parties to the treaty, and proclamation. "Contrary to popular impression, the Senate does not ratify treaties; the President ratifies treaties upon receiving the advice and consent of the Senate to this act."[14] A useful summary of historical interpretations of the Senate's responsibility is found in Howard R. Sklamberg's "The Meaning of 'Advice and Consent': The Senate's Constitutional Role in Treatymaking," *Michigan Journal of International Law* 18: 445–74 (Spring 1997).

The framers of the Constitution were sharply divided on the issue of allowing the president such a central role in treaty making. By and large, the delegates to the Constitutional Convention expected the Senate to dominate the making of foreign policy, certainly to the extent that the

Congress controlled, in Article I, the sole right "to declare war." James Madison felt a president "should be an agent in treaties," where the word "agent" meant a "deputy," one who represents another.[15] John Jay, however, highly approved of the joint responsibility of the Senate and the president in the treaty process.[16] Alexander Hamilton asserted that "if we attend carefully to its operation, [treaty making] will be found to partake more of the legislative than of the executive character, though it does not seem strictly to fall within the definition of either of them."[17] Despite the framers' original intent, historian Leonard W. Levy notes that "Hamilton's position was destined for acceptance by presidents in the twentieth century."[18]

The Vienna Convention on the Law of Treaties defines a treaty as an "international agreement concluded between two states in written form and governed by international law, whether embodied in a single instrument or in two or more related instruments and whatever its particular designation." The State Department's definition of a treaty is "an undertaking between two states which legally binds the parties and an intent is clearly demonstrated by the parties to be governed by its terms."[19]

Executive agreements, on the other hand, are not specifically mentioned in the Constitution; "yet the executive agreement has been used since 1817 when the Rush-Bagot Agreement was reached with Great Britain, limiting naval forces to be kept on the Great Lakes."[20] In recent decades the number of executive agreements concluded has far exceeded that of formal treaties. The distinction between treaty and agreement in practice is the

> submission or nonsubmission of an international instrument to the Senate. . . . Any international agreement which is not submitted to the Senate for its advice and consent is not considered a treaty, even though it may have legislative sanction, whereas any agreement which is submitted to the Senate, be it called a protocol, convention, treaty, agreement, articles, or by some other name, is considered a treaty.[21]

Thus, for treaties the Senate's shared partnership in the process is a central constitutional provision. As such it represents a

> principal means by which the Senate participates in the shaping of American foreign policy. . . . It is fundamental to the logic of the Treaty Clause [in the Constitution] that it does not envisage that the President may unilaterally remake a treaty.

If he could, the Senate's portion of the shared power inherent in the Treaty Clause would be nullified.[22]

Presidents may conclude executive agreements by statutory authority, by a prior treaty provision, or by the Constitution. Moreover, presidents enter into executive agreements concerning property, the initiation of diplomatic relations, cooperation in atomic energy, and trade arrangements. However, NAFTA, the North American Free Trade Agreement Implementation Act (PL 103-182; 107 Stat. 2057), because of its importance, was submitted to both chambers of Congress for approval, followed by a presidential proclamation (Proc. 6641, December 15,1993) and a presidential executive order (EO 12889, December 27, 1993).

The bibliographic apparatus of the president's role in the treaty and agreement process, while not as systematic as one would like, is largely structured in certain publications of the Department of State. The following is a selection of the more useful publications that contain information on treaties and other international agreements.

United States Department of State Dispatch

The *Dispatch* is the latest version of a periodical called the *Department of State Bulletin,* which began in 1939 and was published weekly until January 1978, when it became a monthly. This arrangement lasted until December 1989, when the *Bulletin* abruptly ceased publication. Its demise dismayed librarians and researchers because the *Bulletin* was widely consulted by users for its important textual and bibliographic information.

State Department officials, in trying to justify the *Bulletin*'s termination, stated that its many addresses, news conferences, statements, press releases, presidential proclamations, treaty and agreement information, and other features could be easily found in other sources. This claim was refuted by Lucy DeLuca and David W. Lewis in a closely reasoned content analysis that appeared in the September 1990 issue of *Documents to the People* (DttP). The authors found that in the penultimate issue of the *Bulletin,* fourteen of the twenty-six articles could "not be located in the Homer Babbidge Library" of the University of Connecticut, a federal depository "which receives approximately 90% of the items distributed in the Depository Library Program of the Government Printing Office."[23]

After some lobbying, Congress restored funding for the periodical, renamed the *United States Department of State Dispatch* and issued weekly, an improvement in terms of timeliness. The important upkeep service, "Treaty Actions," was also reinstated, which provides bibliographic information on current international compacts as deposited, entered into force, amended, signed, withdrawn, and the like, with citations to Senate Treaty Documents, TIAS numbers, and UST locations if available (these sources are discussed below). *Dispatch* was reborn as volume 1, number 1, September 3, 1990, and in that issue "Treaty Actions" covered the period January–July 1990. Although this section does not appear in *every* issue of *Dispatch,* when published it is important. *Dispatch* also contains the text of treaties and agreements on a selective basis, the text of the speeches given by the president and high officials in the State Department, ambassadorial appointments, essays, news conferences, and so forth. The weekly being too good to last, *Dispatch* is now a monthly and is indexed in *American Foreign Policy and Treaty Index*'s print edition; on the InfoTrac CD-ROM; EBSCO; and in the *Readers' Guide to Periodical Literature.* Full-text editions include WESTLAW, LEXIS-NEXIS, the National Trade Data Bank; the Department of State Foreign Affairs Network (DOSFAN) Web site (**http://dosfan.lib.uic.edu/index.html**), a partnership of the Department of State, the University of Illinois at Chicago library, and the Federal Depository Library Program; and the Department of State Web site (**http://www.state.gov**). This last Internet address requires knowledge of the specific issue. Figure 6.4, page 200, shows a page from *Dispatch* announcing "Treaty Actions," which includes both bilateral and multilateral pacts. *Dispatch Supplements* are issued on an irregular basis and report on events such as international conferences on topics in which the United States has a vested interest.

Treaties in Force

Treaties in Force (TIF) is an annual volume that contains a bibliographic record of all bilateral and multilateral treaties and agreements in force as of the date of issuance (January 1, [year]). Its index is not satisfactory, but the bibliographic information for each action is updated to include any modifications, additional members joining or leaving multilateral pacts, and citations to the location of the full texts as they have been published in the *Statutes at Large* (prior to 1950), *United States Treaties and Other International Agreements* (UST), *Treaties and Other International Acts Series* (TIAS), *United Nations Treaty Series* (UNTS), *League of Nations Treaty Series* (LNTS), *Treaties and Other*

Figure 6.4. Page from *Dispatch,* "Treaty Actions" section.

Treaty Actions

Treaty Actions
January–July 1990

Multilateral

Agriculture—Diseases
International agreement for the creation at Paris of an International Office for Epizootics, with annex. Done at Paris Jan. 25, 1924. Entered into force Jan. 17, 1925; for the US July 29, 1975. TIAS 8141.
Accession deposited: Burma, Aug. 24, 1989.

Atomic Energy
Amendment of Article VI.A.1 of the Statute of the International Atomic Energy Agency of Oct. 26, 1956, as amended (TIAS 3873, 5284, 7668). Done at Vienna Sept. 27, 1984. [Senate] Treaty Doc. 99-7.
Acceptances deposited: Cote d'Ivoire, Oct. 27, 1989; Jamaica, Dec. 28, 1989; Luxembourg, Jan. 11, 1990.
Entered into force: Dec. 28, 1989.

Amendment of Article VI.A.1 of the Statute of the International Atomic Energy Agency of Oct. 26, 1956, as amended (TIAS 3873, 5284, 7668). Done at Vienna Sept. 27, 1984. Entered into force Dec. 28, 1989. [Senate] Treaty Doc. 99-7.
Acceptances deposited: Mali, Mar. 13, 1990; South Africa, May 25, 1990.

Agreement regarding protection of information transferred into the United States in connection with the initial phase of a project for the establishment of a uranium enrichment installation in the United States based upon the gas centrifuge process developed within the three European countries [Fed. Rep. of Germany, Netherlands, UK]. Signed at Washington Apr. 11, 1990. Entered into force Apr. 11, 1990. *Parties:* Germany, Fed. Rep., Netherlands, UK, US.

Aviation
Convention on offenses and certain other acts committed on board aircraft. Done at Tokyo Sept. 14, 1963. Entered into force Dec. 4, 1969. TIAS 6768.
Accession deposited: German Democratic Republic, Jan. 10, 1989;[1] Marshall Islands, May 15, 1989; Zimbabwe, Mar. 8, 1989.

Convention for the suppression of unlawful acts against the safety of civil aviation. Done at Montreal Sept. 23, 1971. Entered into force Jan. 26, 1973. TIAS 7570.
Accession deposited: Vanuatu, Nov. 6, 1989.

Protocol for the suppression of unlawful acts of violence at airports serving international civil aviation. Done at Montreal Feb. 24, 1988. Entered into force Aug. 6, 1989.[2] [Senate] Treaty Doc. 100-19.
Senate advice and consent to ratification: Nov. 22, 1989.

Protocol relating to an amendment (Article 56) to the convention on international civil aviation (TIAS 1591). Done at Montreal Oct. 6, 1989. Enters into force on the date on which the 108th instrument of ratification is deposited. Protocol for the suppression of unlawful acts of violence at airports serving international civil aviation, supplementary to the convention of Sept. 23, 1971 (TIAS 7570). Done at Montreal Feb. 24, 1988. Entered into force Aug. 6, 1989.[2]
Ratifications deposited: Austria, Dec. 28, 1989; Chile, Aug. 15, 1989; Denmark, Nov. 23, 1989;[3] France, Sept. 6, 1989.[1]

International air services transit agreement. Done at Chicago Dec. 7, 1944. Entered into force Jan. 20, 1945; for the US Feb. 8, 1945. EAS 487.
Acceptance deposited: German Dem. Rep., Apr. 2, 1990.

Convention on international civil aviation. Done at Chicago Dec. 7, 1944. Entered into force Apr. 4, 1947. TIAS 1591.
Adherence deposited: German Dem. Rep., Apr. 2, 1990.

Coffee
Extension of the international coffee agreement, 1983.[4] Done at London July 3, 1989. Entered into force Oct. 1, 1989.
Acceptances deposited prior to Oct. 1, 1989: Angola, Benin, Bolivia, Burundi, Cameroon, Canada, Colombia, Costa Rica, Cote d'Ivoire, Dominican Republic, El Salvador, Equatorial Guinea, Fiji, Finland, France, Gabon, Fed. Rep. of Germany,

Ghana, Guatemala, Guinea, Haiti, Honduras, India, Indonesia, Kenya, Liberia, Madagascar, Malawi, Mexico, Nicaragua, Norway, Panama, Papua New Guinea, Paraguay, Philippines, Portugal, Rwanda, Sri Lanka, Sweden, Switzerland, Tanzania, Thailand, Togo, Uganda, US, Zaire, Zambia, Zimbabwe.
Notifications of provisional application deposited prior to Oct. 1, 1989: Belgium, Brazil, Central African Rep., Cuba, Denmark, Ecuador, Ethiopia, European Economic Community, Greece, Ireland, Italy, Japan, Luxembourg, Netherlands, Nigeria, Peru, Spain, UK, Venezuela.
Accessions deposited: Trinidad and Tobago, Nov. 13, 1989; Singapore, Nov. 28, 1989; Sierra Leone, Nov. 29, 1989.

International coffee agreement, 1983, with annexes, done at London Sept. 16, 1982, as extended July 3, 1989.[4] Entered into force Oct. 1, 1989.
Acceptances deposited: Ethiopia, Mar. 26, 1990; Japan, July 17, 1990; Peru, Mar. 14, 1990; Venezuela, Mar. 2, 1990.
Accession deposited: Jamaica, Mar. 22, 1990.

Conservation
Convention on international trade in endangered species of wild fauna and flora, with appendices. Done at Washington Mar. 3, 1973. Entered into force July 1, 1975. TIAS 8249.
Ratification deposited: Poland, Dec. 12, 1989.
Accession deposited: Burkina Faso, Oct. 13, 1989.

Consular Relations
Optional protocol to the Vienna convention on consular relations, concerning the compulsory settlement of disputes. Done at Vienna Apr. 24, 1963. Entered into force Mar. 19, 1967; for the US Dec. 24, 1969. TIAS 6820.
Accessions deposited: Hungary, Dec. 8, 1989; Nicaragua, Jan. 9, 1990.

Containers
International convention for safe containers, with annexes, as amended. Done at Geneva Dec. 2, 1972. Entered into force Sept. 6, 1977; for the US Jan. 3, 1979. TIAS 9037, 10220, 10914.
Accession deposited: Dem. People's Rep. of Korea, Oct. 18, 1989; Indonesia, Sept. 25, 1989.

Copyright
Berne convention for the protection of literary and artistic works of Sept. 9, 1886, as revised at Paris July 24, 1971, and amended on Oct. 2, 1979. Entered into force for the US Mar. 1, 1989. [Senate] Treaty Doc. 99-27.
Accession deposited: Honduras, Oct. 24, 1989.
Ratification deposited: UK, Sept. 29, 1989.

Cultural Property
Statutes of the International Centre for the Study of the Preservation and Restoration of Cultural Property. Adopted at New Delhi Nov.-Dec. 1956, as amended at Rome Apr. 24, 1963, and Apr. 14-17, 1969. TIAS 7038.
Accession deposited: Mali, Oct. 9, 1989.

Convention on the means of prohibiting and preventing the illicit import, export, and transfer of ownership of cultural property. Done at Paris Nov. 14, 1970. Entered into force Apr. 24, 1972; for the US Dec. 2, 1983.
Acceptance deposited: Australia, Oct. 30, 1989.[12]
Ratifications deposited: Belize, Jan. 26, 1990; Madagascar, June 21, 1989.

Customs
Customs convention on containers, 1972, with annexes and protocol. Done at Geneva Dec. 2, 1972. Entered into force Dec. 6, 1975; for the US May 12, 1985.
Accession deposited: Trinidad and Tobago, Mar. 23, 1990.

Convention establishing a Customs Cooperation Council, with annex. Done at Brussels Dec. 15, 1950. Entered into force Nov. 4, 1952; for the US Nov. 5, 1970. TIAS 7063.
Accessions deposited: German Dem. Rep., Mar. 27, 1990; Iraq, June 6, 1990; Togo, Feb. 12, 1990.

Diplomatic Relations
Optional protocol to the Vienna convention on diplomatic relations concerning the compulsory settlement of disputes. Done at Vienna Apr. 18, 1961. Entered into force Apr. 24, 1964; for the US Dec. 13, 1972. TIAS 7502.
Accession deposited: Hungary, Dec. 8, 1989; Nicaragua, Jan. 9, 1990.

International Agreements of the United States of America, 1776–1949 (Bevans), and the earlier TS and EAS.

TIF is arranged in two parts followed by an appendix. Part 1 includes bilateral treaties and agreements listed by country or other political entity. Part 2 includes multilateral treaties and agreements, arranged by subject, together with a list of nations that are signatories to each pact. The appendix contains a consolidated tabulation of documents affecting international copyright relations of the United States. The latest edition of TIF is updated and supplemented by the information formerly published in "TREATIES: Current Actions" in the *Bulletin* and "Treaty Actions" currently published in the *Dispatch*. TIF may be downloaded in either 3.0 MY PDF format or zipped (compressed) in 2.0 MY PDF format (**http://www.acda.gov/state**). However, this Web site has a "Disclaimer" in which the Treaty Affairs Staff and the Office of Legal Adviser, Department of State, will not vouch for its "accuracy, completeness, formatting, or timeliness."

Treaties and Other International Acts Series

Pursuant to PL 89-479, July 8, 1966 (80 Stat. 271; 1 U.S.C. § 113),

> the Treaties and Other International Acts Series issued under the authority of the Secretary of State shall be competent evidence . . . of the treaties, international agreements other than treaties, and proclamations by the President of such treaties . . . in all the courts of law and equity and of maritime jurisdiction, and in all the tribunals and public offices of the United States, and of the several States, without any further proof or authentication thereof.

This Department of State "Note" is published on the verso of the title page of every *Treaties and Other International Acts Series* (TIAS) numbered pamphlet. The slip treaties in their current form replaced an earlier Treaty Series (TS) and Executive Agreement Series (EAS) in 1945, both of which are still cited, if appropriate, in TIF. The numbering system continued when the earlier series were merged into the TIAS pamphlets; thus, TIAS begins with Treaty 1501 and Executive Agreement 506.

Because of the importance of the TIAS text pursuant to Public Law 89-479, it is regrettable that the State Department has allowed this series to suffer a time lag of several years. This is especially ironic in that

1 U.S.C. § 112b requires publication in a timely fashion, and failure to comply demands "describing fully and completely the reasons for the late transmittal." Figure 6.5 shows a multilateral treaty (TIAS 10561) in pamphlet form. Note that the chronology includes the role of the Senate. Figure 6.6 shows a typical presidential proclamation for a multilateral treaty. Figure 6.7, page 204, shows a chronology of a typical executive agreement. Note the absence of any mention of Senate advice and consent to ratification.

Figure 6.5. Chronology of a multilateral treaty.

MULTILATERAL

Marine Pollution: Intervention on the High Seas in Cases of Pollution by Substances Other Than Oil

Protocol done at London November 2, 1973, as rectified by the proces-verbal of October 14, 1977;[1]

Transmitted by the President of the United States of America to the Senate July 25, 1977 (S. Ex. L, 95th Cong., 1st Sess.);

Reported favorably by the Senate Committee on Foreign Relations June 26, 1978 (S. Ex. Rept. No. 95–24, 95th Cong., 2d Sess.);

Advice and consent to ratification by the Senate July 12, 1978;

Ratified by the President August 3, 1978;

Ratification of the United States of America deposited with the Secretary General of the Inter-Governmental Maritime Consultative Organization September 7, 1978;

Proclaimed by the President April 11, 1983;

Entered into force March 30, 1983.

---

[1] The text of the protocol which appears herein incorporates the corrections set forth in the proces-verbal.

TIAS 10561

Figure 6.6. Presidential proclamation in a TIAS pamphlet.

BY THE PRESIDENT OF THE UNITED STATES OF AMERICA

A PROCLAMATION

CONSIDERING THAT:

The 1981 Protocol for the Sixth Extension of the Wheat Trade Convention, 1971, was open for signature in Washington from March 24 through May 15, 1981, and the Protocol was signed during that period by the respective plenipotentiaries of the Government of the United States of America and certain other Governments;

The text of the Protocol, in the English, French, Russian, and Spanish languages, is hereto annexed;

The Senate of the United States of America by its resolution of December 16, 1981, two-thirds of the Senators present concurring therein, gave its advice and consent to ratification of the Protocol;

The President of the United States of America ratified the Protocol on January 12, 1982, in pursuance of the advice and consent of the Senate;

The Government of the United States of America deposited a declaration of provisional application of the Protocol on June 23, 1981, and deposited its instrument of ratification on January 12, 1982;

Pursuant to the provisions of Article 9 of the Protocol, the Protocol entered into force provisionally for the United States of America on June 23, 1981;

Pursuant to the provisions of Article 9 of the Protocol, the Protocol entered into force definitively for the United States of America on January 12, 1982;

Now, THEREFORE, I, Ronald Reagan, President of the United States of America, proclaim and make public the Protocol, to the end that it be observed and fulfilled with good faith on and after January 12, 1982, by the United States of America and by the citizens of the United States of America and all other persons subject to the jurisdiction thereof.

IN TESTIMONY WHEREOF, I have signed this proclamation and caused the Seal of the United States of America to be affixed.

[SEAL] DONE at the city of Washington this first day of February in the year of our Lord one thousand nine hundred eighty-two and of the Independence of the United States of America the two hundred sixth.

RONALD REAGAN

By the President:
    ALEXANDER M. HAIG JR
    Secretary of State

TIAS 10350

Figure 6.7. Chronology for an executive agreement.

ISRAEL

**Peacekeeping: Multinational Force and Observers—
Privileges and Immunities**

Agreement effected by exchange of notes
Signed at Jerusalem and Tel Aviv September 28 and October 1,
*   1982;*
Entered into force October 1, 1982.

TIAS 10558

United States Treaties and Other International Agreements

Just as public laws are bound together chronologically in the *Statutes at Large,* so the TIAS pamphlets are collected into *United States Treaties and Other International Agreements* (UST). The volumes, published on a calendar year basis beginning January 1, 1950, are accessed by a subject and country index. Before 1950, the full text of treaties and agreements was published in the *Statutes at Large.* The publication delay that afflicts the TIAS pamphlets a fortiori causes UST volumes to suffer a time lag of many years.

Treaties and Other International Agreements of the United States of America, 1776–1949

Earlier collections of treaties have been issued in separate sets known by the names of their compilers: Miller, Malloy, Redmond, Trenwith. With the definitive edition of *Treaties and Other International Agreements of the United States of America, 1776–1949,* compiled under the direction of Charles I. Bevans, the text of treaties and agreements for those years is easily accessed in one twelve-volume set. Each volume has an index, and volume 13 serves as an index to the entire set. This set is known as "Bevans."

Official Supporting Series

Section 114 of the Supplemental Foreign Relations Authorization Act of 1990 established a system for the venerable Foreign Relations of the United States (FRUS) historical series. The records are reviewed by an Advisory Committee on Historical Diplomatic Documentation to ensure that the series "constitutes an authoritative and complete diplomatic record" and to review documents that "may be withheld" within national security and protection of living persons limitations. Published from 1861 through 1951 on an annual basis and thereafter on a triennial schedule, FRUS experiences a time lag of more than thirty years between date of publication and the period covered. Produced by the State Department's Office of the Historian, volumes in the series since 1952 are organized chronologically into subseries according to presidential administrations and geographically and topically within each subseries. Included in the volumes are documents from the State and Defense Departments, White House, National Security Council, Central Intelligence Agency, Agency for International Development, and other foreign affairs agencies. In general, the editors choose documentation that illumines policy formulation and major aspects and repercussions of its execution. The Office of the Historian has a Web site that includes a brief description of the series, pertinent press releases, summaries of recently released volumes, volumes available from the Superintendent of Documents, volumes online, and series completed and in progress from the Kennedy, Johnson, and Nixon administrations (**http://www. state.gov/www/about_state/history/frus.html**).

In 1996 the first volume in the history of the FRUS series devoted entirely to intelligence issues was released. Entitled *Emergence of the Intelligence Establishment, 1945–1950,* the volume traces the creation of the nation's permanent foreign intelligence system from the proposals by senior U.S. policymakers during the last days of World War II to the establishment of the Central Intelligence Agency in 1947. The issue was made available to depository libraries and for sale by the Superintendent of Documents.

American Foreign Policy Current Documents was issued annually from 1956 to 1967 and resumed its annual schedule in 1981. It is a compilation of major official messages; addresses, statements, and interviews; press conference and briefing reports; congressional testimonies; and communications by the White House, the Department of State, and other federal agencies or officials involved in the conduct of foreign policy. *A Decade of Foreign Policy: Basic Documents, 1941–1949* was published in 1950 as Senate Document 81-123.

Since 1981 an annual microfiche supplement has been published that includes important documents that for reasons of space could not be included in the book edition.

The irregularly issued *U.S. Foreign Affairs on CD-ROM* has not only the full text of *Dispatch* but also press briefings, speeches by the president and key Department of State officials, congressional testimony, *Background Notes,* and so forth. *Background Notes,* like *Dispatch,* can be accessed separately and are useful guides that provide information on a country's leaders, politics, economy, and relations with the United States. They appear on the State Department's Web site (**http://www.state.gov/www/background_notes**) before they appear in the GPO print edition for sale and to depository libraries.

International Law Digests

Earlier digests of international law have been the provenance of the State Department since 1877 and are known by the names of the compilers: John L. Cadwalader, Francis Wharton, John B. Moore, Green H. Hackworth, Marjorie M. Whiteman, and Arthur W. Rovine. The last in this distinguished series, *Digest of United States Practice in International Law,* a multivolume set, centers upon the factual and historical settings of cases and incidents and quotes extensively from original sources. But unlike the earlier series, Rovine's work emphasizes international documentation as it relates to U.S. practice. Rovine covered the period 1973 to 1980. Regrettably discontinued as a GPO publication, this estimable endeavor continues to be published in a section of the *American Journal of International Law.*

COMMERCIAL SOURCES FOR TREATIES AND AGREEMENTS

Unperfected Treaties of the United States, 1776–1976, edited by Christian L. Wiktor (Dobbs Ferry, NY: Oceana, 1976), is an annotated, nine-volume set of treaties that did not receive Senate approval or was not ratified by the president.

William S. Hein & Company (Buffalo, NY) issues a series of products and services designed to reduce the time lag of the official treaty and agreement publishing pattern. *United States Treaty Index: 1776–1990 Consolidation,* edited by Igor I. Kavass, affords a more comprehensive access to international acts than its official GPO predecessor sets. Treaties and agreements may be accessed by TIAS number (if available), country or countries, subject, and time frame (chronology).

The guide includes unpublished acts from 1776 to 1950 and current treaties and agreements not yet published in the TIAS pamphlets. The series is updated with "1995 Revision" volumes.

United States Current Treaty Index, edited by Igor I. Kavass, is issued semiannually on CD-ROM and in print and is a supplement to the *1776–1990 Consolidation.* It indexes the treaties and agreements in the above *Consolidation* and contains a TIAS number (if known); chronological, subject, and country indexes; and a KAV (named after the author) and TIAS numerical conversion table.

A Guide to United States Treaties in Force, edited by the assiduous Kavass, consists of two parts. Part I is a "Numerical List and Subject Reference Index," and part II contains a numerical guide, chronological index, and a directory of countries and international intergovernmental organizations (IGOs). The in-depth indexing is a vast improvement over the inadequate TIF index.

Hein also produces two non-print services. *Hein's United States Treaties and Other International Agreements—Current Microfiche Service* offers the full text of treaties that have not yet been published in the TIAS pamphlets with index and other finding aids. Updated bimonthly, this work gives access to the text of treaties and agreements within eight weeks of receipt by Congress.

Oceana Publications, Inc. (Dobbs Ferry, NY) issues a treaty reference service designed, like the products noted above, to rectify the dilatory State Department schedule. Issued quarterly, *Consolidated Treaties & International Agreements* (CTIA) consists of *CTIA: Current Document Service—United States,* which contains the text of unreleased international compacts; *Index: CTIA;* and *CTIA: CD-ROM.* Of undeniable value, the Hein and Oceana products, like those of other commercial firms, are purchased by large research libraries solely because the federal government appears unable or unwilling to provide timely information to the public as required by Title 1, Sections 112a and 112b, *United States Code.* As an alternative to the print sources, coverage from June 1979 of treaties and agreements is accessible online through WESTLAW (database identifier USTREATIES) while coverage of Oceana treaties from 1783 is furnished via LEXIS-NEXIS (Library: INTLAW; File: USTRTY).

In addition to the above, several commercial finding aids may be used for researching treaty and agreement materials. Because of the doctrine of shared powers, many of these sources are mentioned in the discussion of the legislative process in chapter 5.

CIS/Index indexes and abstracts Senate Treaty Documents and Senate Executive Reports, which became part of the United States

Congressional Serial Set beginning with the 96th Congress. Treaty Documents consist of presidential messages transmitting the text of treaties to the Senate Foreign Relations Committee. The Treaty Documents may also contain letters of submittal by the Secretary of State followed by an article-by-article analysis of the treaty as signed, including any memorandums of understanding, procedural protocols, annexes, notes, and the like. A Treaty Document is merely the text of the treaty before Senate committee mark-up and should not be confused with the final version of the treaty as it eventually is issued in the TIAS pamphlets. The text of Senate Treaty Documents is selectively published in the *Department of State Dispatch* and sold through the sales office of the Superintendent of Documents.

Senate Executive Reports emerge from the Senate Foreign Relations Committee and, in the absence of the official TIAS slip treaty, are the closest equivalent to the text of the treaty itself. Often other congressional committees are involved in hearings and reports if the treaty crosses jurisdictional lines and is of grave importance. For example, the Treaty between the United States of America and the Union of Soviet Socialist Republics on the Elimination of Their Intermediate-Range and Shorter-Range Missiles (the INF treaty), signed by Ronald Reagan and Mikhail Gorbachev in December 1987, was duly transmitted to the Senate Foreign Relations Committee. However, this committee received reports from then Senate Majority Leader Robert C. Byrd, the Senate Armed Services Committee, and the Senate Select Committee on Intelligence.[24] The hearings, the Treaty Documents, and the Executive Reports are indexed and abstracted in *CIS/Index* and *CIS Annual*. Figure 6.8 and Figure 6.9, page 210, show the title page of a Treaty Document and an Executive Report, respectively.

CIS Index to US Senate Executive Documents & Reports renders access to Senate action on treaties, nominations, and other presidential submissions from 1817 through 1969 that were not published in the Serial Set. Thereafter the series can be accessed in *CIS/Index*.

American Foreign Policy and Treaty Index (AFPTI), another Congressional Information Service product, began in 1993 as *American Foreign Policy Index* and is issued quarterly in abstracts and index volumes with an annual cumulation. There is an accompanying AFPTI Microfiche Collection containing the full text of the documents indexed. Conceived as a comprehensive guide to foreign policy–related government publications, AFPTI covers a wide range of topics culled from the State Department, the Office of the President, executive branch departments and agencies, independent entities, and the Congress.

Publications include monographs, serials, series, and periodicals. Individual documents and articles announced in AFPTI are available on demand on microfiche or in paper.

Figure 6.8. Title page of a Senate treaty document.

100TH CONGRESS 2d Session	SENATE	TREATY DOC. 100–11

TREATY BETWEEN THE UNITED STATES OF AMERICA AND THE UNION OF SOVIET SOCIALIST REPUBLICS ON THE ELIMINATION OF THEIR INTERMEDIATE-RANGE AND SHORTER-RANGE MISSILES

MESSAGE

FROM

THE PRESIDENT OF THE UNITED STATES

TRANSMITTING

THE TREATY BETWEEN THE UNITED STATES OF AMERICA AND THE UNION OF SOVIET SOCIALIST REPUBLICS ON THE ELIMINATION OF THEIR INTERMEDIATE-RANGE AND SHORTER-RANGE MISSILES, TOGETHER WITH THE MEMORANDUM OF UNDERSTANDING AND TWO PROTOCOLS, SIGNED AT WASHINGTON ON DECEMBER 8, 1987

JANUARY 25, 1988.—Treaty was read the first time, and together with the accompanying papers, referred to the Committee on Foreign Relations and ordered to be printed for the use of the Senate.

U.S. GOVERNMENT PRINTING OFFICE

WASHINGTON : 1988

81–428

Figure 6.9. Title page of a Senate executive report.

100TH CONGRESS *2d Session*	SENATE	EXEC. REPT. 100–15

THE INF TREATY

REPORT

OF THE

COMMITTEE ON FOREIGN RELATIONS
UNITED STATES SENATE

APRIL 14, 1988

U.S. GOVERNMENT PRINTING OFFICE

83-960   WASHINGTON : 1988

CCH Congressional Index, noted in chapter 5, is highly regarded in its bibliographic coverage of presidential actions in which Congress participates within the framework of the Constitution. Volume 1 of *Congressional Index* has a section called "Reorganization Plans—Treaties—Nominations," which tracks current treaty action. For Senate treaty documents, *Congressional Index* shows a cumulative chronology, including dates of removal from the injunction of secrecy, referral to the Senate Foreign Relations Committee, citations to the Senate Executive Reports, ratification, and so forth. With its timeliness and cumulative features, *Congressional Index* is a good current source that develops a retrospective utility with the passage of time.

CQ Weekly (formerly *CQ Weekly Report*) furnishes a lucid exposition of treaty and agreement actions, transforming the stylized language found in official documents into readable prose. With its index, detailed table of contents, and precise citations, *CQ Weekly* establishes bibliographic superiority over prestigious newspapers such as *The New York Times* or *The Washington Post.* This is manifested in its accurate references to the official documents and its detailed voting charts. The weekly is available in print and online with CQ Washington Alert. Its companion volume, the annual *CQ Almanac,* although condensed from the weekly issues, is organized in such a way that the information on treaties is easy to access through its detailed index.

Shepard's United States Citations: Statute Edition can be used to update a treaty by history and treatment. The history function complements the bibliographic information provided in the "Treaty Actions" section of the *Dispatch.* Treatment offers citations to case law and other citing sources that have cited the treaty. In addition to manual access, *Shepard's Statute Edition* is online with LEXIS-NEXIS. Unfortunately, the usefulness of this source is vitiated by the dilatory publication of the treaty series.

Shepard's Acts and Cases by Popular Names, Federal and State is best known for providing citations to federal and state statutes and cases when only the popular name is known. This service also includes the popular names given to treaties. For example, the multilateral Kellogg-Briand Pact [Renunciation of War] of August 27, 1928, which ironically is still in force, is shown to be at 46 Stat. 2343; and the Rio de Janeiro Pact [Reciprocal Assistance] of September 2, 1947, is cited at 62 Stat. 1681.

TREATY INTERNET SITES

I have mentioned some Web addresses in connection with specific publications such as *Treaties in Force* and *Dispatch*. The reality is that there are many places to begin because of the numerous links. The following is a sampling of Internet sites:

- The State Department's Web site is the place to begin (**http://www.state.gov**). The Index (**http://www.state.gov/www. ind.html**) is organized by subjects (Adoption) and forms (Addresses), and the links to sites outside the U.S. government are indicated with an asterisk. The Site Map linked to the same Web page is handy and approaches the information in other ways (by the Department itself, policy, regions, outreach, and services). Select "Search" and you can access the full text of treaties by subject (for example, Extradition) and find collateral documents from such entities as the United States Information Agency and the United States Agency for International Development.

- The status of treaties, which may be accessed through *CIS/Index* as indicated above, and through the "Treaty Actions" section of *Dispatch,* is also available in a serviceable Internet form from the Senate Web site (**http://www.senate.gov/activities/treaties/ html**). The segments include (1) treaties received from the president during the current Congress and referred to the Foreign Relations Committee; (2) treaties reported out by the committee, placed on the Executive Calendar with a sequentially assigned calendar number, and those ready for floor debate and vote; (3) treaties approved by the plenary Senate with links that display the text of the treaty ratification resolutions; and (4) "other actions" such as floor resolutions, understandings, declarations, and the like. Thus you can track these procedures, and along the way you are given the Senate Treaty Document number, the Senate Executive Report number, and the Executive Communication number. When kept current, this is a splendid WWW source.

- GPO Access itself has the full text of hearings, treaty documents and executive reports, and debate and voting in the *Congressional Record* for these initiatives.

- Sometimes overlooked as a source for U.S. treaties, the *United Nations Treaty Series* (UNTS) is available on the United Nations Web site (**http://www.un.org**). The full text of the thousands of bilateral and multilateral treaties in which the United States was a signatory is displayed. The search may be conducted by type of treaty (multilateral, bilateral, original agreements, modification), signature/adoption date, date of entry into force, participants, title, subject, registration number, or any combination thereof. Then you should consult TIF and the later update services to determine if the compact is still in force.

AMERICAN INDIAN LAWS AND TREATIES

There are a number of productive sources for the specialist in Native American laws, treaties, and other presidential and congressional actions germane to this topic. University Publications of America (Bethesda, MD) titles include *The Native Americans Reference Collection: Documents Collected by the Office of Indian Affairs,* which contains some 5,500 congressional documents, reports, and committee hearings, as well as materials published by nongovernmental sources, on 35mm microfilm reels in two parts covering the periods 1840–1900 and 1901–1948; and *Early American Indian Documents: Treaties and Laws, 1607–1789,* edited by Alden T. Vaughan, a multivolume set that comprises treaties with Indian tribes during that period.

Because the United States Congressional Serial Set contains a wealth of information on American Indian affairs, the *CIS US Serial Set Index, 1789–1969* is a valuable guide. The Institute for the Development of Indian Law issued *A Chronological List of Treaties and Agreements Made by Indian Tribes with the United States,* which contains a list of all treaties and agreements, ratified or unratified, covering the period 1778–1909. Volume 7 of the *United States Statutes at Large* contains the text of Indian treaties from 1778 to 1842, and thereafter treaties and agreements with Indian tribes appear in regular chronological order in the *Statutes.* Current law is codified in Title 25 of the *United States Code,* and the regulations of agencies such as the Bureau of Indian Affairs (BIA) and the Indian Claims Commission are found in Title 25 of the *Code of Federal Regulations.* Other contemporary sources on legislative and executive actions include *CIS/Index,* the *Monthly Catalog,* and the *Congressional Record.*

Another source is *Indian Affairs: Laws and Treaties,* edited by Charles J. Kappler (7 volumes. Washington: Government Printing Office,

1904). Reissued and updated in 1972–1979 by the United States Department of the Interior, volume 2 contains bilateral treaties between the United States and Indian tribes, 1778–1871; other volumes contain statutes, executive orders, and other official pronouncements.

Documents of United States Indian Policy, 2d ed., edited by Francis Paul Prucha (Lincoln: University of Nebraska Press, 1990), is a single-volume work that includes almost 200 documents: statutes, Supreme Court decisions, treaties and agreements, and various reports relevant to government policies, past and present, regarding Native Americans.[25] According to John S. Wilson of Baylor University, the "best sources to check for references to government documents are by George Peter Murdock and Timothy J. O'Leary, *Ethnographic Bibliography of North America,* 4th edition (5 volumes), Steven L. Johnson, *Guide to American Indian Documents in the Congressional Serial Set: 1817–1899,"* and Prucha's compilation noted above.[26]

NOMINATIONS

Article II, Section 2, of the Constitution gives the president the power to nominate principal officers of the executive branch and the judiciary, but their appointment is subject to the advice and consent of the Senate. Most presidential nominees are confirmed by the Senate. In the vast majority of nominations, Senate action is a formality. Appointments and promotions of military officers, lower federal court judges, ambassadors, postmasters, and officials in various specialized services are almost automatically given Senate approval. Cabinet positions, sensitive or controversial appointments such as the directors of the FBI and the CIA, and nominations to the Supreme Court receive varying degrees of Senate scrutiny.

The legislative path for nominations consists of a series of steps in which the Executive Clerk of the Senate receives from the president the nomination and refers the name to the appropriate Senate committee. For example, nominees for the federal courts are referred to the Senate Judiciary Committee. There is no prior "executive document" series like the Senate Treaty Documents for international law, but the appropriate Senate committee does issue a Senate Executive Report. Few Senate committees publish an unfavorable report if their votes in committee go against the nominee, and only a simple majority of the plenary Senate is necessary for confirmation.

Senate Executive Reports are indexed and abstracted in *CIS/Index* and *CIS Annual* and are part of the current United States Congressional Serial Set. Other sources providing information on nominations include the "Daily Digest" section of the *Congressional Record,* the *Journal of the Executive Proceedings of the Senate of the United States,* the *Monthly Catalog,* WCPD, and the Public Papers series. Commercial sources include CCH Incorporated's *Congressional Index* and *CIS Index to U.S. Senate Executive Documents and Reports, 1818–1969.* The latter, with its companion text on microfiche, offers a definitive retrospective source for research.

REORGANIZATION PLANS

Reorganization Plans are presidential directives submitted to both chambers of Congress. Under this format, the president may merge, abolish, or transfer functions of designated agencies of the executive branch below the rank of department or independent agency. Following the Supreme Court decision in *Immigration and Naturalization Service v. Chadha,* 462 U.S. 919, 77 L.Ed.2d 317, 103 S.Ct. 2764 (1983), which held that the "legislative veto" is unconstitutional, Congress decided to replace the one-House veto in the executive reorganization statute with a joint resolution of approval. Thus, the president must obtain the approval of both chambers to implement a reorganization schedule, as authorized under the provisions of Title 5, §§ 901–912, *United States Code.* Section 903(c) states that "Any time during the period of 60 calendar days of continuous session of Congress after the date on which the plan is transmitted to it, but before any resolution described in section 909 has been ordered reported in either House, the President may make amendments or modifications to the plan. . . . The President may withdraw the plan any time prior to the conclusion of 90 calendar days of continuous session of Congress following the date on which the plan is submitted to Congress."

Reorganization Plans carry a consecutive number within the year they became effective. They are frequently accompanied by executive orders. For example, the Federal Emergency Management Agency (FEMA) was established by Reorganization Plan No. 3 of 1978 and Executive Orders 12127 and 12148. Minor internal reorganization within existing agencies may be accomplished at the direction of the head of the unit and is frequently announced in the "Notices" section of the *Federal Register.*

The text of *Reorganization Plans* is duplicated in several sources, but they are collected in Title 5 of the *United States Code, Appendix,* which gathers together all pertinent documents such as executive orders implementing them, any other presidential messages pertaining to the *Plans,* historical and revision notes, and cross-references. Following the text of the *Plans* is a "legislative history" similar in outline to that found at the end of a slip law.

Other sources that carry the text of *Reorganization Plans* include the *Congressional Record,* Congressional Serial Set, *Federal Register,* Title 3 CFR, *Public Papers of the Presidents, Statutes at Large, Weekly Compilation of Presidential Documents,* WESTLAW, and LEXIS-NEXIS. FedLaw EasySearch, a CD-ROM product published by Oryx Press (Phoenix, AZ), contains the text of *Reorganization Plans* as well as proclamations and executive orders.

Some presidents, such as Lyndon Johnson, Richard Nixon, and Jimmy Carter, were not shy about transmitting *Reorganization Plans* to Congress for approval. Conversely, George H. W. Bush, Ronald W. Reagan, and William J. Clinton disdained this form, a procedure whose aim, largely unsuccessful, is to galvanize the putatively inert bureaucracy.

UNITED STATES GOVERNMENT MANUAL

The *United States Government Manual,* official handbook of the federal government, furnishes annual information on the departments and agencies of the legislative, judicial, and executive branches, including the independent agencies; government corporations; selective boards, committees, and commissions; some quasi-official entities; and selected bilateral and multilateral international organizations in which the United States participates. Special elements include an alphabetical list of senators and representatives with party affiliation, congressional district (for House members), office building and room number; organization charts; and recent changes of personnel actions. A valuable feature of the current edition is the inclusion of e-mail and Internet addresses for selected departments, agencies, and independent entities. The *Manual* contains an individual name index and a combined agency/subject index. Appendixes include a selective number of acronyms and abbreviations, a complete list of agencies appearing in the CFR, and an appendix titled "Federal Executive Agencies Terminated, Transferred, or Changed in Name Subsequent to March 4, 1933." This last and the main entries contain citations to reorganization plans, proclamations, executive orders, statutes, and the *United States Code.* Figure 6.10 shows a page from the *Manual* in which presidential edicts are cited in this appendix.

Figure 6.10. Page from *United States Government Manual*, Appendix.

conformity in U.S. coins as to fineness and weight. Terminated and functions transferred to Secretary of the Treasury (*see* text) by an act of Mar. 14, 1980 (94 Stat. 98; 31 U.S.C. 363).

Apprenticeship Section, Division of Labor Standards (Labor) Transferred to Federal Security Agency by EO 9139 of Apr. 18, 1942, where it functioned as Apprentice Training Service. Its organizational entity preserved by section 6 of the order. Transferred to War Manpower Commission by EO 9247 of Sept. 17, 1942, where it functioned within Bureau of Training. Returned to Department of Labor by EO 9617 of Sept. 19, 1945. (*See* Bureau of Apprenticeship and Training, text.)

Archive of Folksong (Library of Congress) Renamed Archive of Folk Culture by administrative order of the Deputy Librarian, effective Sept. 21, 1981 (*see* text).

Area Redevelopment Administration Established May 8, 1961, by Secretary of Commerce pursuant to Area Redevelopment Act (75 Stat. 47; 42 U.S.C. 2501) and Reorg. Plan No. 5 of 1950, effective May 24, 1950. Terminated Aug. 31, 1965, pursuant to terms of the act, as amended (79 Stat. 195; 42 U.S.C. 2525). Functions, personnel, and property transferred to Economic Development Administration in Department of Commerce (*see* text) by Department Order 4–A, effective Sept. 1, 1965.

Arlington Memorial Amphitheater Commission Established by act of Mar. 4, 1921 (41 Stat. 1440; 24 U.S.C. 291–295), to report annually to Congress, through the President of the United States, on memorials to be erected and bodies of certain deceased members of Armed Forces to be entombed during next ensuing year within Amphitheater in Arlington National Cemetery in Virginia. Abolished by act approved Sept. 2, 1960 (74 Stat. 739), and functions transferred to Secretary of Defense.

Arlington Memorial Bridge Commission Established by act of Mar. 4, 1913 (37 Stat. 885; D.C. Code (1951 ed.) 8–158), to report to Congress a suitable design for a memorial bridge across the Potomac River from the city of Washington to the Arlington estate. Abolished by EO 6166 of June 10, 1933, and functions transferred to Office of National Parks, Buildings, and Reservations (*see* appendix A).

Armed Forces Medical Library Originally founded in 1836 as Library of the Surgeon General's Office, U.S. Army, and later known as Army Medical Library, it was given title of Armed Forces Medical Library in 1952. The National Library of Medicine Act, approved Aug. 3, 1956 (70 Stat. 960; 42 U.S.C. 275), established the National Library of Medicine in Public Health Service (*see* appendix A) and transferred to it all civilian personnel, property, and funds of Armed Forces Medical Library.

Armed Services Renegotiation Board Established by directive of Secretary of Defense on July 19, 1948, to conduct contract renegotiation with contractors and subcontractors assigned. Board abolished by letter of Secretary of Defense dated Jan. 18, 1952, and functions transferred to Renegotiation Board (*see* appendix A).

Army, Department of the Functions, powers, and duties relating generally to water vessel anchorages, draw-bridge operating regulations, obstructive bridges, tolls, pollution of the sea by oil, and location and clearance of bridges and causeways in navigable waters of the U.S. transferred to Secretary of Transportation by Department of Transportation Act of Oct. 15, 1966 (80 Stat. 931; 49 U.S.C. 1651 note).

Army and Navy Staff College Established Apr. 23, 1943, and operated under Joint Chiefs of Staff. Wartime mission was to train specially selected Army, Navy, and Marine Corps officers for command and staff duties in point operations. Redesignated National War College (*see* text), effective July 1, 1946.

Army Specialist Corps Established in War Department by EO 9078 of Feb. 26, 1942, to marshal outstanding scientific, technical, labor, and business skills directly into the Army in positions where it was not necessary to employ military personnel. Abolished as a separate organization by Secretary of War on Oct. 31, 1942, and functions merged into a central Officer Procurement Service.

Ash Council *See* President's Advisory Council on Executive Organization, appendix A.

Assistance Payments Administration (HEW) Established by Secretary's reorganization of Aug. 15, 1967, to administer assistance programs of certain State grants, Work Incentive Program, and for U.S. citizens returning from abroad and refugees. Transferred by

Published as a special edition of the FR pursuant to 1 CFR 9.1, the *United States Government Manual* began in 1935 as an annual publication of the National Emergency Council. Several other agencies assumed responsibility for its issuances from 1939 until, in 1948, the sponsoring agency became its current provenance, the Office of the Federal Register. From 1935 to 1948 it was titled the *U.S. Government Manual*. In 1949 it became the *U.S. Government Organizational Manual*. The 1973/1974 edition dropped the name *Organization,* according to the compilers, "to reflect a continuing attempt to direct the *Manual* to the general public rather than to the specialist in government." The *Manual* is available in print for sale and to depository libraries and is also accessible via GPO Access. A commercial source, Congressional Quarterly's annual *Washington Information Directory,* is a useful complement to the information found in the *Manual* and sometimes provides more detailed information on smaller entities within departments and agencies than the official *Manual* includes.

SUMMARY

The foregoing has been an attempt to categorize the various publications and collateral sources generated by or for the presidency through official provenances or under commercial imprints. Although the duplication of materials that carry the public record of presidential activity may seem wasteful, such duplication does offer one clear advantage to libraries and other institutions that require this information. By this duplication, libraries large and small, non-depository and depository, may participate in the acquisition of a substantial amount of this documentation in print and non-print formats.

NOTES

1. According to a Department of State ruling, Grover Cleveland is counted twice, as the twenty-second and twenty-fourth president, because his two terms were not consecutive.

2. Nancy P. Johnson, "Presidential Legislation," *Legal Reference Services Quarterly* 2:1 (Spring 1982).

3. Laurence F. Schmeckebier and Roy B. Eastin, *Government Publications and Their Use,* 2d rev. ed. (Washington: Brookings, 1969), p. 341.

4. A brief selection of historical presidential ukases is noted in Mary Woodward, "Executive Orders: A Journey," *Legal Reference Services Quarterly* 10: 126–28 (1990).

5. See *Korematsu v. United States,* 319 U.S. 432 (1943).

6. For earlier official and privately published compilations of presidential materials, see Schmeckebier and Eastin, *Government Publications and Their Use,* pp. 330–47. Unpublished presidential materials before the advent of the presidential libraries program have been collected by the Manuscript Division of the Library of Congress (LC) and are available on microfilm from the LC Photoduplication Division. A CD-ROM version of James D. Richardson's multivolume *Messages and Papers of the Presidents* has been updated to include current chief executives.

7. See *Administrative Notes Technical Supplement* 4: 6 (February 28, 1997).

8. U.S. General Accounting Office, *Compendium of Budget Accounts: Fiscal Year 1999* (GAO/AIMD-98-115), April 1998.

9. *CQ Weekly Report,* May 24, 1997, p. 1207.

10. 62 FR 17288 (April 9, 1997).

11. *Administrative Notes* 19:7 (January 15, 1998). See also *Administrative Notes* 19: 6 (October 15, 1998).

12. U.S. General Accounting Office, *Federal Advisory Committee Act: General Services Administration's Oversight of Advisory Committees* (GAO/GGD-98-124), June 1998, p. 18.

13. 91-2: H. Rep. 1731, p. 5.

14. *The Role of the Senate in Treaty Ratification,* a committee print prepared for the use of the Senate Foreign Relations Committee (Washington, DC: Government Printing Office, 1974), p. 7.

15. Leonard W. Levy, *Original Intent and the Framers' Constitution* (New York: Macmillan, 1988), pp. 38, 41–42.

16. Jacob E. Cooke, ed., *The Federalist* (New York: Meridian Books, 1961), pp. 432–36.

17. Ibid., pp. 503–6.

18. Levy, *Original Intent,* p. 52.

19. Cited in Edwin C. Surrency, "How the United States Perfects an International Agreement," *Law Library Journal* 85: 344 (Spring 1993).

20. Margaret A. Leary, "International Executive Agreements: A Guide to the Legal Issues and Research Sources," *Law Library Journal* 72: 1 (Winter 1979).

21. *The Role of the Senate in Treaty Ratification,* p. 27.

22. Senate Executive Report 100-15 (April 14, 1988), pp. 87–88.

23. *Documents to the People* (DttP) 16: 170–71 (September 1990).

24. Senate Executive Report 100-15 (April 14, 1988), pp. 74–79.

25. Michael L. Tate, "Red Power: Government Publications and the Rising Indian Activism of the 1970s," *Government Publications Review* 8A: 499–518 (1981).

26. John S. Wilson, "Essential U.S. Government Publications for Researching Native Americans," *Documents to the People* (DttP) 24: 233 (December 1996).

CHAPTER SEVEN

ADMINISTRATIVE LAW: REGULATIONS AND DECISIONS

> The rise of administrative bodies probably has been the most significant legal trend of the last century and perhaps more values today are affected by their decisions than by those of all the courts, review of administrative decisions apart. . . . They have become a veritable fourth branch of the Government, which has deranged our three-branch legal theories much as the concept of a fourth dimension unsettles our three-dimensional thinking.
>
> —Supreme Court Justice Robert H. Jackson,
> *FTC v. Ruberoid* (1952)

> *Quis custodiet ipsos custodes?*
>
> —Juvenal (circa A.D. 60–140)

INTRODUCTION

The rulemaking process is a set of formal procedures through which a statute adopted by the Congress and signed by the president is translated into specific written requirements to be carried out and enforced by executive branch and independent agencies. These regulations are usually far more detailed and precise than the statutory provisions to which they are pursuant. The major instruments for transmitting rules and regulations to the public are the *Federal Register* (FR) and the *Code of Federal Regulations* (CFR). As noted in chapter 6, the edicts of the president are published in a special section of the FR and a specific volume (Title 3) of the CFR. In addition, decisions, orders, licenses, advisory opinions, and other documents of agencies with quasi-judicial authority are published in instruments other than the

Federal Register and the *Code of Federal Regulations;* this chapter addresses those sources of information. The FR and CFR are the provenance of the Office of the Federal Register (OFR), National Archives and Records Administration, and are available for sale through the Superintendent of Documents, free to depository libraries in paper or on microfiche, online and on CD-ROM with commercial vendors, and on the Internet via GPO Access and other Web sites.

BACKGROUND

The Federal Register Act of 1935 (49 Stat. 500; 44 U.S.C. § 1501 et seq., as amended) established for the first time in the nation's history a systematic and bibliographically consistent process for promulgating government regulations. Before 1935 there was no central system; each agency did little more than type, sign, and file regulations in agency cabinets. Frequently one had to search out a regulation by going to the agency and tracking it down. This ineffective practice led the government to make a series of miscalculations that resulted in it being embarrassed by a 1935 Supreme Court decision known as the "Hot Oil Case," which was based upon a provision that had been nullified by a later rule.[1] The government's case was dismissed and the Supreme Court denounced all parties for their ignorance of the law. The failure to publicize adequately executive orders and agency regulations came to be known as "hip pocket" law, and its proven lack of effectiveness resulted in a bibliographic structure called the *Federal Register,* the first issue of which was published March 14, 1936. In 1938 the regulations published chronologically in the FR were organized into fifty Titles based upon the structure of the *United States Code;* the CFR became the codified companion to its older sibling (although they behave bibliographically more like fraternal twins, the Castor and Pollux of the federal galaxy).

In 1946 the Administrative Procedure Act (APA), codified in various sections of Title 5, *United States Code,* established a simple process for informal, as opposed to formal rulemaking. Formal rulemaking, required by 5 U.S.C. §§ 556, 557, is activated only in instances where a statute other than the APA requires a rule "to be made on the record after opportunity for an agency hearing." It involves a trial-type procedure presided over by agency members or an administrative law judge and is "seldom used except in ratemaking and food additive cases, and in other limited categories of proceedings."[2]

5 U.S.C. § 553 governs informal, otherwise known as "notice-and-comment," rulemaking, which involves (1) publication of a notice of

proposed rulemaking, (2) opportunity for public participation in the process, and (3) publication of a final rule when specified by the agency but not less than thirty days before the rule's effective date. Whereas the Federal Register Act provided authority for the FR's existence and contents, the APA gave added importance to the document by requiring publication in the *Register* of agency statements of organization, procedural rules, and the public notices mandated for agency rulemaking. During the 1970s Congress enacted a variety of "hybrid" rulemaking statutes, some of which superseded the provisions of the APA. Court-mandated refinements modified the rulemaking procedures of many agencies, and certain presidential executive orders instituted procedural requirements that exceeded APA authority. Add to these events a trend toward deregulation, and the "original unifying effect of the APA" has been somewhat undermined. Moreover, a General Accounting Office (GAO) study determined that "about half of the . . . final regulatory actions published in the Federal Register during 1997 were published without a notice of proposed rulemaking." Responding to this criticism, agencies cited administrative or technical issues with limited applicability, the "time-sensitive" nature of the actions taken, and categorical exceptions permitted by the Administrative Procedure Act.[3] Fortunately for documents librarians, the bibliographic machinery is far less complex than the often arcane formal and informal rulemaking processes.

THE *FEDERAL REGISTER* AND THE *CODE OF FEDERAL REGULATIONS*

The Federal Register Act provides that, in addition to presidential documents, the kinds of information to be published include "documents or classes of documents that may be required to be published by Act of Congress." At present the daily FR includes the following main sections:

- *Presidential Documents:* Discussed in chapter 6, these include executive orders, proclamations, and other presidential actions.

- *Rules and Regulations:* This section includes regulatory documents having general applicability and legal effect; the terms are used interchangeably. When promulgated most of them are keyed to the title and section of the CFR where they are later published according to a quarterly schedule (below). If applicable, the final rules must contain economic, environmental, or international trade impact statements, as well as paperwork reduction requirements and unfunded mandates cost threshold statements. *Emergency Rules* are used infrequently by agencies that can cite as authority statutes other than the APA. For example, the U.S. Fish and Wildlife Service used the emergency rule procedure to declare the San Bernardino kangaroo rat to be an endangered species pursuant to the Endangered Species Act of 1973 as amended. Emergency rules may have an expiration date as well as an effective date.[4] More on the uses of the emergency rule appears later in this chapter.

- *Proposed Rules:* These consist of changes or amendments to already existing regulations or new rules that an agency is considering. Their publication offers timely notice (not less than thirty days) for interested parties to respond to the proposals through hearings or by submitting written statements to the agency.

- *Notices:* This section comprises a potpourri of information other than rules or proposed rules that is applicable to the public. Examples include availability of grants, delegations of authority, filing of petitions and applications, statements of agency reorganization too minor to be submitted as presidential reorganization plans, notices of hearings and investigations, consent decrees, advisory committee meetings, names of defaulted borrowers, listings of gifts to federal employees from foreign government sources, Sunshine Act Meetings, and the like. The Sunshine Act Meetings occupied a separate section of the FR until March 1, 1996, when that section was incorporated into Notices. These are meetings required to be published by authority of the 1976 Government in the Sunshine Act (5 U.S.C. § 552b(e)(3)). Some agencies furnish Internet access to Notices; for example, comments received by the Department of Transportation (**http://dms.dot.gov**).

- *Corrections:* This section consists of editorial corrections of previously published presidential, rule, proposed rule, and notice documents prepared by the Office of the Federal Register.

Other components of the FR include a detailed table of contents, a semiannual Unified Agenda of Federal Regulations, and Readers Aids, including a list of public laws. To provide for agencies' distribution needs, some issues have separate parts, assigned Roman numerals, where agency documents such as final rules are published and that may include presidential documents. A *Federal Register Index,* issued separately, cumulates monthly into an annual.

Just as the *United States Statutes at Large* are codified in the *United States Code,* so the daily issues of the *Federal Register* are codified in the *Code of Federal Regulations.* The titles of the CFR are revised each calendar year on a quarterly schedule as follows:

Titles 1–16	as of January 1
Titles 17–27	as of April 1
Titles 28–41	as of July 1
Titles 42–50	as of October 1

When no amendments or other changes are promulgated in a volume during a quarter, a reprint of the cover of the volume with the new date and a new color is sent to subscribers and depository libraries. This cover can be stapled to the volume and serves to direct that the unrevised issue be retained. With the exception of Title 3, the pamphlet volumes of the CFR are coded by different colors every year. As noted in the previous chapter, Title 3, The President, is a singular annual, color-coded white since 1985. It must be retained until superseded by a cumulative version. That some librarians apparently were discarding Title 3 annual editions was noted in an admonitory paragraph in a 1993 issue of *Administrative Notes.* The terse rebuke said in part that libraries that "have discarded depository copies of Title 3 should replace them. Additionally, all library staff involved in weeding the depository collection should be notified of the special status of Title 3, CFR."[5]

The *Unified Agenda* of Federal Regulations

Under the provisions of the Regulatory Flexibility Act (RFA), PL 96-354; 94 Stat. 1164; 5 U.S.C. §§ 601–612 (September 19, 1980), each agency must prepare an agenda of rules under development that may have a significant impact on a substantial number of small businesses and other small private-sector organizations. The Act defines "agency" broadly so that it encompasses independent regulatory entities as well as executive agencies. Called the *Unified Agenda,* also known as the *Semi-Annual Regulatory Agenda,* the information consists of proposed and final rules that must be published in the *Federal Register* in October and April.[6] As a result, the *Agenda* is voluminous, typically covering more than 1,300 pages in the FR. Because of this and because of its unique schedule, GPO Access maintains this information in a database separate from the *Federal Register* database, which itself runs to more than 60,000 pages a year. The 1997 FR ran 68,517 pages and the 1998 *Register* finished at a robust 72,356 pages.

Section 610 of the RFA requires each federal agency to develop a plan for the review of its rules that have or will have a significant impact on a substantial number of small entities and publish a list of their existing rules that they plan to review in the next year. Although the RFA does not require agencies to use the *Unified Agenda* to publish the required notices, the General Accounting Office (GAO), an investigative agency within the Congress, recommends that they do so. Moreover, Executive Order 12866 requires the administrator of the Office of Management and Budget's (OMB) Office of Information and Regulatory Affairs to specify how federal entities should prepare their *Unified Agenda* entries. At the recommendation of the GAO, the Regulatory Information Service Center within the General Services Administration, beginning with the October 1997 issue of the *Agenda,* prepares an index that lists, by agency, the entries the agencies state are Section 610 reviews.[7]

Privacy Act Notices

Available via GPO Access, Privacy Act Issuances form an annual compilation and contain descriptions of agency records maintained on individuals with accompanying regulations to assist individuals who request information about their records. The two sources of Privacy Act Notices are the CFR for the latest annual cumulation and the FR that updates the CFR. The user selects the agency from a comprehensive list, and the appropriate title and sections of the CFR appear. The Privacy Act of 1974 (PL 93-579, 5 U.S.C. § 552a) serves as the authority for this information.

Congressional Oversight

Under the provisions of Subtitle E, Section 251 of the Contract with America Advancement Act of 1996 (PL 104-121; 5 U.S.C. §§ 801–808, March 29, 1996), two types of rules, major and nonmajor, must be submitted to both the House of Representatives and the Senate before either can take effect. The legislation defines a major rule as one that has resulted in or is likely to result in (1) an annual effect on the economy of $100 million or more; (2) a major increase in costs or prices for consumers, individual industries, government agencies, or geographic regions; or (3) significant adverse effects on competition, employment, investment, productivity, innovation, or on the ability of U.S.-based enterprises to compete with foreign-based enterprises in domestic and export markets. Major rules cannot be effective until sixty days after publication in the *Federal Register* or submission to Congress and the General Accounting Office, whichever is later. The definition of "rule" is broader than the "notice-and-comment" rulemakings under the APA that are published in the FR. "Rule" means "the whole or part of an agency statement of general applicability and future effect designed to implement, or prescribe law or policy."

Although 5 U.S.C. § 801 et seq. is silent about GAO's role relating to the nonmajor rules, the agency's Office of the General Counsel established a database that compiles information about the fifteen to twenty rules GAO receives on average each day. The database captures the title, agency, type of rule, Regulation Identification Number, proposed effective date, date published in the *Federal Register,* congressional review trigger date, and any joint resolutions of disapproval that may be enacted. The database is available on GAO's Web site (**http://www. gao.gov**), but with limited research capabilities.[8]

Content Differences: FR and CFR

If I may pursue the metaphor of siblings, the FR is not only older but more verbose. The conspicuous prolixity of the *Federal Register* extends not just to the obvious; namely, that Proposed Rules and Notices are precluded from the *Code of Federal Regulations.* A great deal of background information published in the FR as a final rule becomes condensed or eliminated when included in the CFR. One example among thousands will suffice. A 1992 final rule authorizing that the Karner blue butterfly be designated as endangered occupied nine pages in the FR. The section was in large part a scientific treatise, meticulously expressed, with that ferocious specificity characteristic of the *Register.*[9] The thousands of words explaining the U.S. Fish and Wildlife Service's determination were reduced to a single line in the CFR.[10]

Constitutional Amendments

One important category of document published in the FR but absent from the CFR is amendments to the Constitution. Beginning with the Twenty-second Amendment, the certifying statement of the Administrator of General Services (the director of the General Services Administration, an independent establishment) that the amendment had become valid was announced at 16 FR 2019 (March 1, 1951).

Additional certifications of validity by the Administrator of General Services were published in the *Register* for the Twenty-third (26 FR 2808, April 3, 1961), Twenty-fourth (29 FR 1715, February 5, 1964), Twenty-fifth (32 FR 3287, February 25, 1967), and Twenty-sixth (36 FR 12725, July 7, 1971) amendments. The Twenty-seventh Amendment was certified as valid by the Archivist of the United States (57 FR 21188, May 19, 1992) because the National Archives and Records Service, formerly an agency within the General Services Administration, became an independent entity in 1984 (98 Stat. 2280) and was designated the National Archives and Records Administration (NARA).

Emergency Rulemaking

As noted above, the Administrative Procedure Act of 1946 clarified the public's role in the rulemaking process. Under normal circumstances, agencies are obliged to publish "proposed rules" so that interested parties have the opportunity to respond either in writing and/or in person at administrative hearings. However, this procedure may be waived under extraordinary circumstances. This happened in dramatic fashion following the deaths of seven Chicago-area residents from cyanide-laced Tylenol in 1982.

Shortly after the deaths generated something approximating a national wave of terror, the Food and Drug Administration invoked a subsection of the APA providing that a general notice of proposed rulemaking need not be published in the *Federal Register* "when the agency for good cause finds (and incorporates the finding and a brief statement of reasons therefor in the rules issued) that notice and public procedure thereon are impracticable, unnecessary, or contrary to the public interest."[11]

The "brief" statement was several pages in length. The FDA noted that the Tylenol killings received wide exposure in the news media and therefore it was "clearly in the public interest to move quickly to establish uniform Federal regulatory standards that will enable manufacturers to implement tamper-resistant packaging and labeling requirements as efficiently and expeditiously as possible" (47 FR 50448). This emergency action appeared as a final rule in the November 5, 1982, issue of the FR. Later, it was codified at Title 21, CFR, Parts 211, 314, and 700. And this is why we may experience some difficulty opening certain types of packaged foods or pharmaceutical products.

SEARCHING THE FR AND CFR

An *embarras de richesses* awaits one who wishes to access the full text of the FR and CFR in all formats: print, fiche, CD-ROM, and online. What follows is a selective list of possibilities.

Commercial Online Databases

The *Federal Register* and the *Code of Federal Regulations* are available via WESTLAW; LEXIS-NEXIS; LEXIS-NEXIS Academic Universe; Legi-Slate, a Windows client program (**http://www.legislate.com**); and CQ Washington Alert. In addition, Counterpoint Publishing (**http://www.counterpoint.com**) sells access to the FR and CFR. Noted in chapter 5 for its excellent coverage of congressional series, CIS Congressional Universe enables one to access the FR by keyword, agency, dates, and type of action (proposed rule, interim rule, final rule, and so forth). Moreover, the CFR is searchable in the same way with Congressional Universe and Academic Universe. Because many of these sources have features that immediately incorporate the final rules and regulations published in the quotidian FR into the appropriate titles and sections of the CFR, the latter is, in effect, being updated daily. In addition, the *Register* is available on DIALOG, which furnishes the full text daily and "Federal Register Abstracts" weekly.

CD-ROM Products

A number of full-text versions of the FR and CFR are available on compact disk. The following is a selection.

- Solutions Software Corporation (Enterprise, FL) publishes the full text of both the FR and CFR on CD-ROM, the former monthly and the latter quarterly. The information is obtained from the GPO Access Web site.

- Counterpoint Publishing (Cambridge, MA) produces the latest six months of the FR on a weekly schedule. The company also issues the CFR monthly.

- The Dialog Corporation (Mountain View, CA) issues the FR on DIALOG ONDISC monthly.

- FastSearch Corporation (Minneapolis, MN) publishes the FR quarterly and the full text of the CFR.

- Management Concepts, Inc. (Vienna, VA) issues the FR quarterly.

- National Technical Information Service (Springfield, VA) issues the CFR on CD-ROM with quarterly updates.

- West Group (Eagan, MN) publishes the CFR on LawDesk, one disk updated monthly; and the CFR with two disks updated monthly. Hypertext links to other West publications are a feature of the latter.

To keep track of this volatile publishing scene, consult the current edition of *CD-ROMs in Print* (Farmington Hills, MI: Gale Group).

Internet Sites

There are several free Web sites that house the full text of either the FR, the CFR, or both databases. As usual, the better part of wisdom is to access the site of a bona fide government agency authorized to mount these publications, such as the GPO; the entity that serves as the provenance of the information, for example, OFR; or a secondary sponsor, such as a GPO Access Gateway, which is obligated to serve as a link to the primary sources. An impeccable imprimatur is the safest way to navigate the Web for legal documents.

In addition to GPO Access, the Office of the Federal Register itself, a component of the National Archives and Records Administration, furnishes access to the FR and CFR. The latter is searchable by keyword for current information, by citation to title and section for current or historical data, by using the *LSA—List of CFR Sections Affected,* and by accessing the "Parallel Table of Authorities and Rules," which is extracted from the latest annual revision of the *CFR Index and Finding Aids* volume (**http://www.access.gpo.gov/nara**). The House of Representatives Internet Law Library (**http://law.house.gov**) provides a link to the NARA Web site. Access to the CFR via the Legal Information Institute (LII) at Cornell University (**http://www4.law.cornell.edu/cfr**) is generated from and links to the official Government Printing Office version. Many other legal Web sites (some of which are noted in chapter 8) have links to the FR and CFR.

Selected regulations are issued by many departments or agencies. Examples include the *Federal Acquisition Regulation* (FAR) (**http://www. gsa.gov.far**); the *Federal Resources Management Regulation* (FRMR) (**http://www.govcon.com**), a free site supported by advertising; a number of agencies within the Labor Department (**http://www.dol.gov**); and the Postal Rate Commission, which supplies *Federal Register* Notices (**http://www.prc.gov**). Selected *Federal Register* documents, such as those of the Environmental Protection Agency, Federal

Highway Administration, and Social Security Administration, are accessible on the Federal Bulletin Board File Libraries via GPO Access (**http://fedbbs.access.gpo.gov**), but this last is an unsystematic and haphazard way to locate rules and regulations.

Print and Microfiche Sources

For commercial access, selected regulations are published in the monthly issues of *United States Code Congressional and Administrative News* (USCCAN) and in the *Advance Service of the United States Code Service* (U.S.C.A.). Congressional Information Service publishes the weekly *CIS Federal Register Index* (1984 to the present), which has a more sophisticated, detailed, and timely index than the *Register*'s own official monthly index. This product is not as useful as it was before the FR became available in electronic formats. The company's *Index to the Code of Federal Regulations* is updated quarterly and, like the weekly product, is superior to the annual *CFR Index and Finding Aids* volume issued by the Office of the Federal Register. Congressional Information Service also contains the full text of both the FR and the CFR on microfiche since their inception in 1936 and 1938, respectively. The *Federal Regulatory Directory,* a publication of Congressional Quarterly, Inc., is revised periodically and profiles in detail more than 100 agencies that have regulatory functions. The *Directory* also includes organization charts, explanations of hearings procedures, and lists of congressional committees with jurisdiction over regulatory matters.

SHEPARD'S CFR CITATIONS

In *Shepard's Code of Federal Regulations Citations,* the CFR is the cited source. The citing sources include the United States Supreme Court, the lower federal courts, state courts in cases reported in units of the National Reporter System, A.L.R. "Annotations," and selected legal periodicals. A value-added feature is the insertion of symbols showing whether the citing source included or failed to include the date of the cited CFR regulation. A triangle symbol indicates failure to include the date, a regrettable oversight considering its importance; and that the correct date was inserted by the editors. An asterisk indicates that the citing source properly included the date. For example, when 42 CFR § 53.111 was cited at 458 F.2d 1117△1972, you know that the appeals court did not include the date. Conversely, when the same title and section of the CFR was cited at 359 FS 911*1973, the asterisk indicates that the district court remembered to include the year the cited source was used in the opinion.

UPDATING THE CFR

With the ease of updating the *Federal Register* online, the methods of keeping the print edition current by contrast appear clumsy and time consuming. To update the CFR, some or all of the following steps may be taken:

1. To locate the title and part/section one is updating, consult the unnumbered *CFR Index and Finding Aids* volume. Revised annually as of January 1, it affords subject access to the CFR volumes. Some CFR titles have their own index, and these titles are noted in the contents page of the volume. The index is an alphabetical arrangement of subjects and agency names. There is also a "Parallel Table of Authorities and Rules," which lists sections of the *United States Code, Statutes at Large,* and numbered public (slip) laws with reference to the appropriate CFR titles and parts. This table is updated in a section of the *LSA—List of CFR Sections Affected* (below).

2. Because of the quarterly publishing schedule of titles, references in the *CFR Index and Finding Aids* include material in the basic CFR volumes as well as amendatory information promulgated in the FR through January 1 but not yet incorporated into the CFR issues. Therefore, researchers should consult a separate publication titled *LSA—List of CFR Sections Affected.* There is no single annual issue of the *LSA—List.* Cumulated monthly, the December, March, June, and September *LSA—List* provides an annual cross-reference for those CFR titles listed on the covers, and these issues must be saved. Organized by CFR titles, chapters, parts, and sections, the *LSA—List* references the page numbers of the FR where amendatory information is announced. The absence of any reference to a title and section means that the rule published in the CFR has not been changed. The page numbers listed to the right of each entry indicate where the specific amendments begin in the *Federal Register.* Boldface page numbers under a particular title show that the

numbers span two years and that device is used to distinguish the previous year from the current year. On October 16, 1998, the *LSA—List* was made available on GPO Access (**http://www.gpo.gov/nara/index.html**). The online LSA service includes the capability to search or browse each monthly publication from 1997 to the present and download documents in either ASCII or Adobe's Portable Document Format (PDF). The page numbers listed to the right of each LSA entry indicate where the specific amendments begin in the FR. These page numbers can be "copied-and-pasted" into the "Retrieve a Federal Register page" in PDF format to access the amendatory actions. In the PDF version, which matches the printed version, the boldface numbers, noted above, show the two-year span. The last two digits of the applicable year, separated from the FR page number by a hyphen, are used in the ASCII text version of the Internet *LSA—List*. When using the "retrieve" feature, the first two digits aid in determining the year to select and require the user to "copy-and-paste" only the page number to receive the appropriate FR page.

3. To complete the updating to the most current issue of the *Federal Register*, consult:

   a. "CFR Parts Affected During [Month]." Located in the Reader Aids section at the back of each daily issue of the FR, this cumulative table also provides references from the CFR titles and parts/sections to *Federal Register* page numbers.

   b. "CFR Parts Affected in This Issue" appears in the front of the daily FR and completes the updating information. This parallel table is similarly arranged.

Figure 7.1, page 234, shows a typical *LSA—List*. An illustration of "CFR Parts Affected During [Month]" is shown in Figure 7.2, page 235. An example of "CFR Parts Affected in This Issue" appears in Figure 7.3, page 236.

(Text continues on page 237.)

Figure 7.1. Page from *LSA—List of CFR Sections Affected.*

TITLE 21—FOOD AND DRUGS

Chapter I—Food and Drug Administration, Department of Health, Education, and Welfare

2.125	(e)(6) added	30334
5.30	(d) revised	62281

List of CFR Sections Affected

	Page
882 Added	51730–51778
895 Added	29221
1000.16 (c) and (d) suspended	44844
Redesignated as 1020.30 (p) and revised	49670, 49671
1002.61 (a)(4) revised; eff. 5–7–80	65357
Technical correction	67655
1010.4 (c) revised	48191
1020.30 (a)(1)(i), (h)(2)(i), (4) introductory text and (i) and (k) revised; (b)(21) amended; (b)(55) added	29654
(b)(3), (d) introductory text, and (e)(2) revised; (p) redesignated from 1000.16 and revised; (b)(56), (57), (d)(3), (e)(3), and (q) added	49671
(m)(1) revised; eff. 12–1–80	68822
1020.31 (g)(1) revised	29654
1020.32 (b)(2)(iv) revised	29654
1040.20 Added; eff. 5–7–80	65357
Technical correction	67655
1040.30 Added; eff. in part 9–7–81	52195
1220.40 (a) revised	30335

Chapter II—Drug Enforcement Administration, Department of Justice

1308.13 (e) introductory text revised	40888
1308.14 (b) introductory text revised	40888
1308.15 (b) introductory text revised	40888
1308.24 (i) table amended	27981
1316.65 (b) revised	42179
(b) and (c) revised	55332
1316.66 Redesignated as 1316.67 and revised; new 1316.66 added	42179
Revised	55332
1316.67 Redesignated as 1316.68; new 1316.67 redesignated from 1316.66 and revised	42179
Amended	55332
1316.68 Redesignated from 1316.67	42179
1316.75 Nomenclature change	

Figure 7.2. Page from "CFR Parts Affected During [Month]."

CFR PARTS AFFECTED DURING DECEMBER

At the end of each month, the Office of the Federal Register publishes separately a list of CFR Sections Affected (LSA), which lists parts and sections affected by documents published since the revision date of each title.

1 CFR
445.........................77127
480.........................74791
490.........................75392

3 CFR

Administrative Orders:

Memorandums:
December 11, 1979........71809
December 14, 1979........74781

Executive Orders:
11223 (Amended by EO 12178).......71807
11322 (Revoked by EO 12183).......74787
11419 (Revoked by EO 12183).......74787
11888 (Amended by EO 12180, 12181).....72077, 72083
11978 (Revoked by EO 12183).......74787
12103 (Amended by EO 12176).......70705
12153 (Amended by EO 12186).......76477
12173.........................69271
12174.........................69609
12175.........................70703
12176.........................70705
12177.........................71805
12178.........................71807
12179.........................71811
12180.........................72077
12181.........................72083
12182.........................72083
12183.........................74785
12183.........................74787
12184.........................75091
12185.........................75093
12186.........................76477

Proclamations:
4705.........................70701
4706.........................71399
4707.........................72348
4708.........................72069
4709.........................74789

Reorganization Plans:
No. 3 of 1979.......69273

Presidential Determinations:
No. 80-8 of December 18, 1979.......77125

4 CFR
6.........................70115
420.........................73001

5 CFR
Ch. I.........................76747
212.........................75615
213.......69611, 70449, 72569, 75615, 77127
214.........................75615
315.........................72569
317.........................75615
737.........................72570
771.........................77127
831.........................76748
870.........................76748
871.......70449, 76748
871.........................76748
890.........................76748
891.........................75914
1250.........................75914
1251.........................75914
1252.........................75914
1253.........................75914
1254.........................75914
1255.........................75914
1256.........................75914
1257.........................75914
1258.........................75914
1259.........................75914
1260.........................75914
1261.........................75914
1262.........................75914
1263.........................75914
1264.........................75914

★ ★ ★ ★ ★

Proposed Rules:
Ch. I.........................69304
229.........................75399
230.........................70349
231.........................72604
239.........................75399
240.........................75399
241.......70189, 72604
249.........................75399

18 CFR
1.......69284, 77155
2.......69935, 71821, 75383, 76482
4.......69642, 69935, 76482, 75383
271.......69642, 69935, 76482, 76778
274.........................76778
284.......69642, 75383
701.........................72583
707.........................69921
713.........................72892

Proposed Rules:
Ch. I.........................70752
35.........................70752
46.........................71428
58.........................70189
280.........................73121
282.........................77198
284.........................73121
292.........................69978

19 CFR
4.........................70458
159.......70138, 75135
171.........................70459
201.........................76458
207.........................76458

Proposed Rules:
4.........................75685
6.........................73122
144.........................75685
151.........................75685
159.........................75685

20 CFR
404.........................73018
676.........................72584

Proposed Rules:
Ch. III.........................72728

21 CFR
Ch. I.........................72585

Proposed Rules:
5.........................75628
10.........................70459
12.........................70459
13.........................70459
14.........................70459
15.........................70459
16.........................70459
176.........................75627
177.........................74816
178.........................69649
201.........................74817
202.........................74817
510.......71412, 74818, 76779
520.......71412, 72586, 74818
522.......71412, 76780
526.........................71412
529.........................72587
548.......69642, 69650
558.......71412, 74819, 76779
701.........................75627
820.........................75627
1000.........................71728
1308.........................71822

Proposed Rules:
Ch. I.......71428, 72728, 75990
25.........................71742
58.........................69666
70.........................75659
131.......69668, 69669, 72613
170.........................75662
182.........................74845
184.........................74845
320.........................69666
333.........................71428
357.........................75666
438.........................69768
452.........................69670
660.........................76811
868.......69673, 70486

22 CFR
42.........................72108

23 CFR
170.........................75552
172.........................75552
420.........................75552
620.........................75552
650.........................72109
713.........................73018

Proposed Rules:
630.........................70191
656.........................70753

Figure 7.3. Page from "CRF Parts Affected in This Issue."

CFR PARTS AFFECTED IN THIS ISSUE

A cumulative list of the parts affected this month can be found in the Reader Aids section at the end of this issue.

7 CFR
53	45320
1464	45115
1806	45115

10 CFR
212	45352

Proposed Rules:
903	45141

12 CFR
201	45115
545	45116

Proposed Rules:
226	45141
509	45175
509a	45175
550	45175
566	45175

13 CFR
107	45120
108	45123

16 CFR
Proposed Rules:
Ch. I	45178
13	45181

17 CFR
Proposed Rules:
1	45192

19 CFR
Proposed Rules:
Ch. I	45333

24 CFR
Proposed Rules:
Subtitle A	45342
Subtitle B	45342

26 CFR
Proposed Rules:
1	45192
601	45192

27 CFR
Proposed Rules:
Ch. I	45326
6	45298
8	45298
10	45298
11	45298

81	45210
162	45218

43 CFR
Public Land Orders:
5675	45133
5676	45133

44 CFR
64	45133
65 (2 documents)	45136, 45137

Proposed Rules:
67 (6 documents)	45225–45227

45 CFR
302	45137

47 CFR
Proposed Rules:
15	45227

50 CFR
32	45137

Proposed Rules:
652	45227

This updating activity can be consummated with a few strokes of the keyboard in a typical online service because the FR cites to the CFR when either a proposed or a final rule is promulgated. Moreover, a "current" issue of the FR in print format is necessarily several days late owing to the Postal Service's ineluctable use of "snail mail."

Page/Date Conversion Tables

The *Federal Register Index* includes at the end of each cumulative monthly issue a parallel table referencing the inclusive page numbers to the date of the daily issue. In addition, the *LSA—List* has a similar "Table of Federal Register Issue Pages and Dates." Moreover, every issue of the FR, in the "Reader Aids" section, has a cumulative "Federal Register Pages and Dates" listing updated daily.

SPECIFICITY AND LANGUAGE

If God is in the details, then the *Code of Federal Regulations,* and especially the *Federal Register,* are leading candidates for secular deification. The user who first makes contact with these publications is fascinated and often appalled by the degree of detail found in the texts. Numerous examples demonstrate this attention to detail. Scan virtually any part and section of Title 21, the Food and Drug Administration (FDA), Department of Health and Human Services, and one will encounter instructions written as precisely as the shimmering ambiguities of the English language allow. For example, 21 CFR § 145.170 regulates the contents of canned peaches. Under § 145.170(a)(4)(iii) one finds that

> Whenever the names of the fruit juices used [to flavor a can of peaches] do not appear in the name of the packing medium as provided in paragraph (a)(4)(ii)(b) of this section, such names and the words "from concentrate" as specified in paragraph (a)(4)(ii)(c) of this section shall appear in an ingredient statement pursuant to the requirements of § 101.3(d) of this chapter.

In the same title, a portion of the requirements for sweet chocolate, found at 21 CFR 163.123(a), requires that the finished product contain

> not less than 15 percent by weight of chocolate liquor calculated by subtracting from the weight . . . of chocolate liquor used the weight of cacao fat therein and the weights therein of alkali and seasoning ingredients, if any, multiplying the remainder by 2.2, dividing the result by the weight of the finished sweet chocolate, and multiplying the quotient by 100.

Efforts to make the FR a document that readers with a lesser IQ than Marilyn vos Savant can fathom seem to have taken on a permanent cast. In 1975, former Director of the Office of the Federal Register Fred Emery issued a *Document Drafting Handbook* in an attempt to assist agencies in improving the clarity of regulatory documents. It contains guidance to help officials create and submit documents that comply with OFR publication requirements and provides numerous examples illustrating common situations and solutions. Now in its October 1998 revision, the *Handbook* furnishes a list of words and phrases devoutly to be eschewed: aforementioned, hereby, provided that, wheresoever, to wit, shall be deemed to be, sole and exclusive, unless and until, null and void, authorized and empowered, may be treated as, hereinafter, and so on. Presidents have attempted to get the agencies to write lucid prose. Jimmy Carter issued EO 12044 (March 23, 1978), which established in Section 1 a policy that "Regulations shall be as simple and clear as possible." On September 30, 1993, William Jefferson Clinton promulgated Executive Order 12866, one of the purposes of which was to make the rulemaking process more accessible and open to the public. On June 1, 1998, Clinton issued a ukase in the form of a Memorandum for the Heads of Executive Departments and Agencies titled "Plain Language in Government Writing." Acting in his role as Schoolmarm-in-Chief, the president averred that "plain language documents [should] have logical organization, easy-to-read design features and use common, everyday words, except for necessary technical terms; 'you' and other pronouns; the active voice; and short sentences." The president directed the bureaucracy to "use plain language in all proposed and final rulemaking documents published in the *Federal Register*" by January 1, 1999, and ordered the Director of the Office of Management and Budget to publish this memorandum in the *Federal Register*.[12]

Shortly thereafter a note appeared on the home page of the Office of the Federal Register offering guidance in "How to Write Plain Language Documents." Among the links were the vice-president's message titled "How to Comply with the President's Memo on Plain Language," a document from the National Performance Review (NPR), Vice-President Gore's initiative "to create a government that works better and costs less."[13] Publications such as *Making Regulations Readable, Drafting Legal Documents,* and the *Federal Register Thesaurus of Indexing Terms,* issued by the Office of the Federal Register; and the classic Strunk and White's *Elements of Style* and other style manuals and grammar guides on the OFR Web site are weapons in the battle against obfuscatory bureaucratese (**http://www.nara.gov/fedreg/plainlan. html**). Still, regulatory activities engender a perennial litany of complaints by companies and corporations: Compliance is costly and outweighs the benefits provided by the rule; some regulations are unreasonable, rigid, or inflexible; paperwork is excessive and too expensive; compliance affects adversely a company's competitiveness; penalties for noncompliance are too severe; and so forth.[14]

THE REGULATORY DILEMMA

There are dozens of agencies within the executive branch that have regulatory authority; in addition, there are more than fifty independent establishments with regulatory power. The distinction is sometimes one of academic punctilio, although the listing in the "Contents" pages of every edition of the *United States Government Manual* will suffice. Although the *Manual* includes government corporations interfiled among the independent entities, it is easy enough to distinguish between the Tennessee Valley Authority, a government corporation, and the Equal Employment Opportunity Commission, an independent agency. It is also useful to identify those independent establishments that perform significant regulatory functions including (but not limited to) the Federal Reserve System, Federal Trade Commission, Federal Communications Commission, National Labor Relations Board, Environmental Protection Agency, Securities and Exchange Commission, and Nuclear Regulatory Commission.

The phrase "independent agency" is somewhat misleading; independence is a relative term. The governing boards of independent agencies are appointed by the president with the advice and consent of the Senate for staggered terms in odd-numbered years that do not coincide with congressional or presidential elections. Moreover, these entities possess what are called quasi-executive, quasi-legislative, and quasi-judicial power. They plan and execute decisions relatively independent of a president's direction. They write regulations largely independent of Congress, which defers to their putative expertise. And they are empowered to render decisions independent of the Article III courts. Checks and balances, however, are inherent in the mandate of independent regulatory bodies. Their degree of independence is circumscribed by a president's appointive power and by the Senate's advice and consent function, by Congress's power of the purse, and by the courts' power of judicial review. No independent establishment can be wholly free from the political dialectic.

Another problem involves oversight. Syndicated columnist and economic guru Jane Bryant Quinn gives this example using tax law:

> As night follows day, regulations follow tax law. . . . Congress smiles in the spotlight when it passes a new tax break. Then it tosses the nascent law to the IRS and says, "Make it work." The IRS, laboring in the fog, has to produce an enforceable rule. Presto! More paperwork, new tax forms and regs that nobody understands. For this, the Congress will ritually bash the IRS, although Congress was the prime mover of the mess.[15]

Substitute any regulation for "tax" and any regulatory agency for "IRS" and you have an apposite generalization. After Congress passes a law requiring the writing of regulations to make the law "work," the bureaucracy begins writing regulations. In theory there are the checks and balances mentioned above, but the reality is not so tidy. If Congress does not exercise oversight, who does? Hence the relevance of the quote by the Roman poet Juvenal at the beginning of this chapter: Quis custodiet ipsos custodes?—Who will watch the watchers? One sure way to reduce the corpulent, distended FR is for Congress to pass fewer laws and to provide oversight for those that are enacted.

While regulation takes center stage most of the time, its opposite, deregulation, has had its ups and downs. During the Reagan Administration, for example, the rush to deregulate resulted in the elimination of thousands of rules deemed burdensome to the private sector, but the total annual pages during President Reagan's tenure still hovered around the 50,000 mark. During the Bush and Clinton administrations the number of pages ballooned to an average of 70,000. The relative brevity of statutory law implies a larger, more protracted role for the executive and independent agencies that must implement the congressional mandate. The Food and Drug Administration is well aware that a container of peaches with incorrect ingredients improperly labeled, when ingested with unpleasant consequences for the consumer, can precipitate a lawsuit with astonishing celerity. Much as business and industry detest these fastidious regulations, they protect both consumers and producers alike. Moreover, the government has a responsibility to balance the public interest with the economic interests of the business community. Rules that are inflexible or even irrational can be removed without eviscerating government's ability to safeguard the public. But with the degree of specificity that inheres in regulatory writing, is it any wonder that the *Federal Register* is such a bloated work and that many individual titles of the *Code of Federal Regulations* themselves are multivolumed?

ADMINISTRATIVE DECISIONS

Reports, decisions, letter rulings, orders, and advisory opinions of regulatory agencies with quasi-judicial authority are published in sources other than the *Federal Register* and the *Code of Federal Regulations*.[16] Tribunals within the agencies adjudicate disputes resulting from the construction of statutes or the regulations pursuant thereto. Boards of review, hearing examiners, or administrative law judges interpret and enforce administrative rulings, and decisions rendered in this context are subject to review by the courts. The publications of these determinations are found in official GPO documents, commercial looseleaf reporters, CD-ROMs, and online in services such as LEXIS-NEXIS and WESTLAW. Commercial sources, print or electronic, are superior to official government publications, which are often poorly indexed and rarely if ever published in a timely manner. However, a growing number of Internet sites maintained by federal government agencies contain administrative orders and decisions, and these records may enjoy greater currency than their comparable print editions. Moreover, in *Shepard's United States Administrative Citations,* the cited sources are decisions and orders of departments and agencies and the citing sources are the United States Supreme Court and the lower federal courts; all state reports; all units of the National Reporter System; A.L.R. "Annotations"; legal periodicals; and other decisions and reports of departments, agencies, independent agencies, and boards as reported in series such as *Public Utility Reports* and *Federal Securities Law Reporter.* In addition, there are parallel citation tables to and from reports or digests of the same decision and orders as reported in the various administrative law commercial or official series.

Some compilations or series of decisions rendered by agencies and published in official government documents are available to depository libraries. Examples include *Agriculture Decisions,* issued semiannually; the biweekly *FCC Record* (1986 to the present), which continues the earlier Federal Communications Commission *Reports,* lst and 2d series; the bound volumes of the *Decisions of the Federal Trade Commission;* the *Decisions and Orders of the National Labor Relations Board;* the *ALJ Decisions of the Occupational Safety and Health Review Commission;* the irregularly issued *Rulings* series of the Social Security Administration, which became an independent agency in 1994,[17] covering old age, survivors, disability, supplemental security income, and black lung benefits; the irregularly issued *Rulings* of the Health Care Financing Administration on Medicare, Medicaid, professional standards review, and related matters; and the *Opinions of the Office of Legal Counsel* of the Justice Department. The Interstate Commerce Commission *Reports,* lst and 2d series, are available, but the ICC was abolished in 1995 (109 Stat. 932), and many of its functions were transferred to the newly created Surface Transportation Board within the Department of Transportation. In addition to lacking timely publication and distribution, these decrees are without the value-added editorial enhancements supplied by commercial publishers.

The databases of WESTLAW and LEXIS-NEXIS are perhaps the best sources to locate these decisions and related pronouncements. These specialized files include the administrative decisions of the Comptroller General, Federal Communications Commission, Federal Trade Commission, defunct Interstate Commerce Commission, Internal Revenue Service, National Labor Relations Board, Occupational Safety and Health Review Commission, Securities and Exchange Commission, and many more.

NOTES

1. *Panama Refining Company v. Ryan,* 293 U.S. 388 (1935). See also Ernest Gellhorn, *Administrative Law and Process in a Nutshell* (St. Paul, MN: West, 1972), pp. 16–18.

2. Benjamin W. Mintz and Nancy G. Miller, *A Guide to Federal Agency Rulemaking,* 2d ed. (Washington: Administrative Conference of the United States, 1991), pp. 3, 45.

3. U.S. General Accounting Office, *Federal Rulemaking: Agencies Often Published Final Actions Without Proposed Rules* (GAO/GGD-98-126), August 31, 1998, pp. 1–2.

4. 63 *Federal Register* 3835 (January 27,1998).

5. *Administrative Notes* 14:4 (January 15, 1993).

6. Mintz and Miller, *Guide to Federal Agency Rulemaking,* pp. 107–8, 111.

7. U.S. General Accounting Office, *Regulatory Reform: Agencies' Section 610 Review Notices Often Did Not Meet Statutory Requirements* (GAO/T-GGD-98-64), February 12, 1998, pp. 1–3.

8. U.S. General Accounting Office, *Congressional Review Act: Update on Implementation and Coordination* (GAO/T-OGC-98-55), June 17, 1998, pp. 1, 2.

9. 55 *Federal Register* 59236-44 (December 14, 1992).

10. 50 CFR 17.11. The one-liner adds, in alphabetical order, the Karner blue butterfly to the List of Endangered and Threatened Wildlife under "INSECTS."

11. 5 U.S.C. § 553(b)(B).

12. Office of the Press Secretary, The White House, Memorandum for the Heads of Executive Departments and Agencies, "Plain Language in Government Writing," June 1, 1998, pp. 1–2. Published at 63 FR 31883 (June 10, 1998).

13. *From Red Tape to Results: Creating a Government That Works Better & Costs Less* (PRVP 42.2:G74), September 10, 1993, p. i.

14. U.S. General Accounting Office, *Regulatory Burden: Measurement Challenges and Concerns Raised by Selected Companies* (GAO/GGD-97-2), November 1996, pp. 58–59.

15. *Albany [New York] Times Union,* November 15, 1998, p. C1.

16. See Veronica Maclay, "Selected Sources of United States Agency Decisions," *Government Publications Review* 16: 271–301 (May/June 1989).

17. The Social Security Independence and Program Improvements Act of 1994, PL 103-296, 108 Stat. 1464 (August 15, 1994).

CHAPTER EIGHT

LEGAL INFORMATION SOURCES

I am not aware that any nation of the globe has hith-
erto organized a judicial power in the same manner as
the Americans. The judicial organization of the
United States is the institution which a stranger has
the greatest difficulty understanding.

—Alexis de Tocqueville

As a litigant I should dread a lawsuit beyond almost
anything else short of sickness and death.

—Judge Learned Hand

INTRODUCTION

Article III of the United States Constitution and the Judiciary Act of
1789 (chapter 20, 1 Stat. 73) established the framework for the federal
judiciary. The judicial branch of the federal establishment forms a pyramid. At the bottom of that pyramid stand the U.S. district, or trial,
courts. The middle level comprises the appellate courts, and the highest
court is at the apex. There are more than ninety district courts. The
appellate system comprises eleven numbered regional circuit courts of
appeal, a twelfth circuit for the District of Columbia, and the Court of
Appeals for the Federal Circuit. The United States Supreme Court is the
only court explicitly mentioned in the Constitution. In addition, special
courts have been established by Congress from time to time to deal with
particular types of cases. Among these are the United States Tax Court,
Court of International Trade, Court of Federal Claims, and Court of
Veterans Appeals. Another special court is the United States Court of
Appeals for the Armed Forces (CAAF), which receives and reviews deci-
sions of the Army, Navy-Marine Corps, Air Force, and Coast Guard
Courts of Criminal Appeals. The former was called the United States
Court of Military Appeals (COMA), while the lower court was formerly

named the Army, Navy-Marine Corps, Air Force and Coast Guard Courts of Military Review. Given the unfortunate acronym, the name change of the highest court in the Uniform Code of Military Justice (UCMJ) system was foreordained. Figure 8.1 shows the structure of the federal court system.

The fact that Congress has empowered certain executive branch and independent agencies with quasi-judicial authority complicates the court structure. The decisions rendered by the tribunals of these administrative units, if appealed, may be reviewed by the district courts or may go directly to the courts of appeals. An explanation of the federal court system is found in a useful brochure issued by the Administrative Office of the United States Courts, *The United States Courts: Their Jurisdiction and Work,* revised periodically. The business of the federal courts is discussed in the Administrative Office of the U.S. Courts *Annual Report of the Director.* The Federal Judiciary home page on the Internet (**http://www.uscourts.gov**) contains much useful information about federal judges, filing a case, juror information, the Judicial Conference of the United States, and job openings in federal courts.

There are also, of course, state courts that have general, unlimited power to decide almost every type of case, subject only to the limitations of state law. The courts located in every city, town, and county are the institutions with which citizens most often have contact. The federal courts, on the other hand, have power to decide only those cases in which the Constitution gives them authority. Article III of the federal Constitution is the soul of brevity, within a document that is nothing if not succinct. Section 1 states that "the judicial Power of the United States, shall be vested in one supreme Court, and in such inferior Courts as the Congress may from time to time ordain and establish." The Congress has indeed from time to time established and abolished various other federal courts. For more extensive background, see Erwin C. Surrency, *History of the Federal Courts* (New York: Oceana, 1987).

Although convention has it that courts cannot be called upon to exercise legislative power, the fact is that "judge-made" law is commonplace where constitutional interpretation is necessary or where provisions of statutes are ambiguous. One cannot determine the meaning of statutes without referring to the cases that interpret them. Congress is often apprehensive that the courts, in explicating the provisions of a statute, will usurp the legislative authority. Yet it is historical fact that the legislative branch has on many an occasion written deliberately equivocal measures, thus forcing courts to perform a legislative function. However, over the decades no consistent approach to statutory construction has informed the courts' deliberations.

Figure 8.1. The United States court system.

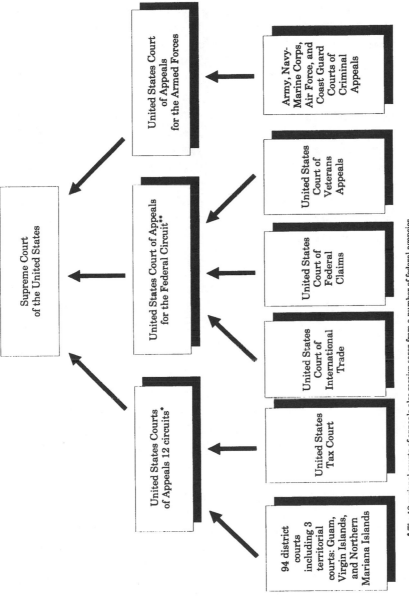

* The 12 regional courts of appeals also receive cases from a number of federal agencies.

** The Court of Appeals for the Federal Circuit also receives cases from the International Trade Commission, the Merit Systems Protection Board, the Patent and Trademark Office, and the Board of Contract Appeals.

Even though federal judges and justices are appointed by the president with the advice and consent of the Senate, their independence is assured by the Constitution. Federal judges hold their positions "during good Behaviour" and can be removed from office against their will only by impeachment. Independence is further ensured by compensation that "shall not be diminished during their Continuance in Office"; that is, neither a president nor the Congress can reduce the salary of a federal magistrate.

Although independence and a concomitant ideal of integrity theoretically characterize the federal judiciary, selection is largely a political process. By tradition, senators of the president's party have the prerogative of naming persons for federal judgeships within their states. Judicial appointment is a powerful patronage lever for an incumbent president. According to famed trial lawyer Vincent Bugliosi, "federal judges, who are appointed for life, are even more insufferably pompous than their state counterparts." In his experience, the "typical judge either has no or very scant trial experience as a lawyer, or has to be educated on the law by the lawyers on both sides, or is pompous and dictatorial on the bench, or worst of all, is clearly partial to one side or the other in the lawsuit."[1]

At the U.S. Supreme Court level, questions regarding a person's qualifications, background, and views are often best discovered by reading—in addition to opinions or other writings by the candidate—the transcript of the nominations hearings held before the Senate Judiciary Committee and distributed by the Government Printing Office in print or via GPO Access. Beguiled by the televising of these hearings, members of this committee and special interest groups have often transformed this crucial part of the nominating process into disingenuous political theater.

THE LEGAL PUBLISHING LANDSCAPE

As a result of several significant mergers and consolidations over the last decades of the twentieth century and ongoing, the legal publishing industry is now under the control of three major companies. The Thomson Financial & Professional Publishing Group, a Canadian conglomerate; Reed Elsevier PLC, an Anglo-Dutch corporation; and Wolters Kluwer, a Dutch firm, bestride the market like colossi. Some of the larger mergers include the following: Thomson purchased the Lawyers Cooperative Publishing company (LCP) in 1989; the Research Institute of America (now called the RIA Group) in the same year; and the West Publishing Company (now called the West Group) in 1996. Reed

Elsevier purchased Congressional Information Service (CIS) in 1979, which is now an affiliate of LEXIS-NEXIS; Martindale-Hubbell in 1990; LEXIS-NEXIS and Michie in 1994; and Matthew Bender and Shepard's in 1998. Wolters Kluwer owns Commerce Clearing House (CCH Incorporated), which it bought in 1995; Aspen Publishers, Inc., including Aspen Law and Business; and Wiley Law Publications, which has been merged with Aspen Law and Business.

In addition, Reed Elsevier acquired more than fifty titles divested by the Thomson Corporation to avoid antitrust action and created a new organization called LEXIS Law Publishing, "which combines the books and CD-ROMs published under the Michie imprint with the United States Code Service, United States Supreme Court Reporter, Lawyers' Edition, and the other acquired titles. Headquartered in Charlottesville, Virginia, LEXIS Law Publishing now provides annotated code services for 35 states and territories, the Law on Disc CD-ROM research system, more than 700 national and state practice publications, and the Shepard's line of citator products."[2] The West Group has a listserv that supplies law librarians and other interested parties with notifications by e-mail of enhancements and changes to customer service offerings and product information. The form for subscribing is located at **http://www. westgroup.com/custserv/servicenews.htm**.

There are, of course, still a smattering of independent publishers such as the Bureau of National Affairs (BNA), but this situation can change from day to day. The best way to keep track of these mergers and acquisitions is to access "A Legal Publishers' List: Corporate Affiliations of Legal Publishers," the University of Colorado Law Library Technical Services home page, compiled and maintained by Rob Richards, University of Colorado law librarian (**http://www.colorado.edu/law/ lawlib/ts/legpub.htm**). Richards updates the information continually. For the sake of sanity, I will refer to the above publishers by their popular names (for example, West Group or, simply, West; Shepard's; LEXIS Law Publishing) or their acronyms, and the reader can consult Richards's Web site for current information on the ever-changing mergers and acquisitions scene.

The fact that Thomson now owns both the West Group and its former main competitor, LCP, is disconcerting. Many librarians and smaller legal publishers fear that this will result in increased prices for legal materials that place a burden on the budget of law libraries and other subscribers. Under the provisions of 38 Stat. 717, as amended (15 U.S.C. §§ 41–58), guidelines for regulating the law book industry are found at 16 CFR Part 256.

REFERENCE AND RESEARCH AIDS

The scope of legal reference and bibliography is vast and seemingly complex. But the bibliographic apparatus adheres to a logic and symmetry not evident in other areas of government publications. Indeed, the list of sources is so specific and unique that library schools often offer a separate course in legal research, and law schools require students to acquire a degree of sophistication in the use of source material. What follows is intended merely to introduce the reader to some salient materials supportive of primary sources. The nature of publications in this field is such that a host of commercial material surrounds and amplifies a relatively small number of official government publications.

Basic Resources

Current print materials that serve as reference resources, guides, or textbooks include Robert C. Berring, *Finding the Law,* 10th ed. (St. Paul, MN: West, 1995); Edward J. Bander et al., *Searching the Law,* 2d ed. (Irvington, NY: Transnational Publishers, 1996); *The Basics of NEXIS for Graduate Schools of Library and Information Science* (Dayton, OH: Lexis-Nexis, 1996–97); Josh Blackman, *How to Use the Internet for Legal Research* (New York: Find/SVP, 1996); Morris L. Cohen and Kent C. Olson, *Legal Research in a Nutshell,* 6th ed. (Eagan, MN: West, 1996); Theodore Herman, *How to Research Less and Find More: The Essential Guide to Computer-Assisted Legal Research* (Eagan, MN: West, 1996); J. Clark Kelso, *Studying Law: An Introduction to Legal Research* (New York: Matthew Bender, 1995); J. S. McKnight, *The LEXIS Companion: A Complete Guide to Effective Searching* (Reading, MA: Addison-Wesley, 1995).

In addition, three books merit comment. Kent C. Olson's *Legal Information: How to Find It, How to Use It* (Phoenix, AZ: Oryx Press, 1998) takes an expansive view of the law, including its value in other disciplines. J. Myron Jacobstein, Roy M. Mersky, and Donald J. Dunn, in *Fundamentals of Legal Research,* 7th ed. (New York: Foundation Press, 1998), cover the United States and law in the United Kingdom. A paperbound abridgment of *Fundamentals* by the same authors is titled *Legal Research Illustrated,* 7th ed. (New York: Foundation Press, 1998).[3] Kendall F. Svengalis's *The Legal Information Buyer's Guide & Reference Manual, 1998–99* (Barrington, RI: Rhode Island Law Press) contains information on all major categories of legal publications, evaluative annotations of more than 1,000 legal treatises in fifty-four major subject areas; a list of primary source materials (codes, administrative regulations, cases, and so forth) with prices, for all states and the

District of Columbia; cost-saving strategies in the selection and purchase of legal materials; and a number of appendixes related to legal publishers, dealers, guides for the lawbook industry, looseleaf services, and the like. The introductory chapters on the legal publishing merger mania are superbly if distressingly informative. The author is the 1998 recipient of the prestigious American Association of Law Libraries Joseph L. Andrews Award for Legal Bibliography.

Citation Forms and Controversies

Print sources include *The Bluebook: A Uniform System of Citation* (16th ed., 1996), published by the Harvard Law Review Association and simply known as *The Bluebook*; a much smaller but quite useful competitor, *The University of Chicago Manual of Legal Citation* (Rochester, NY: Lawyers Cooperative/Bancroft-Whitney, 1989), known as the "Maroon Book"; and Mary Miles Prince, *Bieber's Dictionary of Legal Citations,* 5th ed. (Buffalo, NY: William S. Hein, 1997).

WESTLAW and LEXIS-NEXIS have devised citation systems for their respective cases reported online. For each service, the elements are virtually the same: name of case, document number, year of decision, database identifier (WL for WESTLAW, LEXIS for LEXIS-NEXIS), a unique identifying number, jurisdiction, and date of decision (for example, *Hyperlaw, Inc. v. West Publishing Co.,* No. 94 Civ. 0589, 1997 WL 266972 (S.D.N.Y. May 19, 1997) or *Hyperlaw, Inc. v. West Publishing Co.,* No. 94 Civ. 0589, 1997 US Dist. LEXIS 6915 (S.D.N.Y. May 19, 1997)). *The Bluebook* gives its seal of approval for the use of these headings; however, the LEXIS-NEXIS citation is retained whereas the WESTLAW citation may be dropped once the standard "print" citation appears in the appropriate unit of West's *National Reporter System.*

Universal Citation System

In the early 1990s, some law librarians, judges, and attorneys, becoming increasingly disaffected with the West Group's monopoly on citations that, opponents allege, keep the cost of legal research artificially high, conceived of a universal citation method, one that would be simple, vendor-neutral, medium-neutral, and in the public domain and would encompass both paper and electronic formats. Exercising leadership in this citation reform movement, the American Association of Law Libraries (AALL) published a *Universal Citation Guide* and by 1998 eleven states had adopted some form of vendor-and-medium-neutral citation form; the federal Judicial Conference has appointed a committee to study the matter. Moreover, the AALL Committee on Citation Formats issued a draft copy of its recommendations for a universal statutory citation that was published in the Winter 1998 issue of *Law Library Journal* (pp. 91–112), related to rules set forth in *The Bluebook*.

This is by no means a black-and-white issue. Each side makes cogent arguments for its position, but citation reform proponents must bear the burden of showing that a change is warranted and that the new system will serve the legal community better than the old. The several facets of this issue can be accessed at the AALL Web site (**http://www. aallnet.org**). These competing systems of citation are not to be confused with the function of citators, which are discussed below in the unit on Shepard's citations.

Copyright Issues

Two landmark U.S. Supreme Court copyright decisions enabled commercial publishers of case law to thrive in business. In the early nineteenth century, court reporters were compensated with the sale of official federal and state reports to the legal community and the general public. In *Wheaton v. Peters,* 33 U.S. 591 (1834), the High Court held that its court reporters could not claim copyright on the decisions they reported. Because this decision involved federal case law publishing, states dodged the ruling for a half century by "retaining the copyright to the court reports in the state itself. After all, they argued, the state is the people." This bit of casuistry was finally nullified by the Supreme Court in *Banks & Bros. v. Manchester,* 128 U.S. 244 (1888), which held that no state could copyright its reports, including the preparation of syllabi or other enhancements by its court reporters.[4] However, commercial publishers like the West Publishing Company would win copyright for their own editorial bells and whistles such as headnotes, indexes, tables, editorial commentary, and arrangement of cases by volume, abbreviation of reporter, and page.

So successful was John West, the founder of the famous publishing empire, that every jurisdiction in the federal court system requires citations to West's *Federal Supplement* (now in its second series) and *Federal Reporter* (now in its third series). Whenever a competitor has attempted to use without permission the internal pagination of the West reporters, the company has cried copyright infringement. But copyright law is driven by court decisions, and West may not prevail forever, as the following conflicting opinions reveal.

In June 1985, Mead Data Central (MDC), which at the time owned LEXIS online services (later to become LEXIS-NEXIS), announced a plan to include "star pagination" (the page breaks in the West case reporters) in the text of its court reports by October of that year. West has always contended that its arrangement of cases (for example, 650 F.Supp. 413 denotes volume 650 of West's *Federal Supplement* at page 413) is protected under the provisions of Title 17, United States Code, so it filed suit, claiming that MDC's intention constituted "an appropriation of West's comprehensive arrangement of case reports in violation of" copyright law. A U.S. District Court granted West's motion for preliminary injunction based upon "its determination that West would be able to show that its copyrighted arrangement included the number of pages in each volume." MDC appealed, but the Court of Appeals for the Eighth Circuit upheld the lower court's decision. The appellate court ruled that West's particular arrangement of legal decisions was entitled to copyright protection and that West would suffer irreparable harm from MDC's infringing action. Mead Data Central's petition for writ of certiorari was denied by the Supreme Court.[5] Before a trial on the merits commenced, the companies reached an out-of-court settlement under which MDC agreed to pay a multimillion dollar licensing fee to use West's pagination system in its LEXIS database.[6]

While the Supreme Court declined to hear *West v. Mead Data,* it did hear a dispute that aired similar issues. Rural Telephone Company is a public utility providing service to several communities in Kansas. In accordance with state regulations, it publishes a typical telephone directory consisting of white pages and yellow pages. Subscribers must supply their names and addresses to obtain phone service. Feist Publications, a company that specializes in publishing area-wide phone directories covering a larger geographic range than Rural Telephone, asked the utility to allow it to publish its white pages. When Rural refused, Feist went ahead and extracted the listings it needed without Rural's consent, whereupon Rural claimed copyright infringement. A U.S. District Court held that the white pages were copyrightable, and an appeals court affirmed. Certiorari was granted, but the Supreme Court, in a unanimous decision, reversed.

Justice Sandra Day O'Connor, writing for the Court, argued that the Constitution "mandates originality as a prerequisite for copyright protection," and "while Rural has a valid copyright in the directory as a whole because it contains some forward text and some original material in the yellow pages, there is nothing original in Rural's white pages." O'Connor addressed an error in some past decisions, where courts awarded copyright protection to factual compilations under a spurious theory that came to be known alternatively as "sweat of the brow" or "industrious collection," the notion that "copyright was a reward for the hard work that went into compiling facts." Rejecting this doctrine, the justices held that Rural's compilation of "uncopyrightable facts" did not merit protection.[7]

What might have significant precedential value is a 1997 decision by the U.S. District Court for the Southern District of New York, holding that many of West's value-added features, including its page numbering system, are not worthy of copyright protection. Involving Matthew Bender & Company and Hyperlaw, Inc., who manufacture and market compilations of judicial opinions stored on compact disks, as plaintiffs, the court held that excepting the headnotes, virtually all other "changes" West makes to the text of its published cases are "trivial" or "sweat of the brow" efforts. Citing the *Feist* decision several times, the court concluded that West's pagination, among other features, does not qualify as "original works of authorship" as required by 17 U.S.C. § 102(a) of the Copyright Law.[8] West appealed but the U.S. Second Circuit Court of Appeals, in a 2 to 1 decision on November 3, 1998, upheld the district court's decision. When the Supreme Court declined to hear the appeal (67 U.S.L.W. 3732, June 1, 1999), the appellate decision was upheld, and West's arrangement of cases in its reporters is no longer protected by copyright.

Encyclopedias

Two general legal encyclopedias dominate the field and afford topical coverage of the law in narrative form: *American Jurisprudence Second* (Am.Jur.2d) and *Corpus Juris Secundum* (C.J.S.). The former was published by Lawyers Cooperative Publishing until it became a West Group product; the latter has been published by West since 1936. Both encyclopedias include coverage of every field of law, substantive and procedural, civil and criminal. Am.Jur.2d has been available on WESTLAW since 1997. Insta-Cite (now KeyCite), West's case history and citation verification service, has contained references to *Corpus Juris Secundum* since 1991.

Both Am.Jur.2d and C.J.S. are multivolume works arranged alphabetically by topic, with multivolume general indexes plus an index in each volume. References in C.J.S. traditionally purported to cite all reported cases; but in the 1980s the editors signified their intention to offer less comprehensive coverage with a new subtitle, "A Contemporary Statement of American Law as Derived from Reported Cases and Legislation." Revised volumes do not reference every case but do include some citations to statutory law. Ironically, this trend more closely approximates the editorial philosophy of Am.Jur.2d. Important differences between the two major national encyclopedias nevertheless remain and are discussed in chapter 16 of the seventh edition of *Fundamentals of Legal Research* (pp. 374–77).

An encyclopedia for the layperson is the twelve-volume *West's Encyclopedia of American Law* (WEAL), issued by the West Group in 1998. It replaced *The Guide to American Law: Everyone's Legal Encyclopedia,* which was first published by West in 1983. Containing more than 4,000 entries, volume 12 of WEAL consists of an index to the set and a dictionary.

Dictionaries

Standard one-volume dictionaries include *Black's Law Dictionary,* 6th ed. (West, 1990) and Bryan A. Garner's *A Dictionary of Modern Legal Usage,* 2d ed. (New York: Oxford University Press, 1995). The former is online via WESTLAW; the latter, online with LEXIS-NEXIS. Stephen H. Gifis's *Law Dictionary,* 4th ed. (Hauppauge, NY: Barron's Educational Series, 1996) defines more than 2,000 legal terms in language for the layperson. West's multivolume dictionary, *Words and Phrases,* lists alphabetically terms that the courts have judicially defined, with citations to cases that have construed them. These words and phrases first appear in the advance sheets of the various units of West's *National Reporter System,* federal and state. The *'Lectric Law Library* (**http://www.lectlaw.com**) is a free Web site that contains thousands of legal words, terms, and phrases. The site bills itself as the "Net's most extensive legal dictionary." In the site's "Legal Lexicon's Lyceum" pages are thousands of definitions of legal terms, phrases, and concepts. Ignore the puerile commentary by the cybernerds who run the site and you find a surprisingly good dictionary; the definitions marked with an asterisk are thorough and detailed, with citations to cases. See, for example, the entry for *stare decisis.*

Directories

The most comprehensive legal directory is the multivolume *Martindale-Hubbell Law Directory.* Martindale-Hubbell, a member of the Reed Elsevier PLC Group, has its headquarters in New Providence, New Jersey. Published annually, this multivolume directory lists virtually all lawyers admitted to the bar, providing typical directory information on attorneys, law firms, state bars, law schools, legal market services and suppliers, and a "confidential" rating approximating each lawyer's legal ability. In addition the *Directory* contains law digests of states and foreign countries; information on U.S. copyright, patent, and trademark law; and uniform model acts and codes such as the Uniform Commercial Code. It is available in paper, on CD-ROM, and online through LEXIS-NEXIS. It also maintains a Web site called the Martindale-Hubbell Law Locator (**http://www.martindale.com**), which offers basic information about individual attorneys, such as address, date of birth, date admitted to the bar, and college and law school attended.

BNA's Directory of State and Federal Courts, Judges, and Clerks (Washington: Bureau of National Affairs), published approximately every two years, contains comprehensive information about the courts of record in the federal court system, the fifty states, the District of Columbia, American Samoa, Guam, the Northern Mariana Islands, Puerto Rico, and the Virgin Islands. *BNA's Directory* contains a personal name index, a list of federal and state-level administrators, a list of reporters of judicial decisions, and an index by geographic jurisdiction. Charts depicting court structure and information on the use of the Internet to find texts of decisions and related materials are helpful finding aids.

The U.S. Administrative Office of the Courts publishes the *United States Court Directory* annually, providing names, mailing addresses, and telephone numbers for U.S. court judges and for librarians of those courts. The current edition of the *Judicial Staff Directory* (Mount Vernon, VA: Staff Directories) contains accurate and timely information about the judiciary and extensive biographical data for the federal courts. The same company's *Staff Directories on CD-ROM Plus* contains the full text of the congressional, federal, and judicial staff directories, as well as the Central Intelligence Agency's annual *World Factbook*. Moreover, there are biographical directories, historical and current, and directories on the Internet such as the *Directory of Legal Academia* (**http://www.law.cornell.edu**) and the American Association of Law Libraries' *AALL Directory and Handbook* (**http://www. aallnet.org**).

Legal Periodical Literature

The vast periodical literature of the law would be as useless as a book misshelved in the stacks of a library without appropriate finding aids, the most important of which are good indexes.

Indexes

The market for legal periodical indexes is dominated by two major publishers. *Current Law Index* (CLI) and *Legal Resources Index* (LRI), both of which began publication in 1980, are products of the Gale Group. CLI is a print edition published monthly with quarterly and annual cumulations. LRI is available online via WESTLAW, LEXIS-NEXIS, and DIALOG. LegalTrac is the CD-ROM edition of the online LRI. It has the feature of providing letter grades, such as A, B, or C, for books reviewed. More than 800 periodicals are indexed in these sources.

The H. W. Wilson Company's *Index to Legal Periodicals & Books* (ILP) enjoyed a virtual monopoly on large-scale coverage of legal journal articles from 1908 until 1980. ILP covers about 600 periodicals and other titles, such as a selection of yearbooks, proceedings of annual institutes, and annual reviews of a particular topic or in a given field, published in the United States, Canada, Great Britain, Ireland, Australia, and New Zealand. In 1994 ILP began indexing law-related monographs. ILP is online with WILSONLINE and on compact disk with WILSONDISC. Both ILP and LegalTrac have author and subject indexes, a table of cases, a table of statutes, and book reviews; but Legal-Trac also provides access by title.

Periodical Citators

In *Shepard's Law Review Citations,* the cited sources are articles in about 200 legal periodicals. The citing sources are federal and state courts and other law review articles. Conversely, in Shepard's *Federal Law Citations in Selected Law Reviews,* the cited sources include the United States Constitution, the *United States Code,* federal court rules, and the decisions of the federal courts, while the citing sources are articles appearing in some nineteen prominent law school law reviews. *Shepard's Citations* generally are discussed below.

Digests

Even in the age of computer-assisted legal research (C.A.L.R.), digests can be useful tools for conducting legal research, and no chapter on the subject would be complete without mention of them. The many types of digests include those covering specific states or types of courts, those covering multiple jurisdictions, and those covering federal courts. Because case reporters are chronologically organized, the digest's main function is to rearrange all cases within the covered jurisdiction by broad topics. Cases are not reprinted; only abstracts, or "digests," are provided. Accompanying a digest are a separate table of cases and a Descriptive-Word Index that allows the user to work from a very specific term or phrase to the broader one under which like cases on points of law are abstracted. Thus, "Animals" is a topic and #47 is the key number representing the subheading "running at large."

Anyone who uses the printed court opinions of the various states would do well to read one of the basic research guides cited earlier to develop an understanding of the National Reporter System, the various components of which publish cases from all jurisdictions; the American Digest System, which supplies headnotes (also called abstracts, digest paragraphs, or annotations) of those decisions in subject arrangement; and the Key Number System. The Key Number System, described by West as a "permanent, or fixed, number, given to a specific point of case law," was developed by the West Publishing Company to classify all cases under any of more than 435 legal concepts.[9]

Every headnote (a more appropriate term because virtually all digest "paragraphs" consist of one sentence) has most or all of the following elements: the court that decided the case from which the point of law was assigned a headnote, the jurisdiction, and the year; the digest itself summarizing a point of law identified by its topic and key number; statutory authority; and citations that may include the case's subsequent history. When West Group headnote editors review a case, they identify the points of law it contains and write a headnote for each one. Then the key number classification editors assign them topics and key numbers. The system is not static, however. As the law evolves, old key numbers are removed, new ones are added, and the affected headnotes are reclassified. Thus quaint topics of a bygone age (Common Scold, Dueling, Livery Stable Keepers) are no longer in today's classification scheme.

The WESTLAW Key Number Service permits access to the digest system topic and key number outline. The well-known symbol of the key, a registered trademark of West, on WESTLAW is replaced with the letter "k." Thus Digest Topic 110 (Criminal Law), key number 393 (compelling accused to incriminate himself) is cited as 110k393. The Key Number Service can also be accessed from the display of case headnotes in West-reported cases using the jump feature. The headnotes have been enhanced on WESTLAW with full classification hierarchies shown for each headnote, including both current and former topic and key numbers. Jump references will automatically access the Key Number Service or link from a digest paragraph to the corresponding text in the case, a useful hypertext feature. Moreover, obsolete topics and key numbers can be converted to current classifications merely by accessing the appropriate database: Type the old topic/key number in the "Terms and Connectors Query" text box and click "Search." The defunct class is preceded by the word "Formerly" and the current class appears above the "Formerly" line.

A more time-consuming print strategy requires use of West's multivolume *U.S. Supreme Court Digest,* which abstracts all decisions of the High Court using the Key Number System. A similar service is called *Digest of United States Supreme Court Reports, Lawyers' Edition* (LEXIS Law Publishing), also multivolumed, which uses a corresponding system of headnotes composed of topics and section numbers (for example, Courts § 128—tax immunity for federal contractors—role of Congress). Whichever set is used, the researcher must check the appropriate supplements for later case material. Indeed, all print sources of the law are accompanied by supplementation, whether it is in annual pocket parts or periodically issued separate pamphlets or both.

Encompassing digests of decisions from the lower federal courts is the West series that begins with the *Federal Digest,* covering all cases before 1939; *Modern Federal Practice Digest* (1939–1960); *West's Federal Practice Digest,* 2d (1961–November 1975); *West's Federal Practice Digest,* 3d (December 1975–); *West's Federal Practice Digest,* 4th, which "began in 1989 and was completed in 1993" and overlaps with the 3d series. "Specifically for the period December 1975 through 1983, both the 3rd and 4th must be consulted to assure comprehensive coverage. For cases from 1984 forward, only the 4th needs to be consulted."[10] Specialized digests keyed to West's topical reporters cover bankruptcy, claims, education, military justice, and so forth. In this instance, as elsewhere, the online search capabilities permit the researcher to bypass the printed series of digests.

Annotated Law Reports

American Law Reports (A.L.R.) comprise a selective number of court decisions. Published by LCP (now part of West), the series is useful for its "Annotations," which carry a specific meaning in the A.L.R. context. Written by experts in the field, "Annotations" present an organized commentary on previously reported like decisions, and they range in length from one or two pages to over three hundred pages. Cases chosen for "Annotation" treatment are either those that lend themselves "to an exhaustive treatment of an important subdivision of the law of a major topic" or those that treat "limited areas of the law which are not covered at all or are covered insufficiently in other law books."[11]

The American Law Reports are published in the following series: A.L.R, covering 1919–1948; A.L.R. 2d, 1948–1965; A.L.R. 3d, 1965–1980; A.L.R. 4th, 1980–1992; A.L.R. 5th, 1992 to date; A.L.R. Fed., 1969 to date, which includes only leading decisions of the federal courts; and L. Ed. 2d. For A.L.R. 5th and volume 111 (1993) of A.L.R. Fed., and L. Ed. 2d, the illustrative cases follow rather than precede the "Annotations" in the volumes.

Finding Aids

A five-volume *Index to Annotations* affords subject access to all A.L.R. series but the first. For that, a separate, one-volume *Quick Index* is available. The *Index to Annotations* is kept current by annual pocket-part supplements. It lacks a table of cases, but it is thorough and collateral "Annotations" are provided.

Electronic Services

LEXIS-NEXIS offers the "American Law Reports Articles Library" (Library and file: ALR), which contains the full text of A.L.R. 2d through 5th, A.L.R. Fed., and Lawyers' Edition 2d. This last contains "Annotations" for selected cases published in LCP's *United States Supreme Court Reports, Lawyers' Edition*, 2d series (below). WESTLAW's A.L.R. database contains "Annotations" for A.L.R. 3d. A.L.R. 4th, A.L.R. 5th, and A.L.R. Fed.[12] Currency is a plus for these online versions; both databases are updated more frequently than the print series, which are updated annually with pocket-part supplements. A CD-ROM edition of the American Law Reports called *LawDesk* comprises A.L.R. 3d, A.L.R. 4th, A.L.R. 5th, and A.L.R. Fed. *LawDesk* features folio software, is published by the West Group, and has a jump-cite function. However, the CD-ROM lacks the Total Client-Service Library References (now called "Research References"), which appear in the print edition on the page preceding the "Annotation" and furnish cross-references to appropriate provisions of publications such as Am.Jur.2d, the A.L.R. series, the *United States Code Service,* and various form books such as *AmJur Pleading and Practice Forms.* In addition, the subject index on the compact disk is nowhere near as user-friendly as the printed multivolume *Index to Annotations.*

Looseleaf Reporters

Before the growth of online legal products and services, looseleaf reporter services were extremely useful in accelerating convenience of access to important statutes, regulations, and cases in a "one-stop shopping" package. These commercial ventures were replete with editorial enhancements (bells and whistles) and specified a wide variety of topics from accounting to taxation. At one time the field was dominated by Commerce Clearing House (Chicago) (**http://www.cch.com**), the Bureau of National Affairs (Washington, DC) (**http://www.bna.com**), and Prentice-Hall. The last was sold and its considerable stable of reporters either terminated or acquired by other companies. With acquisitions and mergers, most of the Prentice-Hall looseleaf services ended up in the catalog of the Research Institute of America (RIA) (**http:riatax. com**), a New York–based publisher. The company has "pursued a publishing philosophy which aims to translate varied primary sources into a form which is understandable to the practitioner." Commerce Clearing House, now named CCH Incorporated but known simply as CCH, remains the largest publisher of looseleaf services, with more than 200 topics with an emphasis on tax and business reporters. The Bureau of National Affairs (BNA) issues more than forty looseleaf products and is a "major provider of information in the fields of environmental, intellectual property, labor, securities, and tax law."[13]

These three and a number of other national and regional publishers of looseleaf services now issue many products in electronic as well as print format. Many CCH and RIA publications and "almost all Bureau of National Affairs publications are available online in LEXIS-NEXIS and WESTLAW."[14] The definitive source for ascertaining what services are current is Arlene L. Eis, comp., *Legal Looseleafs in Print* (Teaneck, NJ: Infosources Publishing). An annual, its entries are organized alphabetically by title with full bibliographic information. There are indexes by publisher, subject, and electronic formats, with individual indexes for services on CD-ROM, on diskette, and online.

Shepard's Citations

Because the law is a dynamic process, the legal researcher must know what acts or cases are valid and may properly be cited as authority. Citators give current information on valid authority, and the most complete set of books and services for determining this is known as *Shepard's Citations,* formerly owned by McGraw-Hill but now under LEXIS-NEXIS.

The word "Shepardizing" is used in legal parlance to describe the procedure whereby the applicability of cases, statutes, and other documents as authority is determined. To find out if the case or statute you have researched is still good law, you must Shepardize that case or statute. The hackneyed rhyme "Not to Shepardize is to jeopardize" is painfully true. Of numerous examples, one will suffice. In a state of New York ruling, the "court was astounded to find that the case upon which so much reliance was placed by defendant's counsel was reversed by the Appellate Division. . . . [O]n the point in question, and this reversal was affirmed by the Court of Appeals."[15] Failure to Shepardize can be manifest evidence of malpractice for an attorney and devastating to his or her client.

In Shepard's terminology, the word *citation* typically signifies a reference in a later authority to an earlier authority. The earlier authority is known as the "cited" source (case, statute, and so forth), and the later authorities are referred to as the "citing" sources. Anyone familiar with citation indexes such as *SSCI—Social Science Citation Index* will recognize the concept. Through the appropriate Shepard's units, one can determine two important things: (1) the history of a cited source—whether a decision has been reversed by a higher court, a statute repealed, the Constitution construed, a treaty amended, and so on; and (2) the treatment—how other courts (and relevant secondary sources such as law review articles or A.L.R. "Annotations") have remarked the cited source. For judicial decisions, treatment can be as important as history. For instance, if later court cases (the citing sources) have "criticized" the merit of the cited case, its worth as authority is vitiated. Conversely, if subsequent cases "followed" (cited as controlling) the earlier, cited case, its value as authority is reinforced.

Shepard's Federal Units

Mentioned above are special Shepard's units covering legal periodicals, and in earlier chapters units covering statutes and the *Code of Federal Regulations* were assayed. Two other federal citators are worth noting in this context:

1. *Shepard's United States Citations* covers Supreme Court cases; the Constitution, statutes, court rules, and treaties; decisions and orders of some administrative entities; and copyrights, trademarks, and patents.

2. *Shepard's Federal Citations* includes citations to the courts of appeals, district courts, and selected special reporters such as *Federal Claims Reporter* and *Federal Rules Decisions,* the latter consisting of district court cases construing the federal rules of criminal procedure, published in the Appendix to Title 18, *United States Code*; and the federal rules of civil procedure, appellate procedure, and evidence, published in the Appendix to Title 28, *United States Code.*

Case Names Citators

Shepard's United States Supreme Court Case Names Citator and *Federal Case Names Citators* are billed as companion volumes to *Shepard's United States Citations.* The former furnishes the case name, date of decision, and correct citation for each reported Supreme Court case from 1900 to the present. When available, citations to the official *United States Reports* and, of course, to the more timely West commercial editions are shown. For the latter, a separate volume(s) is issued for each of the federal circuits.

Electronic Versions

No better example of the merits of computer-assisted legal research (C.A.L.R.) can be found than in Shepardizing. To search the printed Shepard's units, with their numerous columns, minuscule print, and abbreviations, requires patience and persistence. Shepardizing online or on compact disk, by contrast, is almost effortless. One can determine history by using Auto-Cite, available on LEXIS-NEXIS, or KeyCite (formerly called Insta-Cite), available on WESTLAW. For history and treatment, Shepard's is available on LEXIS-NEXIS and on CD-ROM. In 1996 Reed Elsevier, the parent company of LEXIS-NEXIS, acquired the citator division of Shepard's/McGraw-Hill. Subsequently, LEXIS-NEXIS did not renew the contract to provide WESTLAW with the database, but by that time the West Group had developed KeyCite, which has all the features of Shepard's (history and treatment) and also offers negative indirect history. Both Shepard's on LEXIS-NEXIS and KeyCite on WESTLAW are updated daily. Shepard's also furnishes subscribers with its services via a fee-based Internet site (**http://www.shepards.com**). You log on for daily updates using your Shepard's customer number as the password. Moreover, the home page has links to LEXIS-NEXIS Xchange and "Shepard's on Matthew Bender." Also, at the LEXIS-NEXIS home page (**http://www.lexis-nexis.com**) there is a link to LEXIS-NEXIS Xchange for Shepardizing.

Popular Names of Cases

In addition to citators, a famous publication is *Shepard's Acts and Cases by Popular Names, Federal and State*, which I have mentioned as a reference for determining the popular names for statutes and treaties. Popular names given to cases are easy to find. For example, the Manila Prize Case may be found at 188 U.S. 254, 47 L.E. 463, 23 S.C. 415; the Federal Skywalk Cases are located at 680 F.2d 1175. Other popular name tables are located in special digests, but *Shepard's Acts and Cases* is considered the most comprehensive.

Other Legal Sources

United States legal sources also encompass opinions of the attorneys general, treatises, restatements of the law, uniform laws, model codes, jury instructions, canons of professional ethics, form books, and so on. For these and other legal tools, the reader is advised to consult one of the basic sources noted earlier in this chapter. In addition, a reliable checklist for information on current and retrospective legal sources is Oscar J. Miller and Mortimer D. Schwartz, eds., *Recommended Publications for Legal Research* (Littleton, CO: Rothman), an annual published since 1970, with letter-grade (A, B, and C) ratings.

FEDERAL COURT REPORTS

> A judge is a law student who marks his own examination papers.
>
> —H. L. Mencken

The magisterial bibliographic apparatus created and maintained by commercial publishers such as the West Group is necessary in large measure because of the doctrine of *stare decisis*, which holds that the "principle underlying the decision in one case will be deemed of imperative authority, controlling the decisions of similar cases in the same court and in lower courts within the same jurisdiction, unless and until the decision in question is reversed or overruled by a court of competent authority."[16] From this construct, it follows that an attorney must have access to the latest decisions to advise his or her client correctly. Commercial publishing of case law is geared to prompt reporting, not only of the opinions and decisions of courts but also of the indexes and other finding aids. The process is crucial to effective legal deliberation.

Decisions relied upon as precedent are usually those of appellate courts. Consequently, availability of published decisions increases in ascending order of the federal court hierarchy. Whereas only selected decisions of district courts are readily available, virtually all written decisions of the appellate courts and the Supreme Court are reported either in their official edition and/or commercially. However, in recent years, the federal courts of appeals have increasingly rendered decisions without published opinions. These are noted in the *Federal Reporter* series in tabular form by title (plaintiff-defendant order) referencing docket number, date, disposition (affirmed, reversed, dismissed, petition for review denied, and so forth), and a citation to or geographical abbreviation of the lower court from which the case was appealed. "It has long been the practice of the federal courts of appeals to ban the citation of unpublished opinions." But because of the "ready availability of these opinions online," a trend toward reversing that appellate court practice may be discerned.[17]

Federal court reports can be placed within the context of West's *National Reporter System* (NRS), a network of reporters that includes the opinions of state, federal, and special courts. For state reports there exists within the NRS a series of seven regional reporters that cover the opinions of several contiguous states and separate units that cover the courts of New York, California, and Illinois. The federal courts and the special courts are covered in the NRS as described below.

District and Appellate Courts

During most of the nineteenth century, decisions of the U.S. district courts and courts of appeals were published in a number of separate series cited by the names of their official reporters. This "nominative" reporting, which caused bibliographic confusion, was rectified by the publication of a multivolume series known as *Federal Cases* (West). Covering the period 1789–1879, *Federal Cases* is arranged alphabetically by name of case and numbered consecutively. Some 18,000 lower federal court decisions are reported in this series.

For the years 1880 to the present, three units of West's *National Reporter System* must be consulted. There are no official government editions of these major federal court cases.

Federal Reporter

The *Federal Reporter* consists of three series. The first series (F.) comprises 300 volumes (1880–1924). The second series (F.2d) began anew with volume 1 and concluded with volume 999 (1924–1993). The current series (F.3d), begun in 1993, continues *Federal Reporter* to date. Over time, this series has reported not only appellate, but also district court cases and cases of selected special courts, some of which have since been abolished or reorganized.

Federal Supplement

The *Federal Supplement* (F.Supp., F.Supp.2d) reports decisions of the district courts since 1932, as well as decisions of other courts during various periods, such as the Customs Court, Court of International Trade, Court of Claims, and so forth.

Federal district court decisions, however, are published selectively. Some cases that the West editors chose not to print may nevertheless be located online, others by using looseleaf services in a particular topical area, still others by contacting the clerk of the appropriate court. Cases in both the *Federal Reporter* and the *Federal Supplement* series may be accessed in print by using the appropriate *West Federal Practice Digest* series, which has parties to the case in plaintiff-defendant order and the reverse; the appropriate unit of Shepard's to match these court reports is *Shepard's Federal Citations*. The full text of lower court reports is available on CD-ROM, on LEXIS-NEXIS and WESTLAW, and on a few Internet sites.

Other Lower Court Reporters

Specific units of the West Publishing Company include *Federal Rules Decisions,* which publish selective district court cases that construe the federal rules of civil and criminal procedure; *Bankruptcy Reporter,* pursuant to changes mandated by the Bankruptcy Reform Act of 1978; and the reporters covering the so-called Special Courts, designated as Article I, or legislative, courts, and having functions that "are prescribed by Congress independently of section 2 of Article III."[18] These include the West Group's *Military Justice Reporter, Federal Claims Reporter,* and *West's Veterans Appeals Reporter.* Official reports published by the Government Printing Office include those of the Tax Court, Court of Veterans Appeals, and an annual *United States Reports: Selected Reports* on microfiche, but they should not be used because they are not updated sufficiently nor do they feature the editorial enhancements of the commercial reporters. For example, case law generated in the United States Tax Court is far better covered in the online or print looseleaf services.

The United States Supreme Court

The United States Supreme Court consists of nine justices, one of whom is the chief justice, and all of whom are appointed for life by the president with the advice and consent of the Senate. The Court's continuous annual term extends from the first Monday in October and is typically concluded by late June or early July of the following year. Popular opinion holds that the Supreme Court is an ultimate court of appeals for all, a bulwark of freedom to which every citizen can press his or her claim under federal law or the Constitution. In actual fact, the Supreme Court is quite limited in its jurisdiction. It hears disputes between states, disputes between a state and the federal government, cases in which a federal court or the highest court of a state has held a statute unconstitutional, and a few other categories. Moreover, it has broad discretionary power to decline to hear a large number of appeals. Indeed, of "the cases brought to federal and state courts, the Supreme Court actually hears only a fraction of 1 percent."[19] Clerks, hired by the justices on the basis of their performance in law school and other criteria, do the initial screening of petitions and write memoranda about each case summarizing the facts and the issues and often recommend whether the case should be accepted for review. Based on the clerks' memoranda and occasional independent research, the justices meet privately to decide whether to grant or deny certiorari. If four of the nine justices decide that a case warrants review, it is docketed for oral arguments. Fewer than 100 cases are accepted each term. Before a case is argued, some justices have clerks write a "bench memo" summarizing the case and on occasion suggesting questions the justices could ask during oral arguments. After a case is argued, the justices meet in private to take an initial vote and assign the writing of the majority and dissenting opinions. Clerks usually write the first drafts, which are then circulated to other justices for editing and revision. Clerks are often the conduits for communicating and negotiating between justices about the final wording. When the written opinions are handed out under the names of the justices, the clerks, of course, are never mentioned.[20]

The first meeting of the Supreme Court was held on February 1, 1790, in the Royal Exchange on Broad Street in New York City. Only three of the six justices were present, hence no quorum was achieved. They reconvened the next day and formally organized themselves as the Supreme Court. One of the justices did not show, then declined appointment. John Jay of New York was the first Chief Justice. The names of the first Associate Justices are now forgotten, mere footnotes in history. For some time the justices "wore black robes with a wide scarlet facing and gold piping and 12- or 14-inch scarlet cuffs." Attempts to ascertain when and why the Court eventually eschewed this sartorial splendor have met with no success.[21] At Jefferson's request, however, they first discarded "the monstrous wig which makes the English judges look like rats peeping through bunches of oakum."[22]

With its power of judicial review—the authority of the Court to strike down federal, state, and local acts it deems unconstitutional—the decisions of this tribunal are both legally and politically of momentous consequence. Lawyers are accustomed to say that the truth is in the Supreme Court record; that is to say, it is not unusual for the passage of time to reveal that some dissenting justice saw the case more clearly than did the majority. Justice Robert H. Jackson, whose aphoristic wit rivaled that of Benjamin Disraeli and Oscar Wilde, expressed the High Court's influence thus: "We are not final because we are infallible, but we are infallible because we are final."[23]

Official Supreme Court Series

The official GPO edition of Supreme Court reports is issued in three stages. In order of recency, they are as follows:

- *Slip opinions* in pamphlet form are printed individually when rendered by the High Court. Information includes the docket number, date of argument, date of decision, and a syllabus prepared by the Reporter of Decisions for the convenience of the reader. Figure 8.2 shows a page from an official slip opinion.

- *Official Reports of the Supreme Court: Preliminary Print* are issued in paperbound form and generally cover a two- or three-week period. They contain an index and cumulative table of cases reported. The pagination of the preliminary prints is the same as that which will appear in the bound volumes. Because they are two to three years behind schedule, and because, like slip opinions, they are subject to correction by the Court, they are virtually worthless as sources of information.

Figure 8.2. Official slip opinion.

NOTICE: This opinion is subject to formal revision before publication in the preliminary print of the United States Reports. Readers are requested to notify the Reporter of Decisions, Supreme Court of the United States, Washington, D.C. 20543, of any typographical or other formal errors, in order that corrections may be made before the preliminary print goes to press.

SUPREME COURT OF THE UNITED STATES

No. 95–891

OHIO, PETITIONER *v.* ROBERT D. ROBINETTE

ON WRIT OF CERTIORARI TO THE SUPREME COURT OF OHIO

[November 18, 1996]

CHIEF JUSTICE REHNQUIST delivered the opinion of the Court.

We are here presented with the question whether the Fourth Amendment requires that a lawfully seized defendant must be advised that he is "free to go" before his consent to search will be recognized as voluntary. We hold that it does not.

This case arose on a stretch of Interstate 70 north of Dayton, Ohio, where the posted speed limit was 45 miles per hour because of construction. Respondent Robert D. Robinette was clocked at 69 miles per hour as he drove his car along this stretch of road, and was stopped by Deputy Roger Newsome of the Montgomery County Sheriff's office. Newsome asked for and was handed Robinette's driver's license, and he ran a computer check which indicated that Robinette had no previous violations. Newsome then asked Robinette to step out of his car, turned on his mounted video camera, issued a verbal warning to Robinette, and returned his license.

At this point, Newsome asked, "One question before you get gone: [A]re you carrying any illegal contraband in your car? Any weapons of any kind, drugs, anything like that?" App. to Brief for Respondent 2 (internal quotation marks omitted). Robinette answered "no" to these questions, after which Deputy Newsome asked if he could search the car. Robinette consented. In the

- *United States Reports* (U.S.) are the bound, permanent edition of the decisions. Once the bound volume is received, libraries may discard the individual opinions and the preliminary prints. The bound version contains a table of cases reported, a table of statutes cited, and a topical index. As with the material included in the preliminary prints, the *United States Reports* include per curiam decisions, orders, and chamber opinions as well as the full text of decisions. The volumes experience a printed time lag of from four to five years. About the only useful point that can be made here is that the official series volumes are all available free to depository libraries.

Congressional Information Service publishes a CIS *US Reports* microfiche file containing the full text of all signed opinions and per curiam decisions, a record of orders granting or denying petitions for writ of certiorari, and High Court rulings on its obligations to review cases on appeal, from 1790. From 1969 the file also contains opinions of individual justices "in chambers," ruling on applications, such as a stay of execution, addressed to them in their capacity as justices for particular circuits. Official opinions from 1992 to 1998 are available from the Federal Bulletin Board home page (**http://fedbbs.access.gpo.gov**). A number of commercial sources, some of which are noted above, carry the unannotated opinions of the Supreme Court, years of coverage varying from one Web site to another.

United States Supreme Court Reports, Lawyers' Edition

Now published by LEXIS Law Publishing (formerly published by LCP) and cited as L.Ed. or L.Ed.2d, depending on the series, this commercial version of Supreme Court reports is issued first in *Advance Reports,* published twice monthly. The page numbering is identical with that which will appear in the bound volumes. *Advance Reports* contains a "Current Awareness Commentary"; the names of the justices; a cumulated table of federal constitutional provisions, statutes, court rules, and regulations cited; a table of classifications to the *United States Supreme Court Digest, Lawyers' Edition;* memorandum cases; a table of cases; and a topical index. Case summaries and headnotes, which are classified to the *Digest,* precede the text of each opinion. As the number of cases accumulates, bound volumes are issued that supersede the *Advance Reports.* Like the official edition, opinions are arranged in chronological order within each volume. This edition is useful for its

A.L.R. "Annotations" and for the summaries of briefs of counsel. Bound volumes have pocket-part supplementation that includes a "Citator Service" and a "Later Case Service." The text of the "Syllabus by Reporter of Decisions" and the justices' opinions are prepared from the official GPO *Preliminary Prints,* which are subject to corrections. Figure 8.3, pages 272–73, shows the first page of an opinion and a page showing "Research References," formerly called "Total Client-Service Library References."

Supreme Court Reporter

Cited as S.Ct., this unit of West's *National Reporter System* contains the typical features of West's topic and key number classification system in addition to the cases themselves. Headnotes referencing topic and key number are classified to the American Digest System. Features of the advance sheets, issued biweekly, and the bound volumes include a semimonthly summary of grants of certiorari and other activities titled "United States Supreme Court Actions"; names and allotments of the justices; a cumulative table of cases; "Judicial Highlights," which are summaries of selected decisions from state and federal courts; parallel tables from the official *United States Reports* to the *Supreme Court Reporter;* Supreme Court rules, federal rules of civil procedure, federal rules of evidence, and so forth; cumulative federal sentencing guidelines; cumulative words and phrases; a cumulative key number digest; table of dispositions; memorandum decisions; and the text of cases. Figure 8.4, page 274, shows a page from a decision published in an advance sheet of West's *Supreme Court Reporter.*

United States Law Week

Published by the Bureau of National Affairs (BNA), *United States Law Week* (U.S.L.W. or simply LW) is a weekly topical reporter that consists of two looseleaf binders. The Supreme Court section supplies the full text of all High Court cases, with several editorial features that enhance research capabilities. Noteworthy is a section called "Supreme Court Today," which has a separate index and features a summary of cases acted upon, a journal of the High Court's proceedings, cases docketed, a summary of cases recently filed, a summary of oral arguments, and several other useful finding aids. The weekly edition of U.S.L.W. has been available on WESTLAW since January 1986, and LEXIS-NEXIS has carried a daily edition since June 1987.

(Text continues on page 275.)

Figure 8.3(a). First page of opinion.

U.S. SUPREME COURT REPORTS   129 L Ed 2d

BOARD OF EDUCATION OF KIRYAS JOEL VILLAGE SCHOOL
DISTRICT, Petitioner

v

LOUIS GRUMET, et al. [No. 93-517]

———

BOARD OF EDUCATION OF MONROE-WOODBURY CENTRAL SCHOOL
DISTRICT, Petitioner

v

LOUIS GRUMET, et al. [No. 93-527]

———

ATTORNEY GENERAL OF NEW YORK, Petitioner

v

LOUIS GRUMET, et al. [No. 93-539]

512 US —, 129 L Ed 2d 546, 114 S Ct 2481

[Nos. 93-517, 93-527, and 93-539]

Argued March 30, 1994. Decided June 27, 1994.

Decision: New York statute creating public school district for Hasidic
Jewish village held to violate First Amendment's establishment of religion
clause.

SUMMARY

Members of the Satmar Hasidic sect, practitioners of a strict form of Judaism, incorporated the village of Kiryas Joel within the town of Monroe,
New York, pursuant to a New York statute which gave almost any group of
residents who satisfied various procedures the right to form a new village.
Children in the village generally were educated in private religious schools,
but the public school district within which the village fell provided special
services to the village's handicapped children at an annex to one of the
private schools. After this arrangement was ended in response to United
States Supreme Court decisions holding unconstitutional a state's provision

Figure 8.3(b). "Research References."

bilingual and bicultural special education is offered by a public school district to handicapped children of members of a religious sect at a neutral site near one of the sect's parochial schools, where such a scheme is administered in accordance with neutral principles that would not necessarily confine special treatment to members of the sect.

Schools § 10 — handicapped children
8. Under New York law, parents who are dissatisfied with their handicapped child's educational program have recourse through administrative review proceedings.

RESEARCH REFERENCES

16A Am Jur 2d, Constitutional Law § 481; 68 Am Jur 2d, Schools §§ 29, 33, 37, 338

16A Am Jur Legal Forms 2d, Schools §§ 229:22-229:25

3 Americans With Disabilities: Practice and Compliance Manual § 11:4.5

USCS, Constitution, Amendment 1

L Ed Digest, Constitutional Law § 982

L Ed Index, Jewish Faith; Schools and Education

ALR Index, Jews; Religion and Religious Societies; Schools and Education; Separation of Church and State

Annotations:

Establishment and free exercise of religion clauses of Federal Constitution's First Amendment as applied to public aid to sectarian schools or students at such schools—Supreme Court cases. 125 L Ed 2d 793.

Establishment and free exercise of religion clauses of Federal Constitution's First Amendment as applied to public schools—Supreme Court cases. 96 L Ed 2d 828.

Supreme Court cases involving establishment and free exercise of religion clauses of Federal Constitution. 37 L Ed 2d 1147.

Auto-Cite®: Cases and annotations referred to herein can be further researched through the Auto-Cite® computer-assisted research service. Use Auto-Cite to check citations for form, parallel references, prior and later history, and annotation references.

SYLLABUS BY REPORTER OF DECISIONS

The New York Village of Kiryas Joel is a religious enclave of Satmar Hasidim, practitioners of a strict form of Judaism. Its incorporators intentionally drew its boundaries under the State's general village incorporation law to exclude all but Satmars. The village fell within the Monroe-Woodbury Central School District until a special state statute,

Figure 8.4. Decision published in advance sheet, *Supreme Court Reporter* (West).

2246   118 SUPREME COURT REPORTER

Angel Jaime MONGE, Petitioner,

v.

CALIFORNIA.

No. 97–6146.

Argued April 28, 1998.

Decided June 26, 1998.

Defendant was convicted in the Superior Court, Los Angeles County, Sam Cianchetti, J., of multiple drug offenses, and was sentenced under three strikes law as prior felony offender and given enhancement for prior prison term. Defendant appealed. The Court of Appeal affirmed defendant's conviction but remanded for resentencing. After granting review, the California Supreme Court, 16 Cal.4th 826, 66 Cal.Rptr.2d 853, 941 P.2d 1121, reversed in part. Certiorari was granted. The United States Supreme Court, Justice O'Connor, held that Double Jeopardy Clause does not preclude retrial on prior conviction allegation in noncapital sentencing context.

Affirmed.

Justice Stevens dissented and filed opinion.

Justice Scalia dissented and filed opinion in which Justices Souter and Ginsburg joined.

1. Double Jeopardy ☜30, 107.1

The Double Jeopardy Clause does not preclude retrial on a prior conviction allegation in the noncapital sentencing context. U.S.C.A. Const.Amend. 5.

2. Double Jeopardy ☜1

The Double Jeopardy Clause protects against successive prosecutions for the same offense after acquittal or conviction and against multiple criminal punishments for the same offense. U.S.C.A. Const.Amend. 5.

3. Double Jeopardy ☜30

An enhanced sentence imposed on a persistent offender is not to be viewed as either a new jeopardy or additional penalty for the earlier crimes but as a stiffened penalty for the latest crime, which is considered to be an aggravated offense because a repetitive one. U.S.C.A. Const.Amend. 5.

4. Double Jeopardy ☜103, 109

Where an appeals court overturns a conviction on the ground that the prosecution proffered insufficient evidence of guilt, that finding is comparable to an acquittal, and the Double Jeopardy Clause precludes a second trial. U.S.C.A. Const.Amend. 5.

5. Double Jeopardy ☜1

The Double Jeopardy Clause does not provide the defendant with the right to know at any specific moment in time what the exact limit of his punishment will turn out to be. U.S.C.A. Const.Amend. 5.

6. Double Jeopardy ☜32, 112.1

The guarantee against double jeopardy neither prevents the prosecution from seeking review of a sentence nor restricts the length of a sentence imposed upon retrial after a defendant's successful appeal. U.S.C.A. Const.Amend. 5.

7. Criminal Law ☜1208.1(6)
  Homicide ☜358(1)

It is of vital importance that the decisions made in the penalty phase of a capital trial be, and appear to be, based on reason rather than caprice or emotion.

8. Double Jeopardy ☜5.1

The Double Jeopardy Clause prevents states from making repeated attempts to convict an individual for an alleged offense, thereby subjecting him to embarrassment, expense, and ordeal and compelling him to live in a continuing state of anxiety and insecurity, as well as enhancing the possibility that even though innocent he may be found guilty. U.S.C.A. Const.Amend. 5.

9. Criminal Law ☜1208.1(6), 1213.7

In capital cases the fundamental respect for humanity underlying the Eighth Amendment requires consideration of the character and record of the individual offender and the circumstances of the particular offense as a constitutionally indispensable part of the process of inflicting the penalty of death. U.S.C.A. Const.Amend. 8.

Nominative Reporting

Early state and federal reports were often named after their reporters rather than after the courts whose names they reported. The first ninety volumes of the *United States Reports* were originally cited using the names of seven reporters who covered the period 1789 through 1874. These volumes were later numbered consecutively, but when they are cited it is customary (although not mandatory)[24] to include the reporter's name and the volume of his series parenthetically. Thus a citation to an early report would be phrased as follows: *Marbury v. Madison,* 5 U.S. (1 Cranch) 137, 2 L.Ed. 60 (1803). In this citation William Cranch's reports, in nine volumes, were renumbered volumes 5 through 13, and the famous case may be read either in the official edition or in the *Lawyers' Edition* (first series). West's *Supreme Court Reporter* did not begin its series until the October term of 1882.

Supreme Court Records and Briefs

A brief is a written argument concentrating on legal points and authorities, which is used by the attorney to convey to a higher court the essential facts of his or her client's case and a statement of the questions of law involved. In addition, briefs are often filed by a "friend of the court" (amicus curiae) backing one side of the case on appeal. The "record on appeal" that accompanies the brief consists of items introduced in evidence in the lower court, as well as a compilation of pleadings and motions, instructions to the jury, cross-examination of witnesses, and so forth. Together these materials are of signal importance to researchers in many disciplines.

Congressional Information Service's *CIS US Supreme Court Records & Briefs* microfiche collection comprises all argued cases since 1897 and since 1975 all "non-argued" cases (including *in forma pauperis*) in which one or more justices wrote a dissent from the per curiam decision to deny certiorari. CIS also sells microfiche files of the records and briefs of the Court of Appeals of the District of Columbia circuit.

Supreme Court briefs are available from the October 1979 term on LEXIS-NEXIS (Library: GENFED; File: BRIEFS). Records and briefs are not really "published"; rather, they are "produced in relatively small quantities . . . [and] are 'deposited' with selected libraries. But academic law libraries are discarding these consequential documents, and not everyone can travel to a designated library or to the National Archives to access them."[25] This makes microfiche collections like CIS's all the more valuable.

Supreme Court Oral Arguments

The oral arguments of the attorneys before appellate courts expose the strengths and weaknesses of a case and usually reveal the courts' concerns. Some useful sources for oral arguments include:

- Congressional Information Service's *Oral Arguments of the US Supreme Court* is a microfiche service for the transcripts for all argued cases with a current service and a retrospective collection from the 1969/1970 term. Moreover, the Warren Court Collection preserves all transcribed arguments from the 1953/1954 term through the 1968/1969 term.

- The Supreme Court releases all its audiotapes to the National Archives in November following the term in which cases were argued. The Archives accessions the audio materials and makes copies for use by researchers.

- *Landmark Briefs and Arguments of the Supreme Court of the United States: Constitutional Law* (Bethesda, MD: University Publications of America) makes available selected cases of the High Court from 1793 to 1973. Term supplements began in 1974. Starting with the 1989 term, the *Landmark* series includes an "Opinions" supplement issued with the volumes of briefs and oral arguments. These volumes include the full text of written opinions for all the selected cases. Special supplements include *Landmark Right-to-Die Cases* and *Landmark Abortion Cases*. Other titles include the multivolume *Antitrust Law: Major Briefs and Oral Arguments of the Supreme Court of the United States, 1955 Term–1975 Term.*

- Oyez, Oyez, Oyez (**http://oyez.nwu.edu**), a product of the Academic Technologies Department of Northwestern University, contains hundreds of hours of audio files (RealAudio). "Oyez" uttered three times takes its name from the phrase by which the Marshall of the High Court calls the courtroom to order. The word means "hear ye" and comes from the Anglo-Norman oyez, the plural imperative of oyer (to hear). On the Frequently Asked Questions (FAQ) pages of this site, one is informed that the files cannot be downloaded and the materials are protected by copyright. However, one can purchase a CD-ROM with a silly title, *The Supreme Court's Greatest Hits,* which consists of a select set of materials from fifty cases encompassing more than eighty hours of audio. The Oyez Project also features a "virtual" tour of the Supreme Court building and has a link to the nonpareil FindLaw Internet site.

Judicial Conference Records

Records of the US Judicial Conference: Committees on Rules of Practice and Procedure, a publication of Congressional Information Service, permits researchers to ascertain the intent of rules and rules revisions, determine why certain proposals were rejected, see how rules were affected by specific court cases, and track changes in judicial thought about fairness and efficiency in procedural issues. CIS's microfiche collection of these records and a companion printed index cover the period since 1935. The types of records in this collection include minutes and transcripts of meetings, correspondence among members, and comments from the legal profession and the public. The Judicial Conference of the United States, the governing body of the federal judicial system as a whole, functions as an entity of general oversight and recommendation. Presided over by the Chief Justice of the Supreme Court, the Conference includes in its membership the chief judge from each of the circuit courts of appeals and a district judge from the nearly 100 federal district courts.

ELECTRONIC SOURCES AND SERVICES

The migration of legal materials to the Internet has been, and continues to be, the fastest-growing enterprise in the legal publishing industry. In addition, the commercial online services continue to provide systematic searching structures not always available at legal Web sites. The following is a very selective summary of both resources.

Evaluative Tools

Although this is a field where print materials obsolesce with frightful velocity, two sources may be of use: James Evans's *Law on the Net,* 2d ed. (Berkeley, CA: Nolo Press, 1997) and Don MacLeod's *The Internet Guide for the Legal Researcher* (Teaneck, NJ: Infosources Publishing, 1997). On the Internet, The Argus Clearinghouse has a ratings system of one to five checks for each of the following five criteria: level of resource description; level of resource evaluation; guide design; guide organizational schemes; and guide meta-information: information about other information, that is, a description of the site itself, its mission, how it was researched and constructed, qualifications of the authors, frequency of updating, and so forth (**http://www.clearinghouse.net/ratings.html**). A useful resource is the Virtual Chase: A Research Site for Legal Professionals, where the criteria for evaluating sites is based on objectivity, expediency, timeliness, accuracy, and authenticity. Virtual Chase has, in addition to a checklist for determining quality, a Webligraphy (**http://www.virtualchase.com/Quality.htm**). The Scout Report (**http://wwwscout.cs.wisc.edu/scout/report**) is published weekly on the Web and by e-mail. By selecting the SIGNPOST link and then accessing "Law," you can get a report card on a number of legal sites graded by content, authority, information maintenance, presentation, availability, and, if applicable, cost.

Project Hermes

Project Hermes, named after the ancient Greek messenger of the gods (who was also celebrated as the god of cunning and theft), offers electronic transmission of the text of decisions within eight to twelve hours of their release by the High Court to the GPO Access databases and to a consortium of information-oriented organizations. The files are sent in ASCII and in Adobe Portable Document Format (PDF).

Commercial Online Services

LEXIS-NEXIS and WESTLAW, recipients of Project Hermes, offer full-text coverage of the Supreme Court, the courts of appeals, district courts, and Article I special courts. Each employs its version of natural language searching, a device that retrieves citations to documents that have the highest likelihood of matching the concepts in the description one entered. WESTLAW's is named WIN (WESTLAW Is Natural) and LEXIS-NEXIS's is called FREESTYLE; both search strategies can be modified by the usual parameters (date, judge, and so forth). Both databases support voice recognition software. WESTLAW's version is called LawTALK; LEXIS-NEXIS has a program called TalkTime. Moreover, WESTLAW sports a Web-based interface to its databases (**http://www.westlaw.com**). The opinions of the federal courts are, of course, transmitted without editorial enhancements; within weeks the West editors add their well-known digest paragraphs and other bells and whistles.

LEXIS-NEXIS has a point-and-click Windows service, and its LEXIS-NEXIS Xchange, (**http://www.lexis.com/xchange**), in addition to Shepardizing, gives current information on motions and certiorari petitions, summary affirmances and dismissals, and related actions.

Moreover, in a feature called "The Prognosticator," a legal guru attempts to guess the outcome of cases after oral arguments are presented. And LEXIS-NEXIS Academic Universe offers, among many other databases, searchable files on federal cases and court rules. As noted, a daily edition of *United States Law Week* is available through LEXIS-NEXIS.

A list of other online subscription services and commercial legal publishers is found in FindLaw, where you can click on a number of these services to find content and ordering information (**http://www. findlaw.com/casecode/commercial.html**).

CD-ROM Products

There are a number of federal court decisions on CD-ROM, led by the West Group's coverage of the Supreme Court and the lower federal courts. LEXIS Law Publishing issues the *United States Supreme Court Reports, Lawyers' Edition*, covering cases from 1789 to date on two disks with quarterly updates. Several other smaller companies are in the CD-ROM market. These are announced, with prices, Internet addresses, phone numbers, and periodicities, in Kendall F. Svengalis's *Legal Information Buyer's Guide and Reference Manual, 1998–99* (pp. 71–75).

Internet Sites

In addition to the evaluative sites noted above, a number of Web sites furnish opinions of the district courts, circuit courts of appeal, and special (Article I) courts, as well as the Supreme Court. As always, I am inclined to list a few sites that either have excellent links to other sites or have attributes that set them apart from, if not above, other sources. Herewith, in addition to Oyez 3, is a selective roundup:

- *FindLaw* (**http://www.findlaw.com**). This is as good a Web site for the law as can be found. One of its fourteen topical areas, "Laws: Cases and Codes," has access to Supreme Court decisions from 1893, all federal circuit court decisions, selective district court decisions, and decisions of some of the Article I special courts. Moreover, FindLaw has an impressive number of links, including those to several excellent legal Web sites sponsored by accredited law schools. FindLaw Legal News, a free service, is a virtual daily newspaper for the serious reader (**http://legalnews. findlaw.com**).

- *Hieros Gamos* (**http://www.hg.org**). This site bills itself as "The Comprehensive Legal Site," and is divided into three categories. HG I claims to be a directory "of every organization, association, law school, firm, vendor, etc. directly or indirectly involved with the legal profession." HG II furnishes lists of some 200 areas of law practice and links to hundreds of discussion groups. HG III, our immediate area of interest, includes links to decisions of state and federal courts. This site, which has been promiscuously praised by legal eagles, is in my opinion overrated. This is also the opinion of The Argus Clearinghouse, which gave HG a ranking of two checks out of a possible five.

- *World Wide Web Virtual Library: Law* (**http://www.law.indiana**). The virtue of this site is its collection of subject-related Web sites maintained by institutions worldwide. Materials are arranged by organization type (for example, United States Government Servers, Law Journals on the WWW, and so forth) and there exists a superior list of linkages to virtually all the sites that comprise useful information.

- *Legal Information Institute* (LII) (**http://www.law.cornell.edu**). This is one of the major Internet sites at the Cornell Law School and offers, among many other services, a collection of recent and historic Supreme Court decisions.

- *The Federal Court Locator* (**http://www.law.vill.edu**). Sponsored by the Villanova University Center for Information Law and Policy, this site provides federal courts of appeals opinions from about the mid-1990s to the present.

- *Fedworld/FLITE* (**http://www.fedworld.gov/supcourt**). The Federal Legal Information Through Electronics (FLITE) database was developed by the Judge Advocate General, United States Air Force and was limited to federal, state, and local government agencies. Now available to the public, the site provides access to thousands of Supreme Court opinions from FedWorld, a vast Internet site sponsored by the National Technical Information Service (NTIS).

- *FedLaw* (**http://www.legal.gsa.gov**). Sponsored by the General Services Administration, this site covers the *United States Code,* including a popular names table; the *Code of Federal*

Regulations; congressional legislation; and links to federal court reports from the Villanova site (Federal Court Locator).

- *Rominger Legal* (**http://www.romingerlegal.com**). This is a competent site with lots of links to Supreme Court and federal appellate decisions as well as professional law directories, state legal series, and numerous other categories.

- *Georgia State University College of Law* (**http://law.gsu.edu**). The home page of this interesting site links to, inter alia, GSU's Meta-Index for U.S. Legal Research, which simply links to search tools at many other sites. Each search tool starts with a "default" entry as an example with a brief abstract of the site and its coverage. Thus, for U.S. Supreme Court opinions you are sent to FindLaw, the acme of legal Web sites.

In addition, excellent sites may be found at Pace University School of Law (**http://www.law.pace.edu**), Emory University School of Law (**http://www.law.emory.edu**), and several other law schools. There are enough links in most of the above sites to re-create the Great Chain of Being.[26] And if, from time to time, one seeks risible relief from the sober strictures of the law, a Web site featuring odd enactments may be your cup of cappuccino. Access **http://www.dumblaws.com** and discover that in California no vehicle without a driver may exceed 60 miles per hour and that it is illegal to herd more than 2,000 sheep down Hollywood Boulevard at one time.

SUMMARY

While many eminent men and women have served on the federal bench, the name of John Marshall, the fourth Chief Justice of the Supreme Court, looms like the legendary Helios of Rhodes over the juridical landscape. Marshall served as the nation's highest judicial officer for thirty-four years, and during that time he wrote the opinion of 508 of the more than 1,000 cases he participated in; but no decision of Marshall's is more famous or more consequential than *Marbury v. Madison.* In this case Marshall cleverly expounded the doctrine of Judicial Review, the idea that a federal court, and ultimately the Supreme Court, can examine an act of Congress to determine its constitutionality. This was instant precedent, the Big Bang of jurisprudence. The summarizing words of Marshall have been oft quoted but bear repeating: "It is emphatically the province and duty of the judicial department to say what the law is. . . . This is of the very essence of judicial duty."[27]

Although the framers of the Judiciary Act of 1789 seem to have envisaged the position of the Supreme Court as ultimate arbiter of the constitutionality of acts of Congress, that authority is not explicit in the Constitution. Accordingly, Marshall extended the "checks and balances" feature of our tripartite system to include the third branch as a coequal entity, a singular riff on Montesquieu's memorable political melody.

Similarly, the bibliographic fibers woven into the activities of the Congress, the executive branch, the independent agencies, and the federal courts "is a complex web—perhaps not always seamless, but often ingenious in its inter-relationships and sometimes even beautiful in its harmony. . . . To understand a statute, one needs the decisions which have interpreted it; to understand a court's decision, one needs the statute which it has applied; to understand an administrative regulation, one must see the statute by which it was authorized."[28] This paradigm of functional unity is often difficult to descry, but I hope that the information furnished in the last three chapters conveys a perception of its presence.

NOTES

1. Vincent Bugliosi, *And the Sea Will Tell* (New York: Norton, 1991), pp. 282–83.

2. Kendall F. Svengalis, *The Legal Information Buyer's Guide and Reference Manual, 1998–99* (Barrington, RI: Rhode Island Law Press, 1998), p. 11.

3. Individual issues of *Noter Up,* a semiannual publication updating the *Fundamentals of Legal Research* and *Legal Research Illustrated,* include current materials in a section titled "New Publications in Legal Research, Writing, and Bibliography."

4. Thomas A. Woxland, "'Forever Associated with the Practice of Law': The Early Years of the West Publishing Company," *Legal Reference Services Quarterly* 5: 122 (Spring 1985).

5. *West Publishing Company v. Mead Data Central, Inc.,* 616 F.Supp. 1571, 1575 (1985), *aff'd,* 799 F.2d 1219 (1986), *cert. denied,* 497 U.S. 1970 (1987).

6. "West and Mead Data Settle Copyright Dispute," *National Law Journal* 6 (August 1, 1986).

7. *Feist Publications, Inc. v. Rural Telephone Service Company, Inc.,* 499 U.S. 340, 111 S.Ct. 1282, 1285, 1291 (1991).

8. *Matthew Bender & Company, Inc., Plaintiff, v. West Publishing Company, Defendant. Hyperlaw, Inc., Intervenor-Plaintiff, v. West Publishing Company, Defendant,* 1997 U.S. Dist. LEXIS 6915, 42 U.S.P.Q. 2d (BNA) 1930 (May 19, 1997).

9. *West's Law Finder: A Legal Research Manual* (Eagan, MN: West, 1989), p. 11.

10. J. Myron Jacobstein et al., *Fundamentals of Legal Research,* 7th ed. (New York: Foundation Press, 1998), p. 108, note 7.

11. Miles O. Price et al., *Effective Legal Research,* 4th ed. (Boston: Little, Brown, 1979), pp. 172–73.

12. *Password* 16: 1, 3 (November/December 1996).

13. Svengalis, *The Legal Information Buyer's Guide,* pp. 608, 610, 614.

14. Jacobstein, *Fundamentals of Legal Research,* p. 322.

15. *Rosensteil v. Rosensteil,* 251 N.Y.S.2d 565, 578–79 (1964).

16. Price, *Effective Legal Research,* p. 145.

17. *Noter Up,* August 1994, p. 9.

18. Office of the Federal Register, *United States Government Manual, 1997/98 ed.* (Washington: Government Printing Office), p. 75.

19. Laurence Baum, *The Supreme Court,* 4th ed. (Washington: Congressional Quarterly Press, 1992), p. 12.

20. *USA Today* 16: 13A (March 13–15, 1998).

21. *Congressional Record* (daily edition), February 1, 1990, p. H196.

22. Samuel Eliot Morison, *The Oxford History of the American People* (New York: Oxford University Press, 1965), pp. 321–22.

23. *Brown v. Allen,* 344 U.S. 433 (1953).

24. See *The University of Chicago Manual of Legal Citation* (Rochester, NY: Lawyers Cooperative Publishing Company, 1989), p. 16.

25. Margaret A. Leary, "The Case of the Disappearing Briefs: A Study in Preservation Strategy," *Law Library Journal* 85: 357 (Spring 1993).

26. See Robert A. Piliwsky, "A Bibliographic Essay on Law-Related Internet Sites," *The Serials Librarian* 35: 77–96 (1999).

27. *Marbury v. Madison,* 5 U.S. (1 Cranch) 137, 177–78.

28. Morris L. Cohen, ed., *How to Find the Law,* 7th ed. (Eagan, MN: West, 1976), p. xvi.

CHAPTER NINE

STATISTICAL SOURCES

> [T]he very term statistic derives from the Greek denoting "of state affairs." And if the statistics themselves are frequently dour, statisticians are the most cheerful, even playful, of beings, combining the sheer joy of mathematics with the more enduring satisfactions of hard but cumulative labor.
>
> —Daniel Patrick Moynihan

> Statistics: a group of numbers looking for an argument.
>
> —Anon.

INTRODUCTION

Henry James called Washington, DC, the city of conversation. Most of the time the media attend to, and are an integral part of, the chattering classes and confer upon one another a faux punditry. But inside the Beltway there are productive tribes that labor in relative silence, for the nation's capital is also a city of statisticians with redoubts where legions of demographers encamp. A wag once said that demographers don't care what you do, so long as they can count it. I am reminded of the famous witticism attributed to Mrs. Patrick Campbell, the nineteenth-century actress: "My dear, I don't care what they do, so long as they don't do it in the street and frighten the horses." What do they count? Just about everything you can imagine.

A voluminous amount of material has been written about the federal statistical project. In this chapter I attempt to identify and describe a few basic statistical sources, in print and on the Internet, and examine some of the Census Bureau's strategies designed to make "Census 2000" more accurate than its 1990 decennial count.

The statistical enterprise of the federal government is decentralized. Many agencies gather various kinds of numerical information and report these data for the use of both the private sector and governments at all levels. Congressional hearings also generate a wealth of data on a wide array of public policy issues. Statistics help measure the quality of life; furnish the basis for modifications of union contracts, child support, and Social Security payments; determine where the United States stands in relation to other countries; and address a host of other economic, social, and scientific matters. For example, the Consumer Price Indexes (CPI) measure the average change over time in the prices paid by urban consumers for a fixed market basket of goods and services. The Bureau of Labor Statistics (BLS) has been producing the index since 1913 and makes comprehensive adjustments every ten years and technical adjustments on an ongoing basis. Two versions of the CPI are published each month by the BLS, a major statistical-gathering entity of the government within the Department of Labor. The CPI-U includes expenditures by urban wage earners, professional, managerial, and technical workers; the self-employed; short-term workers; the unemployed; retirees; and others not in the labor force. The CPI-W is based only on expenditures patterns of hourly wage earners or persons holding clerical jobs.

A General Accounting Office (GAO) report concluded that the CPI expenditure rates should be updated more frequently than the standard ten-year pattern to make them more representative of consumer spending. "Because federal tax brackets and federal payments . . . are adjusted for inflation, a CPI that more accurately measures inflation could affect the federal budget."[1] Cost-of-living adjustments (COLAs) for many activities and payments—collective bargaining contracts, Social Security, military and civil service employees, food stamp recipients, school lunches, and so forth—are linked to the CPI by law. As William Claude Dukenfield (a.k.a. W. C. Fields), the legendary actor and world-class quaffer of spirituous beverages, remarked during an inflationary period in the 1920s, "I can't see how the human race is going to survive now that the cost of living has gone up two dollars a quart."[2]

Another example is the way in which information gathered by or for the Bureau of the Census is used to define societal issues. The following is a selective list:

- determining compliance with the Voting Rights Acts and amendments;

- allocating funds from federal grant programs;

- identifying areas requiring bilingual education;

- assessing the need for equal employment opportunity programs;
- developing programs to reduce unemployment;
- establishing fair market rent values;
- enforcing fair lending practices;
- identifying areas requiring child assistance programs;
- establishing occupational and vocational education programs;
- analyzing population growth;
- developing programs for the elderly and handicapped;
- selecting sites for retail stores and new plants;
- planning school district boundaries and school construction programs;
- establishing regional transportation systems.[3]

The reluctance of Congress and the administration to fund adequately the nation's statistical undertaking is irrational when one contemplates the manifold ways in which statistics are used by federal, state, and local governments and by the private sector. The 1980s and 1990s have witnessed spasms of government parsimony that have curtailed the gathering, analyzing, and disseminating of statistics. Congress wants agencies to conduct their statistical activities with robust reliability and minimal funds, and arguments over the Census Bureau's methods of ensuring greater accuracy in the decennial census are examples of the lawmakers' ambivalence. However, concepts must constantly be refined, statistical collection methods updated, and redundancies among agencies' data programs evaluated; and these operations cost money. But ultimately they are worth doing well and well worth doing, because a nation's ability to survive and prosper in the highly competitive global economy depends upon reliable data made available as swiftly as possible.

The government's present policy of making an increasing number of formerly printed statistical reports available only on electronic bulletin boards and other sources available via the Internet has its downside. Because these sources are available online for limited periods of time, and because they are never issued in print, they cannot be retrieved once they are removed from their servers. At least one organization,

Congressional Information Service (CIS), downloads these reports and indexes, abstracts, and microfilms them as part of their *American Statistics Index* microfiche series; in addition, the full text of numerous statistical series is permanently archived in the firm's *Statistical Universe* database. The potential evanescence of electronic access and the mischief it can cause are manifest when a prominent purveyor of federal statistics like CIS feels obliged to resort to this strategy for the benefit of data users.

SELECTED INTERNET RESOURCES

The migratory habits of the government with respect to statistical information are as precipitant as those of other types of information discussed in previous chapters. Federal agencies and the private sector dominate the ether in offering users more numeric data than ever before. The following is a review of commercial and governmental products available through the Internet.

COMMERCIAL SOURCES

The most comprehensive source of federal statistical publications is Congressional Information Service's *American Statistics Index* (ASI). Published since 1974, ASI indexes and abstracts statistical publications of the executive branch, Congress, the judiciary, the independent regulatory agencies, and other federal entities. A subscription offers paperbound monthly index and abstracts issues for the current calendar year plus the previous year's clothbound annual cumulation of index and abstracts volumes from 1974. Starting with the 1987 annual, an index of SuDocs classification numbers is included. An initial three-volume set published in 1974, titled *ASI Annual & Retrospective Edition,* provides indexing and abstracting on a selective basis for series issued from the early 1960s through 1973. Index cumulations are available for intervals covering 1974–1979, 1980–1984, 1985–1988, 1989–1992, 1993–1996, and so forth.

Contents of *American Statistics Index*

For current monthly issues, data are provided by subject, issuing agency, name (personal and corporate), type of data breakdown (by city, occupation, or educational attainment), publication title, and agency report number. Each index entry cites an accession number that references a specific publication description in the abstracts section. ASI carries every type of statistical publication: periodicals, series, annuals, biennials, monographs, and so forth, including both depository and nondepository items. As with most of the CIS products, the full text of the publications announced in ASI is available on microfiche or individually in paper or microfiche through the company's Documents on Demand service. Figure 9.1, page 290, shows a sample abstract from *American Statistics Index.*

Statistical Universe

ASI was formerly available on *Statistical Masterfile* (SMF), a CD-ROM product that included *Statistical Reference Index* (SRI) and the *Index to International Statistics* (IIS). SRI announces statistical publications of state governments, associations and institutes, business and commercial publishers, and universities. IIS covers titles published by international intergovernmental organizations (IGOs) such as the United Nations and its specialized agencies, the European Union, the Organization of American States, the Council of Europe, and other prominent IGOs. Just as *Congressional Masterfile* 2 on CD-ROM was replaced by Congressional Universe (see chapter 5), *Statistical Masterfile* was superseded by Statistical Universe, a Web-based product that encompasses ASI records from 1973 to the present, links to more than 800 full-text documents published from 1994 and stored on LEXIS-NEXIS (CIS's parent company), and links to more than 2,000 publications on federal agency Web sites. The full-text series consists in about equal measure of depository and nondepository items. These are available for viewing in HTML and PDF formats; all charts and tables are available as GIF images stored at 300 dots per inch.

Statistical Universe confers some advantages over SMF. The former is updated monthly, whereas *Masterfile* subscribers received quarterly disk updates. Because you are searching on LEXIS-NEXIS, you have the option of doing advanced searches; you will be able to exclude serials from the searches, thereby eliminating duplicate titles in the answer set in cases where the government produces the same types of data every year; and you will retrieve a more precise answer than was available on SMF.

While Statistical Universe expands its full-text coverage, it provides links to other Web sites to supplement its records, a feature that is available from the 1996 ASI entries. This service, accessible by referring to the "List of Links" on Statistical Universe, connects to such prominent sites as the *Statistical Abstract of the United States,* STAT-USA, FedStats, and CenStats, all of which are discussed later in this chapter. Moreover, Statistical Universe maintains a consistent user interface to

Figure 9.1. Sample abstract from *American Statistics Index*.

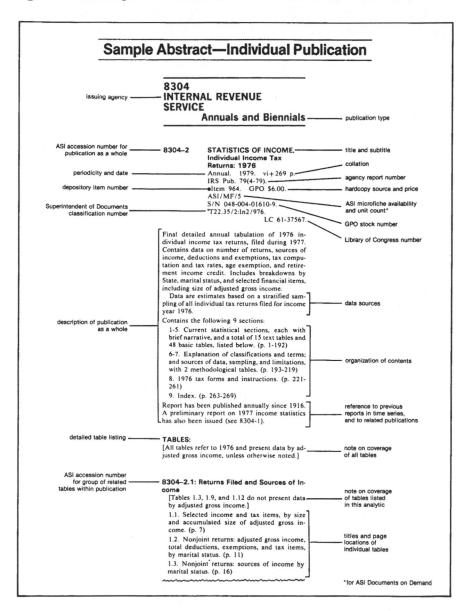

the full text, which differs within and among government Web sites. All full texts on Statistical Universe are presented in similar fashion. Finally, as noted but worth repeating, CIS and LEXIS-NEXIS have made a commitment to archive these texts on a permanent basis.

GOVERNMENT SOURCES

Statistical information is available in many formats: Print still survives but competes with microfiche, computer tape reels or tape cartridge, floppy diskette, CD-ROM, and online media. The electronic dissemination of federal government statistics has become the primary means of transmitting numeric information, especially small data that would require many huge and clumsy volumes of print to contain. Leading statistical agencies such as the Census Bureau and the Bureau of Labor Statistics maintain flourishing Web sites; but, as noted, important statistical series compiled by or for the many statistic-gathering federal entities increasingly appear in electronic format only. In hindsight it seems inevitable that vast quantities of numeric data would end up on the Internet, once it slipped the surly bonds of print and of its predecessor, the ARPANET, with its limited command and control mission.

STAT-USA

STAT-USA, a division of the Commerce Department's Economics and Statistics Administration, bills itself as the federal government's premier electronic publisher of trade and economic information. Formerly named the Office of Business Analysis, STAT-USA (**http://www.stat-usa.gov**) is actually a suite of products and services. It presumably fills the gap vacated when a product called the National Economic, Social, and Environmental Data Bank, which was issued quarterly on CD-ROM from October 1992 to August 1995, was discontinued.

The most prominent component of STAT-USA is STAT-USA/ Internet, which provides one-stop electronic browsing for business, economic, and trade information from more than fifty federal agencies and a few nongovernmental entities. Broad topics include daily economic news; frequently requested statistical releases; information by subject such as export and international trade, domestic economic news, and statistical series; business leads and procurement opportunities; STAT-USA databases; and selected publications of interest. STAT-USA/Internet is free for use in depository libraries, but users at home or at their offices must pay a modest annual or quarterly subscription because STAT-USA is required to operate in a cost-recovery mode.

Begin at STAT-USA's home page and visit the State of the Nation (SOTN) Library for current and historical economic and financial releases and economic data, and/or access the GLOBUS & National Trade Data Bank (NTDB) area for current and historical trade-related releases, international market research, trade opportunities, country analysis, and much more. Within these areas, you can find a trove of statistical information. A number of these series are available in print through SuDocs subscriptions and free to depository libraries, but some information is available only through this site or the Internet pages of the individual agencies that contribute their data to STAT-USA. The SOTN files include:

- daily releases such as bond rates, the *Daily Treasury Statement,* and foreign exchange rates;

- general economic indicators such as the aforementioned Consumer Price Indexes, the Producer Price Indexes (called in print version the *PPI Detailed Report,* which foreshadows trends that subsequently develop in the CPI and which was formerly called *Wholesale Prices and Price Indexes*), gross domestic product, export sales from the Department of Agriculture, personal income and outlays, and so forth;

- housing and construction data such as housing vacancies, housing starts and building permits, new home sales, and housing vacancies;

- employment statistics such as the employment cost index, unemployment, metropolitan area employment and unemployment;

- manufacturing and industry figures such as advance retail sales, auto and truck sales and production, durable goods, shipment and orders, and more;

- monetary information such as bank credit, weekly foreign exchange rates, selected interest rates, and aggregate reserves;

- economic policy information such as the *Monthly Treasury Statement of Receipts and Outlays of the United States Government*, statements by the Chairman of the Board of Governors of the Federal Reserve System from his aerie high atop Mount Olympus, and the "Beige Book." This last is the popular title for *Current Economic Conditions,* a report issued at irregular intervals on business cycle fluctuation in economic activity for each Federal Reserve District in support of Federal Open Market Committee meetings. The Beige Book has been issued since July 1983 and has been indexed and abstracted in ASI since March 1991.

If these databases do not contain the information you seek, you can consult the SOTN Library for an additional 3,000 files or visit the Economic News Archive.

The NTDB and GLOBUS databases are equally impressive in the range of statistics they provide. A select list of files includes:

- global business opportunity information and statistics such as those from the Defense Logistics Agency, agricultural trade leads, international marketing reports rates, historical trade opportunity leads going back two years, and Commerce Business Daily (CBD). This last is a worthy periodical that carries notices of proposed government procurement actions, contract awards, sales of government property, and other procurement information. CBD is of particular value to firms interested in bidding on federal government purchases and surplus property offered for sale, or in seeking subcontract opportunities from prime contractors. It is also available in paper copy for sale or free to depository libraries.

- current exchange rates posted twice a day, the 10 A.M. midpoints and the noon buying rates;

- international trade statistics, including U.S. exports and imports by commodity and country;

- market and country research comprising industry sector analysis and foreign agricultural market reports, country commercial guides, and so forth;

- current press release data covering foreign trade series (FT 900) supplemental tables, export and import price indexes, and so forth;

- contacts such as commercial service international contacts, export yellow pages, and state-by-state export resource listings;

- miscellaneous such as the Asia Commercial Overview. There is also a link at this segment for searching the entire NTDB if desired rather than specific sites noted above.

The Omnibus Trade and Competitiveness Act of 1988 (PL 100-418; 102 Stat. 1107) requires the Secretary of Commerce to manage and operate the NTDB for the purpose of trade analysis and export promotion. The basic concept, capably implemented in this popular service, holds that the NTDB will distribute major categories of data covering almost every aspect of U.S. trade and international economics. Almost any series remotely associated with trade will likely find its way into this service, and this is the NTDB's strength and weakness. You are never really sure what information will pop up in the bank's commodious database, but if you look you will probably find what you need. The NTDB is available on CD-ROM as well as via STAT-USA/Internet. The former product is free to depository libraries and their clientele but requires a subscription for other users. STAT-USA publishes a free quarterly periodical titled *STAT-USA/The Newsletter* as a service to its customers.

USA Trade

USA Trade, a product in the National Trade Data Bank CD-ROM series, is issued monthly from January 1998. It is the result of a partnership between the Foreign Trade Division (FTD) of the Bureau of the Census, which is the official provenance of federal government export and import statistics, and STAT-USA, which has a proven track record in assembling all kinds of trade information. A subscription to this CD-ROM product furnishes you with access to some 17,000 import and 9,000 export commodities at the highest level of the Harmonized System (HS), representing data for the 240 trading partner countries of the United States as well as fifty statistical districts. The software allows you to choose various levels of HS commodity classifications. Using USA Trade, you can sort and isolate commodity data by country; and anytime the Census Bureau revises earlier HS level statistics, the changes will be reflected in the next USA Trade disk.

Bureau of Export Administration

The Bureau of Export Administration (BXA) controls the export of commercial products, called "dual use" items, which may also be used for military purposes. BXA publishes regulations that establish guidelines for exporters to determine whether the products they want to see are dual use and therefore must be licensed. Other entities, such as the State Department, the Department of Energy, and the Nuclear Regulatory Commission, are involved in the export licensing process. To guide exporters through this maze, BXA has mounted a Web site (**http://www. bxa.doc.gov**) to introduce exporters to the Bureau and to answer most of the general questions frequently asked. The site also provides schedules of upcoming seminars hosted across the country for manufacturers, wholesalers, shippers, and other businesses involved in exporting and serves as a "What's New" bulletin board, publishing press releases and announcing new regulations or other changes to the export process.

TIC Export Information

The International Trade Administration of the Commerce Department has a Trade Information Center (TIC) whose experienced trade specialists are available to help companies navigate the complex tributaries of documentation, licensing, and regulations that make selling a product to a buyer in Rwanda more complicated than selling to one in Rhode Island. TIC specialists furnish information, counseling, and assistance for countries in Western Europe, Asia, the Western Hemisphere, Africa, and the Near East. The TIC's Internet site (**http://www.ita. doc.gov**) offers resources under links such as answers to frequently asked questions, export programs, country and regional market information, international trade offices nationwide, trade promotion events, trade lead information, and financing information.

FedStats

The Federal Interagency Council on Statistical Policy maintains the FedStats (a.k.a. FEDSTATS) site (**http://www.fedstats.gov**) to provide easy access to the full range of statistics and related information produced by more than seventy federal agencies. Although agency statistics are bound to overlap with STAT-USA compendia, the sites together offer a vast array of data. The FedStats Home Page provides links to the following pages: the agencies that provide the statistics; programs by broad subjects, from agriculture to transportation; state, county, and local area data; press releases announcing new products and services; whom to call or write with your questions on statistical content; budget documents, working papers, and *Federal Register* notices; "FastFacts," in which publications such as the *Statistical Abstract of the United States* are summarized with links to their full contents in Adobe PDF; and an in-depth search capability using the A to Z index, from Acute Conditions (colds and influenza) to Weekly Earnings. FedStats, like STAT-USA, is a site guaranteed to gratify the needs of the most fervent statistical wonk.

White House Site

The White House Home Page (**http://www.whitehouse.gov**) links to the White House Briefing Room, which includes, among other useful loci, a selection of federal economic and social statistics reported by agencies and a link to FedStats.

MAJOR STATISTICAL AGENCIES

Many agencies participate in gathering and disseminating statistical information, but the two most prominent (and newsworthy) agencies that are involved in the federal statistical enterprise are the Bureau of Labor Statistics and the Bureau of the Census. The following represents a discussion of selected series from each of these entities.

BUREAU OF LABOR STATISTICS

The Bureau of Labor Statistics (BLS) is, as noted above, an agency within the Labor Department. According to its mission statement posted on its Internet site (**http://stats.bls.gov**) and published in the latest edition of its *Customer Service Guide,* the BLS

> is the principal fact-finding agency for the Federal Government in the broad field of labor economics and statistics. BLS . . . collects, processes, analyses, and disseminates essential statistical data to the American public, Congress, other Federal agencies, State and local governments, business, and labor. BLS also serves as a statistical resource for the Department of Labor. BLS data must satisfy a number of criteria, including relevance to current social and economic issues, timeliness in reflecting today's rapidly changing economic conditions, accuracy and consistently high statistical quality, and impartiality in both subject matter and presentation.

The Bureau's data come from voluntary responses to surveys of businesses or households conducted by BLS staff, by the Census Bureau on a contract basis, or in conjunction with cooperating state and other federal agencies. This information can be accessed not only on the Internet but also in print, by fax on demand, through recorded telephone message systems in more than twenty-five metropolitan areas, and by direct contact with BLS representatives in eight regional offices located in major cities throughout the United States. Important printed information includes the BLS Bulletin series and several periodicals, most of which are available for sale by the Superintendent of Documents and free to depository institutions. There are more than 200 BLS series announced in the *List of Classes of United States Government Publications Available for Selection by Depository Libraries* under the "L2." class stem of the SuDocs class notation.

Employment and Unemployment

Arguably the most politically volatile of the BLS data sets, employment and unemployment figures have toppled presidents and registered temblors in the body politic. They can also represent personal tragedies for individuals and households. Some of the prominent series in this category are as follows:

- The BLS sponsors the collection and production of data from the National Longitudinal Surveys (**http://stats.bls.gov/nlshome. htm**). Each survey gathers information at multiple points in time on the labor market experiences of five groups of American men and women. Each group selected is considered to have special problems in the labor market. The individuals in the sample are representative of the larger population of like Americans born during a given time period and include minorities, youth, women, and the economically disadvantaged. Each group consists of 5,000 or more members, some of whom have been surveyed for decades. These data offer researchers the opportunity to study large segments of American men and women over significant periods of their lives.

- Covered Employment and Wages (**http://stats.bls.gov/ cewhome.htm**) produces a comprehensive series for workers protected by state unemployment insurance laws and is a virtual census of payroll employment. The data include monthly employment; total quarterly wages; and number of establishments by four-digit Standard Industrial Classification for the nation, all states, and all counties. Printed annual publications in the BLS Bulletin series include *Employment and Wages, Annual Averages.*

- Occupational Employment Statistics (**http://stats.bls.gov/ oeshome.htm**) is a survey that collects national data on employment by occupation and industry for wage and salary workers in approximately 750 occupations and 400 nonfarm industries. In the print BLS Bulletin series is the annual *Occupational Employment Statistics* for selected industries.

- Mass Layoff Statistics (**http://stats.bls.gov/lauhome.htm**) comprises two series. The quarterly series covers layoffs of at least thirty-one days in duration that involve fifty or more individuals from a single establishment filing initial claims for unemployment insurance during a consecutive five-week period. The monthly series covers layoffs of fifty workers or more regardless of duration. For both series, data are provided on the reason for layoffs, initial unemployment insurance claims, geographic distribution by state of initial layoffs and initial claimants, industry distribution of the layoffs, and recall expectations.

- Employment, Hours, and Earnings by Industry (**http://stats.bls.gov/ceshome.htm**) surveys payroll records of more than 390,000 businesses on a monthly basis and provides detailed industry data on these three data sets for workers on nonfarm payrolls for the nation, all states, the District of Columbia, Puerto Rico, the Virgin Islands, and more than 270 metropolitan areas.

- The Current Population Survey (CPS) of households is conducted monthly by the Census Bureau for the BLS and provides data on employment, unemployment, and persons not in the labor force (which includes discouraged workers and persons not in the labor force for other reasons). Beyond that, studies based on the CPS cover a broad range of topics, including the nation's overall labor market situation, as well as those of special worker groups such as minorities, women, school-age youth, older workers, disabled veterans, persons living in poverty, contingent workers, and displaced workers. These national labor force statistics may be accessed at **http://stats.bls.gov/cpshome.htm.** Union membership, formerly issued in the Collective Bargaining Agreements file, which ceased data collection at the end of 1995 (**http://stats.bls.gov/lmrhome.htm**), is one of the twenty-five special categories collected in the population survey.

- State and Metropolitan Area Labor Force Statistics (**http://stats.bls.gov/lauhome.htm**) furnishes monthly labor force, employment, and unemployment data for some 6,950 areas, including all states, the District of Columbia, Puerto Rico, metropolitan areas, counties, cities of 25,000 population or more, and all cities and towns in New England. Annual averages of employment status are available by demographic groups, occupation, industry, and full- or part-time status.

For the last three divisions within the employment/unemployment category, the BLS issues many press releases on a periodic basis and the monthly printed periodical *Employment and Earnings,* a sales selection and a depository item.

An interesting commercial work attesting to the popular game of ranking jobs is Les Krantz's *Jobs Rated Almanac* (New York: St. Martin's Press, 1999), in which the author, using statistics from the BLS, the Census Bureau, professional organizations, and telephone surveys, identified 250 occupations and ranked them according to six variables: income, stress, physical demands, potential growth, job security, and work environment. Not surprisingly, nine of the top ten were in computer or math-related fields, with Web site managers atop the list. The worst-ranked were manual labor jobs in traditionally troubled and dangerous fields, such as fishermen (No. 248), lumberjacks (No. 249), and roustabouts in oil fields (No. 250). The presidency ranked number 229: lots of stress, a stagnant salary, and no room for job growth.

Prices and Living Conditions

The specter of inflation, like that of unemployment, brings fear and trembling to politicians. Following are some noteworthy issuances in this category.

- The Consumer Price Indexes (**http://stats.bls.gov/cpihome. htm**), as noted above, measure the average change over time in the prices paid by urban consumers for a fixed market basket of consumer goods and services. User fees, such as for water, and sales and excise taxes paid by the consumer, are included. Not included are income taxes and investments such as stocks and life insurance. Low unemployment and little or no inflation, something the country enjoyed in the fin de siécle years of the twentieth century, makes for happy times and typically favors incumbency. The CPI began during World War I (it was then called the cost-of-living index) as a way of determining a fair wage scale for the shipbuilding industry, and it has undergone several major revisions in methodology since then. But the determination of the index population and the categories of goods measured continues to remain controversial and is the subject of many scholarly analyses and criticism.

  Much is at stake in the construction of the CPI. Millions of workers are covered by collective bargaining contracts that provide for increases in wage rates based on increases in these indexes. Moreover, various federal statutes mandate adjustments in wages and benefits as the CPI rises or falls. And the index affects the official definition of poverty, which is the basis for eligibility in numerous health and welfare programs at the federal, state, and local government levels. The print equivalent of the online data is called the *CPI Detailed Report,* a monthly sales and depository publication filled with statistical tables and technical notes.

- The Producer Price Indexes (**http://stats.bls.gov/ppihome. htm**) measure the average change in the selling prices received by domestic producers for their output. They include price changes for the entire output of the domestic goods-producing sector for agricultural, forestry, fisheries, mining, scrap, and manufacturing industries and also furnish price changes for a growing portion of the output of the domestic services sector (transportation, help supply services, and health services). The PPI often foreshadows trends that subsequently develop in consumer prices. The print version of the Internet information is the *PPI Detailed Report* (formerly known as *Wholesale Prices and Price Indexes*), which is published monthly with an annual supplement. Like the *CPI Detailed Report,* this journal is a sales and a depository issuance.

- The Consumer Expenditure Survey (**http://stats.bls.gov/ csxhome.htm**) provides data on the buying habits of American consumers by socioeconomic characteristics. These data are used to update from time to time the CPI market baskets and for research by government, business, labor, and academic analysts. It is unique among federal surveys in allowing users to associate the complete range of consumer expenditures with the income and characteristics of those consumers. The program consists of two surveys, the quarterly interview survey and the diary survey, each with its own questionnaire and sample. Interview data furnish information on relatively large or recurring expenditures. Diary data offer detailed expenditure information on small, frequently purchased items. The information available from these surveys provides expenditures classified by income, age, consumer unit size, and other demographic characteristics of consumer units since 1984. A biennial print version in the BLS Bulletin series is called *Consumer Expenditure Survey.*

Other BLS Series

Several other Bureau of Labor Statistics series include the National Compensation Survey; Employment Cost Trends; Employee Benefits Survey; Occupational Compensation Survey; Occupational Injuries and Illnesses, which produces the *Occupational Injuries and Illnesses Classification Manual* (**http://stats.bls.gov/oshoi**); Quarterly Labor Productivity; Industry Productivity; Multifactor Productivity; Employment Projections; and international data covering comparative information on labor statistics and developments abroad, such as United States Import and Export Price Indexes and Foreign Direct Investment data.

Frequently used series and periodicals not mentioned above are available in print, fiche, and electronic formats. The following publications are available online in PDF from the Bureau's home page by clicking on the "Publications & Research Papers" box.

- The *Monthly Labor Review* (MLR) features articles on employment, prices, compensation, working conditions, productivity, social indicators, foreign labor developments, and other topics. In addition, the *Review* contains fifty tables of current labor statistics, book reviews, and occasional columns on workplace performance and legal issues. The Current Labor Statistics section of MLR contains links to all preformatted data tables available on the BLS Web site as well as a PDF file of the tables appearing in the print edition of MLR. The MLR is a very useful source, and the *Periodicals Supplement* to the *Monthly Catalog* shows its many indexing and abstracting services.

- *Compensation and Working Conditions,* a quarterly, includes articles on occupational pay, employee benefits, employer costs for employee compensation, occupational injuries and illnesses, and other workplace issues. The periodical also presents occupational wage and employee benefit statistics. *Conditions* is a sales publication and a depository item.

- *The Occupational Outlook Handbook,* a well-known biennial BLS Bulletin series noted in chapter 6, covers several hundred occupations, indicating for each occupation information about the nature of the work, places of employment, educational requirements, potential earnings, the projected employment outlook, and the like. The first *Handbook* was prepared at the request of and with the financial support of the Veterans Administration (now the Department of Veterans Affairs), which was authorized by law to furnish World War II veterans with information concerning the need for general education and for trained personnel in the various trades, crafts, and professions. Accordingly, it was first issued in August 1946 as VA Manual M7-1, *Occupational Outlook Information,* but was given its present name in 1949 when it was made available for sale to the public for use in schools, colleges, VA regional offices and guidance centers, employment service offices, community organizations, and other agencies engaged in the vocational guidance of young people, veterans, and workers.

To help job seekers, employment planners, and guidance counselors keep abreast of current occupational and employment trends between editions of the *Handbook,* the BLS issues the *Occupational Outlook Quarterly,* which consists of articles and statistics on selected vocations. Both the biennial and the quarterly products are available for sale and for deposit.

- *BLS Update* is a handy, free, quarterly printed newsletter that contains highlights of selected new BLS publications, a list of BLS regional offices, telephone hotline numbers at the several cities, and an order form for sales publications from the Superintendent of Documents. Most of this information is also available and with greater recency on the BLS Web site.

BUREAU OF THE CENSUS

Of all the statistics-generating federal entities, the Census Bureau is, deservedly, best known. Census publications are the core of a library's collection of statistical information and may be required by anyone from the most sophisticated researcher to the parent who, high school student in tow, asked ever so seriously to see the "consensus on demagoguery." The Bureau's primary function is to collect, process, compile, and disseminate numeric data for the use of other government agencies, federal, state, and local; groups in the private sector; and the general public. It publishes more statistics than other agencies do, covers a wider range of subjects, and serves a greater variety of needs. Moreover, Article I, Section 2 of the Constitution, construed by the one-person, one-vote principle established by the U.S. Supreme Court, requires congressional redistricting based upon population shifts recorded in the decennial census. In *Wesberry v. Sanders,* 376 U.S. 1, 11

L.Ed.2d 481, 84 S.Ct. 526 (February 17, 1964) the High Court held that, as nearly as practicable, one person's vote should be worth as much as another's. Later that year, in *Reynolds v. Sims,* 377 U.S. 533, 12 L.Ed.2d 506, 84 S.Ct. 1362 (June 15, 1964), the Court ruled that state legislative districts must be as nearly of equal population as practicable. The two decisions, in theory, were supposed to eliminate or reduce dramatically the pernicious practice of gerrymandering. In a number of subsequent decisions involving apportionment disputes, the Court has followed the precedents set in *Wesberry* and *Reynolds.* However, to paraphrase Mark Twain, reports of the demise of the practice of gerrymandering are greatly exaggerated.

The first census was taken in 1790, and the process has been repeated each succeeding decade. In 1902, the Bureau of the Census was established as a permanent office (32 Stat. 51). By laws codified in Title 13 of the United States Code and by virtue of Article I, Section 2 of the Constitution, the Bureau is enjoined to take a census of the population every ten years. Although media attention tends to focus on the decennial census of population and housing, other lesser-known censuses are taken on a five-year schedule, currently for years ending in "2" and "7." These quinquennial censuses include the census of governments and the so-called economic censuses comprising financial, insurance, and real estate; manufactures; mineral industries; retail trade; wholesale trade; service industries; transportation, communications, and utilities; and business owners, including Hispanics, Blacks, women, and other minorities.[4]

For more than 150 years, the Census Bureau and its predecessor the Census Office conducted a five-year agriculture census. In 1996 the responsibility for that quinquennial snapshot was transferred to the Department of Agriculture's National Agricultural Statistics Service (NASS). Accordingly, the 1997 Census of Agriculture was conducted by NASS with the assistance of the Census Bureau. The NASS Web site (**http://usda.gov/nass**) has data for the 1997 census and various intercensal surveys conducted by NASS, which collects information on every facet of the U.S. agricultural scene.[5]

In addition, the Census Bureau collects statistics on outlying areas, including Puerto Rico, Guam, the U.S. Virgin Islands, Northern Mariana Islands, and American Samoa; and conducts various U.S. and foreign censuses and surveys in its international research and foreign-trade programs. In 1790, the federal government began publishing annual general statistics on U.S. foreign commerce and navigation, and the task of compiling these statistics from figures submitted by customs inspectors was first given to the Treasury Department. Since 1941, the Census Bureau has been doing the job pursuant to Title 15, Chapter 30, *Code of Federal Regulations,* the authority for which is Title 13, Chapter 9, *United States Code.*

Because users need information far more frequently than on a decennial or quinquennial schedule, the Bureau conducts intercensal activities on a continual basis. Moreover, the Census Bureau's vigorous Web site (**http://www.census.gov**) provides virtually up-to-the-minute data at its home page by clicking on "Current U.S. Population Count" (known as the Bureau's POPClock).[6]

Basic Information Sources

The Census Bureau's Web site, noted above, is the most convenient way to keep current about Census information; its more than 60,000 bibliographic and textual products, plus the latest information on "Census 2000," make it an indispensable source. Information about virtually every census product available can be found on the site. Abstracts are presented online at the time each new product becomes available, and the complete text of all printed reports released since January 1996 is accessible in PDF at the direct URL **http://www.census. gov/prod/www.titles.html**. Moreover, an increasing amount of background information and tables supplement published articles and studies. Indeed, it is becoming commonplace for an article that has been printed in a Census Bureau series to refer the reader to statistical tables available only on a Web site, whether it is the Bureau's or another agency for which the Bureau has collected data. Whether this bifurcation is desirable or not, it is becoming an inevitable fact of Internet life; and the integrated use of the two formats to produce a document is expected to grow in the future.

The following is a selection of informative, recurring Census Bureau issuances. Check the Web site, with its legions of links, if you want to access the information therein via the Internet or in another medium; in addition to the online availability, the Bureau's products come in print, microfiche, maps and charts, computer tape, diskettes, and CD-ROM.

Census Catalog & Guide

The *Census Catalog & Guide,* published annually, is sometimes organized by subject into chapters, sometimes grouped by media (print, CD-ROM, and so forth) and within media by subject (agricultural, economic, international). Beginning with the 1998 edition, URLs for all listed products were given. Be sure to read the "Introduction" because new editions are often designed to supplement or serve as a companion volume to the previous catalog. A PDF version of the *Catalog & Guide* can be accessed from the Bureau's Web site, and the specific URL is always published on the first page of the current catalog. Free to users, the catalog is a depository item and order forms are provided.

Historical Catalogs

In addition to the current *Census Catalog & Guide,* a basic collection for research purposes should include several other titles. The *Bureau of the Census Catalog of Publications, 1790–1972* is a large volume that provides a comprehensive historical bibliography of sources issued by the Bureau covering those years. This volume combines the previously issued *Catalog of United States Census Publications, 1790–1945,* prepared by Henry J. Dubester, who was chief of the Census Library Project, Library of Congress, with the *Bureau of the Census Catalogs* from 1946 to 1972. Kevin L. Cook's *Dubester's U.S. Census Bibliography with SuDocs Class Numbers and Indexes* (Englewood, CO: Libraries Unlimited, 1995) covers Dubester's 1790–1945 catalog with Superintendent of Documents classification numbers added to the original bibliography and subject index, thus making it unnecessary for users to search in two sources for these materials.

Monthly Product Announcement

The *Monthly Product Announcement* (MPA) serves to supplement the current *Census Catalog & Guide.* A free paper copy of this valuable pamphlet is available by e-mail (<majordomo@census.gov> and follow directions) or on the Internet (**http://www.census.gov/mp/ www/mpa.html#MPA**). Each issue offers bibliographic, including ordering, information for publications in paper copy, data files on computer tape, CD-ROM, diskettes, and, as noted, those on the Bureau's Web site. Most publications are available through the Bureau's Customer Services or the sales and depository divisions of the SuDocs, and Census Bureau order forms are provided. One can also order by phone or fax unless the entry gives other instructions. URLs are given for the majority of entries in MPA. For the most current information about Census Bureau products and how to obtain them, access CenStore by selecting the CenStore/Catalog option from the Bureau's home page. In 1999 the Bureau instituted a service called "Online Shopping," which allows customers to order CD-ROM products directly from CenStore. Using standard Internet shopping techniques, users can place orders twenty-four hours a day, seven days a week.

Census and You

Census and You is a monthly subscription newsletter available for sale by the SuDocs and free to depository libraries. It keeps users informed about current censuses and surveys; plans for upcoming censuses; products and programs, including computer tapes and other unpublished data sources; seminars and conferences the Bureau conducts periodically; local contact sources for specific Bureau activities and products; and, periodically, an announcement of statistical products from other federal agencies. There is very little overlap between *Census and You* and MPA.

CenStats Replaces CENDATA

CenStats is an electronic subscription service that provides convenient access to popular Census Bureau databases, including detailed import and export information; data currently available on selected CD-ROMs, such as USA Counties, ZIP Business Patterns, and County Business Patterns; and ways of accessing a street address and getting a neighborhood population profile. Customers can obtain a quarterly or annual subscription. CenStats replaced CENDATA, which was offered via DIALOG and CompuServe.[7]

Major Statistical Compendia

According to Norman Cousins, we the people "cannot understand our own country or any other or our lives or anyone else's without adequate data. We may not be able to make judgments on statistics alone, but we make better judgments if they rest on a solid base."[8] Following are some selections from statistical florilegia.

Statistical Abstract of the United States

It has been called Uncle Sam's Reference Shelf, the Census Bureau's best-seller, the National Data Book. It is the people's Guide to Sources—of data from the Census Bureau, other federal agencies, and private organizations. It covers all aspects of American life; and when a new edition is published, it gets the kind of media attention normally reserved for the latest John Grisham novel. I refer, of course, to the *Statistical Abstract of the United States,* considered one of a handful of federal government sources that may be proclaimed indispensable. This annual compendium of statistics began as a publication of the Treasury Department and is now the provenance of the Bureau of the Census. Published since 1878, the earliest volumes give no hint of its present scope and range. The first edition is almost wholly devoted to aspects of foreign trade, shipping, and public finance; data on imports of gold, silver coin, and bullion take up 11 of its 154 pages. Nearly 108 pages concern imports and exports. What might be called social statistics are confined to three tables, one summarizing the population of the several states as recorded by each decennial census from 1790 to 1870 and the other two summarizing immigration by nationality and year.

By the 1920s, the *Statistical Abstract* had come to resemble in many respects the familiar volumes of the present day. By the end of the Eisenhower era, the *Abstract* exceeded 1,000 pages, of which roughly 1 in 4 was devoted to social statistics. The 1959 volume, for example, carried a table showing enrollments in "white schools" and "Negro schools" in eighteen southern states. The editions of this seminal work mirror the concerns of the nation, and virtually every edition contains new tables. The 1990 volume included, for the first time, deaths from AIDS and summary data on the growth of computer technology in the office environment. New features in the 1994 edition were Dow Jones market data, health care expenditures, and foreign stock and bond activity. According to a piece in *Census and You* promoting the 1996 edition, good and bad things were reduced to statistics. On a typical day in the United States, 343 juveniles were arrested for violent crimes, 196 businesses failed, and 3,211 motor vehicles were stolen. On the other hand, 6,500 marriages occurred, 1,344 immigrants arrived, and 2 million gallons of ice cream were produced.[9] The 1997 edition carried ninety-seven new tables covering topics such as hate crimes, pet ownership, and consumer finance. New tables in the 1998 edition included women's health, school violence, home-based businesses, and bank fees and services.

While each edition adds, drops, or refines features, the contents, divided into sections, typically cover more than thirty broad areas such as population, vital statistics, education, elections, energy, science, prices, and business enterprise. The *Statistical Abstract* includes source notes (footnotes) that refer the user to government and private-sector publications where more detailed information is available; an appendix that references tables in the *Abstract* to earlier data shown in the *Historical Statistics* (below); and a reliable index. A nifty recurring feature is a table and map of the United States showing the "Center of Population," a balance point that in 1790 was approximately twenty-three miles east of Baltimore, Maryland, and that by 1990 was a densely wooded area in Crawford County, Missouri. Based on the decennial censuses, the map clearly shows a west-by-southwest movement of the population in the last two centuries, statistical evidence of the doctrine of Manifest Destiny.

The *Abstract* is sent to depository libraries in print and on CD-ROM, and the print version is available for sale by the Superintendent of Documents, National Technical Information Service (NTIS), Hoover's Inc., Amazon.com, and Bernan Press. This last costs a few dollars more than the official clothbound edition but has a Smyth-sewn, hardcover binding and the type size for tables is 25 percent larger. Moreover, recent editions have been available on the Internet in Adobe PDF either through a link from GPO Access and, as noted, from FedStats; or directly via **http://www.census.gov/statab/www.** This site also provides selected features from the latest editions of the *Abstract* and *USA Counties;* links to *USA Statistics in Brief;* state rankings by categories such as resident population, infant mortality, average annual pay, and many more; frequently requested tables; state and county profiles; and a guide to state statistical abstracts.

Historical Statistics of the United States, Colonial Times to 1970

This massive, two-volume supplement to the *Statistical Abstract* contains more than 12,500 time series, largely annual, on U.S. social, economic, political, and geographic development from 1610. The compilation includes source notes for additional information, definition of terms, a descriptive text, and a detailed subject index. As noted, an appendix in the annual *Statistical Abstract* serves as an index to many (but not all) tables that continue *Historical Statistics* tables, thus saving the researcher an extra index-checking step. The Census Bureau has plans to supplement this basic history to cover the period 1940–1990 and to add new series that begin in the post–World War II period and that link to tables in the *Abstract.* A commercial edition is available on CD-ROM.

An elegant online companion to the paper edition of the *Historical Statistics* is the United States Historical Census Data Browser **(http://fisher.lib.Virginia.edu/census).** The data displayed at this address were initially created by the Inter-university Consortium for Political and Social Research (ICPSR) under a grant from the National Science Foundation, and the site is intended to aid in browsing the ICPSR data files. Data selection follows guidelines developed by the American Historical Association and describes the people and the economy of the United States for each state and county from 1790 to 1970. Sources include the decennial censuses as well as statistics from the

Department of Agriculture and the National Council of Churches of Christ of the United States.

State and Metropolitan Area Data Book

Available through a link from FedStats or directly at the Census Bureau's Web site (**http://www.census.gov/statab/www/smadb.html**), this source covers smaller geographic areas. Begun in 1979, the *Area Data Book*, now in its fifth edition, is published every five or six years and presents statistics on social and economic conditions in the United States at the state and local levels, including data for component counties and central cities of metropolitan areas. Tables cover population, income, the labor force, business enterprises, trade, education, construction, banking, health care, crime, and much more. The *Data Book* includes state and metropolitan area ranking tables for a number of variables such as employment, pay, housing, and trade. Metropolitan area definitions such as the Metropolitan Statistical Area (MSA) are determined by the Office of Management and Budget and revised periodically. The *Area Data Book* is also a sales publication and is sent to depository libraries; moreover, the 1997–1998 edition is available on CD-ROM.

County and City Data Book

Another so-called supplement to the *Statistical Abstract* is the *County and City Data Book,* which is issued about every five years and helps businesses identify potential new markets for their products and services. The 1994 edition of the *Data Book* contains official statistics for 1,078 cities, 3,141 counties, and 11,097 places of 2,500 or more inhabitants. It features socioeconomic and housing data from the 1990 census and the reports and surveys that update them, medium income, tax base, and more than 100 other variables for counties and cities nationwide. Like other Census Bureau products, the *Data Book* is issued in print, on CD-ROM, and on the Internet (**http://www.census. gov/statab/www/ccdb.html**).

Related to the *Data Book* is *CountyScope,* a Census Bureau CD-ROM product that brings together county and subcounty data from various data files such as some of the 1990 Summary Tape Files (STFs); economic censuses of retail, service and manufacturing data for ZIP code areas; county business patterns; TIGER/Line files, and others. These figures will again be useful when updated after the results of

Census 2000 have been compiled. Likewise, it is hoped that, post 2000, *USA Counties,* a 1996 CD-ROM product available to depository libraries that includes all the data published for counties from the earlier editions of the *State and Metropolitan Area Data Book* and the *County and City Data Book,* will be released in an updated revision.

CENSUS DEPOSITORY LIBRARIES

The Census Bureau still maintains approximately 129 Census Depository Libraries. In 1950, the agency initiated its own depository system and, at its height, more than 400 libraries participated. With enactment of the Depository Library Act of 1962, a large number of these libraries joined the Title 44 depository program. Moreover, the Bureau no longer adds new member libraries. The 129 libraries designated are required to select the Censuses of Population and Housing for their individual state. They have the option to select a variety of other census information found, for example, in the quinquennial censuses. A list of Census Depository Libraries, arranged by state, was published in the June 15, 1989, issue of *Administrative Notes.* Because some of these institutions directly administered by the Census Bureau are also Title 44 depositories, confusion may arise over which agency is providing which materials. The information in *Administrative Notes* 10: 1 (June 15, 1989) clarifies this issue. Other sources for Census Bureau products and services include the State Data Center program, the National Clearinghouse for Census Data Services, the Bureau's regional offices, and the Department of Commerce and International Trade Administration (ITA) offices; all of these entities support Internet sites.

PERSONAL CENSUS RECORDS SEARCHING

By law individual records from the federal population censuses are confidential for seventy-two years. Population census schedules from 1790 through 1920 are available to the public on 35mm positive microfilm at the National Archives and its regional offices or through sales and rental programs. Most of the 1890 schedules, however, were destroyed by fire in 1921. Records of the 1930 census will be opened to the public in 2002.

Researchers looking for specific names in the 1790 census should consult a publication titled *Heads of Families at the First Census of the United States Taken in the Year 1790.* Special Soundex indexes that show the page and line number on the appropriate census schedules are available for 1880, 1900, 1910, and 1920. In the intradecennial years, particularly during the nineteenth century, a number of state and territorial censuses were also taken. These are described in Henry J. Dubester's *State Censuses: An Annotated Bibliography of Censuses Taken After the Year 1790, by States and Territories of the United States.* An appendix in that volume provides information on the location of existing records.

Census staff will search the records of federal censuses of population from 1910 to date, stored at Jefferson, Indiana, and provide, for a fee, official transcripts of personal data to individuals who lack birth or citizenship documents. The transcripts may be used for various purposes: to qualify for Social Security benefits, to get a job, to obtain naturalization papers, to get a passport, to establish a claim to an inheritance, to get an insurance policy, or to trace ancestry. The transcripts generally show age at the time the census was taken (not date of birth), sex, relationship to the householder, and, where requested, race. Application forms with more detailed information can be obtained by contacting the Personal Census Search Unit, Bureau of the Census, P.O. Box 1545, Jefferson, IN 47131.

STATE DATA CENTERS

The State Data Center (SDC) Program was initiated by the Census Bureau in 1978 to improve access to the many statistical products available from the agency. The Bureau furnishes products, training in data access and use, technical assistance, and consultation to the states, which, in turn, disseminate the products and provide assistance in their use to county and local governments, nonprofit organizations, and other users. All states, the District of Columbia, Puerto Rico, the U.S. Virgin Islands, Guam, and the Commonwealth of the Northern Mariana Islands have SDC programs.

A typical SDC has a tripartite hierarchy: a lead entity such as a state executive or planning agency, coordinating units such as the state library or a large research university, and several affiliates such as regional planning commissions and public and private colleges and universities. However, anyone with a computer and modem can access census data on the Bureau's Web site, information formerly available only on Summary Tape Files or CD-ROM. This phenomenon may not make the State Data Centers obsolete, but it has shifted their function from providing data to training affiliate personnel in ways to interpret data, always the more difficult task.

The names, addresses, contact person, telephone and fax numbers, and e-mail address for the lead agency and the coordinating agencies (but not every affiliate for all states) can be visited from the Bureau's home page by clicking on "Subjects A–Z" for "S" or directly (**http:// www.census.gov/sdc**).

CENSUS GEOGRAPHY

Although geography is the foundation of census activities, it was always the least reliable component of data evaluation. In decennial counts taken before 1990, the Geography Division of the Census Bureau prepared traditional enumerator assignment maps, and field workers relied on direct observation to assign each household to the correct geographic location. These methods were prepared in separate, complex clerical operations by hundreds of workers who, inevitably, made different errors on each product.

Then a system called TIGER (Topologically Integrated Geographic Encoding and Referencing), introduced in the 1990 census, all but eliminated the problems described above. TIGER is not a map itself. Rather, it is a digital database that allows a user to integrate map features with other data; in other words, a powerful Geographic Information System (GIS).

Due to the TIGER technology, consistency in the geographic products generated was achieved. One can combine the geographic and cartographic data of a TIGER/Line file with other statistical information using mainframe computers, microcomputers, workstations, or personal computers and appropriate software for various applications. The design of the TIGER database adapts the principles of topology, graph theory, and associated fields of mathematics to provide a disciplined description for the geographic structure of the United States: the location and relationship of streets, rivers, railroads, and other features to one another and to the numerous geographic entities for which the Bureau tabulates data from its censuses and sample surveys. It is designed to assure no duplication of these features or areas. Examples include thematic or other types of mapping, geocoding of spatially referenced data for marketing research, routing or dispatching, address matching, redistricting, as well as a variety of applications using GIS (see chapter 12).

One year after the 1990 census, the Library Programs Service (LPS) began distribution of the Bureau's TIGER/Line CD-ROMs to depository libraries state by state. Some of the smaller states could be stacked onto a single disk, whereas California and Texas required three and four disks, respectively.

TIGER Mapping Service

During the 1990s, TIGER grew in sophistication. With demand for Internet-based dissemination of census data growing, the Bureau began to develop, in conjunction with Lawrence Berkeley National Labs, a project called the TIGER Mapping Service (TMS), the main purpose of which is to provide a high-quality, national scale, street-level map to Web users. This service is freely accessible to the public and based on an open architecture that allows other Web developers and publishers to use public domain maps generated in their own applications and documents. One result: high-quality street maps with simple GIS capabilities such as point display (by latitude/longitude or address) and statistical choropleth mapping.

In March 1998, the Bureau entered into a partnership with a commercial firm, GeoResearch, Inc., of Bethesda, Maryland, to improve the geographic database. The cooperative enterprise provides for the use of GeoResearch's GeoLink software to verify and update information on the TIGER system. GeoLink uses satellite technology to obtain the geographic coordinates of residential addresses and other map features. Since the mid-1980s, GeoResearch has performed Global Positioning System/Geographic Information System field mapping, data collection, and database development for a wide range of customers, including many state and local governments.

TIGER Mapping Service goals are available via its home page (**http://tiger.census.gov**). The Census Bureau, required by law to provide the information it gathers on a cost-recovery basis, finds the Internet (and specifically the Web) to be more accessible and less costly than other media. During 1997, the TMS servers generated 25,000 to 30,000 free maps per day, and only lack of congressional funding precludes the addition of statistical mapping features helpful to the many users of this service.

INTERCENSAL PUBLISHING

Most of us are aware of the Census Bureau only when the decennial enumeration, with its congressional quarreling and budgetary battles, commands the media's attention. Even the quinquennial censuses pass unremarked, like lone freight trains in the night. As noted above, the assiduous workers at the Bureau conduct intercensal activities continually. Certain reports may be issued annually, quarterly, monthly, and weekly, based upon random sampling of various populations. Moreover, special population censuses, such as those requested by local governments and school districts, and other surveys and studies also update and supplement the major five- and ten-year counts.

The best place to track the Bureau's laudable industry is in the pages of *Monthly Product Announcement* in print or from the Bureau's Internet site. In addition, a free e-mail subscription to the *Census I-Net Bulletin* (**http://www.census.gov/apsd/inet**) is another fast means of accessing bibliographic and textual information on intercensal publications.

OTHER STATISTICAL SOURCES

Commercial and governmental data sources tend to merge and blur because numeric data are in the public domain (unless protected by trade secret or related intellectual property laws). A sampling of official and private sources of statistical information, current and retrospective, follows.

- Suzanne Schultze's three-volume Population Information (Phoenix, AZ: Oryx Press) set is composed of *Population Information in the Twentieth Century Census Volumes: 1950–1980* (1988), *Population Information in the Twentieth Century Census Volumes: 1900–1940* (1985), and *Population Information in the Nineteenth Century Census Volumes* (1983).

- Congressional Information Service (CIS) offers an annual *Guide to 1990 US Decennial Publications* in print with a companion microfiche full-text service. Indexes and abstracts are adapted from the *American Statistics Index* (discussed earlier in this chapter) and the fiche collection is drawn from the ASI Microfiche Library. Other retrospective CIS products include the 1980 and 1970 decennial counts with a similar format to the 1990 enterprise; non-decennial series, originally filmed by Greenwood Press, cover the periods 1820–1945 and 1946–1967 and are based on Dubester's cumulative catalog for the former years and annual census catalogs for the latter years.

- Other commercial sources include Bernan Press (Lanham, Maryland), which publishes compilations of series that have been discontinued by the government agency formerly responsible for issuing the data, owing to misguided budgetary rescissions of the

Congress and the administration. Examples include Patrick A. Simmons, ed., *Housing Statistics of the United States* (1997); Courtney M. Slater, ed., *Business Statistics of the United States* (1997); and John E. Cremeans, ed., *Handbook of North American Industry: NAFTA and the Economics of Its Member Nations* (1997). This last is a blend of informative articles on the North American Free Trade Agreement and tables and charts supported by narrative analyses. These sources represent but an example of titles by commercial vendors that have taken advantage of the federal penchant for parsimonious publishing.

- *The Socioeconomic Status and Health Chartbook, 1998,* located at the FastFacts page of the FedStats Internet site, is a comprehensive report on the relationship between socioeconomic status and health in the United States.

- The Government Information Sharing Project at Oregon State University was initiated with funding from the Department of Education and presents data provided by the Census Bureau, the Bureau of Economic Analysis (Commerce Department), the National Center for Education Statistics, and the MESA Group. This last is a private company based in Alexandria, Virginia, which specializes in the development of demographic, economic, and management systems. As of early 1999, the Sharing Project's home page (**http://govinfo.kerr.orst.edu**) displayed a number of point-and-click categories, including USA Counties 1996; the 1990 census of population and housing; population estimates by age, sex, and race, 1900–1997; the equal opportunity employment file, 1990; school district data book profiles, 1989–1990; and more. A link to "Other Government Web Sites" directs you to the U.S. Government Printing Office (from which in turn you can click on GPO Access), the White House, Congress's THOMAS Web site, the Library of Congress, the Federal Web Locator, and selected subject resources (including agriculture, the historical documents list from Project Vote Smart, law, periodicals, reference, scientific and technical reports, and so forth).

- The *Annual Survey of Manufactures* (1949–) covers the same topics as the quinquennial census of manufactures, but there is less product detail. Title 13 of the *United States Code* requires the survey and mandatory responses. Data obtained include kind of business, location, ownership, value of shipments, payroll and employment, cost of materials, inventories, new capital expenditures, fuel and energy costs, hours worked, and payroll supplements. This survey can be viewed at the Census Bureau Internet site.

- The *Survey of Current Business,* issued monthly by the Commerce Department's Bureau of Economic Analysis, incorporates cyclical indicators that were formerly published in the defunct *Business Conditions Digest.* In addition to information on trends in industry and the business situation and outlook, it is the source of current national income and product account tables, data on federal fiscal programs, and the like. The substantial "Current Business Statistics" section of the periodical generates the essential reference component of this publication. Available via STAT-USA, the *Survey* is also published as an annual CD-ROM; both the monthly and the annual are available for sale and are sent to depository libraries.

- In the social welfare field, no government journal arguably holds greater prominence than the quarterly *Social Security Bulletin.* Articles often present well-documented time series and analyses of both public and private social welfare expenditures from 1965 to date. Of great value is a recurring feature titled "Current Operating Statistics," tables on topics such as Medicare benefits, income maintenance programs, and black lung benefits. An annual *Statistical Supplement to the Social Security Bulletin* presents similar social data for 1955 onward. Access Social Security Administration data at **http://www.ssa.gov**.

Many other government annuals and periodicals that provide statistical tables and analyses, far too numerous to mention in this selective roundup, serve an important reference function. Now that most of this information is on the Internet, librarians do not have to worry that their print versions are relegated to distant shelves and stacks.

SELECTED AGENCIES

The Census Bureau's dominance in the federal statistical world is in part due to its contractual arrangements to gather data for many other government departments and agencies, which in turn publish the data under their own provenance. Some agencies that issue statistics and their Internet addresses follow. For a complete list, consult current issues of *American Statistics Index,* and for easy access use Laurie Andriot's Internet site (**http://www.fedweb.com**). In the print companion to this extremely useful site, *The Internet Blue Pages* (Medford, NJ: CyberAge Books, 1998), "statistics" as an index entry has more than 100 subheadings, from "accident" to "workplace safety and health."

- Department of Agriculture (USDA): The National Agricultural Statistics Service (**http://www.usda.nass**) links to the five-year census of agriculture database and provides, among other data, prices paid and received by farmers and statistics on field crops, fruits, and vegetables; farm animals; farm employment; and agricultural chemical use. As mentioned earlier in this chapter, the Department of Agriculture now assumes responsibility for its quinquennial census.

- USDA: The Economic Research Service (**http://www.econ.ag.gov**) furnishes data for farm sector income and employment, trade, specialty agriculture, and so forth.

- Department of Commerce: In addition to the Census Bureau, the Economic Development Administration (**http://www.doc.gov/eda**) and the International Trade Administration (**http://ita.doc.gov**), to name just a couple of agencies, spew out tons of statistics. For example, the Bureau of Economic Analysis (**http://www.bea.doc.gov**) prepares and disseminates data on corporate profits, national defense purchases, personal taxes, gross domestic product, national income, personal consumption expenditures, personal saving rate, trade balance, and more.

- Department of Education: The National Center for Education Statistics (**http://nces.ed.gov**) collects, analyzes, and reports data on virtually every aspect of American education.

- Department of Justice: The Bureau of Justice Statistics (**http://www.ojp.usdoj.gov/bjs**) includes, inter alia, homicide rates by age, personal theft and household crime rates, arrests for drug abuse violations, violent crime measures, and national correctional populations (a euphemism for prison inmates).

- Department of Labor (DOL): In addition to the Bureau of Labor Statistics, belabored above, the Employment Standards Administration (**http://dol.gov/dol/esa**) has links to its several units, such as the Wage and Hour Division, which provides data on working conditions, minimum wages, family and medical leave, equal employment opportunity in businesses with federal contracts and subcontracts, prevailing wages in construction and services, and so forth.

- DOL: The Employment and Training Administration (**http://www.doleta.gov**) presents statistics on dislocated workers, NAFTA, labor surplus areas, unemployment insurance claims, and much more.

- Department of Transportation: The Bureau of Transportation Statistics (**http://www.bts.gov**) "is a statistical agency, a mapping agency, and an organization for transportation analysis. No other federal agency combines these activities under one roof."[10] Statistics include boating accidents, highway data, on-time statistics for airlines, truck inventory—almost every mode of transport.

- Department of Health and Human Services (HHS): The Centers for Disease Control and Prevention (CDC) (**http://cdc.gov**) employ the epidemiological sleuths who track down outbreaks of the greater and lesser menacing diseases with which the planet is continually affrighted and recommend vaccines for the population. Their renowned *Morbidity and Mortality Weekly Report* (MMWR), in existence since 1952, with its quarterly "CDC Surveillance Summaries" and annual summary, presents data reflecting the concerns of the intrepid scientists and physicians who work for paltry wages and who bring to our attention public health problems amenable to prevention strategies. One critic described the weekly as "brisk and businesslike, redolent of competence and devoid of levity" with a "crisp, lucid, oddly vivid style suggestive of Hemingway as retold by Strunk and White."[11] MMWR and other issuances from the Center can be accessed online from the agency's home page.

- Social Security Administration (**http://www.ssa.gov**): From this capacious site all manner of numeric information tumbles. One link in particular is to Research and Data, including Research, Evaluation, and Statistics.

- Securities and Exchange Commission (**http://www.sec.gov**): The SEC's monthly *Official Summary of Security Transactions and Holdings* provides figures showing owners, relationships to issues, amounts of securities bought or sold by each owner, their individual holdings at the end of the reported month, and types of securities. Other data series include statistics on stock initial public offerings (IPOs), securities registration, and option markets. Also included in the SEC's Web site is a link to the well-known EDGAR (Electronic Data Gathering, Analysis, and Retrieval) database, which consists of a large number of corporate filings required by federal securities laws and the regulations promulgated in 13 CFR Parts 200 et seq. Among the better-known forms are the 10K annual reports that most reporting companies file with the SEC and the 10Q reports filed quarterly by most reporting companies. The latter include unaudited financial statements and provide a continuing view of the company's financial situation during the year.

It would be difficult indeed to find an agency or quasi-entity of the federal establishment that did not in some fashion publish statistics, at least in its annual report. But there are problems involved. As the Internet expands, we tend to celebrate our accessibility to ever greater sums of information. Yet the corollary is that as information mounts, so does our ignorance; we have not mastered the ability to convert so much data into useful knowledge, much less wisdom. And, as Juri Stratford points out, the Web

> exacerbates the problem of replicating data or research. While government agencies have always published revised data as new information becomes available, one can usually recreate a history of those revisions from paper copy held in archival collections. . . . However, when agencies publish revised series on the Internet, they frequently withdraw the older versions. . . . [Moreover], if researchers are able to extract their own subsets via online retrieval engines, how does one cite the "source" of these data in a meaningful way that will allow others to replicate their extractions, aggregations, or findings?[12]

THE CENSUS OF POPULATION AND HOUSING

If the census could be described solely in historical terms, one might call it "from horseback to cyberspace, 1790–2000." The first census was taken by U.S. marshals on horseback and their assistants, trying to find scattered settlers. It is the oldest of the censuses taken, and it has been enumerated every decade since 1790. The first census of housing was taken in 1940, although counts of "dwelling houses" were obtained in earlier censuses of population. Today published reports in print and electronic formats covering both results refer to the combined Census of Population and Housing. Technology has always been merely the means. The uses of census data are the important matters: reapportionment, congressional redistricting, assisting federal agencies in managing their responsibilities, allocating federal aid, helping state and local governments plan for and provide services, and helping businesses provide new services and products and tailor existing ones to demographic changes. And, in case you think that controversy about the decennial census is a recent development, consider this comment:

> The [first] census was to have taken 9 months, but actually it took 18 months. President George Washington believed that the count of 3.9 million people was too low. Congress, however, accepted the data and proceeded to apportion the number of representatives in accordance with the census data. Immediately, the debate about how exactly to implement the apportionment began, and this controversy has continued in one form or another for over 200 years.[13]

The growth of the decennial count for the two centuries since that first census is shown in Figure 9.2, from Appendix II in GAO report GGD-98-103.

HISTORICAL OVERVIEW

A succinct but excellent historical overview of the census is found in a report by the United States General Accounting Office (GAO) titled *Decennial Census: Overview of Historical Census Issues* (GAO/GGD-98-103, May 1998). In addition to the brief history and a general discussion of Census Bureau plans for the 2000 decennial count, the report includes useful tables, the most frequently asked questions about the decennial census, and a bibliography of non-GAO publications and sources.

Figure 9.2. Growth of the decennial census from 1790 to 1990.

Census year	Total U.S. population (millions)	Number of enumerator staff	Number of headquarters and/or office staff	Total cost of census (thousands of dollars)
1790	3.9	650	a	$44
1800	5.3	900	a	66
1810	7.2	1,100	a	178
1820	9.6	1,188	a	208
1830	12.9	1,519	43	378
1840	17.1	2,167	28	833
1850	23.2	3,231	160	1,423
1860	31.4	4,417	184	1,969
1870	38.6	6,530	438	3,421
1880	50.2	31,382	1,495	5,790
1890	63.0	46,804	3,143	11,547
1900	76.2	52,871	3,447	11,854
1910	92.2	70,286	3,738	15,968
1920	106.0	87,234	6,301	25,117
1930	123.2	87,756	6,825	40,156
1940	132.2	123,069	9,987	67,527
1950	151.3	142,962	9,233	91,462
1960	179.3	159,321	2,960	127,934
1970	203.2	166,406	4,571	247,653
1980	226.5	458,523	4,081	1,136,000
1990	248.7	510,200	6,763	2,600,000

aThere was no official headquarters staff for the first four censuses. In addition, the records for the 1790, 1800, and 1810 Censuses were accidentally destroyed; the numbers shown are estimates.

Sources: The Story of the Census—1790-1915, Bureau of the Census, Department of Commerce, 1915; The Bureau of Census, adapted by A. Ross Eckler, Bureau of the Census, 1972; Margo J. Anderson, American Census: A Social History (New Haven: 1988); Modernizing the U.S. Census, National Research Council, 1995; Statistical Abstract of the United States—The National Data Book, Bureau of the Census, Department of Commerce, October 1996.

CONSTITUTIONAL ISSUES

Article I, Section 2, Clause 3 of the Constitution concerns the composition of the House of Representatives:

> Representatives and direct taxes shall be apportioned among the several states . . . according to their respective numbers. . . . The actual enumeration shall be made within three years after the first meeting of the Congress . . . and within every subsequent term of ten years, in such manner as they shall by law direct.

The Constitution was not specific about how to apportion the representatives; neither did it fix the number of seats there should be in the House nor how the states were to elect their representatives. Thus the debates over the years about methods of apportionment ostensibly focused on mathematics but actually were a matter of political power. The brevity of the Constitution in this matter has led to court decisions mandating congressional districts of equal size and the configuring of districts to reflect minority populations (an issue revisited by the courts), alleging an undercount in large cities, and, more recently, challenging the use of statistical sampling to improve the census accuracy.

This last problem arose from the congressional mandate to make the millennial census more accurate and less costly than the 1990 census turned out to be. Article I, section 2 requires an "actual enumeration" (see above); in addition, Congress has the authority to conduct censuses "in such a manner as they shall by law direct." However, the legislators have delegated that authority to the Secretary of Commerce through Title 13 of the *United States Code.* In 1997, the Bureau let it be known that it planned an aggressive program to count 90 percent of every neighborhood and then to account for the rest through sampling techniques first utilized by the Bureau in the 1940 census.

Bipartisan legislation in Congress created a distinguished panel of experts from the National Academy of Sciences, who concluded in 1994 that the use of sampling to estimate the number and characteristics of the nonresponding 10 percent of households would reduce costs and nonresponse bias, increase accuracy, and reduce differential undercoverage. In other words, failing to include sampling as an element of Census 2000 would produce results worse than those obtained for the 1990 census. Moreover, the conclusions of this panel were reaffirmed by a second panel that issued interim reports in 1992 and 1996. Thus fortified by expert opinion, in 1996 the Census Bureau outlined its plans for a re-engineered Census 2000 based on initiatives recommended by the Academy.

In 1997, not long after Dr. Martha Farnsworth Riche, then Director of the Census Bureau, released these findings on the Bureau's Web site, opposition among members of Congress and state and local governments emerged. In early 1998 two sets of plaintiffs filed separate suits challenging the legality and constitutionality of the plan, one of the parties being the House of Representatives filing in the U.S. District Court for the District of Columbia. That district court (11 F.Supp. 2d 76) held that the plan violated the Census Act. Moreover, in the District Court for the Eastern District of Virginia, the defendants and various intervenors filed motion to dismiss, and the plaintiffs, consisting of residents of four counties and thirteen states, filed motion for summary judgment. A three-judge panel of this District Court granted plaintiffs' motion for summary judgment and permanently enjoined the Bureau's proposed use of statistical sampling (19 F.Supp.2d 543). On direct appeal (the so-called fast track), the Supreme Court consolidated the lower court cases. In a 5 to 4 decision (*Department of Commerce v. United States House of Representatives,* 119 S.Ct. 765, 67 USLW 4090, January 25, 1999), the High Court issued a limited ruling against the use of sampling, based upon an interpretation of two ostensibly contradictory sections of Title 13 of the *United States Code,* the statutory authority for the duties and responsibilities of the Census Bureau.

The Commerce Department argued that 13 U.S.C. § 141(a) authorizes the Secretary of Commerce to "take a decennial census . . . in such form and content as he may determine, including the use of sampling procedures." However, this broad grant is tempered by 13 U.S.C. § 195, which states that "*Except* (my emphasis) for the determination of population for purposes of [congressional] apportionment. . . , the Secretary shall, if he considers it feasible, authorize the use of . . . statistical . . . 'sampling' in carrying out the provisions of this title." Therefore, although § 195 permits the Secretary to use sampling in assembling the myriad demographic data that are collected in connection with the decennial census (the "long form"), it maintains the long-standing prohibition on the use of such sampling to calculate the population for congressional apportionment.

The Supreme Court, in its decision based on the relevant provisions of the statute, avoided the constitutional question; and this, plus the closeness of the decision, was considered good news for the Census Bureau and the Clinton administration, which championed sampling. In addition, the Court did not foreclose allowing sampling for the drawing of political boundaries within each state (gerrymandering) and the allocation of billions of dollars in federal funds for the numerous social programs that are tied to census counts.

Several political struggles remain. The Congress must decide whether it is willing to fund a census that has one set of numbers for apportionment and another set for other purposes, as allowed by §§ 141(a) and 195 of Title 13. One month after the High Court's decision, the Census Bureau announced that it would "issue a traditional count to be used for apportionment . . . and a second set of adjusted figures to be used to redraw political boundaries and distribute nearly $200 billion in federal funds each year." But some federal officials now estimated that, as a result, Census 2000 would cost $6 to $7 billion, "a dramatic increase over the $4 billion price tag attached to the Census Bureau's initial plan. The higher cost stems primarily from the need to hire 250,000 additional census takers to collect information from every household" and to produce two population numbers, the traditional door-to-door count and a statistical sampling method to compensate for people missed in the head count.

It is ironic that many of the same lawmakers who insisted that the bureau bring in an accurate census on the cheap found themselves advocating a less accurate count at greater expense. As it has since George Washington's tenure, the issue boils down to politics. "It is widely believed that the adjusted figures are more likely to benefit Democrats because they will produce higher counts in neighborhoods that tend to vote Democratic."[14] But the final outcome of this brouhaha will have to await the dawn of a new millennium.

CENSUS 2000 STRATEGIES

The 1990 count was called the Bicentennial Census in celebrating two centuries of decennial enumerating; it is followed by the Millennial Census or, as some would say, the Y2K Census (not the more common usage of overwrought computer "compliant" concerns, but simply as a catchy abbreviation). As noted, because of dissatisfaction with the results of the 1990 census, the Congress and the administration ordered the Census Bureau to improve the accuracy, simplify the questionnaire, and make the 2000 count less costly (adjusted for inflation) than the 1990 count. Historians will no doubt remember three aspects of this millennium: frenetic voices prophesying eschatological events; ostentatious celebrations, bacchanals of wretched excess; and the decennial census: in short, the sacred, the profane, and the statistical.

Amid all the turmoil of partisan politics, the Census Bureau has been proceeding with its plans for the millennial census, plans that, as in previous censuses, began before the decennial snapshot was taken a decade ago. Naturally, the Bureau wants to avoid the embarrassment of the 1990 count, the first in fifty years to be less accurate than its predecessors by undercounting millions of Americans, especially children and members of racial and ethnic and minority groups. The net undercount, defined as people missed minus people included erroneously, was about 4 million persons, or about 1.6 percent of the population. Moreover, the Bureau estimated that about 6 million persons were counted twice, while 10 million were missed. The sum of these numbers, 16 million, represents the gross undercount. And this tally does not include other errors, such as persons assigned to the wrong locations.

The Bureau is not wholly to blame for that situation. Some populations are significantly more difficult to count than others, and clearly the Bureau underestimated the magnitude of the problem. But in Washington, where promise breakers far outnumber Promise Keepers, the agency stands as a beacon of probity, beset by shameless advocacy groups and feckless members of Congress, the latter pinning the entire blame for the undercount on the Bureau and ordering them to be more accurate and less putatively profligate, as if an estimated $4 billion constituted an exorbitant amount to secure vital data for a nation with a Gross Domestic Product that exceeds $7.5 trillion.

The Census Bureau hoped to correct these mistakes by two sampling procedures, including the one described above, which was designed to reduce the time required for, and expense of, following up on the millions of housing units that may not respond to the questionnaires. The other, referred to as the Integrated Coverage Measurement (ICM), was intended to adjust the population counts obtained from census questionnaires and nonresponse follow-up procedures to eliminate the persistent differential undercount of minorities. It was also meant to replace the old, inherently flawed, post-enumeration survey.[15] The Supreme Court decision, however, shot down the ICM plan and the Bureau has replaced it with a plan called the Accuracy Coverage Evaluation (ACE), a scheme to produce an adjusted set of figures. This reversal of fortune represents a triumph of politics over reason. Nevertheless, the Bureau adopted four major strategies for making Census 2000 as good as possible: partnership, simplicity, technology, and methods.

- Form partnerships with state, local, and tribal governments; community groups; the private sector; and the United States Postal Service. The local governments and the community groups know their constituents better than the Census Bureau and can alert the Bureau to problems and advise the agency of opportunities to publicize the count. For example, the Bureau, working with organizations such as the National Urban League, AFL-CIO, and National Congress of American Indians, hopes to persuade people in minority communities to cooperate and be counted. To that end, plans include placing advertisements in the ethnic press to recruit some of the temporary employees the Census Bureau uses for its decennial count. Indeed, the Bureau expects to hire more than 500,000 part-time workers and is expecting older Americans, both retirees and working people seeking to supplement their income, to form the backbone of this civilian army, which the agency calls "the nation's largest peacetime mobilization."[16] Moreover, private companies can be of great assistance because they can process forms and promote Census 2000 visibly and effectively. To avoid costly duplication of effort, the Bureau will, for the first time, be allowed to use address information provided by the Postal Service. Letter carriers will be the primary, and logical, source of information on vacant housing units.

It is extremely difficult to get an accurate count of people who do not live in traditional households, such as residents of nursing homes, college dormitories, and migrant worker camps; runaway youth; people in remote areas; and shelters for battered women and the homeless. On the nights of March 20–21, 1990, the Bureau conducted a special "shelter and street night" (S-night) operation, a separate count of the homeless population. Because the number of homeless is a controversial and emotional issue, the official results, which were published in Summary Tape File (STF) 1A, came under criticism by special interest groups for this segment of the population. The Census Bureau acknowledged that a count of this population can never be wholly accurate because a portion of the homeless remains elusive. Moreover, radical advocacy groups, whose agenda is to keep homeless data inflated, urged their "subjects" to avoid the census takers to the greatest extent possible. For Census 2000, the emphasis will shift from finding the homeless on street corners, sleeping on sidewalks, under bridges, and at the entrances to buildings, to identifying them through the organizations that assist them.

- Keep it simple. The bureau devised user-friendly forms that it hopes will not be mistaken for junk mail (as was thought to have happened with the 1990 questionnaires) and enlisted community leaders to distribute language-specific forms in neighborhoods where English is not the primary language. About 83 percent of housing units will receive the short-form questionnaire; it will require the least number of questions in 180 years. For Population you will be asked for name, sex, age, relationship, Hispanic origin, and race. For Housing, one question: tenure (whether the dwelling is owned or rented). The long form furnishes socioeconomic detail needed for the wide range of government programs and federal requirements mentioned above, and will be sent randomly to about one out of every six housing units. It includes the same seven questions as the short form but in addition consists of twenty-seven more, fourteen under Population and thirteen under Housing. By law, the Census Bureau cannot share your answers with others, including welfare agencies, the Immigration and Naturalization Service, the Internal Revenue Service, courts, the police, and the military. Anyone who violates this injunction faces up to five years in prison and $5,000 in fines. The law works: Seldom in the nation's history have these data been released inappropriately, and not once in the 1990 census data.

- Use technology intelligently. The 1990 census was microfilmed and key entered. In Census 2000 the forms, for the first time, will be scanned directly into computers that can read handwriting. The completed forms will then be read directly into computer files ready for tabulation. Sophisticated software will spot duplications.

- Use statistical methods, if Congress appropriates enough money for the Bureau to effect this properly.[17] I have discussed this in detail above, but I cannot resist quoting John Allen Paulos, professor of mathematics and author of the highly acclaimed book *Innumeracy: Mathematical Illiteracy and Its Consequences,* who averred that the "name of the game in statistics is the inferring of information about a large population by examining characteristics of a small, randomly selected sample."[18]

Figure 9.3 shows F.A.Q.s about the census as published in Appendix I of GAO report GGD-98-103.

If all the strategies mesh, if Congress doesn't use its fiscal wrecking ball to demolish the Bureau's effort to employ sampling where it is allowed by statute and case law, if advocacy groups with their possessive agendas rein in their temper tantrums against the agency, and if Lady Luck deals the right cards, the Census Bureau will engineer the greatest comeback since Truman bested Dewey half a century earlier.

Figure 9.3. F.A.Q.s and answers about the decennial census.

Appendix I

Most Frequently Asked Questions and Answers About the Decennial Census

Question	Answer
Why is a census count taken?	For constitutionally mandated reapportionment and other statutory requirements.
What is reapportionment?	Allocation of the 435 members in the House of Representatives among the states according to the population from the decennial census.
What is the latest count?	248.7 million people per the 1990 Census.
Who is counted?	All persons residing in the United States, regardless of their citizenship status.
How long does it take to count and report results?	Nine months, with extensive research, pretesting, and planning.
How much does it cost?	$2.6 billion for the 1990 Census; about $4 billion is the projected cost for the 2000 Census.
How many workers are needed?	Over 500,000 temporary workers and about 6,800 permanent employees were used during the 1990 Census.
How is the census taken?	Mostly self-enumeration, by mail, using standardized short and long form questionnaires and door-to-door follow-up for nonresponding households.
What questions are asked?	Population, economic, demographic, and housing issues.
Are statistical procedures used?	The long form or sample questionnaire is filled out by one-sixth of the population and used to project national results. The Census Bureau plans to use statistical sampling and estimation procedures in 2000.
At what levels are the results available for public uses?	Computerized data are available by state, county, city, municipalities, etc., in various enumerations.
What publications are available?	Standardized and special publications are available on paper, computer tapes, CD-ROM, and the Internet.

Note: The plans for the 2000 Census are not final. Depending upon decisions made by the Bureau and Congress, operational procedures may change, and costs must then be adjusted.

BEYOND 2000

Getting the millennial census right is only the beginning. What happens after the year 2000 is equally crucial to the nation's well-being. Two efforts that will have an impact upon the coming years are worthy of note: the *American Community Survey* and the *American FactFinder*.

American Community Survey

The *American Community Survey* (ACS) is an ambitious project designed to replace the long form by the 2010 census. Although Congress keeps reducing funds for ACS to gain maximum operational effectiveness, a number of selected counties have been surveyed since 1996. The first CD-ROM containing the data for four counties tested in that year was distributed to depository libraries in 1998 (C 3.297; depository item 154-B-14). The data available on the compact disk include profiles of communities and population groups, summary tables similar to the 1990 Summary Tape Files, and Public Use Microdata Samples (PUMS) for users to customize the data.

Subject to congressional budgeting (I realize this sounds like a broken record, but the caveat is regrettably necessary), the ACS will be an ongoing monthly household survey furnishing estimates of housing, social, and economic characteristics every year for all states, cities, counties, metropolitan areas, and population groups of 65,000 persons or more. Smaller entities, for example, rural areas and city neighborhoods, and population groups of less than 15,000 people, will take two to five years to accumulate a sample the size of the decennial census. Sample data extracted from the decennial long form are dated within two years after the census is taken, and their usefulness declines every year thereafter. Consequently, the billions of government and business dollars divided up among jurisdictions and population groups are based on flawed social and economic profiles. The ACS will provide more accurate and current profiles annually instead of every ten years.

Once the survey is in full operation, the multi-year estimates of characteristics will be updated each year for every governmental unit, for components of the population, and for census tracts and block groups. It is a logical solution to the long-form problem. Information about the ACS can be accessed directly from the Bureau's home page, furnishing detailed facts and figures about the system.

American FactFinder

The *American FactFinder* is a data retrieval system inaugurated in 1999, which permits users to access information about their community, their economy, and their society. For the first few months of its existence, *FactFinder* offered the 1990 decennial census, the 1997 economic censuses, the 1998 dress rehearsal census, and the 1997 and 1998 *American Community Surveys.* The prototype for *American FactFinder* was called Data Access and Dissemination System (DADS), which became extinct when the Bureau introduced the new phrase.

Basic information will be freely available through the Internet, but there will be fees for custom tabulations of microdata, extracting and downloading large files and segments of files, and special tabulations of data in formats such as CD-ROMs, paper, or computer tape. The first data sets from the prototypical DADS included the 1990 decennial census. Updated series will include the 1999 *American Community Surveys,* and ultimately Census 2000 and beyond.

According to Customer Services,[19] this product also replaces the *Factfinder for the Nation* series, which consisted of useful, irregularly issued numbered brochures that described the range of census materials available on a given topic. No new *Factfinder for the Nation* series items have been published or revised since the mid-1990s. Information about *American FactFinder* can be accessed via **http://factfinder. census.gov**.

SUMMARY

It could be said, glibly, that statistics are too important to be left to the politicians. Yet that is how the system works. In 1980 Vincent P. Barabba, Director of the Census Bureau, wrote, "The challenge we face is to realize the full potential of statistical information in helping to solve the issues society now faces and will face in the future. To the degree that the providers and users of data can answer that challenge, American society . . . will have the means to make a smooth transition into the realities—and the opportunities—of the 1980s and beyond."[20] As we enter the twenty-first century, those words speak to us with greater resonance than ever.

NOTES

1. U.S. General Accounting Office, *Making the CPI More Reflective of Current Consumer Spending* (GAO/T-GGD-98-115), April 29, 1998, p. 5.

2. Lawrence Sanders, *McNally's Gamble* (New York: G. P. Putnam's Sons, 1997), p. 9.

3. U.S. Bureau of the Census, *Census '90 Fact Sheet #2* (D-3224.2), October 1988, p. 1.

4. An entire issue of *Government Information Quarterly* (v. 15, no. 3, 1998) is devoted to the 1997 Economic Censuses, including an article on the North American Industry Classification System, discussed in chapter 6.

5. *Census and You*, August 1996, p. 7.

6. "Dynamic POPClocks," accessed from the Bureau's home page, include minute-by-minute U.S. and world population estimate projections.

7. Telephone conversation with representative, Customer Service, Bureau of the Census, March 15, 1999.

8. Norman Cousins, "Preface," in *Reflections of America: Commemorating the Statistical Abstract Centennial* (Washington: Bureau of the Census, 1980), p. v.

9. *Census and You,* December 1996, pp. 1–2.

10. Laurie Andriot, comp., *The Internet Blue Pages* (Medford, NJ: Cyber-Age Books, 1998), p. 177.

11. Cullen Murphy, "Misfortune's Catalog," *The Atlantic Monthly* 253: 14–15 (February 1984).

12. Juri Stratford, "Responding to Reference Queries for Numeric Data and the Problems Inherent in Interpreting Statistical Sources: A Note," *Journal of Government Information* 25: 417 (1998).

13. U.S. General Accounting Office, *Decennial Census: Overview of Historical Census Issues* (GAO/GGD-98-103), May 1998, p. 9.

14. Barbara Vobejda, "Double Census Count Might Cost $7 Billion," *The Washington Post,* February 24, 1999, p. A19.

15. GAO, *Decennial Census,* pp. 29–30.

16. *AARP Bulletin* 40: 21 (February 1999).

17. U.S. Bureau of the Census, Economic and Statistics Administration, *Creating a Census for the 21st Century: The Plan for Census 2000* (February 1997), pp. 3–8. See also GAO, *Decennial Census,* p. 27.

18. John Allen Paulos, *Innumeracy: Mathematical Illiteracy and Its Consequences* (New York: Hill and Wang, 1988), p. 114.

19. Telephone conversation with representative, Customer Service, Bureau of the Census, March 26, 1999.

20. Vincent P. Barabba, "The Future Role of Information in American Life," in *Reflections of America,* p. 202.

CHAPTER 10

INTELLECTUAL PROPERTY

> Intellectual property may be broadly, but fairly, said to be the promotion of the progress of humankind.
>
> —Dr. Kamil Idris, Director General of the World
> Intellectual Property Organization (WIPO)

INTRODUCTION

Intellectual property may be divided into four categories: trade secrets, patents, trademarks, and copyright. They comprise ingenious, abstruse, or transitory areas of the law that evolve in response to technological change. Indeed, more than a century and a half ago, Supreme Court Justice Joseph Story found that copyright and patent jurisprudence come "nearer than any other class of cases belonging to forensic discussions, to what may be called the metaphysics of the law where the distinctions are, or at least may be, very subtle [sic] and refined, and, sometimes, almost evanescent."[1]

TRADE SECRETS

Trade secrets may be defined as "any formula, pattern, device or compilation of information which is used in one's business, and which gives him [or her] an opportunity to obtain an advantage over competitors who do not know or use it."[2] However, attorney Stephen Elias avers that "there is no crisp, clear definition of what [trade secrets] are. Rather, the context in which a dispute over ownership of information arises will determine whether a court will treat the information as a trade secret. As a general rule, information that has commercial value and that has been scrupulously kept confidential will be considered a trade secret; the owner of the information will be entitled to court relief against those who have stolen or divulged it in violation of a duty of trust or a written nondisclosure agreement."3 More specifically, the term embraces "all forms of financial, business, scientific, technical, economic, or engineering information, including patterns, plans, compilations, program devices, formulas, designs, prototypes, methods, techniques, processes, procedures, programs or codes . . . if (A) the owner thereof has taken reasonable measures to keep such information secret; and (B) the information derives independent economic value, actual or potential, from not being generally known to, and not being readily ascertainable through proper means by the public."4

There are several factors used to determine if subject matter qualifies as a trade secret. Among these are the extent of measures taken by the trade secret owner to guard the secrecy of the information and the ease or difficulty with which the information could be properly acquired or duplicated by others. Based on these considerations, the general rule is that subject matter cannot be successfully protected as a trade secret if it is widely distributed. However, if adequate security measures are taken to ensure that access to the subject matter being distributed is treated as secret, the subject matter may still be considered a trade secret.5

Activities that the courts commonly treat as trade secret theft include

- disclosures by key employees occupying positions of trust in violation of their duty of trust toward their employer;

- disclosures by current and former employees in violation of a confidentiality agreement entered into with their employer;

- disclosures by suppliers, consultants, financial advisors, or others who signed nondisclosure agreements with the trade secret owner, promising not to disclose the information;

- industrial espionage;

- disclosures by any person owing an implied duty to the employer not to make such disclosure, such as directors, corporate officers, and other high-level salaried employees.

When a disclosure is considered wrongful, the court "may also consider use of the information wrongful and issue an injunction preventing its use for a particular period of time." The court may also award punitive damages to punish the wrongdoer. In extreme cases, "criminal antitheft laws may be invoked and the trade secret thief subjected to criminal prosecution."6

Trade Secrets Federalized

Until 1996, trade secrets laws were solely the province of the states by adoption of the Uniform Trade Secrets Act. In that year the Economic Espionage Act (P.L. 104-294, October 11, 1996; 110 Stat. 3488; 18 U.S.C. § 1831) was passed making the theft of trade secrets a federal criminal offense. The Act gives the Department of Justice sweeping authority to prosecute trade secret theft whether it is inside or outside the United States. The federal act generally tracks the definition of a trade secret in the Uniform Trade Secrets Act but expands the definition to include the new technological ways that trade secrets are created and stored. The extraterritorial provisions of the act give the Justice Department broad authority to prevent the willful evasion of liability for trade secret misappropriation by using the Internet or other means to transfer the trade secret information outside the United States.[7]

As with other types of property, such as goods, accounts receivable, patents and trademarks, trade secrets may be sold by one business to another. Sources of statutory and case law in this area include WESTLAW, LEXIS-NEXIS, and several Internet sites, including the fee-based LEXIS-NEXIS Academic Universe.

PATENTS

> The issue of patents for new discoveries has given a spring to invention beyond my conception.
> —Thomas Jefferson

On April 10, 1790, the first president of the United States, George Washington, signed into law the bill that established the foundations of the American patent system. Three years earlier, the Constitutional Convention had given Congress the power to "promote the progress of science and the useful arts by securing for limited time to authors and inventors the exclusive right to their respective writings and discoveries." These powers were made manifest by incorporation in Article I, Section 8, Clause 8 of the Constitution.

The United States patent system was the first to recognize by law the inherent right of an inventor to limited protection and to provide for the systematic scrutiny of applications by qualified examiners working at the United States Patent and Trademark Office (PTO), an agency within the Department of Commerce. This legal enforcement has become the model for the patent system of numerous foreign countries. However, before the federal Constitution was adopted, the several Colonies issued patents. The first patent on this continent was granted by the Massachusetts General Court to Samuel Winslow in 1641 for a novel method of making salt. Colonial and state patents, unlike modern patents, were issued only by special acts of the appropriate legislatures. There were no general laws providing for the granting of patents, and in every instance it was necessary for inventors to make a special appeal to the governing body of their colony or state. When the delegates from the several states met in Philadelphia to frame the Constitution, the clause concerning patents (and copyright) was adopted. On March 4, 1789, government under the new Constitution commenced, and President Washington urged the representatives to give "effectual encouragement . . . to the exertion of skill and genius at home." A year later, the patent bill became law pursuant to the constitutional mandate.

Recipients of patents throughout the history of the United States read like a drumroll of the famous. Abraham Lincoln, who said of invention "I know of nothing so pleasant to the mind, as the discovery of anything which is at once new and valuable," was granted on May 22, 1849, a patent for "A Device for Buoying Vessels over Shoals." In addition to Lincoln, a brief list of patents awarded would include Harry Houdini, George Washington Carver, Frank Lloyd Wright, Samuel Colt, Mark Twain, Louis Pasteur, Samuel F. B. Morse, Alexander Graham Bell, Guglielmo Marconi, Enrico Fermi, Orville and Wilbur Wright, and, of course, that most celebrated of inventors, Thomas Alva Edison, the "Wizard of Menlo Park," whose creativity accounted for a record 1,093 patents.[8]

Although U.S. patents began to be numbered in 1836, more than 10,000 unnumbered patents were issued before that year, including Eli Whitney's cotton gin and Cyrus McCormick's reaper. Six years before Lincoln was awarded Patent No. 6469, Henry Ellsworth, the United States Commissioner of Patents, implied that the naive nineteenth-century doctrine of perfectibility was close to consummation. "The advancement of the arts from year to year," he exclaimed, "taxes our credulity, and seems to presage the arrival of that period when human improvement must end."[9] And in 1899, Charles H. Duell, another Commissioner of Patents, declared that "Everything that can be invented has been invented."[10] So much for the art of crystal-ball gazing. Before the millennium, more than 6 million patents had been granted by the USPTO. Lincoln, who was a keen student of the patent process, stated in 1859 that before the incorporation of the system and its legitimacy in law, "any man might instantly use what another had invented; so that the inventor had no special advantage from his own invention. The patent system changed this and thereby added the fuel of interest to the fire of genius, in the discovery and production of new and useful things."[11] History has abundantly justified his eloquent and prescient statement.

Types of Patents

Patent laws provide for the granting of patents in three major categories. Utility patents are awarded to anyone who invents or discovers any new and useful process, machine, manufacture, or composition of matter, or any new and useful improvement thereof. In turn, utility patents are subdivided into general and mechanical, electrical, and chemical. Design patents are granted to any person who has invented a new, original, and ornamental design for an article of manufacture. In design patents, the appearance of the article is protected. Plant patents are bestowed upon anyone who has invented or discovered and asexually reproduced any distinct and new variety of plant, including cultivated sports, mutants, hybrids, and newly found seedlings, other than a tuber-propagated plant or a plant found in an uncultivated state. The term of a utility patent used to be seventeen years, but PL 103-465, December 8, 1994, amended § 154 of Title 135, *United States Code,* "to provide that the term of a [utility] patent will commence on the date of issue, and end twenty years after the date on which the application resulting in the patent was filed. . . . This provision is necessary to comply with the requirements of Article 4 *bis*(5) of the *Paris Convention for the Protection of Industrial Property*" (108 Stat. 4295-96). Like a utility patent, a plant patent's term is twenty years from the date on which the application was filed in the United States. For design patents, however, the term is fourteen years from the grant and no fees are necessary to maintain a design patent in force. In every instance the inventor must file an application with the Commissioner of Patents and Trademarks. Then examiners of the USPTO search prior patents and, if appropriate, the literature of the discipline involved, whether that be the scientific and technical (for example, Patent No. 5,000,000) issues of *American Bicyclist & Motorcyclist* (for example, Patent No. D308500), or the Frederick's of Hollywood Catalog (for example, Patent No. 5,163,447). The examiners are seeking to determine whether the application presents something that is novel and not obvious; that is, something patentable.

It is not unusual for the same inventor to apply for and receive both a utility and a design patent. For example, on July 5, 1994, Ted Webb was awarded U.S. Patent D348,502 for the ornamental design of a bouncing swing he had sculpted (design class 21, design subclass 246). And on August 30, 1994, Webb was awarded utility Patent Number

5,342,245 for the apparatus itself (class 472, subclass 118). Plant patents, on the other hand, usually stand by themselves. My favorite is PP9,707, awarded to Melvin Ohrazda and David Mathison November 26, 1996. Titled "Lucky Rose Golden Apple Tree" (plt/34.1; 1 claim, 12 drawing figures), it is a new variety "which bears apples with a deep red blush on areas exposed to sunlight." Perhaps the horticulturists who created and nurtured this masterpiece were inspired by the last line of Yeats's great poem, "The Song of Wandering Aengus."

Claims and Prior Art

When renowned rock guitarist Edward L. (Eddie) Van Halen was awarded Patent No. 4,656,917 for a stringed musical instrument support, he was able to itemize twenty-two claims.[12] Utility patents must include in the written specifications one or more claims, "brief descriptions of the subject matter of the invention . . . reciting all essential features necessary to distinguish the invention from what is old." Indeed, the claims are "the operative part of the patent. Novelty and patentability are judged by the claims; and, when a patent is granted, questions of infringement are judged by the courts on the basis of the claims."[13] Clearly, the more claims that can be documented, the greater the chance of winning approval from the PTO examiners, who are thorough and unforgiving. For both design and plant patents, on the other hand, only one claim is permitted; the patent is granted to the entire design, or to the whole plant.

The often difficult and tortuous search for justifying one's invention involves searching prior patents, journal articles, and monographs. To make any claims stand up, this research, known as prior art, must be conducted. Sources found are cited in the "References" section of the patent and are displayed in the CD-ROM and Internet editions of the patents. Almost all inventions are extensions of prior art, therefore each novel feature (claim) must be significant and substantially different from those previous inventions in the searcher's class and subclass. Prior art serves to define the state of the art at the time a patent application is filed. Specific items of prior art may serve as the basis of denying patentability; thus it is imperative that all sources of information that relate to an invention be integrated into patentability determinations. For example, an appellate court ruled *In re Hall*, 781 F.2d 897, 899 (1986) that a publicly cataloged doctoral dissertation in a publicly accessible library is properly considered a prior art document.

When Patents Expire

When a patent expires it simply means that the new or novel features (the claims) that made the invention distinctive and protected the inventor or assignee from infringement are no longer protected. The invention described by the patent falls into the public domain and can be used by anyone without permission. Competitors can then use the feature or features to produce a similar product (called a knockoff) perhaps more cheaply, and gain some share of the market. Often the fortunes of a company are profoundly affected by the expiration of a patent. Companies that have survived expiration have planned well ahead to stay competitive. For instance, the patent on Prozac (the best known of the antidepressant drugs) is owned by Eli Lilly & Company and has accounted for nearly one-third of Lilly's entire revenue. Prozac's main claim is its key ingredient, a chemical called fluoxetine. The competing antidepressants on the market will be able to use this chemical once Prozac's patent expires. But Lilly is working on a number of new drugs to aid other illnesses, and the company hopes that these endeavors will fill the sales vacuum when Prozac inevitably loses some of the market share it now enjoys. Diversify and survive is the motto of successful companies.

The fact that an invention or discovery is in the public domain does not mean that subsequent developments based on the original invention are also in the public domain. Rather, new inventions that improve public domain technology are continually being conceived and patented. The vast majority of awarded patents are extensions of basic technologies that are no longer covered by in-force patents.

When a patent expires on a brand-name drug, other pharmaceutical companies can introduce competitive generic versions of the brand-name product. The aggressively competitive world of pills for every need or urge generates patents galore. It takes an average of nine years from the time a drug is first tested to final Food and Drug Administration (FDA) approval. The generic or chemical name is assigned by the FDA; for example, "Tagamet" is the brand name for the generic drug "cimetadine." The generic product is manufactured in compliance with the FDA's Good Manufacturing Practices regulations; contains identical amounts of the same active ingredients; is in the same dosage form, strength, and purity; and is analyzed and rated for bioequivalency. In other words, until a patent expires, or unless a manufacturer decides to permit others to manufacture the drug, only one brand of the drug is allowed on the market. Most pharmacies post or have current rosters of brand-name drugs with their generic equivalents. There is no need to buy an expensive product with a well-recognized brand name when a comparable generic product is available for one-half the cost. Consider this when you automatically reach for a product that has insinuated itself into your memory through the Pavlovian repetition of seductive advertisements.

Basic Information Sources

Because one can still search manually as well as in electronic formats, the following sources can be useful. *Basic Facts About Patents,* a free brochure, presents a brief, non-technical overview about the patent application process and supplies answers to frequently asked questions. *Attorneys and Agents Registered to Practice Before the U.S. Patent and Trademark Office* (also known as the Attorney Roster and Patent Attorney Roster File) contains names and addresses of patent attorneys and agents authorized to represent inventors before the PTO. This source is on CD-ROM (Patents ASSIST), floppy diskette, magnetic tape, and in print from the Superintendent of Documents (SuDocs). Another source for names of attorneys and agents is the Yellow Pages of one's local telephone directory. *General Information Concerning Patents* is available from the SuDocs, and on the PTO Web site it is accompanied by a variety of useful information for the aspiring inventor.

Manual Searching

Before the advent of electronic retrieval of patent information, one of the more stimulating tasks of the reference librarian was assisting users who were conducting a patent search. In that ancient and pristine time, only print and microform were available. Thus librarians directed their wanna-be inventors to the appropriate sources they needed for the oft hazardous prior art journey. Though used far less frequently now that electronic search sources are available, these durable sources still exist. One can begin with the *Index to the U.S. Patent Classification System.* At the beginning of this annual is an alphabetical list of about 430 classes and 140,000 subclasses, but the *Index* itself is a "subjective list of relevant terms, phrases, synonyms, acronyms, and trademarks that have been selected over the years to aid the user in identifying and describing products, processes, and apparatus of patent disclosure."[14] Approach the *Index* as you would any other finding aid in the universe of useful bibliographic tools, but beware: It is a complex listing, as intricate as a Bach partita, and your client must select with great care synonymously related words and phrases that will describe unique claims for your invention. The pitfalls are real. Class 12 is titled BOOT AND

SHOE MAKING, but class 36 is BOOTS, SHOES, AND LEGGINGS. The first listed class is PLANTS, but Class 47 is PLANT HUSBANDRY. And these are just the easy examples.

The user can then be directed to the *Manual of Classification,* a looseleaf updated periodically, which furnishes the list of classes and subclasses. Each Class Schedule is divided into major groups of subclasses, headed by a major subclass in CAPITAL LETTERS. This major unit is then divided into coordinate subclasses, indented with a single dot. The coordinate subclasses are further divided into subordinate subclasses, indented with two or more dots. For example, Class 365, "STATIC INFORMATION STORAGE AND RETRIEVAL," has, as the first listed of several subclasses, MAGNETIC BUBBLES, with one of several coordinate and subordinate subclasses.[15] And on it goes, rivaling cladistics in its hierarchical complexity. Users are advised to review the entire Class Schedule and refine their search by following the indentations until they discover the smallest entity that can be claimed as a novel feature of their invention. The *Manual* is as formidable as it is indispensable and, like the *Index,* requires meticulous attention to detail.

United States Patent Classification Definitions, a detailed description of each class and subclass, is updated semiannually. The *Definitions* indicate the subject matter found in or excluded from a class or subclass, limit or expand the precise manner in which the meaning is intended for each subclass title, and serve as a guide to the *Manual* by eliminating, as much as possible, the subjective and varying interpretations of the meanings of the subclass titles. In addition, notes are included to illustrate the kinds of information that can be found in a subclass and direct the searcher to other related subclasses that may contain relevant information.

If inventors aspire to the famous Emersonian apothegm on building better mousetraps,[16] they will come to class 43, "FISHING, TRAPPING, AND VERMIN DESTROYING," but may need to decide which of several subclasses is most appropriate to their novel mousetrap. Here the *Definitions* provide the distinguishing nuances. For example, subclass 58 of class 43 includes devices "which lure animals not domesticated or take advantage of some habit of the same and by which reason of some voluntary action on the part of the said animals catch or would or paralyze or kill the same or in general render them helpless, that man may work his will upon them," that last phrase revealing a poet hiding inside a bureaucrat. But the invention of a wire mesh rodent screen that is inserted in the end of a corrugated plastic drainage pipe to prevent rodent incursions into the pipe was awarded U.S. Patent No. 5,581,934 (December 10, 1996) under class 43, subclass 64 rather than 58. Traps like this "reset themselves under the influence of gravity." Class 43 distinguishes between traps for vermin such as mice and those designed to capture fish and insects. Moreover, if the invention is a letter box trap or a coin trap, you need to access class 232, "DEPOSIT AND COLLECTION RECEPTACLES," which comprises subclasses 47+ for letter box traps and subclasses 55+ for coin traps.

"Subclasses with a plus sign . . . are intended as a reminder that this is only a starting point. The searcher should continue scanning down the schedule until a relevant subclass is found."[17] In class 84, Music, the *Definitions* note that "[I]nstruments furnishing a sound of only one pitch, even if it might be used for musical purposes, are generally to be found in Class 116, Signals and Indicators, Class 446, Amusement Devices: Toys, subclasses 207+ and 397+, but "bellows and wind flow regulators, unless specifically adapted to musical instruments are to be found in Class 60, Power Plants, subclasses 407+." Eternal vigilance is the price of liberty and the shibboleth for the conduct of a successful patent search.

In earlier times the reference librarians would have sent our Edisonian wanna-bes to a *Microfilm List* that comprised a complete enumeration of patent numbers by class/subclass from 1836 to 1969, which was sold by the PTO but was not a depository item. The drudgery of writing down all the individual patent numbers was one of the unhappy tasks of pre-electronic patent searching. To bridge the gap between that source and the present, users may consult the annual *Index of Patents,* a massive two-volume work that contains a list of patentees and a subject index by class/subclass.

Finally, the searcher can be directed to the *Official Gazette of the United States Patent and Trademark Office—Patents,* a weekly listing of current inventions in numerical sequence. Nicknamed OG or POG, the *Official Gazette* contains, among other bibliographic data, a selected drawing and at least one representative claim for each patent granted. It also contains indexes to patents by classification, state, and patentee; a list of patents available for license or sale; and general information, notices, and changes in rules.

Patent and Trademark Depository Libraries

With the exception of the *Microfilm List,* all of the above sources are available for sale from the Superintendent of Documents and free to Title 44 depository libraries. In addition, there is a growing network of more than eighty specialized Patent and Trademark Depository Libraries (PTDLs) located in almost all states, the District of Columbia, and

Puerto Rico. A majority of these designated PTDLs are also Title 44 depositories. They afford access to many of the same products and services offered at the PTO search facilities located in Arlington, Virginia; all PTDLs have CASSIS and other CD-ROM products for searching patent and trademark information. However, it is advisable to call a particular library in advance because the PTDLs vary in the scope of their collections, hours of operation, services, and fees for making paper copies of patents and trademarks from the paper or microfilm collections. PTDLs offer the following products and services:

- back-file collections and current issues of patents;

- *Official Gazette—Patents;*

- *Official Gazette—Trademarks;*

- reference assistance and referrals;

- patent classification research instruction;

- supplemental reference materials;

- young inventor programs;

- public seminars and training opportunities.

Two Partnership PTDLs offer enhanced services for which fees are charged. The Sunnyvale Center for Innovation, Invention and Ideas, Sunnyvale, California, and the Great Lakes Patent and Trademark Center at the Detroit (Michigan) Public Library offer online patent text and image searching. PTO has authorized the partnerships to order file wrappers, assignment documents, and certified copies for their customers and to accept disclosure documents on-site. Libraries with Automated Patent System capability, PTDL Partnership locations, and a complete list of PTDLs by state are located through the USPTO Web site address, noted below.

Automated Patent System

The Automated Patent System (APS) is presumed to eventually replace the CASSIS series in Patent and Trademark Depository Libraries. APS contains the full text of each patent issued and was developed for the PTO under contract with private-sector companies. Databases include the Classification Search and Image Retrieval (CSIR) and the Automated Patent System—Text Search (APS—Text Search). Updated weekly on two magnetic tapes, searches are available to the public at the Patent Search and Image Retrieval Facility in Arlington, Virginia. There is also a Patent Full Text file available on magnetic tape. Both products are highly expensive, averaging between $8,000 and $9,000 for a year's subscription.

Patent Search Room

In the same complex in Arlington is the Patent Search Room, which contains copies of all U.S. patents issued from 1790 to the present. The collection in paper form is arranged by technology classification by the patent classification system and also available by patent number on 16mm microfilm and in bound paper volumes. There, as in the PTDLs, automated searching is available to the public using the CASSIS CD-ROM products and APS—Text Search. Staff members are available to help customers locate files and reference materials.

Patents on the CASSIS CD-ROM Series

The Classification and Search Support Information System (CASSIS) began publication in 1989 after a pilot program to test the feasibility of using CD-ROM to replace an aging online system. Originally distributed only to the Patent and Trademark Depository Libraries, the series, with one exception, is now available to Title 44 depository libraries and by subscription to the public. The series includes the following:

- Patents ASSIGN: U.S. Patents Assignments Recorded at the USPTO. Includes data derived from assignment deeds for patents granted since 1971, which were recorded at the PTO after August 1980. Updated quarterly.

- Patents ASSIST: Full Text of Patent Search Tools. A compilation of a number of patent search tools including the above-mentioned print sources and *Attorneys and Agents Registered to Practice Before the U.S. Patent and Trademark Office; Classification Orders Index,* a list of classifications abolished and established since 1976; and the current edition of the *United States Patent Classification to International Patent Classification Concordance,* a product of the World Intellectual Property Organization (WIPO), an international intergovernmental specialized agency affiliated with the United Nations. Updated quarterly.

- Patents BIB: Selected Bibliographic Information from U.S. Patents Issued 1969 to the Present. Contains bibliographic information for utility patents issued from 1969 to the present and for other types of patent documents issued from 1977 to date. Included, inter alia, are the current classifications, patent title, date of issue, and abstracts. Patents BIB also refers to patent image locations on USAPat, discussed below.

- Patents CLASS: Current Classification of U.S. Patents Issued 1790 to the Present. Permits one to create a complete subclass list that contains current classification information for all patent types, as well as defensive publications and statutory registrations issued from 1790 to the present. Updated bimonthly.

- Patents SNAP: Concordance of U.S. Patent Application Serial Numbers to U.S. Patent Numbers. Provides a concordance (not to be confused with the WIPO concordance noted above) between U.S. patent numbers and application serial numbers. Includes data for patents with an application date from January 1, 1977, through the date specified on the disk. Updated annually.

- USAPat: Facsimile Images of United States Patents. Contains facsimile images of patents from 1994 to the present. An "image" is an actual page of the patent, including all drawings, that looks exactly like the printed document. It must be emphasized that USAPat is a document delivery system, not a search system; retrieval is by document number only, from a cumulative index. About 150 disks are issued each year, averaging three disks per week. (See USAMark, discussed on page 356.)

- CASSIS Sampler: Samples of CD-ROM Products Published by the USPTO. Includes most of the products currently available in the CASSIS CD-ROM series, but with sample data only. This product is not available to Title 44 depository libraries but can be used free of charge at the PTDLs.

Internet Sites

The USPTO's site is **http://patents.uspto.gov**. In October 1992 an agreement was reached between the National Science Foundation (NSF), an independent agency of the federal establishment, and the Center for Networked Information Discovery and Retrieval (CNIDR), a private-sector entity that performs software research and custom development, to create a clearinghouse for networked information. This project resulted in several prototype systems involving standards for client-server applications, including those of the National Library of Medicine, the National Aeronautics and Space Administration, the United States Geological Survey, and the PTO. As a result of this sub-vention, the PTO offers Internet access to patents in major databases: the U.S. Patent Full-Text Database, Bibliographic Database, and the International AIDS Patent Database. The last includes full text and images of acquired immune deficiency syndrome (AIDS)–related patents issued by the U.S., European, and Japanese patent offices.

A "What's New" page on the Web site contains recent changes or improvements to the system and is updated periodically. Unfortunately, one can only conduct a preliminary prior art foray from 1976 to the present. The Patent Full-Text Database contains hyperlinks to the full-page images of each patent. New images become available each Tuesday and are 300 dpi Tagged Image File Format (TIFF). Displaying them requires either a TIFF plug-in for your browser or a properly installed and configured application to which your browser sends TIFF images for display. Full-page images can be accessed from each patent's full-text display by clicking on the "Images" button at the top of the display page. This will bring up the image of the first page of the document along with navigation buttons for retrieving the other pages of the document. The additional buttons include the identifiable sections of each patent: front page, drawings, specifications, claims, certificates of correction (if any), and re-examinations (if any). Moreover, patent images must be retrieved one page at a time. The PTO suggests that images may best be printed using the plug-in's print button rather than the browser's print function. There are more than thirty patent field codes for searching. They include but are not limited to year or groups of years, ranked chronologically or by relevance to the key words or phrases, and accessed by abstract (a brief summary and description of the patented item); date the application for the patent was filed; application number; assignee name, city, state, and country; primary and/or assistant patent examiner; government interest; inventor name, city, state, and country; legal representative; patent number; patent title; references to previous patents, journal articles, and other publications (prior art); and U.S. class/subclass. This last used to be called "original class" (OCL); but in May 1997 was replaced by Current Class (CCL) data, which include any changes to the issued classification of the patent resulting from reclassification of the technology groupings containing the patent. The "Tips on Fielded Searching" page of the PTO Web site gives more information on the several fields.

In addition, May 1997 saw several new fields added to both databases: foreign priority, foreign references, other references, U.S. references, PCT Information; reissue data, and related U.S. application data. Note, however, that these added fields do not represent added data, only new ways to narrow one's search. There are other Web sites that contain patent information:

- The Intellectual Property Network (IPN) (**http://www.patents.ibm. com**), sponsored by IBM, permits viewing of patent documents from the United States and Europe as well as patent applications published by WIPO. Searchable fields include patent number, title, abstract, claims, assignee, inventor(s), and attorney/agent. Bibliographic data and text from 1971 and images from 1974 are provided. Fun features include a "Gallery of Obscure Patents" and "Wacky Patent of the Month," both devoted to recognizing inventions that range from the unconventional to the bizarre. Among the former are Patent Number 5,351,436 (Fly Swatter with Sound Effects) and Patent Number 5,457,821 (Hat Simulating a Fried Egg). For an example of a Wacky Patent, see the first paragraph on page 351. A copy of the full patent specification can be ordered through Optipat, Inc., for a fee by mail or fax. Optipat also supplies images in CD-ROM format.

- QPAT-US (**http://qpat2.qpat.com**) offers coverage of U.S. patents from January 1, 1974. Bibliographic information includes inventor's name, patent number, date awarded, abstract, description, U.S. classification notation, and prior art. This "front page" information is free, but the full text is accessible to paying subscribers only. QPAT-US is produced by Questel-Orbit, an international information provider specializing in patent, trademark, scientific, chemical, business, and news information.

- Micropatent (**http://www.micropat.com**), unlike the sites above, requires users to open a minimum $50 deposit account from which the cost of usage is deducted. The name given to this search engine is PatentWeb. The registration page on this Web site has the appropriate phone and fax numbers, and links for general information, registering, technical support, billing, and sales.

Commercial Online Databases

A number of vendors produce databases for specialized patent searching, among them Pergamon, DIALOG, Questel, BRS Technologies, Derwent, and others. These cover patents pending and awarded in disciplines such as petroleum refining, petrochemicals, and related fields. Two major online services for patent searches and related information are WESTLAW and LEXIS-NEXIS. WESTLAW contains the full text of more than 2 million patents; the database identifier (PATENTS-US) includes all statutory invention registrations; granted utility, design, plant, and reissue patents; and defensive publications issued since 1974. Exact facsimiles of patent drawings can be viewed and printed as they appeared in the *Official Gazette*. In addition, WESTLAW affords extensive access to federal intellectual property in the areas of U.S. and international case law, statutes and legislative history, administrative law, public records and filing, news and information, and practice guides such as *Restatements of the Law*. Moreover, DIALOG intellectual property databases on WESTLAW include Claims/U.S. Patent Abstracts, 1950 to date, Claims/U.S. Patent Abstracts Weekly, Claims/Reassignment & Reexamination, and Inpadoc/Family and Legal Status.

LEXIS-NEXIS has two libraries and many files for patent information. The Patent and Trademark Office Library (LEXPAT) furnishes access to the full text of U.S. patents from 1976 as well as updated information on assignments, certificates of correction, term extensions, adverse decisions, re-examination certificates, reissues, disclaimers, dedications, and litigation notices. The Patent Law Library (PATENT) contains all the material available in the LEXPAT plus patent-related federal case law, legislation, decisions of the Commissioner of Patents and Trademarks, patent law periodicals, and extensive prior art research files.

International Patent Classification

Mentioned above, the *United States Patent Classification to International Patent Classification Concordance* (also known as the *USPC-IPC Concordance and Concordance File*) consists of parallel tables and is revised periodically. The *Concordance* maintains the correlation between any class and subclass of the U.S. Patent Classification (USPC) System and the corresponding class and subclass of the International Patent Classification (IPC) System published by the World Intellectual Property Organization. It is intended only as a guide because there are some differences in the philosophies of the two systems and it should not be considered to depict a one-to-one relationship. It is, nevertheless, very important. For example, inventions such as the jack-in-the-box constitute a field of search that includes U.S. class 46 and various subclasses. Patent 3,691,675 was awarded for a Jack-in-the-Box Sounder equipped with a bellows extending between the pop-up figure and the box so that the bellows expands when the figure emerges from the box. An air-operated sounder makes a distinctive noise when the air is expelled through a passageway. This momentous invention was given, inter alia, a 46/118 class/subclass designation, described in the *Manual of Classification* as "Amusement Devices. Toys. Figure Toys. Combined. With Sound. Movable Figure." The *Concordance* shows that particular U.S. class to be equivalent to international class A63h 13/16, with a descriptive breakdown as follows: "Human Necessities (A). Sports; games, amusements (63). Toys (h). Toy figures with self-moving parts, with or without movement of the toy as a whole (13/00). Boxes from which figures jump (13/16)." The international classification notation is given in the bibliographic information for the *Official Gazette* entries, on the Internet, and on the appropriate CASSIS CD-ROMs.

Other Patent Publications

In addition to the sources mentioned above, the PTO issues publications on floppy diskette, magnetic tape, microfiche, and in print in support of patents and the process of securing this property right. These are listed, with brief annotations, in the current edition of the *Products and Services Catalog,* an annual publication from the Information Dissemination Organizations (IDO) of the PTO. When a product is available on CD-ROM, magnetic tape, and paper, the *Catalog* describes all three under the same product title. When different formats are supplied by different IDO sources or are available from the Superintendent of Documents, the *Catalog* has ordering information and order forms for all of the suppliers. In addition, the *List of Classes* itemizes over thirty series available to Title 44 depository libraries on CD-ROM, microfiche, and in print.

Patent Law

The American patent system is codified in Title 35 of the *United States Code* and the regulations of the PTO are promulgated in Chapter I, Title 37, of the *Code of Federal Regulations.* But advances in what can be patented are usually governed by case law. If patent examiners reject the claims of applicants, they may first appeal to the Board of Patent Appeals and Interferences, an administrative tribunal within the USPTO with quasi-judicial powers. If the board's decision is adverse to applicants, the plaintiffs may carry their appeal further to the Court of Appeals for the Federal Circuit or file civil action against the agency in the U.S. District Court for the District of Columbia.

Through the decades, as the number of patents granted increased, so did the volume of patent litigation. In recent times, the courts, "keenly aware that a patent could be used to stifle competition," have tried "to restrict the patent to genuine novelty, to individual skill," as a reaction to the increasing phenomenon of "corporate mass production of small improvements."[18] The Supreme Court has tried to clarify words such as "new" ("never known before"), "useful" ("operative—that is having and accomplishing a purpose"), and "inventive" ("something beyond the skill of an ordinary skilled person—in the field of the idea").[19] It is questionable whether this attempt at secular hermeneutics has slowed the onrushing corporate juggernaut.

That said, the judiciary plays an important role in redefining what is patentable. For example, in *Diamond v. Chakrabarty,* 447 U.S. 303, 100 S.Ct. 2204, 65 L.Ed.2d 144 (1980), the Supreme Court ruled, in a 5 to 4 decision, that a "live, human-made micro-organism is patentable subject matter" under the provisions of 35 U.S.C. § 101. Less than a year later, biologist Ananda M. Chakrabarty was awarded Patent No. 4,259,444 (March 31, 1981), with the title "Microorganisms having multiple compatible degradative energy-generating plasmids and preparation thereof," in plain English, a microbe to clean up oil spills. The patent was assigned to the General Electric Company. Chakrabarty had initially filed his application on June 7, 1972. The mills of justice, like those of God, often grind slowly. Since then, however, scientists have patented genes, cell lines, and genetically remodeled animals from mice to abalone. Now biologists want to patent ways to make human-animal chimeras. A mouse with a human gene? Once human DNA enters the picture, the legal situation becomes murky, but some bioethicists have invoked the Thirteenth Amendment to the U.S. Constitution (slavery or involuntary servitude) as supporting a ban on patenting chimeras.

As Harwell points out, "Basic knowledge of patent law concepts enhances the patent searcher's ability to identify material that is pertinent for prior art patentability assessments and for other purposes. The role of the library and library staff is to provide information assistance rather than legal advice. This role can best be fulfilled by . . . allowing the patron to take responsibility for the results of the search and for any subsequent decisions and actions." By refusing to answer substantive questions, the librarian "can avoid the unauthorized practice of law."[20] Of course, patrons can be referred to the several international treaties that bind nations in protecting inventors, among them the Patent Cooperation Treaty of 1970, as amended in 1979 and modified in 1984, and the Eurasian Patent Convention of 1994.

Once you have learned enough to become comfortable with patent searching, you may congratulate yourself using the "Pat on the back apparatus," a gadget with a "simulated human hand carried on a pivoting arm. . . . The hand is manually swingable into and out of contact with the user's back to give an amusing or important pat on the back." This landmark device was assigned Patent No. 4,608,967 and awarded to Ralph R. Piro on September 2, 1986 (class 601/subclass 107); subsequently, it was honored with a "Wacky Patent of the Month" award at the IPN database, mentioned above.

Figure 10.1 shows a drawing of a battery-powered electric tractor, issued as Patent No. 4,662,472. Its U.S. classification designation in original classification (OR) is 180/235; its international classification is B60K 17/30; HO2P 5/16. In the full-patent specification, the inventors articulated twenty-eight claims and included five "Drawing Figures." The prior art search yielded twelve patents. When this patent was announced in the *Official Gazette,* only the basic bibliographic information, the abstract, and one drawing were provided.

Figure 10.1. Drawing from full patent specification.

U.S. Patent   May 5, 1987   Sheet 1 of 4   **4,662,472**

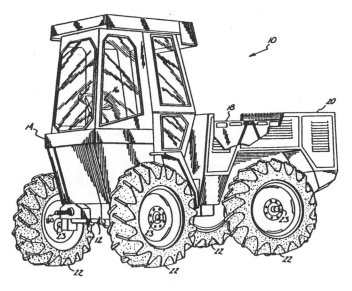

TRADEMARKS

The General Accounting Office reported to the Senate Judiciary Committee that in fiscal year (FY) 1995, "about three-fourths of PTO's funding . . . and staff were devoted to the patent process. Other major activities in PTO include the trademark process, the agency's executive direction and administration, and the dissemination of information."[21] Yet trademark searching is just as challenging and rewarding as patent searching.

Federal trademark authority is embodied in the Lanham Trademark Act (15 U.S.C. § 1051 et seq.) as amended and is based on the commerce clause of the Constitution (Article I, Section 8, Clause 3). To obtain a federal trademark registration, the owner of a mark must demonstrate that the mark is used in a type of commerce that may be regulated by Congress. However, unlike patent and copyright law, federal trademark law coexists with state and common-law trademark rights. Therefore, registration at either the federal or state level is not necessary to create or maintain ownership rights in a mark. For example, priority of trademark rights between owners of confusingly similar marks, regardless of whether the marks are federally registered, is based upon first use of the mark. A trademark, when duly registered by the PTO, gives the registrant the same legal protection against infringement granted to a patentee. The symbol ® on a product indicates that the PTO has issued the registrant formal notification of acceptance, subject initially to an appeal in opposition. If no party or parties come forth to challenge the mark within thirty days of PTO approval, the registration becomes active and its owner has, in effect, a contract signifying ownership and all the commercial and legal benefits that derive by virtue of registration. Use of the letters "TM" is a way of showing ownership, but it is unnecessary because the mark's use in commerce is sufficient to confer ownership.

Unlike patented and copyrighted works, trademark rights can last indefinitely, as long as the mark continues to be used in commerce. The time period of federal trademark registration is ten years, with ten-year renewable terms, on into the future. There are well over 1 million active, expired, abandoned, or canceled trademarks, and one sees those currently in use so often that they appear to be ubiquitous. There are the golden arches of McDonald's, the CBS eye, the NBC Peacock, the Jolly Green Giant, the Hallmark crown, the Gerber baby, Mister Donut, the circle "W" of Westinghouse Electric Corporation, and hundreds of thousands more. Less obvious are all the words and phrases with or without an accompanying design or symbol. Simply look in your kitchen and bathroom cabinets, for starters, or browse through a magazine with many advertisements, and you will find multitudes of brand names with the familiar ® or SM denoting official PTO approval.

Types of Trademarks

A trademark may consist of a distinctive word, phrase, symbol, design, fragrance, shape, color, sound, series of letters, or combinations thereof (15 U.S.C. § 1127). Trademarks that are suggestive or evocative (Slenderella diet food products, Netscape Communicator), "coined marks" (Exxon, Kodak), and fanciful words (Double Rainbow ice cream), because their intrinsic nature serves to identify the particular source of products, are entitled to protection. In addition, "trade dress" is protected under the Lanham Trademark Act. Trade dress may consist of a distinctive uniform worn by employees of an establishment, a product that has come to be known by its distinctive shape, or a service that has come to be known by its distinctive decorating motif (Taco Cabana's chain of fast-food restaurants). The general rule is that an identifying mark is protected if it is inherently distinctive or has acquired distinctiveness through "secondary meaning." Examples of the latter include Sears (department stores), Ben and Jerry's (ice cream), and Howard Johnson (hotels and lodges). Conversely, "weak marks" consist of common or ordinary words that have not acquired customer recognition through long usage. Examples abound and include people's names (Fred's Auto Supplies, Grandma's Country Kitchen) or geographic terms (Western Pest Control). These categories receive less protection under federal or state laws. Unprotectable trademarks include generic marks (aspirin and cellophane began as distinctive but became generic over time); surnames unless distinctive (what McDonald's has become over time); and names for businesses, called trade names (except those that are distinctive, such as Apple computers).[22]

Service Marks

When used to identify and promote a service, a trademark can be called a service mark (SM), although the word "trademark" is typically used as the generic term to include service marks. As a rule, a trademark for goods appears on the product or on its packaging, whereas a service mark is commonly used in advertising to identify the owner's services. Thus, Fidelity Investments is a registered trademark, but its motto ("Where 12 million investors put their trust") is Fidelity's registered service mark. The name Marriott (the hotel chain) is registered as a trademark, but the hotel's slogan "Got a suitcase? Gotta Join" is a service mark.

Basic Information Sources

Basic Facts About Trademarks, revised periodically, is a free brochure from the PTO, providing brief, non-technical information about the trademark registration process; filing requirements; sample written applications, drawings, and specimens; a list of PTDLs; and selected trademark application forms. Commercial sources are numerous. Ably representing the many aspects of trademark law and practice, both in the United States and internationally, are the publications of the International Trademark Association (**http://www.inta.org**), a New York–based organization with more than 3,200 members in 117 countries.

Electronic Data Protected

Case law accepts electronic transmission of data as protected trademark registration. In *In re Metriplex, Inc.,* 23 U.S.P.Q. 2d 1315 (1992), the PTO's Trademark Trial and Appeal Board (TTAB) authorized registration of a mark identifying "data transmissions services accessed via computer terminal," and accepted, as evidence of use of the mark, a printout of the mark as it appeared on the computer screen during transmission. Other federal court decisions have held that photographs and copies of video games as part of a computer bulletin board system and copies of video games are protected by trademark law.[23]

Depository Library Logo

On August 25, 1992, the PTO granted a service mark for the Federal Depository Library System (FDPL). The logo, an eagle's stylized head and wing curved around an open book, was assigned Certificate of Registration No. 1710513. This mark, which had its first use in commerce September 30, 1977, is intended for Title 44 depository libraries and library groups in applications associated with the FDPL. Assigned U.S. class 107 (Education and Entertainment) for "library services; namely, providing information and publications from the federal government on various subjects to libraries in the United States and its territories," the "drawing is lined for the colors red and blue." The Government Printing Office (GPO) also developed an electronic depository logo; all depository libraries that register for GPO Access receive a certificate recognizing this initiative, as well as decals with the GPO's logo of the electronic FDPL.[24]

The classification of trademarks does not have the subclass feature that permits precise searching in patent classes. The well-known Bell telephone system, for example, is classed in several categories. U.S. classes 21, 26, 38, 101, 103, 104, and 107 cover electrical, scientific, printed matter, advertising and business, construction and repair, education and entertainment, and miscellaneous services. The familiar symbol of a bell enclosed in a circle, owned by all the "Baby Bells" since the divestiture of "Ma Bell" in 1984, stands for computers, telephone directories, its use in advertising, the installation and maintenance of telecommunications systems, computer retail store services, seminars and workshops, and a number of other verbal descriptors. These U.S. classes correspond to class numbers 9, 16, 35, 37, 41, and 42 in the international schedule of classes of goods and services (see *Official Gazette: Trademarks,* September 5, 1989, p. TM 13).

Design Phrase

The trademark application must have a clear and precise written description of the mark. "This description is defined as the Design Phrase (PH=) field" and "is the weak link in the system because it does not have a controlled vocabulary, and because only about 30 percent of the records with a design have a design phrase." When the design phrase is "far fetched," it is difficult for the searcher to be able to retrieve the image. In the well-known chocolate delicacy, the Hershey "Kiss" (Class 46: Foods and Ingredients of Foods), first registered in 1924, the design phrase reads "Plume extending out of wrapper."[25] That is presumed to be the singular distinguishing element, a duplication of which would imply infringement. Thus, the descriptive quality of the design phrase facilitates an accurate trademark search, especially with a design-only mark.

Trademarks on the CASSIS CD-ROM Series

The CASSIS CD-ROM series, described for patent searching above, contains the following trademark disks, all of which are available to depository libraries and by annual sales subscription.

- Trademarks ASSIGN: U.S. Trademarks Assignments Recorded at the USPTO. Includes data derived from trademark assignment deeds recorded since 1955 with ten searchable fields. Includes the searchable text of the *Trademark Manual of Examining Procedures* and the *Goods and Services Manual,* which lists goods and services with their corresponding international and U.S. classifications. Updated bimonthly.

- Trademarks PENDING: Bibliographic Information from Pending U.S. Trademarks. Contains the text of trademark applications that have been filed but not yet approved for registration, with twenty-five searchable fields. Includes the two manuals listed above. Updated bimonthly.

- Trademarks REGISTERED: Bibliographic Information from Active, Registered U.S. Trademarks. Contains the text of all active registered trademarks from 1884 to the present with twenty-nine searchable fields. Includes the two manuals noted above. Updated bimonthly.

- Trademarks ASSIST: Full Text of Trademark Search Tools. Includes the two manuals noted above and the *Trademark Trial and Appeal Board Manual of Procedure,* the *Trademark Statute and Rules* (Trademark Act of 1946 and the Rules of Practice), the *Trademark Examination Trial and Notes,* the *Trademark Telephone Index,* and the *IDO Products and Services Catalog.* Issued approximately twice a year.

- USAMark: Facsimile Images of Registered United States Trademarks. Like USAPat, this CD-ROM consists of facsimile images of registered U.S. trademarks from 1884 to the present, an "image" being an actual page of the trademark that looks exactly like the original printed document. And like its counterpart, USAMark is a document delivery system, not a search system. The inaugural back file consists of approximately 100 disks covering registrations through December 31, 1996. Beginning in January 1997, the CD-ROM has been updated monthly, covering registrations that become available during a month and delivered within fifteen days of the end of the month covered. When enough images accumulate to fill a disk, a new back-file disk is issued that supersedes the monthly updates that it incorporates. This product became available to depository libraries in 1998.

- CASSIS Sampler. Includes a small sample of the several products noted above. As with patents, the products demonstrated on the CASSIS Sampler disk can be used free of charge at the many PTDLs throughout the nation and in Puerto Rico.

Official Gazette—Trademarks

Several products are available on CD-ROM and magnetic tape, including the *Official Gazette of the United States Patent and Trademark Office—Trademarks* (sometimes called TOG). Like its companion periodical for patents, the print edition of the trademark *Gazette* is issued every Tuesday. It contains an illustration of each trademark published for opposition and salient bibliographic information. And like its sister serial, it is a depository item and is for sale from the Superintendent of Documents.

Internet Sites

PTO Web Trademark Database (**http://www.uspto.gov/tmdb**) is a free database that includes bibliographic information for pending and registered trademarks as of July 1, 1998. One can search by word mark, registration or serial number, Boolean connectors, or search expression. If you seek information on registration number 1257722, you will see that included are the word mark (I can't believe it's not butter!), pseudo mark (I cannot believe it is not butter!), owner name and address (for registrant and last listed owner, if different), attorney of record, serial and registration numbers, filing and registration dates, mark drawing code, disclaimer (no claim is made to the exclusive right to use "butter" apart from the mark as shown), register, date published for opposition, affidavits, type of mark (trademark, service mark), international class number, and description of goods and services provided, including date of first use and date of first use in commerce.

To provide another example, the description for Alliance Capital A, an investment consulting service, states that the mark consists in part of a fanciful depiction of the letter "A" and the date it was first used in commerce was June 30, 1985. Not mentioned on the Web site is the service mark phrase used in its advertisements: "Because Later Is Sooner Than You Think" (SM).

Like the CD-ROM products, Trademarks Pending and Trademarks Registered, this database is updated bimonthly and initially included only the information listed above. By 1999, the number of trademarks that contained images had dramatically increased and this will only expand with time. The site includes a link to a page titled "Important Notice: Limitations Regarding The PTO's Web Trademark Database," which is required reading so that users do not waste time searching for information that is not available. For example, the absence of a mark in this database does not necessarily mean that it is not currently used in commerce.

Micropatent (**http://www.micropat.com**), discussed in connection with patent searching above, also has a daily, monthly, or annual TrademarkWeb subscription. There is a link to the page at which information about this service is given.

Trademark Search Library

The Trademark Search Library in Arlington, Virginia, contains a copy of every registered United States trademark. All active marks are available in cross-referenced alphabetical and design sections. Like patents, trademarks on 16mm microfilm and in bound volumes are in numerical order. Also available are records on microfilm of trademark applications, abandoned applications, and expired registrations. Automated searching is available by using the CD-ROM series, the Trademark Reporting and Monitoring System (TRAM), and X-Search. This last is an improvement over a flawed word and imaging search tool called T-Search, which trademark examiners and private users alike found inadequate. The *X-Search User Manual,* a looseleaf notebook available for sale, was developed as a reference guide for those who have completed PTO-provided training. It includes the design codes manual used by the trademark examiners.

Commercial Online Databases

Several commercial vendors make trademark information available. Three of the better-known and used sources are

- DIALOG: File 226 is a database called TRADEMARKSCAN-U.S.—FEDERAL, which covers all active registered marks and applications filed at the PTO. The database includes cross-references to assist retrieval of corrupted spellings and unconventional presentations of words. Each record covers the requisite bibliographic information. Coverage is from 1884 to the present. A CD-ROM version of this database is also available from the vendor.

- WESTLAW: The advantage of using WESTLAW and LEXIS-NEXIS for information on intellectual property is that they include, in addition to search capabilities, comprehensive coverage of statutes, cases, administrative rulings, foreign countries, and many secondary sources that provide news and scholarly analysis. TRADEMARKSCAN-U.S.—FEDERAL is also available on WESTLAW, where one can retrieve the same alternative usages the DIALOG edition has. In WESTLAW (FIP-TM is the database identifier) the Rotated Trademark Text and Enhancements box permits one to retrieve alternate spellings (quick! retrieves kwik), slang expressions (mosquito! & eater! retrieves skeeter eater), plays on words (so! & what! retrieves sew what), and other odd uses of words and numbers (anyone! & for! & tennis! retrieves NE14 10S).

- LEXIS-NEXIS: The Trademark and Unfair Competition Law Library (TRDMRK) contains both federal and state trademark and unfair competition case law and codes. In addition, the Library contains several files for regulatory materials (Title 37, *Code of Federal Regulations*), trademark registrations, newsletters, and intellectual property journals, including the intellectual property listings found in the *Martindale-Hubbell Law Directory* (Library: TRDMRK; File: MHINTP).

Domain Names and Trademark Issues

As of late 1998 there were seven top-level domains (TLDs) in the United States: "com," which represents commercial organizations; "edu" for four-year, degree-granting colleges and universities (branches of the ".us" domain are provided within each state for schools (K12), technical schools (TEC), community colleges (CC), and libraries (LIB)); "org" for miscellaneous entities that do not fit anywhere else; "int" for organizations established by international treaties, or international databases; "net" for entities and computers that represent part of the Internet's infrastructure; "mil" for military sites; and "gov" for federal government offices only (registration for state and local entities is made under the ".us" domain). The term preceding the top-level domain is the "second-level domain" (SLD) name (for example, the "uspto" of the "uspto.gov" designation). Both .com and .org are considered generic TLDs. Country codes such as .fr (France) and .to (Tonga) are non-generic because they refer to specific geographic areas. Only one party can possess a particular second-level domain name to be associated with a particular top-level domain; and for the federal government the most succinct policy has been "one agency, one name."

Network Solutions, Inc. (NSI), a private, nongovernmental organization, ran the InterNIC (Internet Information Center) registration service from 1993 until March 1998, when the National Science Foundation (NSF), an independent agency, did not renew its contract with NSI to handle Internet domain registrations. To fill the vacuum, the Department of Commerce asked the Geneva-based World Intellectual Property

Organization (**http://www.wipo2.wipo.int**) to develop recommendations for the protection of trademarks on the Internet. Domain names have created problems under trademark law, because only one entity can possess a second-level domain name. A substantial number of companies do business with the identical name (for example, Santa Fe Industries, Santa Fe Restaurant, Santa Fe Designs), but there is no confusion because either their products or services are patently different or they are geographically remote from one another. Under U.S. trademark classification practice, if the goods or services of two parties using the same name or a homophone thereof are sufficiently different that consumers will not be confused by the source or origin of the goods or services, then both parties may use the same name. Internet domain names, however, do not offer this luxury because of the limited number of top-level domains. In other words, there is essentially only one classification for all commercial goods and services (.com), whereas there are more than forty different classifications in the trademark system. Suggestions have been floated to expand the TLDs to include words like "firm," "shop," and "info," but companies fear that they will need to register all their trademarks with each new suffix to protect themselves.

Moreover, conflict arises from a disconnect between the systems for registering trademarks and domain names, the former administered by the PTO, the latter by a nongovernmental organization on a first-come, first-served basis. This has resulted in numerous instances of registrants who were innocently (and, in some cases, with malice aforethought) registering second-level domain names that infringed the trademark rights of another party. In 1995 NSI developed a policy to resolve this problem, and now WIPO is attempting to create "a standard approach to resolving disputes over domain names, a fixed process for determining ownership of famous names on the Internet, and a plan to determine trademark ownership when new top-level domain names . . . are launched. . . . Several high-profile trademark disputes have already erupted over domain name registration on the Internet. Many companies demand that they should have the right to domain names associated with their brand . . . even if those domains have been previously registered by another entity."[26]

Some companies have responded by registering every conceivable variation of whatever trademarks they already own as alternative Web sites. For example, NIKE has registered not only NIKE.com but airjordan.com, swoosh.com, justdoit.com, and others. Proctor and Gamble has registered more than 130 Web addresses, ranging from toothpaste.com to badbreath.com to pampers.com. Preying on the anxieties companies feel about consumer product recognition, some profiteers hoard and sell domain names to the highest bidder. By the end of 1998, there were almost 2 million domain names. It has been forecast that this number will rise exponentially, and there are those who contend that the Internet will be the world's largest vehicle for commerce into the twenty-first century. A number of committees and coalitions have become involved in studying the problems and issuing "white papers" replete with recommendations. The consensus seems to favor a nonprofit corporation to oversee Internet addresses; the aim is to eventually privatize management of the domain name system. The stakes are high. Whether WIPO or the Internet Corporation for Assigned Names and Numbers (ICANN) resolves this problem, piquant terms like "cybersquatting" and "cyberpiracy" have already entered the language.

Trademark Law

Trademark disputes follow the pattern described for patent litigation. Once the PTO Examining Attorney approves the mark and it is published in the *Official Gazette—Trademarks,* any other party has thirty days to oppose the registration or request an extension of time to oppose. Oppositions are held before the Trademark Trial and Appeal Board (TTAB), an administrative tribunal in the PTO. If that board's ruling is unfavorable to the party or parties opposing the mark, action may be taken in federal district court, with the possibility of appellate action. The PTO makes available a Trademark Annual Trial and Appeal Board File, which contains all TTAB adversary proceedings, including the proceeding number, transaction date, date of filing, date of status, correspondence address, and TTAB status. This file is on the Trademark Web site and is contained on one magnetic tape, current as of the end of each December.

Trademark law expanded dramatically in the late nineteenth and early twentieth centuries. As Friedman notes, "The first injunction in a trademark case was granted in 1844," and "from this acorn grew a mighty oak." In a mass-production economy where numerous goods and services almost identical except for package and name compete zealously for consumers' dollars, trademark litigation flourishes. Lawsuits were (and still are) "acrimonious" and "relatively frequent," and trademark cases record "the activity of many jackals of commerce who tried to make off with values that inhered in another man's product."[27]

Both the Lanham Trademark Act and the basic underlying principles of trademark law describe the broadest possible universe. Section 1127 of the Act states that trademarks "include any word, name, symbol, or device, or any combination thereof." Since that embraces almost everything capable of carrying meaning, this language in theory is not restrictive. Hence the courts, the PTO, and the TTAB over the years have authorized many categories of marks: a particular sound (NBC's three chimes), color (the pink of Owens-Corning fiberglass insulation; a special shade of green-gold on the pads that Qualitex Company makes and sells to dry cleaning firms for use on dry cleaning presses), scent (plumeria blossoms on sewing thread), shape (Coca-Cola bottle), and so forth.

Blatant infringement of a trademark is obvious, but some cases may appear to the general public as frivolous or even ludicrous. For example, Mead Data Central, owner of the LEXIS-NEXIS trademark for its computerized legal research services (the company was sold to Reed Elsevier in 1994 and renamed LEXIS-NEXIS), brought action in 1988 against the Toyota Motor Corporation, which had announced in August 1987 that it planned to name a new line of luxury cars LEXUS. The U.S. District Court (S.D.N.Y.) ruled in Mead Data's favor under the tight statutory language of New York State's "antidilution" law (McKinney's General Business Law, § 368-d). On appeal, however, the U.S. Court of Appeals for the Second Circuit reversed and vacated without a published opinion.[28] Mead Data Central may have reasoned that if the LEXUS line of cars turned out to be lemons, the public might mistakenly associate the name with the database and draw untoward conclusions. This homophonic dispute is by no means unusual in trademark litigation, such is the assiduity with which companies guard their symbolic assets of commerce. In his written opinion, the district court judge noted that the "law of trademarks and unfair competition in this country has traditionally been based on the law of fraud or deceit."[29] One is reminded of the couplet penned by the eminent British jurist Sir Edward, Lord Coke (1552–1634):

Ask thou, why in such swelling volumes law do flow?
The cause is in the need; fraud in the world doth grow.[30]

Trademark treaties include the Madrid Agreement Concerning the International Registration of Marks of 1891, as amended; and the Stockholm Act of 1967, as amended in 1979.

COPYRIGHT

The same constitutional mandate governing patents applies also to copyright: Its privileges are conferred upon authors by virtue of Article I, Section 8, Clause 8 of the Constitution. Statutes are published in Title 17, *United States Code;* regulations are promulgated in Title 37 of the *Code of Federal Regulations;* and numerous court cases construe the code and the regulations. The Copyright Act of October 19, 1976, is codified at 17 U.S.C. § 101 et seq. It became effective January 1, 1978, and the basic text and amendments since that time represent the most complete revision of the copyright law. But technological developments in subsequent years bid fair to upset the equity that the act of 1976 attempted to secure.

The first Copyright Act of 1790 (1 Stat. 124) granted an author "sole right and liberty of printing, reprinting, publishing and vending" a "map, chart, book or books" for fourteen years, renewable for one additional fourteen-year term. Authors had to deposit a printed copy of their work with the clerk of the federal court in their district before publication, and another copy had to be delivered "within six months to the secretary of state as well. In 1831, the original term was extended to 28 years," and by this time the act "covered musical compositions, designs, engravings, and etchings" in addition to maps, charts, and books. In 1856, the copyright statute "was amended to include dramatic productions; in 1865, to cover photographs and negatives."[31] Various amendments added categories of "original works of authorship" until the Copyright Act of 1909 (35 Stat. 105) effected significant changes in the law. By the 1970s, the 1909 law, as amended in 1947, had proved woefully inadequate to accommodate technological advances. Today, 17 U.S.C. § 301 protects a copyrighted work for the length of an author's life plus seventy years. In the case of joint works, copyrighted protection is granted for the length of the life of the last surviving joint author plus another seventy years. "In cases where the creator is a business, the copyright lasts between 75 and 100 years."[32] The Act of 1976, as amended, is complex, and case law construing its provisions represents an ongoing effort, especially in the area of electronic publishing.

Exclusive Rights

Section 106 of the Act of 1976 empowers the owner of copyright to do, and authorize any of the following:

- reproduce the copyrighted work in copies or phonorecords;

- prepare derivative works based upon the copyrighted work;

- distribute copies of phonorecords of the copyrighted work to the public by sale or other transfer of ownership, or by rental, lease, or lending;

- perform the copyrighted work publicly, in the case of literary, musical, dramatic, and choreographic works, pantomimes, and motion pictures and other audiovisual works;

- display the copyrighted work publicly, in the case of literary, musical, dramatic, and choreographic works, pantomimes, and pictorial, graphic, or sculptural works, including the individual images of a motion picture or other audiovisual work.

Works Protected

Section 102(a) of the Copyright Act of 1976 sets forth the subject matter eligible for protection as subsisting "in original works of authorship fixed in any tangible medium of expression, now known or later developed, from which they can be perceived, reproduced, or otherwise communicated, either directly or with the aid of a machine or device." From this provision, the courts have derived three basic requirements for copyright protection: originality, creativity, and fixation. To be original, a work must not be simply copied from another. There is no requirement that the work be novel, as in patent law. To be creative, there must be merely a modicum of creativity, and the level required is exceedingly low. Fixation means that protection attaches automatically to an eligible work of authorship the moment the work is sufficiently fixed, that is (metaphorically), "when the ink dries on the paper." There are no prerequisites, such as registration or affixation of a copyright notice, for obtaining or enjoying copyright protection. Works are not sufficiently fixed if they are "purely evanescent or transient" in nature, such as those projected briefly on a screen, shown electronically on a television or cathode ray tube, or captured momentarily in the "memory" of a computer. Although electronic network transmissions from one computer to another, such as e-mail, may only reside on each computer in random access memory, that has been ruled to be sufficient fixation.[33]

Works Not Protected

Section 102(b) of the Copyright Act states that copyright does not extend to any "idea, procedure, process, system, method of operation, concept, principle or discovery, regardless of the form in which it is described, explained, illustrated, or embodied" in such work even if it meets the criteria of originality, creativity, and fixation. Section 105 precludes works of the U.S. government from protection with a few exceptions. The U.S. Postal Service, for example, can use the law to prevent the reproduction of postage stamp designs for private or commercial non-postal services. Sometimes just what can or cannot be protected has resulted in differing appellate decisions. As mentioned in chapter 8, in 1986 the Court of Appeals for the Eighth Circuit upheld a lower court's decision that the West Publishing Company's arrangement of legal decisions was entitled to copyright protection, and the Supreme Court denied certiorari.[34] Four years later, however, the Supreme Court, reversing lower courts' decisions, held that the white pages of a telephone directory are not copyrightable, an issue some critics assert is essentially the same as West's claim of copyright.[35] West lost copyright protection. As in patent and trademark law, court decisions based on copyright statutes reflect in their subtle nuances the complexity of the statutory provisions case law is called upon to interpret.

Fair Use

Section 107 of the 1976 act sets forth the doctrine of fair use, one of the murkier areas of copyright law. Fair use limits the rights of copyright owners by exempting certain uses from liability. But the statute contains no clear and direct answers about the scope of fair use and its meaning in specific situations. Instead, it sets forth four factors in determining fair use: the purpose and character of the use, its nature, the amount and substantiality of the portion used in relation to the work as a whole, and the effect on the potential market for or value of the work. As a result of these general factors, case law is crucial in determining fair use from one instance to the next. In a 1994 decision involving fair use (*Campbell v. Acuff-Rose Music, Inc.,* 510 U.S. 569, 127 L.Ed.2d 500, 114 S.Ct. 1164), the Supreme Court, reversing the ruling of the appellate court, held that the rap music group 2 Live Crew's commercial parody of the song "Oh Pretty Woman" did not infringe Acuff-Rose's copyright and is fair use within the meaning of § 107. Fair use doctrine requires case-by-case analysis and not rigid application of bright line rules.

Section 107 ends with these words: "The fact that a work is unpublished shall not itself bar a finding of fair use if such finding is made upon consideration of all the above factors." In a celebrated 1980s case, reclusive author J. D. Salinger successfully brought suit against the Random House publishing company and biographer Ian Hamilton on the grounds that the biographer used Salinger's unpublished letters to others (which were available for perusal at collections in university libraries) without permission. An appellate court held that Hamilton could not describe the correspondence in such a way that it caught the spirit of Salinger's writing style. A sufficient number of "infringing" quotations and paraphrases in the manuscript of Hamilton's biography (which a friend of Salinger's had surreptitiously sent to him in that form) resulted in an interpretation of the Copyright Act that had a chilling effect on publishers and biographers. The court reached the conclusion that the "biography, in its present form, infringes Salinger's copyright in his letters" and unpublished materials enjoy the same protection as published, copyrighted materials. Hamilton had to rewrite his biography, *In Search of J. D. Salinger* (New York: Random House, 1988), but it ended up as more of a diatribe against the court's interpretation of the law than a solid biographical portrait.[36] Classroom guidelines generally permit the copying, for educational purposes, of short extracts of works. Moreover, §108 provides additional exemptions for libraries.

Copyright Arbitration Panels

The Copyright Royalty Tribunal Act of 1993 (PL 103-198, 107 Stat. 2304) transferred the functions of the Copyright Royalty Tribunal to the Library of Congress (LC) and the Copyright Office, an agency within LC. The law established ad hoc arbitration panels consisting of three members to be appointed by the Librarian of Congress. Rate making and distributions of copyright royalties collected under the compulsory licenses of the Copyright Act are entrusted to the Copyright Arbitration Royalty Panels, and the rules of procedure of the Panels are codified at Title 37, § 251 of the *Code of Federal Regulations*. Like the Board of Patent Appeals and Interferences and the Trademark Trial and Appeal Board for their respective jurisdictions, the Panels are authorized to adjudicate controversies among claimants regarding the distribution of royalty fees.

Internet Sites

The Copyright Office has a hearty home page (**http://www.loc.gov/copyright**) with numerous links to general information, publications, current and pending legislation and regulations, international copyright (WIPO), *Federal Register* notices, Copyright Office press releases, and a link to "related resources" including GPO Access and Library of Congress information. In addition, users may subscribe to a free electronic service called NewsNet, which offers the latest information on hearings, deadlines for comments, new and proposed regulations, new publications, and other copyright-related subjects of interest. The Copyright Office emphasizes that NewsNet is not an interactive discussion group or chat room, but rather a current awareness service.

Among several non-governmental Web sites, the useful *Librarians' Index to the Internet* has a copyright button and the "Search Results" include links to other sites that discuss copyright and fair use, an online tutorial (copyright for dummies?) on the subject, an extensive annotated index of copyright sites of interest to educators, and many specific resources (**http://sunsite.berkeley.edu/cgi-bin**).

Commercial Online Databases

- DIALOG. File 120: U.S. Copyrights supplies access to details for all active copyright and "mask work" (defined at 17 U.S.C. § 901) registrations on file at the Copyright Office. Like DIALOG'S trademark database, this file is designed as a fast screening tool for checking the ownership and registration status of a particular work or an individual's or entity's portfolio of registered works. The database holds monographs, which contain information on the initial registration and renewal of a work; and legal documents, which contain information on assignments of ownership status.

- WESTLAW. All copyright and mask work registrations on file with the Copyright Office since January 1978 are available in the U.S. Copyrights database (COPYRIGHT is the db identifier). The database allows one to check the ownership and registration status of a copyrighted work. In addition to the title, owner, author, or registration number, COPYRIGHT contains monographs, legal documents, and serial publications. Approximately 80 percent of the records are monographs, the documents that attest to the initial registration or renewal of a work. Legal documents provide information about the ownership status of a work, usually in the context of assignments. Serial publications include newspapers, magazines, and catalogs that are issued in successive parts for an indefinite period. In addition, the federal intellectual property database (FIP), as noted above, includes case law, the *United States Code*, The Bureau of National Affairs' *United States Patents Quarterly* (USPQ), legislative history, administrative law and regulations, news, information, and practice guides.

- LEXIS-NEXIS. Like WESTLAW, LEXIS-NEXIS has many files on cases, statutes, regulations, and secondary sources. Their Copyright Law Library (COPYRT) consists of all federal court decisions, *Congressional Record* information, bills, monographs, journal articles, newsletters, and recent topical developments in the law.

Official Copyright Publications

At the Copyright Office home page there is a link to "Publications." There one can find useful publications such as the Copyright Information Circulars, a numbered series that serves various purposes such as conducting a copyright search and international copyright relations that the United States enjoys as a signatory to the Universal Copyright Convention (UCC) and the Berne Convention. The *Catalog of Copyright Entries* (CCE), which began in book form and was followed by microfiche editions, is now available only via the Internet, by selecting "Library of Congress" at the United States Copyright home page. The *Compendium of Copyright Office Practices,* now issued as "Compendium II," is a link on the home page and a depository item in paper format. In addition, the *Decisions of the United States Courts Involving Copyright,* an annual containing substantially all copyright cases since 1789 that have been decided by the federal and state courts; and the *Annual Report of the Register of Copyrights* on microfiche are made available to Title 44 depository libraries.

Shepard's Citator

In *Shepard's Intellectual Property Law Citations* (formerly *Shepard's United States Patents and Trademarks Citations*) the cited sources include patents, trademarks, and copyrights, as well as court and administrative decisions involving intellectual property law, and pertinent provisions of the *United States Code* and the *Code of Federal Regulations.* Citing sources are obtained from five types of source material: federal court decisions, state court decisions, specialized intellectual property sources such as the *Official Gazette—Patents* and the *Official Gazette—Trademarks,* selected law reviews, and A.L.R. "Annotations."

Three in One

There are some instances in which copyright, patent, and/or trademark intersect or overlap. For example, Equal is a registered trademark of the Nutrasweet Company, which was awarded Patent No. 3,800,046 for its artificial sweetening formula. The ingredients listed on a packet of Equal are copyrighted. In other instances, a trademark can be licensed to others for royalties. This felicitous occurrence happened to Class of 2000, Inc., a San Diego, California–based manufacturer of T-shirts, sweatshirts, hats, and shorts. The registrant, Odysseus Demetriadi, was granted the trademark in 1996 (Registration number 2018220; Mark Drawing Code: Typed Drawing) in anticipation of millennium madness, and since then the company has added the mark to jewelry, cigars, bottled water, and many other items. It turns out that any number of other manufacturers are willing to pay royalties of between 8 and 10 percent to the California firm for licensing rights.[37]

Copyright Law

Like patent and trademark law, copyright law generally advances by cases that construe the statute. As noted in chapter 8, *Wheaton v. Peters* (1834) was a landmark decision, in which the "Supreme Court held that there was no common-law right of literary property. An author's sole source of protection was the federal copyright statute. . . . As in the law of patents, there was a tension between the (monopoly) rights of creators and the free-market interests of the business community. In *Wheaton v. Peters,* the Supreme Court leaned away from the monopoly aspects of copyright, by confining copyright to the terms of the federal statute."[38] International treaties include the Berne Convention for the Protection of Literary and Artistic Works of 1886; the Stockholm Act of 1967; and the Paris Act of 1971, as amended in 1979. Moreover, the United States International Trade Commission, an independent agency, has quasi-judicial powers to take action against unlawful methods of competition in import trade, specifically infringement of a valid and enforceable U.S. copyright, patent, trademark, or mask work. The agency's home page is at **http://www.usitc.gov**, and there is also a link to the home page and to the decisions of the USITC from the Federal Bulletin Board Web site (**http://fedbbs.access.gpo.gov**).

The Digital Millennium Copyright Act

The Digital Millennium Copyright Act (DMCA), Public Law 105-304, 112 Stat. 2860, passed in 1998, contains detailed rules for online service providers that must be followed to obtain protection from liability for infringement. Not only must OSPs register with the Copyright Office, but educational institutions are also required to educate their communities about copyright law and compliance. Other provisions of PL 105-304 require the community to develop processes for collecting information and conducting studies to ensure the long-term protection of fair use and other copyright exceptions. This amendment has significant implications for libraries, archives, and institutions of higher education.

WHAT THE FUTURE MAY HOLD

It would be an act of foolish bravado to try to predict the future of any government activity involving the Internet. It is clear, however, that the legal battleground will be dominated by "the access and transmission of intellectual property in the digital realm." In 1998, Marybeth Peters, the U.S. Register of Copyrights, seemed to advocate a middle ground regarding fair use of the access and transmission of intellectual property in the digital realm. "Publishers want meaningful protection and libraries want meaningful exceptions, and I support both goals," Peters said in an interview reported in *Library Journal.* Concerning government information, Peters averred that "databases produced by or for the government are excluded from [copyright] protection. I don't know of any moves by the government to reduce the availability of information. In my agency we are making more and more information available for free through the Internet."[39]

NOTES

1. *Folsom v. Marsh,* 9 Fed.Cas. 342, 344, No. 4,901 (1841).

2. *Restatement of Torts* § 757, Comment b (1939).

3. Stephen Elias, *Patent, Copyright & Trademark: A Desk Reference to Intellectual Property Law* (Berkeley, CA: Nolo Press, 1996), p. 14.

4. R. Mark Halligan, Esq., *The Economic Espionage Act of 1996: The Theft of Trade Secrets Is Now a Federal Crime (c) 1996–1997.* Available at **http://www.execpc.com/~mhalligan/crime.html** (Accessed June 17, 1998).

5. Bruce A. Lehman (chair), *Intellectual Property and the National Information Infrastructure: The Report of the Working Group on Intellectual Property Rights* (Washington: Information Infrastructure Task Force, 1995), p. 174.

6. Elias, *Patent, Copyright & Trademark,* pp. 16–17.

7. Halligan, *The Economic Espionage Act of 1996.*

8. U.S. Patent and Trademark Office, *The Story of the U.S. Patent and Trademark Office* (Washington: USPTO, 1988), pp. iii–v et passim.

9. *Annual Report of the Commissioner of Patents* (1843), p. 5. Cited in Suzy Platt, ed., *Respectfully Quoted: A Dictionary of Quotations Requested from the Congressional Research Service* (Washington: Library of Congress, 1989), p. 287.

10. *Newsweek,* January 27, 1997, p. 86.

11. Platt, *Respectfully Quoted,* pp. 287–88.

12. *Official Gazette: Patents,* April 14, 1988, p. 703.

13. U.S. Patent and Trademark Office, *General Information Concerning Patents* (Washington: USPTO, April 1989), p. 15.

14. Susan B. Ardis, *An Introduction to U.S. Patent Searching: The Process* (Englewood, CO: Libraries Unlimited, 1991), p. 98.

15. Ibid., p. 177.

16. Ralph Waldo Emerson: "If a man can write a better book, preach a better sermon, or make a better mousetrap than his neighbor, though he builds his house in the woods the world will make a beaten path to his door."

17. Ardis, *An Introduction to U.S. Patent Searching,* p. 51.

18. Lawrence M. Friedman, *A History of American Law,* 2d ed. (New York: Simon & Schuster, 1985), p. 437.

19. Kay Ollerenshaw, "How to Perform a Patent Search: A Step by Step Guide for the Inventor," *Law Library Journal* 73: 1 (Winter 1980).

20. Kevin Harwell, "Legal Issues Relating to Patent Searching in Publicly Accessible Libraries," *Journal of Government Information* 25: 44 (January/February 1998).

21. U.S. General Accounting Office, *Intellectual Property: Patent Examination and Copyright Office Issues* (GAO/T-RCED/GGD-96-230), September 18, 1996, p. 4.

22. Elias, *Patent, Copyright & Trademark,* pp. 324–28.

23. Lehman, *Intellectual Property and the National Information Infrastructure,* pp. 171–72, notes 497, 498.

24. The GPO logo is reproduced in *Administrative Notes* 13: 2 (October 15, 1992).

25. N. J. Thompson, "DIALOGLINK and TRADEMARKSCAN-FEDERAL: Pioneers in Online Images," *Online,* May 1989, pp. 16, 18–19.

26. *Infoworld* 20: 58 (July 20, 1998).

27. Friedman, *A History of American Law,* pp. 437–38.

28. *Mead Data Central, Inc. v. Toyota Motor Sales, U.S.A., Inc.,* 702 F.Supp. 1031, 1033 (1988); *rev'd,* 875 F.2d 308 (1989).

29. *Mead Data Central, Inc.,* 702 F.Supp. 1031, 1041 (1988).

30. Lord Coke, *Twyne Case,* 3 Coke 80, 1 Sm.L.Cas.1.

31. Friedman, *A History of American Law,* pp. 256–57, 437.

32. Elias, *Patent, Copyright & Trademark,* p. 66.

33. Lehman, *Intellectual Property and the National Information Infrastructure,* pp. 24–25, 28.

34. *West Publishing Company v. Mead Data Central, Inc.,* 799 F.2d 1219 (1986); *cert. denied,* 479 U.S. 1070 (1987).

35. *Feist Publications, Inc. v. Rural Telephone Service Company, Inc.,* 499 U.S. 340 (1991).

36. *Salinger v. Random House, Inc.,* 811 F.2d 252, 253 (1987).

37. *Albany [New York] Times Union,* October 11, 1998, p. C2.

38. Friedman, *A History of American Law,* p. 257.

39. Evan St. Lifer, "Inching Toward Copyright Detente," *Library Journal,* August 1998, pp. 42–43.

CHAPTER ELEVEN

SELECTED DEPARTMENTS AND AGENCIES BY FUNCTION

> The nearest approach to immortality on earth is a government bureau.
>
> —James F. Byrnes

INTRODUCTION

The purpose of this chapter is to draw the reader's attention to selected categories of materials issued by or for departments and agencies, other than those visited in previous chapters. I am aware that by imposing this limitation, everyone's favorite agency, series, or function may be omitted. But rather than providing a lengthy recital of individual titles, which in any event change with the vicissitudes of time and events and which would require a multivolumed work, I am convinced that selectivity and exemplification are the better parts of virtue in this context. For elaboration the reader is referred to the several reference sources discussed in chapter 4.

SCIENTIFIC RESEARCH AND DEVELOPMENT

The Title 44 depository library system, although it is composed of thousands of series, does not encompass all federal publishing. One of the more prominent categories in this area is the technical report or translation. Technical reports are generally issued as "non-GPO" publications by a wide variety of agencies and their contractors and are not subject to bibliographic control or distribution by the sales or depository divisions of the Office of Superintendent of Documents. A small number of series are itemized in the *List of Classes of United States Government Publications Available for Selection by Depository Libraries,* cataloged in the Library Programs Service, and announced in the *Monthly Catalog*.

For various reasons, this vast body of federally sponsored technical report literature lies largely outside the Title 44 depository program. Some materials may be classified, some may be reports that the various sponsoring agencies have simply neglected to distribute, others may fall within the provisions of 44 U.S.C. § 1903 exempting certain self-sustaining categories of information from distribution to depository libraries. Whatever the reasons, these publications reflect the federal commitment to research and development (R&D), an obligation made manifest by multitudes of contracts and grants awarded by federal agencies to corporations, universities, think tanks, specialized consultants, and professional organizations and societies. The volume of technical reports produced in any given year depends upon the degree of federal largesse for R&D.

Citations to technical reports are often cloaked with acronyms for issuing agencies or with series of numbers prefixed by "codes" designating the originating agency. Clues that a title falls within the technical report category frequently emerge in the form of a contract or grant number or an accession or series report number. Virtually all of the bibliographic sources generated by the report-granting agencies include indexes by contract/grant number and by accession/report series codes. For a chronological guide to many of the earlier indexes to the technical report literature, see Yuri Nakata's *From Press to People*.[1]

NATIONAL TECHNICAL INFORMATION SERVICE

Although many agencies disseminate technical reports, they distribute primarily those created as a result of their own R&D efforts. The National Technical Information Service (NTIS), however, produces relatively little but is the main conduit for technical reports in general. NTIS is a self-supporting agency within the Technology Administration of the Department of Commerce. It is self-sustaining because all costs associated with collecting, abstracting, indexing, archiving, reproducing, and disseminating the information it gathers are paid for by the sales of its products and services.

NTIS was established in 1970 to simplify and improve access to data files and to scientific and technical reports produced by federal agencies and their contractors. Its origins are found in the Publications Board (PB), created by EO 9568 in 1945 to handle the release of thousands of technical reports (both captured German documents and other classified materials) to U.S. industry following World War II. Also in 1945 the Secretary of Commerce established an Office of Declassification and Technical Services, which was redesignated the Office of Technical Services the following year and absorbed the functions of the Publications Board and the Director of War Mobilization. The Office of Technical Services was superseded in 1965 by the Clearinghouse for Federal Scientific and Technical Information, which in turn gave way to NTIS. Today, the agency is the nation's permanent repository and primary disseminator of U.S. and foreign government–sponsored research and development, not only in all areas of science and technology, but owing to a generous 1954 Comptroller General's definition of "technical information," to include the soft sciences and even "federal tax forms and White House documents on the Internet."[2] Participating in the NTIS program are more than 200 federal agencies, some state and local governments, and sources outside the United States, which make up about 30 percent of the total incoming research documents. In addition, NTIS is authorized to work with the private sector to build strategic alliances through the use of contracts or cooperative agreements. This program, under the provisions of the National Technical Information Act of 1988 (PL 100-519, 102 Stat. 2594, 15 U.S.C. § 3701 et seq.), allows NTIS to enter into joint ventures with businesses to create new information products from and distribution channels for U.S. government-produced data and software. The Act also requires that NTIS "make selected bibliographic information products available in a timely manner to depository libraries as part of the Depository Library Program of the Government Printing Office."

In past years, the agency had to rely on voluntary submission of source documents by the various federal agencies, many of which have their own outlets for disseminating their research results. This inadequacy was remedied by passage of the American Technology Preeminence Act (ATPA) of 1991, which requires that federal agencies deposit their scientific and technical documents with NTIS in print and electronic formats. As a result, "annual additions to the [NTIS] collection increased from 84,000 in 1994 to 104,000 in 1996."[3] The total number of titles in the NTIS collection approaches the 3 million mark and includes, in addition to the basic scientific and technical publications, electronic datafiles, audiovisuals, software, and standards.

The NTIS Mandate

NTIS is governed by the provisions of Title 15, *United States Code,* sections 1151–1157 and by the two acts noted above. Save for bibliographic products, NTIS has consistently maintained that it is exempt from participation in the Federal Depository Library Program (FDLP). 15 U.S.C. § 1153 states in part "that the general public shall not bear the cost of publications and other services which are for the special use and benefit of private groups and individuals." As a consequence of this statutory authority, the *List of Classes* itemizes more than twenty newsletters, catalogs, bibliographies, indexes, directories, and related titles available to Title 44 depositories, but the vast majority of publications announced in these sources are excluded from depository distribution.

NTIS Access Tools

The NTIS Database (**http://www.ntis.gov**) provides full descriptive summaries of more than 400,000 titles that NTIS has received from the participating government departments and agencies since 1990. The following represent different ways in which these titles are bibliographically announced. Subscribers can order any NTIS document directly on the Web.

- NTIS OrderNow, a quarterly catalog on CD-ROM, replaces two titles: *Government Reports Announcements & Index* (GRA&I), a semimonthly indexing and abstracting service and its companion, *Government Reports Annual Index.* The former ended its illustrious run with the December 1996 issue; the latter with its 1994 edition. After an unseemly spat, NTIS, ethically if not technically bound by the provisions of the Act of 1988 to make selected bibliographic products available to depository libraries, agreed to send the CD to Title 44 institutions that had subscribed to GRA&I and its annual index. For individual and corporate subscribers, the catalog costs $250 a year. It contains descriptions for more than 100,000 titles added to the collection within the previous two years. Users must access GRA&I for documents covering the period 1975 to 1996, but when the annual index folded two years earlier, searching became arduous with the print indexes. However, this is mitigated by several commercial online vendors such as DIALOG, DATA-STAR, OCLC, and STN International/CAS; and CD-ROM resources, including SilverPlatter and DIALOG OnDisc.

- A free updating service is NTIS OrderNow Online (**http://www. ntis.gov.ordernow**). The database is said to contain information on products added to the NTIS collection within the most recent thirty-day period, but I have found bibliographic citations to titles with much earlier publication dates. Product descriptions can be accessed by Product Id; title; abstract; key words; subject; language; country of publication; source; personal author(s); performing organization; and document type. The resulting product description includes the above information with price in paper copy or on microfiche and ordering information, by phone, fax, or e-mail.

- The NTIS Advanced Search page (**http://www.ntis.gov/ advance.htm**) covers the entire NTIS Web site, which includes information about 400,000 technical reports and related information products received by NTIS within the latest ten-year period. This site is searchable by keyword, agency, or order number.

- The FedWorld Information Network (**http://www.fedworld.gov**) was established in 1992 by NTIS to function as the online locator service for an extensive inventory of information disseminated by federal agencies. It covers publications housed within NTIS's capacious data bank but also acts as an electronic gateway for more than 100 government bulletin boards. The variety is suggested at FedWorld's home page, where you are invited to browse the Federal Job Announcement Database; plan your vacation or business trip by surfing the US Customs Traveler Information site; access the Internal Revenue Service to review and download tax forms, instructions, and publications; and be guided by US Business Advisor. FedWorld is constantly expanding, and "to bring government closer to the public" is their slogan. FedWorld's databases are truly something to behold. A very selective sample includes free as well as fee-based products: Supreme Court decisions, certain titles of the *Code of Federal Regulations,* the Environmental Protection Agency's Clean Air Act database, and numerous meta-databases, defined as "systems that point to the actual data or how to get it," among which are more than 100,000 military, federal and industry standards, thousands of trade-related documents, more than 1,500 descriptions of federal audiovisual products, and so forth.

- GOV.Research_Center (**http://grc.ntis.gov**) is a subscription service that comprises, in addition to the entire NTIS database, several other large files. The AGRICOLA (Agricultural Online Access) database contains bibliographic records for documents acquired by the National Agricultural Library (NAL) of the Department of Agriculture. Updated monthly, AGRICOLA consists of more than 3.6 million records from 1970. AgroBase integrates AGRIS International, which corresponds in part to Agrindex, a database sponsored by the Food and Agriculture Organization, a specialized agency within the United Nations family; and AGRICOLA. Also updated monthly, this combined database contains more than 5.5 million records since 1970. The Energy Science and Technology Database (EDB) is a multidisciplinary file containing worldwide references to basic and applied scientific and technical research literature in the wide field of energy and energy-related research. Updated monthly, EDB contains more than 3 million records since 1976. The Federal Research in Progress (FEDRIP) database offers access to current government-sponsored research projects in the fields of health, the physical and life sciences, agriculture, and engineering. Updated monthly, FEDRIP contains more than 150,000 records from the current two years. The National Institute for Occupational Safety and Health (NIOSH), an entity within the Centers for Disease Control and Prevention (CDC), maintains the NIOSHTIC database, which consists of about 160 English-language technical journals, is updated quarterly, and contains more than 200,000 records, some going back to the nineteenth century, in the field of work-related illness and injury. A companion database, the RTECS file, contains toxicological information compiled, maintained, and updated by NIOSH. From any of these files, you can order reports directly on the Web.

- SRIM (Selected Research in Microfiche) offers subscribers microfiche copies of the full text of reports from the NTIS database. You can choose from more than 350 existing subject areas or even have a new subject area customized to meet a specific need. As soon as new reports in a given field enter the NTIS collection, customers will receive a microfiche copy. Detailed information about SRIM can be accessed at **http://www.ntis.gov/srim.htm**.

- NTIS Alert is a fortnightly subscription service that gives customers the latest titles of newly acquired information available in sixteen subject areas such as environmental pollution and control, materials science, transportation, communication, energy, and health care. The service was formerly known as *Abstract Newsletters* and before that, *Weekly Government Abstracts*. Information on this service is available at **http://www.ntis.gov/ alerts.htm**.

Document Accession Notation

What is now called the "Product Id" (above) has also been named the NTIS Order Number and the Document Accession Number. Whatever the nomenclature, each report announced in NTIS OrderNow and its predecessors is assigned a prime document accession number; all numbers have alpha prefixes. Certain prefixes are used exclusively for report collections input from specific entities, a sampling of which follows:

- AD <Unclassified reports received from the Department of Defense (DoD), January 1964–present. This prefix is a holdover from the old Armed Services Technical Information Agency (ASTIA) document designation.>

- BTHE <Reports received from the British Standards Institution for their Technical Help to Exporters service, November 1976–present.>

- ED <Federally sponsored reports announced for the Educational Resources Information Center (ERIC), January 1972–present.>

- FIPS <Reports received from the National Institute of Standards and Technology (formerly the National Bureau of Standards), November 1976–present.>

- JPRS <Translations received from the Joint Publications Research Service, January 1964–present.>

- N <Reports received from the National Aeronautics and Space Administration, January 1964–present.>

- PB <Reports indexed, cataloged, and abstracted by NTIS for other agencies, January 1964–present.>

Pricing Methods

As noted, NTIS is a self-sustaining agency and is authorized by statute to charge market prices so it can generate sufficient revenue to offset operational costs. By contrast, the Government Printing Office (GPO), as noted in chapter 2, is obliged by law to provide dissemination services at the least cost to the government, and its pricing mechanism is based on recovering only the incremental costs for reproducing and disseminating a product plus a legislated 50 percent surcharge for these services. Thus there are instances in which NTIS, which sells titles that vary in provenance from the biennial *Occupational Outlook Handbook* issued by the Bureau of Labor Statistics to the Central Intelligence Agency's well-known annual *World Factbook,* will charge higher prices for a publication, whether in print or on CD-ROM, than GPO. It is best to consult the Superintendent of Document's *Sales Product Catalog* before ordering a publication from the latest edition of the *NTIS Catalog of Products* or another of the many NTIS order information sources.

DEPARTMENT OF ENERGY

The Department of Energy (DOE) was established in 1977 (91 Stat. 569, 42 U.S.C. § 7131) to consolidate major federal energy functions in one executive department. Transferred to DOE were all responsibilities of the Energy Research and Development Administration; the Federal Energy Administration; the Federal Power Commission; and the Alaska, Bonneville, Southeastern, and Southwestern Power Administrations, formerly components of the Department of the Interior, as well as the power-marketing functions of the Bureau of Reclamation. Also transferred to DOE were certain functions of the defunct Interstate Commerce Commission, the Department of the Navy, and the Department of Housing and Urban Development. The vast majority of DOE's R&D and testing are carried out by contractors who operate government-owned facilities. Their management and administration are executed in DOE operations offices located throughout the country, from Idaho Falls, Idaho, to Oak Ridge, Tennessee. These offices are a formal link between DOE headquarters in Washington and its field laboratories and other operating facilities.

Department of Energy Databases

With the demise of the monthly, and before that, semimonthly *Energy Research Abstracts* (1976–1995), accessing documents produced or obtained by the Department of Energy has become a function of commercial vendors and of the Internet. Updated twice a month, the Energy Science and Technology Database is a multidisciplinary file consisting of worldwide references to basic and applied scientific technical research material. The results of this research are transmitted to the public via commercial firms, including Cambridge Scientific Abstracts (**http://www.acsa.com**), DIALOG Corporation (**http://www.dialog.com**), NERAC, Inc. (**http://www.nerac.com**), and STN International/Chemical Abstracts Service (**http://www.cas.org**). The Web site of DOE's Office of Scientific and Technical Information (OSTI) (**http://www.osti.gov**) has a page titled "Information Resources" that permits the user to access a number of OSTI-sponsored and -maintained sites; prominent links include the following:

- The DOE Information Bridge, a component of EnergyFiles, provides free access to the full text and bibliographic records of DOE reports in physics, chemistry, materials, biology, environmental sciences, energy technologies, engineering, computer and information science, renewal energy, and other topics. This information, produced by DOE and its contractors, has been received and processed by OSTI since January 1996. It is available via GPO Access (**http://gpo.osti.gov**) because of an interagency agreement between the Director of OSTI and the Superintendent of Documents. The names and locations of depository libraries maintaining the DOE full-text collections in paper or on microfiche can be accessed at **http://www.doe.gov/dra/dra.html**.

- The Department of Energy Reports Bibliographic Database contains citations for DOE-sponsored scientific and technical reports from January 1, 1994 to the present. This continues *Energy Research Abstracts,* a monthly indexing-abstracting service that once was available to depository libraries. The Internet version can be searched by keywords, title, personal author/affiliation, Energy Science and Technology Database (EDB) Subject Category descriptors or subject category numbers, FDLP Item Number, date of publication, and WAIS Entry Date (**http://apollo.osti.gov**). The information retrieved includes comprehensive bibliographic data and abstract, and citations are updated weekly. The site links to NTIS or GPO for ordering information; DOE employees, contractors, and international partners such as INIS, the International Nuclear Information System, and ETDE, the Energy Technology Data Exchange, may also purchase reports from DOE's Office of Scientific and Technical Information. A related database is INIS Atomindex, which replaced the defunct Atomic Energy Commission's *Nuclear Science Abstracts*. INIS Atomindex is not available to depository libraries because it is published by the International Atomic Energy Agency, an international intergovernmental organization (IGO) within the United Nations system. The INIS Secretariat is located in Vienna, Austria, but OSTI serves as the INIS national center for the United States. The ETDE system is similar to INIS: a cooperative venture among several foreign governments to conduct and share energy-related R&D. Because the United States is a member, OSTI serves as the central receiving and processing unit for this information, which it then disseminates to national centers in other participating countries.

- OpenNet (**http://www.doe.gov/opennet**), the instrument employed to carry DOE's Openness Initiative of Public Awareness, Public Education, Public Input, and Public Access, is intended to make information that is no longer classified available to the public. It includes references to declassified energy and energy-related documents made publicly available after October 1, 1994. In addition to the declassified materials, OpenNet references older document collections from several DOE sources. There are degrees of declassification among the holdings. Some have been wholly declassified. Others have had some sensitive information removed to produce a "sanitized" copy; the term "redacted" is sometimes used to refer to these documents. The redacted documents are recognizable by the blank spaces that can be found in them. A few documents of historical interest are included here; these are termed "never classified."

Other DOE Resources

In 1982, OSTI entered into an agreement with GPO under which GPO would distribute to depository libraries on microfiche a series of Contractor Reports and Publications. The series comprises more than forty categories, ranging from "Arms Control" to "Wind Energy." Now available via DOE's Web site, each entry in this series comprises full bibliographic information, including the depository item number (O430-M-46) and depository library ordering information when retrieving microfiche from library collections.

There are more than 200 series available to Title 44 depository libraries in the DOE collections, including publications of units within the Department such as the Federal Energy Regulatory Commission and the Energy Information Administration (EIA). The latter's Web site (**http://www.eia.doe.gov**) and the quarterly CD-ROM product, *Energy InfoDisc* (a depository item), offer the full text of EIA materials.

NATIONAL AERONAUTICS AND SPACE ADMINISTRATION

The National Aeronautics and Space Administration (NASA) was established in 1958 as an independent agency (72 Stat. 426, 42 U.S.C. § 2451). The principal statutory responsibilities of NASA are to conduct research to solve problems of flight within and outside the Earth's atmosphere and develop, construct, test, and operate aeronautical and space vehicles. Like DOE, NASA executes its R&D programs largely through contracts with the private sector. It operates various research facilities throughout the United States, from the Ames Research Center in California to the George C. Marshall Flight Center in Alabama, through which NASA's Office of Space Flight plans, directs, and executes the development, testing, and operation of the Space Shuttle Program.

NASA Scientific and Technical Information Program

The agency's Scientific and Technical Information Program (STI) offers access to more than 3 million aerospace and related citations (**http://www.sti.nasa.gov**). This service is administered by the NASA Center for Aerospace Information (CASI) for the Program's lead R&D facility, the Langley Research Center, Hampton, Virginia. Its Web site offers enough links to build a suit of chain-mail armor. In addition to the standard policy directives, procedures and guidelines for documentation and dissemination, a grammar handbook, and fact sheets in PDF, the site contains a Government Information Locator Service (GILS), declassified documents announcements, and a section titled "STI Products." Within these pages are links to a proprietary database called the IEEE/IEE Electronic Library (IEL), which contains full-page images of the collection of publications from the Institute of Electrical and Electronic

Engineers, Inc. (IEEE) and the Institute of Electrical Engineers (IEE); Electronic Selected Current Aerospace Notices (E-SCAN); NASA Image eXchange (NIX), by which you can search distributed photo databases at NASA centers; a NASA Thesaurus; STI Program Bibliographic Announcements, electronic versions of publications produced by the STI Program; listservs; *Spinoff* and *STI Bulletin ONLINE;* and other resources including a NASA Search-the-Web service that allows you to search from one place by keyword or phrase; the results are sorted by best match.

NASA RECONplus

Amidst this smorgasbord of information is CASI's Technical Report Server, the NASA RECONplus database. This has become the on-line equivalent of STI's *Scientific and Technical Aerospace Reports* (STAR), once available for sale and to depository libraries, which bibliographically announces the unclassified report literature related to all aspects of aeronautics and space R&D, including energy development, conservation, oceanography, environmental protection, urban transportation, and other topics of national priority. The NASA RECONplus database can be searched by title, author, abstract, report number, major and minor subject terms, contract number, accession number, language, and corporate source (**http://www.sti.nasa.gov/ RECONselect.html**). Full bibliographic information and an abstract are retrieved. Moreover, the full text of the STAR documents is available free in PDF via **http://www.sti.nasa.gov/Pubs/star/Star.html**.

NASA at Forty

In 1998 the *New York Times* celebrated NASA's four decades of space exploration, recalling the high and the low points, with articles about historic missions, dramatic video, and photos from the newspaper's archives, and made the special report available on their Web site (**http://www.nytimes.com/library/national/science/nasa/index. html**).

DEFENSE TECHNICAL INFORMATION CENTER

The Defense Technical Information Center (DTIC) is a component of the Department of Defense (DoD) Scientific and Technical Information Program in support of the Office of Under Secretary of Defense for Acquisitions and Technology, Defense Research and Engineering. That mouthful is typical of the hierarchical structure of large federal entities such as the DoD, an octopus with many tentacles. DTIC's headquarters is located at Fort Belvoir, Virginia, with regional offices in Boston; Dayton, Ohio; Albuquerque, New Mexico; and Los Angeles. DTIC is a member of CENDI, an interagency working group composed of senior Scientific and Technical Information (STI) managers from several major programs in various federal agencies. All government entities are aficionados of abbreviations, but the Pentagon's products and services seem especially salted with more acronyms than alphabet soup at full boil.

The DTIC collection includes technical reports, management summaries at the technical effort level, independent research and development summaries, and special materials such as captured German and Japanese documents from World War II. The scope of the collection includes what one would normally assume—military science, missile technology, nuclear science, and the like—but owing to DoD's wide research interests, the collection also contains information on disciplines such as biology, chemistry, energy, environmental sciences, oceanography, computer sciences, sociology, logistics, and human factors engineering. Also included in the collection are DoD directives and instructions and the Defense Federal Acquisition Regulation Supplement (FARS), the last being the primary regulation used by agencies requesting supplies and services.

A visitor to DTIC's Internet home page (**http://www.dtic.mil**) finds several buttons linking to, among other pages, "Products and Services" and "Search Database" features. Some of the collections are unclassified and available; others are classified and only available to eligible personnel in government agencies and private-sector contractors and grantees. An interactive arrangement, Defense RDT&E Online System (DROLS), gives direct access to major fee-based collections, by which you can search, retrieve, display, and order products from the following three major databases:

Technical Report Database

The Technical Report (TR) database is a collection of reports describing the progress or results of research efforts and other scientific and technical information. The reports convey the results of DoD-sponsored research, development, test, and evaluation (RDT&E) activities. The TR database contains some 2 million citations in print and non-print formats. Included are DoD patents and patent applications, studies and analysis reports, open source literature from foreign countries, conference proceedings, reprints, and theses. DTIC also carries Library of Congress Federal Research Division records, which cover a variety of foreign and domestic subject areas. Reports are assigned "AD" prefix notations (see above).

Technical Effort and Management System Database

Formerly called Work Unit Information System (WUIS), the Technical Effort and Management System (TEAMS) database describes ongoing DoD research and technology efforts. Containing more than 250,000 records, the collection includes summaries of completed and terminated research. The audience for these brief annotations is government scientists, engineers, and managers, as well as their contractors in industry and academia. The collection encompasses a broad range of scientific disciplines and technologies.

Independent Research and Development Database

The Independent Research and Development (IR&D) collection consists of more than 140,000 descriptions of products initiated by DoD contractors but not required under a contract.

Selected Internet Reference Tools

TopicLINKS directs the user to locations and sources of information available from the Internet on topics that categorize the areas of scientific and technical interest DTIC's field and group structure is based upon. The *DROLS Retrieval Reference Guide* gives examples of search strategies and displays formats for the three databases noted above. The *TRGUI Manual* contains a point-and-click Windows interface for searching DROLS. *DTIC Cataloging Guidelines* contains instructions for applying the Committee on Scientific and Technical Information (COSATI) cataloging rules to the descriptive cataloging of technical reports, a useful source not only for DTIC products. The *DTIC Thesaurus* consists of a multidisciplinary subject term vocabulary used to index and retrieve information from DTIC's databases.

EDUCATION

Since Plato's *Republic,* nations have attempted to articulate the role of government in the business of educating its citizens. On May 4, 1980, the newly minted Department of Education officially began operations, culminating a century-long debate in the United States about the appropriate federal role in education. Federal involvement in education in effect goes back to the Northwest Ordinance of 1787, which authorized land grants for the establishment of educational institutions; in 1867 a Department of Education Act (14 Stat. 434) created an agency to collect and disseminate information about education in the states and territories. The following year the agency's name was changed to the Office of Education; it functioned with a small budget in the Interior Department for the next seventy years. In 1939 the Office was transferred from the Department of the Interior to the new Federal Security Agency. When the FSA was abolished in 1953, the Office of Education became part of the newly created Department of Health, Education, and Welfare (HEW). The same act that established the Department of Education renamed HEW the Department of Health and Human Services (HHS). With the overblown rhetoric that often comes back to haunt and embarrass public officials, President Jimmy Carter said about the Department of Education that it "will profoundly transform . . . the quality of education in our nation." Relative to departments such as Defense and HHS, the federal education establishment is small, and perhaps that is the way it should remain.

EDUCATIONAL RESOURCES INFORMATION CENTER

The Educational Resources Information Center (ERIC), a nationwide information network, is part of the National Library of Education (NLE), a unit of the Office of Educational Research and Improvement (OERI) within the U.S. Department of Education. Established in 1966, its purpose is to acquire, select, abstract, index, store, retrieve, and disseminate timely education-related materials for the use of teachers, administrators, researchers, librarians, students, and other interested persons. This is accomplished by a central coordinating staff in Washington and a decentralized network of sixteen full and several adjunct clearinghouses located at universities and professional organizations across the country. Each clearinghouse is responsible for a particular subject area of education or related disciplines and for collecting relevant materials of value on that topic. "Adjunct clearinghouses are organizations that, at no cost to ERIC, assist ERIC in covering a specialized segment of the literature of education."[4] Examples include art education, child care, clinical studies, consumer education, and test collection. Examples of regular clearinghouse areas include rural education and small schools; adult, career, and vocational education; educational management; and information and technology (formerly information resources).

ERIC/IT

This last clearinghouse, known as ERIC/IT, is located at Syracuse University's Center for Science and Technology and is affiliated with the university's School of Information Studies and the School of Education. ERIC/IT specializes in library and information science and educational technology. Like the other clearinghouses in their respective areas of expertise, ERIC/IT acquires, selects, catalogs, indexes, and abstracts documents and journal articles in these subject areas for input into the ERIC database. The clearinghouse publishes monographs, digests, and minibibliographies in the two fields. The staff of ERIC/IT also issues a print periodical, *ERIC/IT Update,* which announces new clearinghouse products and developments, and *ERIC/IT Networkers,* an online series of help sheets that contain information for using ERIC-related resources on the Internet. Moreover, "ERIC in Action," a fifteen-minute video describing the basic structure of the ERIC system, is available from ERIC/IT to anyone interested in accessing current education information.

Bibliographic Sources

Two major indexing-abstracting services provide the bibliographic control and announcing of educational materials screened by the clearinghouses and accepted into the ERIC database. *Resources in Education* (RIE) announces "document" literature, and *Current Index to Journals in Education* (CIJE) covers the "journal" literature. They both use a common indexing vocabulary established by the *Thesaurus of ERIC Descriptors* (Phoenix, AZ: Oryx Press), with its descriptors and identifiers, which is revised periodically and available from the publisher and on microfiche to depository libraries. Peripheral files include, in addition to the *Thesaurus,* an Identifier Authority List (IAL), a semicontrolled list of additional content identifiers; a Source Directory, which contains an authority list of organizations that have prepared or sponsored documents processed by ERIC; and ERIC Digests in full text. Free publications include *All About ERIC* and *The ERIC Review.*

Resources in Education

RIE is still issued monthly in print, is listed in *U.S. Government Subscriptions* as a sales subscription, and is available to depository libraries in print or on microfiche. Depending upon subscription levels, RIE may continue in print or be phased out. Categories include conference papers, student seminar papers, speeches, studies, unpublished manuscripts, and books published commercially, this last since 1993.

Also available are ERIC Digests, short reports on current education topics produced by each of the sixteen clearinghouses. As Figure 11.1 shows, an "ED" number is assigned sequentially to documents as they are processed, and each clearinghouse has its own alpha prefix followed by a sequential number. The majority of documents announced in RIE, like those listed in NTIS OrderNow and its predecessors, are non-depository titles.

Figure 11.1. Sample entry from RIE.

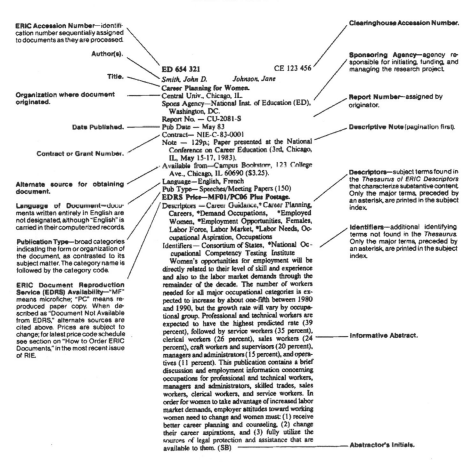

After the entries, which include the appropriate bibliographic information and an abstract called a "resume," there are several indexes: by subjects, personal authors, institutions, publication types (for example, 041: doctoral dissertations; 101: computer programs); and temporary ERIC Clearinghouse Accession Numbers cross-referenced to the permanent ERIC Document (ED) accession numbers. Other features of RIE include additions and changes to the *Thesaurus of ERIC Descriptors,* how to submit documents to ERIC, ERIC price codes (paper copy, microfiche), ordering information, and a current list of ERIC clearinghouses. The full text of ED documents can be found on the ERIC microfiche at many large libraries and from the ERIC Document Reproduction Service in Springfield, Virginia (**http://edrs.com**).

Current Index to Journals in Education

CIJE is a monthly guide to periodical literature in education and related subjects. Since 1969, articles published in more than 800 journals, including many library-oriented periodicals, are indexed and abstracted by the same clearinghouses. The main entry section of CIJE includes full bibliographic information and an "annotation" or abstract of the article. There are indexes for subjects, personal authors, journal contents, and source journals. As seen in Figure 11.2, there are an "EJ" accession number and a specific clearinghouse number, the alpha prefixes followed by a sequential processing notation. CIJE is available to depository libraries on microfiche and sold by Oryx Press. The articles are available in libraries, from University Microfilms International, the Institute for Scientific Information, and the CARL Uncover Document Delivery Service, but no article reproduction firm carries 100 percent of ERIC-indexed journal titles.

Electronic Editions of RIE and CIJE

Electronic versions of RIE and CIJE are searchable as an integrated service. The semiannual indexes to RIE were discontinued by GPO with the 1994 issue. (The annual index, produced by Oryx Press in print format, will continue as long as there are sufficient subscribers.) If that decision was a harbinger of things to come, the print and fiche formats may be targeted for extirpation, because the ERIC database has been searchable on the Internet since 1989 (**http://www.askeric.org**). Indeed, various systems offer unrestricted Internet access from sites announced in "Internet Access Points to ERIC" from the current online issue of the *Networker* (**http://ericir.syr.edu/ithome/networkers**).

Figure 11.2. Sample entry from CIJE.

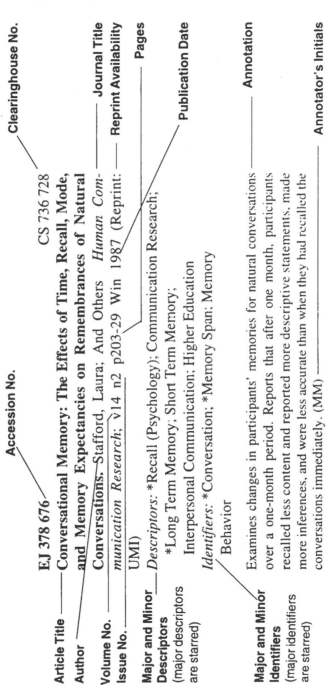

Main Entry Section

Complete information about each article included in *CIJE* is given in the Main Entry Section, which is arranged by Clearinghouse and sequential EJ numbers.

Accession No.

Clearinghouse No.

CS 736 728

EJ 378 676

Article Title ——— **Conversational Memory: The Effects of Time, Recall, Mode, and Memory Expectancies on Remembrances of Natural**

Author ——— **Conversations.** Stafford, Laura; And Others   *Human Com-* ——— **Journal Title**

Volume No. ——— *munication Research;* v14 n2 p203-29 Win 1987 (Reprint: ——— **Reprint Availability**

Issue No. ——— UMI)

Pages

Major and Minor ——— *Descriptors:* *Recall (Psychology); Communication Research;
Descriptors   *Long Term Memory; Short Term Memory;
(major descriptors   Interpersonal Communication; Higher Education
are starred)

Publication Date

Identifiers: *Conversation; *Memory Span; Memory
Behavior

Major and Minor ——— Examines changes in participants' memories for natural conversations ——— **Annotation**
Identifiers   over a one-month period. Reports that after one month, participants
(major identifiers   recalled less content and reported more descriptive statements, made
are starred)   more inferences, and were less accurate than when they had recalled the
conversations immediately. (MM) ———

Annotator's Initials

ACCESS ERIC

In 1989 ACCESS ERIC, a comprehensive outreach and dissemination program for the entire ERIC system, was established. There are two components to this system: (1) By calling 1-800-LET-ERIC, you can obtain information about the subject-specific clearinghouses, find out how and where to search the ERIC database, and obtain free publications as noted above; (2) through the systemwide Web site (**http://www.accesseric.org:81**), you can search all RIE and CIJE citations with a link to electronic document delivery, read or print the publications, and link to other ERIC-sponsored databases such as the Calendar of Education-Related Conferences and the Education Resource Organizations Directory.

New features are perennially cropping up, such as the Virtual Reference Desk; Microsoft/AASL's KidsConnect page; the Gateway to Educational Materials (GEM); and so forth. Moreover, the **http://www.askeric.org** upgraded Web site is the preferred starting place for Internet-based educational resources. Launched in April 1999, users can customize the site to reflect their needs. The site also provides information about ASKERIC corporate sponsors.

GEM, which was introduced on the Web January 30, 1998, was developed because standard Internet searching technologies did not effectively meet the needs of users searching for educational materials scattered across the Internet. GEM solves this problem by using metadata, a term that refers to information concerning the content, condition, quality, or other characteristics of data. Just as Hypertext Markup Language (HTML) tags define the appearance of a resource on the Internet, metadata tags define its content. Search engines no longer need to scan the entire resource looking for keywords. Instead, they are able to return documents tagged with metadata that meet the search criteria, and this tagging leads to more efficient and precise searching. Thus GEM records, individual packets of metadata that describe and identify an object in "card catalog" fashion, constitute a "virtual card catalog." Records are collected at a central location to form the Gateway. Using *Personal Library* searching software, users can search GEM to find educational resources that meet their needs. GEM may be accessed at **http://the gateway.org**. The service is a consortium effort, and collection holders range from large organizations such as the Smithsonian Institution and the Library of Congress to high schools and even individual teachers.[5]

In addition to free Internet access, online vendors, such as Ovid Technologies, OCLC, and DIALOG, and CD-ROM vendors such as DIALOG, SilverPlatter and NISC, permit integrated searching of the databases.

FDLP/ERIC Digital Library Project

As noted, the vast majority of titles announced in RIE are contract reports or other studies (a number of library school students, for example, have their seminar papers and theses accepted in RIE). A small percentage of ERIC documents, however, are available to depository libraries on microfiche in a series titled "Education Documents Announced in RIE." This number, perhaps 10 percent of the total, reflects only those documents prepared or sponsored by the Department of Education that have been issued by OERI (ED 1.310/2; 466-A-3). Libraries that subscribe to the full ERIC collection would have duplicate copies of this small subset of depository materials. In 1998 the GPO, NLE, and Online Computer Library Center (OCLC) began a pilot project to make this subset of public domain reports available free to depository libraries via the OCLC FirstSearch service. The ERIC reports in Tag Image File Format (TIFF) are indexed for storage "in eight robotic automatic cartridge systems that . . . can hold some 12.8 billion typewritten pages." The storage systems are housed at OCLC headquarters in Dublin, Ohio.[6]

DECLASSIFIED INFORMATION

The researcher can pursue many avenues when seeking access to documents that may have been, at one time, classified or elusive and that, when pieced together, reflect policy decisions made at the highest level of government. Much of this material has been collected, indexed, and made available by private publishers rather than through the government itself. But this is changing; the development of "Freedom of Information Act" pages within the Web sites of several agencies marks a willingness on the part of the government to bring these declassified materials to the public. What follows is a selective account of public and private-sector access to once-classified information.

CENTRAL INTELLIGENCE AGENCY

Although the Superintendent of Documents has assigned to Central Intelligence Agency (CIA) publications PREX 3 SuDocs class numbers, an author symbol under the Executive Office of the President, the entity is an independent agency within the executive branch. The Director of Central Intelligence (DCI) is the president's chief advisor on intelligence matters and both the Director and Deputy Director of the Agency are appointed by the president with the advice and consent of the Senate. As noted in chapter 6 (under "The Black Budget"), the CIA is one of several intelligence-gathering agencies in the federal establishment, although the disproportionate media attention the CIA is given obscures that fact. Established under the National Security Council by the National Security Act of 1947 (61 Stat. 495, 50 U.S.C. § 401 et seq.), it now functions, as amended, under that statute; Executive Order 12333 of December 4, 1981; and other edicts.

Although its activities are largely classified, it may come as a surprise to the public that the CIA issues several useful reference works that are available through the FDLP, the sales program of the SuDocs and NTIS, and through the Documents Expediting Project (Doc Ex). Among the items available to depository libraries are the CIA Maps and Atlases series, a listing of all unclassified maps; Directory of Officials series, covering certain countries, typically those with whom the United States has less than cordial relations; the *Handbook of Economic Statistics* and *Handbook of International Statistics,* both annuals; and the *World Factbook* in print and on CD-ROM, a comprehensive resource of facts and statistics on more than 250 countries and other entities.

The CIA Web Site

Like other government units, the CIA has done its share of migrating to the Internet. Before gaining entry to the home page, your attention is riveted by a statement in bright red:

> You are entering an Official United States Government System, which may be used only for authorized purposes. Unauthorized modification of any information stored on this system may result in criminal prosecution. The Government may monitor and audit the usage of this system, and all persons are hereby notified that use of this system constitutes consent to such monitoring and auditing.

Once you pass this admonition the CIA site is quite friendly (**http://odci.gov/cia**). Several bullets access different pages. "Publications," for example, includes a menu of many of the publications noted above for depository distribution. Some make the full text available (*World Factbook*); others (CIA Maps) give only the year, country, NTIS Order Number, and price. Other selections at this page include a suggested reading list of intelligence literature, GILS records (hosted by the GPO), and specific reports of various investigations conducted by the Inspector General.

The button titled "CIA Connections" gets you to several links, among them the "Freedom of Information Act" (FOIA) site (**http://www.foia.gov**), which contains Agency records declassified under the FOIA and released to the public since November 1996. The database is periodically updated to reflect the release of newly declassified information. Some of the older mimeographed documents retrieved are smudged, indistinct, and hard to read; but the information is valuable to scholars researching the turbulent history of the Cold War.

Foreign Broadcast Information Service

The Foreign Broadcast Information Service (FBIS) operates under the aegis of the CIA and oversees a worldwide network of broadcast monitoring units that are responsible for reviewing foreign media. The information selected is based on a set of intelligence requirements and is translated and disseminated to consumers. The majority of FBIS reports are currently unclassified and available to the public.

The FBIS was established in 1941, when the demand for information from enemy sources was pressing, as the Foreign Broadcast Monitoring Service, which recorded, translated, analyzed, and reported to other government agencies broadcasts from foreign countries. Until 1946 reports were issued by the now defunct Federal Communications Service; in that year its functions were transferred to the Central Intelligence Agency. FBIS reports are disseminated in two major categories. The FBIS Daily Report series covers regions of the world divided as follows: Central Eurasia, East Asia, East Europe, Latin America, China, Near East and South Asia, West Europe, and Sub-Saharan Africa. The FBIS Publications Reports series comprises topics such as arms control and proliferation, environment and world health, and narcotics. The information is obtained from full text and summaries of newspaper articles, conference proceedings, television and radio broadcasts, periodicals, and nonclassified technical reports. In singing the praises of FBIS materials, one author averred that they "probably come as close as any reasonable source to being a transparent medium accurately conveying overseas reaction to the news."[7]

Joint Publications Research Service

Originally the reports described above were prepared for the use of government officials and agencies by the Joint Publications Research Service (JPRS); they were transferred to the FBIS in 1979. Many libraries that have a separate collection of federal publications in the SuDocs classification scheme will have the JPRS publications organized under earlier class numbers, for example, Y 3.J66; PREX 7.13 and PREX 7.14 through 7.23. The Readex Microprint Edition of JPRS Reports covers the period 1956 to 1980. *Transdex Index* (Wooster, OH: Bell & Howell), from 1975 to 1996 when it ceased publication, offered a valuable way of locating specific items. *Transdex: Bibliography and Index to the U.S. JPRS Translations* (New York: Macmillan Information, 1970–1974) provides indexing by country, subject, publication title, and author. Mary Elizabeth Poole's *Index to Readex Microprint Edition of JPRS Reports* (New York: Readex Microprint, 1964) covers the period 1958 to 1963. The *Subject Index to United States Joint Publications Research Service Translations* (New York: CCM Information Services, 1966–1968) is a biannual index to JPRS social science translations from 1966 to 1968; this source gives JPRS numbers and conversion tables to microfilm collections. But neither the *Monthly Catalog* nor *Government Reports Announcements & Index* lists the titles of every JPRS article.

Dissemination of FBIS Series

Depository libraries used to receive the FBIS Daily Report and Publications Reports series on microfiche. The format was switched to CD-ROM beginning with the period June–September 1996. Although each issue is preceded by a contents page, anyone lacking the specific date of an event found researching the fiche difficult. Newsbank/Readex rectified this problem with the creation of a useful *FBIS Index on CD-ROM* to subscribers. World News Connection (WNC) is a fee-based news service available on the Web. FBIS supplies the National Technical Information Service with its reports, and NTIS enters new information into WNC every business day. Generally, this information is available within forty-eight to seventy-two hours from the time of original broadcast or publication. More information on search strategies and "profile subscribers" is available at **http://www.fedworld.gov/ntis**.

Copyright Caveat

NTIS pays royalties to the media sources that supply FBIS with information, so it needs to recover their costs for dissemination. This results in the depository distribution limitation of the GPO's CD-ROM product. As a result, this policy statement from FBIS was published in *Administrative Notes:*

> Federal depository libraries may make the FBIS on CD-ROMs available to the public for research. They may do this only on a stand-alone machine, and should not install it on a LAN. Federal depository libraries . . . may not legally permit the public to print or download the information contained on the For Official Use Only CD-ROM. Any other use may result in a claim of copyright or contract infringement from the original copyright holder(s). Public customers should be referred to NTIS' World News Connection Service.[8]

COMMERCIALLY AVAILABLE DECLASSIFIED DOCUMENTS

The outpouring of declassified documents is not solely a function of FOIA requests, a cumbersome process at best. As a result of Executive Order 11652, signed by President Richard Nixon in 1972 and amended by subsequent chief executives, thousands of post–World War II documents originally classified as Top Secret, Secret, or Confidential were declassified under the mandatory review provision of that ukase. Carrollton Press, Inc. (Washington) subsequently began to acquire, index, abstract, film, and make these titles available to the public. Initially, the *Declassified Documents Retrospective Collection* (2 volumes, 1976–1977) and the *Declassified Documents Quarterly Catalog* (volume 1, 1975–) in print format were published, and corresponding microfiche collections were also made available for purchase. The declassified materials range from one-page telegrams, correspondence, and unevaluated field reports to extensive background studies, detailed minutes of cabinet-level meetings, and situation reports. Entries provide information on the classification level that had been assigned to the document, the date of publication, and the date each was declassified. A better sense of what *Declassified Documents* contains may be gained when one knows what was excluded from the source. Intentional exclusions were noted in the "Foreword" to volume 1, number 1, of the *Quarterly Catalog* (January/March 1975):

> (1) documents which were declassified automatically in bulk following expiration of the 30 year rule, (2) documents which already have been given wide public dissemination (such as parts of the "Pentagon Papers," documents included in Foreign Relations of the U.S., and research reports indexed and published on microfiche by NTIS, AEC, or NASA), and (3) documents which we believe to be of marginal interest to anyone other than the requester.

Since 1986, Research Publications International (Woodbridge, CT), has produced the *Declassified Documents Catalog,* consisting of bimonthly issues combining abstracts and a subject index, and an annual cumulated subject index. The full-text microfiche collection is issued bimonthly. Arrangement of the abstracts is alphabetical by the names of the government agencies in which the documents originated or for which they were prepared. Documents are numbered consecutively throughout the abstracts for each year.

Although one would have to access many separate agency Web sites to find a trove comparable to what this collection has assembled under one continuing series, the index is not easy to use. While subject terms include persons, events, and headings such as armaments, communism, and atomic warfare, subjects are broad and heavily geared to country names. When countries are accessed, the user is required to search extensively to locate detail. For many countries, the subheadings "Politics and government" and "Foreign relations with the United States" typically contain so many identification numbers that the researcher may spend a great deal of time determining the relevance of any one entry to a specific inquiry. Figure 11.3 shows a page from the catalog.

Another good source for declassified materials, especially those of a foreign policy nature, has been collected using the Freedom of Information Act since 1985 by the National Security Archive (NSA), an independent research institute affiliated with George Washington University (Washington, DC). The NSA has microfilmed numerous sets of topically oriented documents obtained in this manner and sells the collections to libraries and other institutions. Now these collections have been made available for a fee via the Web in an enterprising activity called *The Digital National Security Archives: The Secret Documents That*

Figure 11.3. Page from *Declassified Documents Catalog*.

State Department (continued)

Iraq (continued)

A.   [Reports of disturbances in Baghdad exaggerated; reaction to Nuri
       Said's appointment as Prime Minister mixed.] Am Cons Basra, Air-
       gram A-8. Jan. 12, 1949. 2 p. CONFIDENTIAL.

B.   Iraq: Political Review, January 22, 1948 [Prime Minister Nuri Said
       takes stand against opponents; pressure for war in Palestine is relieved;
       dissident foreign Arab papers are banned; student demonstrations are
       broken up.] Am Emb Baghdad, Airgram A-27. Jan. 22, 1949. 3 p.
       CONFIDENTIAL.

C.   [Description of Communist and Independence Party demonstration
       in honor of Baghdad's "Martyrs".] Am Cons Basra, Airgram A-14.
       Jan. 26, 1949. 2 p. CONFIDENTIAL.

D.   [Situation in Basra: police arresting "Communist" agitators; economy
       slumping.] Am Cons Basra, Airgram A-19. Feb. 2, 1949. 1 p. CON-
       FIDENTIAL.

E.   Iraq: Political Review, February 14, 1949 [Prime Minister Nuri Said
       answers critics of government policy on: British recognition of Israel;
       arrests of political opponents; handling of Palestine War]. Am Emb
       Baghdad, Airgram A-58. Feb. 14, 1949. 4 p. RESTRICTED.

F.   Notes on Current Events and Opinions in Iraq [reaction to US and
       British recognition of Israel; possibility of incorporation of Arab
       Palestine into Transjordan; possible approval of union with Syria
       (Greater Syria Plan)]. Am Emb Baghdad, Airgram A-60. Feb. 14,
       1949. 2 p. RESTRICTED.

G.   [Executions of Communists Yousif Salman Yousif and Hussain
       Mohammed El-Shabibi; economic outlook.] Am Cons Basra, Air-
       gram A-26. Feb. 16, 1949. 2 p. CONFIDENTIAL.

H.   Prime Minister Nuri As Said Talks Frankly to Parliament about Iraq's
       Economic and Political Difficulties. Am Emb Baghdad, Airgram A-
       78. Feb. 25, 1949. 2 p. RESTRICTED.

Made U.S. Policy (Alexandria, VA: Chadwyck-Healey). Access to more than 35,000 documents was made available in 1999 with more collections scheduled in future years. Collections are grouped by subject or country; for example, Berlin Crisis, Iran-Contra Affair, Nicaragua, Military Uses of Space, and South Africa. Documents are searchable by several access points, including level of classification, and some collections include photographs. Visit this site at **http://www.seas. gwu.edu/nsarchive**.

Primary Source Media, a division of the Gale Group, makes available selected declassified documents released by presidential libraries. These digital facsimiles can be downloaded and printed as needed, and corresponding text files are fully searchable. Called the Declassified Documents Reference System, U.S., the information is accessible at **http://www.ddrs.psmedia.com**.

LIBRARY AWARENESS PROGRAM

Before Presidents George Bush and Boris Yeltsin proclaimed a formal end to the Cold War February 1, 1992, paranoia metastasized throughout the intelligence-gathering agencies of the U.S. government and even infected libraries. During the 1980s, the Federal Bureau of Investigation (FBI) waged a war of harassment against library users with "foreign" names, pestering directors of libraries to cooperate in identifying certain users of unclassified documents readily accessible through online and print sources such as *Government Reports Announcements & Index* and *Scientific and Technical Aerospace Reports*. To add insult to injury, the FBI had the chutzpah to designate this incursion its "Library Awareness Program." The American Library Association (ALA) discovered that the Program was "a broader government effort than originally believed. . . . [I]t has been determined that 22 federal agencies, under CIA direction, are involved in the program as part of an interagency Technology Transfer Intelligence Committee." Moreover, these government entities "are empowered by their legitimate statutory charge to investigate domestic intelligence gathering by foreign nationals." Legal counsel advised ALA's Intellectual Freedom Committee that a "permanent injunction against these agencies to cease and desist would not be granted because the courts would construe that the Awareness Program was legal under the statutes and that [libraries] would be unable to demonstrate sufficient injury."[9]

As prominent library educator Herbert S. White noted at the time, the "diligent search of the unclassified literature for potential nuggets has been an old game, and generally an acknowledged one. . . . The Soviet embassy was, and I suspect remains, one of the best customers of the National Technical Information Service, and the CIA library did (and perhaps still does) provide interlibrary loan materials to that same embassy."[10]

It transpired that the FBI had collected more than 3,000 pages of documents connected to the Library Awareness Program in which librarians were asked by FBI personnel to report library use by possible foreign agents. In settlement of a Freedom of Information Act lawsuit filed by the National Security Archive (noted above) in June 1988, the agency "acknowledged that its agents had searched FBI files for information on over 100 individuals affiliated with libraries and library organizations." In congressional hearings, the FBI Director testified that "the program had focused on 21 libraries, mostly in the New York City area." However, a list attached to the court order, prepared by ALA's Office for Intellectual Freedom, showed that agents had visited more than a dozen other libraries around the country, from Princeton University in the 1960s to UCLA in January 1988 and the University of Utah in April 1988.[11] The tortuous semantic efforts to call these documents that were putatively being secreted away by spies "unclassified but sensitive" only made the government appear more foolish.

Eventually the FBI ceased its "counterintelligence investigations" and the principled librarians who refused to comply with the agency's outrageous demands were aptly celebrated. What this was all about raised the question: Were we to become an informed nation or a nation of informers?

AUDITS AND EVALUATIONS

It is probably true that the federal government performs better than its reputation, but not well enough. The wilder tales of government waste and incompetence usually turn out to be, upon closer examination, grossly exaggerated. That new government programs malfunction or established ones falter is no different than the failure of new products from the private sector. Watchdog organizations from outside of government—the media, activist groups with an agenda, reputable institutions such as Common Cause—remind us daily of the ineptitude of government. But federal departments and bureaus have their internal inspectors general, and the Congress has a unique agency that blows the whistle on the mismanagement of funds, personnel, mission, or all of the above.

GENERAL ACCOUNTING OFFICE

Established by the Budget and Accounting Act of 1921 (96 Stat. 887, 31 U.S.C. § 702) as an independent agency, the General Accounting Office (GAO) was not recognized as a unit within the Congress until 1945. Over the years, the Congress has expanded GAO's audit authority, added new responsibilities and duties, and taken steps to increase the agency's ability to act independently. Today, the GAO assists the Congress, its committees, and its individual members in carrying out their legislative and oversight responsibilities; performs legal, accounting, auditing, and claims settlement functions with respect to federal government programs and operations; and makes recommendations designed to render government operations more effective.

The GAO's chief officer, the Comptroller General of the United States, serves for a fifteen-year term. This long tenure secures for the agency a degree of independence from both the executive branch and the Congress, because GAO includes other congressional agencies (for example, the Government Printing Office) in its audits and investigations. Moreover, the "discretion that characterizes the transmittal of reports to Congress affords the Comptroller General a certain sanction in his dealings with agencies since officials are ordinarily hesitant about having Congress apprised as to shortcomings alleged by the Comptroller General." Internal GAO procedures mandate that "individual reports to the Congress should be prepared if one or more of the following purposes would be served: comply with a specific statutory requirement; call attention to important matters requiring or warranting action by the Congress; communicate useful information on important matters of interest to the Congress."[12]

Despite the fact that the GAO accounts of incompetence and chicanery by agencies or their contractors are trumpeted by the media, it is probably safe to say that the General Accounting Office is one of the lesser-known entities of the federal establishment. Indeed, the GAO produces "hundreds of reports and decisions as well as testimony before Congress that deal with an enormous variety of facets of American government and society."[13] Yet, as former Senator William Proxmire averred, "Few people have heard of the General Accounting Office. Few know what it does. Fewer still know that it is an arm of the United States Congress."[14]

GAO Print Resources

A monthly abstracting service titled *Reports and Testimony* (formerly known as the *Month in Review*) consists of a number of annotated titles arranged under broad topics such as energy, information management, national defense, and veterans affairs. In recent years this publication has increased the information in its contents. In March 1997 the monthly added GAO legal decisions, opinions, and reports on agency rules (see chapter 7). In April 1997 the *Reports* included the titles of GAO correspondence. Designated by the letter "R," these reports are of limited scope and contain no major recommendations. Correspondence is not posted on the Internet but can be ordered from GAO's Document Distribution Center. An annual *Index of Reports and Testimony: Fiscal Year [yr.]* is organized similarly but lacks the annotations found in the monthly reports and testimony schedule. Neither finding aid has detailed subject, title, or author indexes, but the monthly issues are relatively easy to browse, and the abstracts are generously detailed.

Other GAO publications available to depository libraries include more than fifty titles in print, microfiche, and electronic formats found in the *List of Classes*. Like the Library of Congress and several other entities, the GAO has its own field printing facility. Other GAO series are announced in *Subject Bibliography No. 250*.

GAO Legislative Histories

Since its inception, the GAO has compiled and maintained legislative histories of public laws to assist the agency and its divisions in their mission. A discussion of this source is found in chapter 5.

The GAO's Web Site

I have always found the GAO to be one of the most responsive agencies in the federal establishment, and its Internet site only reinforces that impression. It is perhaps no coincidence that the General Accounting Office was the first database not created at the Government Printing Office to be included in GPO Access. Its home page (**http://www.gao.gov**) has links to, inter alia, the full text of the *Reports and Testimony* noted above; Comptroller General Decisions and Opinions; reports on agency regulations before they are implemented; GAO Policy/Guidance Publications; GAO FraudNET, reporting allegations of fraud, waste, abuse or mismanagement of federal funds; and the *Daybook*. This last is a daily listing of released GAO *Reports and*

Testimony posted to the home page every business day. In addition to commentary on agency regulations, GAO's Office of General Counsel regularly issues legal opinions and decisions involving bid protests. Figure 11.4 shows a title page from the transcript of testimony by a GAO official before a congressional committee.

Figure 11.4. Page from GAO *Testimony*.

United States General Accounting Office

GAO

Testimony

Before the Committee on Labor and Human Resources,
United States Senate

For Release on Delivery
Expected at 10:00 a.m.
Tuesday, May 19, 1998

HMO COMPLAINTS AND APPEALS

Plans' Systems Have Most Key Elements, but Consumer Concerns Remain

Statement of Bernice Steinhardt, Director
Health Services Quality and Public Health Issues
Health, Education, and Human Services Division

GAO/T-HEHS-98-173

SUMMARY

One major characteristic shared by these diverse sources of information is that the individual titles within series or categories typically are not listed in the *Monthly Catalog* or available to Title 44 depository libraries. There are exceptions, of course; for example, GAO documentation is available on GPO Access and in print. One thing is clear: As the amount of information available in electronic formats increases, as is surely the case, the importance of the print or microfiche report will decline. In formulating federal dissemination policy in an electronic environment, Congress must see to it that statutory language and legislative intent embrace the concept of equity among unequal user groups.

NOTES

1. Yuri Nakata, *From Press to People* (Chicago: American Library Association, 1979), pp. 100–104.

2. John T. Cocklin, "FedWorld, THOMAS, and CBNet: United States Federal Government Information Dissemination in the 1990s," *Journal of Government Information* 25: 400 (1998).

3. Ibid.

4. Ted Brandhorst, "Educational Resources Information Center," in *The Bowker Annual Library and Book Trade Almanac,* 39th ed. (New Providence, NJ: Reed Elsevier, 1994), p. 174.

5. For example, see *ERIC/IT Update* 19: 1, 8 (Summer/Fall 1998).

6. *ERIC/IT Update* 20: 2 (Winter 1998); *Administrative Notes* 19: 1–2 (February 15, 1998).

7. John Merrill, "Bringing the World to the Classroom: Using the FBIS Reports in the Int'l Politics Course," *NEWS for Teachers of Political Science* (Fall 1984).

8. *Administrative Notes* 18: 3 (April 15, 1997).

9. *Cognotes,* January 8, 1989, p. 1.

10. Herbert S. White, "Librarians and the FBI," *Library Journal* 113: 54–55 (October 15, 1988).

11. *American Libraries,* June 1989, p. 481. See also Herbert N. Foerstel, *Surveillance in the Stacks* (Westport, CT: Greenwood, 1991).

12. Joseph Pois, *Watchdog on the Potomac: A Study of the Comptroller General of the United States* (Washington: University Press of America, 1979), p. 206.

13. Frederick C. Mosher, *The GAO: The Quest for Accountability in American Government* (Boulder, CO: Westview Press, 1979), p. 2.

14. William Proxmire, "Foreword," in Richard E. Brown, *The GAO: Untapped Source of Congressional Power* (Knoxville: University of Tennessee Press, 1970), p. v.

CHAPTER TWELVE

GEOGRAPHIC
INFORMATION SOURCES

This land is your land, this land is my land,
From California to the New York island,
From the redwood forest to the Gulf Stream waters,
This land was made for you and me.
                    —Woody [Woodrow Wilson] Guthrie

INTRODUCTION

According to William A. Katz, geographic sources "may be subdivided into three large categories: maps and atlases, gazetteers, and guidebooks."[1] The last include a number of brochures issued by the Forest Service, the Bureau of Reclamation, the Fish and Wildlife Service, the Bureau of Land Management, and the National Park Service containing information on camping, picnicking, hiking, skiing, and other pursuits. These titles are announced in *Subject Bibliography No. 17,* "Recreational and Outdoor Activities," and usually include maps and geographic names. The American Guide Series, produced during the 1930s by the Federal Writers' Project of the defunct Works Progress Administration, includes more than 150 volumes, some of which are still in print. Frequently reprinted and issued by numerous publishers, the series is still useful and is distinguished by its detailed contents and style of writing.

Millions of maps and charts have been and continue to be distributed to depository libraries. Within the government are entities that produce maps but do not issue or sell them, as well as agencies that both produce and sell their cartographic products. Task forces over the years have recommended that a single civilian unit be established to coordinate these diffuse activities, but the single-agency concept remains unconsummated.

407

This chapter focuses on federal mapping, charting, geodesy, surveying, and gazetteer endeavors. As in other federal enterprises, the Internet has captured the several geographic activities of departments and agencies, and I shall mention exemplary Web sites that feature sources of geographic information. Moreover, Geographic Information Systems (GIS) have revolutionized the production and management of geographic information, and these systems are given appropriate attention.

FEDERAL CARTOGRAPHIC ACTIVITIES

Cartography is defined as "the production of maps, including construction of projections, design, compilation, drafting, and reproduction."[2] This enterprise is one of the oldest activities of the U.S. government. Recognizing the need for large-scale maps based on field surveys, the Continental Congress in 1775 authorized General George Washington to appoint a Geographer of the Army. The corps of surveyors that compiled sketch maps of terrain, prepared plan maps of military posts, and laid out routes for troop movements was the predecessor for permanent mapping agencies with both military and civil functions.[3]

According to Charles A. Seavey, an expert in these matters, "Maps are probably among the most valuable and least understood government publications available today. Yet, the government agencies of the world (national, state, and local) account for over 80 percent of all maps published in a given year."[4]

Major Mapping and Charting Agencies

Although a number of agencies prepare cartographic products for various purposes, the leading producers of maps and charts are the National Ocean Service, National Imagery and Mapping Agency, and the United States Geological Survey.

National Ocean Service

The National Ocean Service (NOS), an agency within the National Oceanic and Atmospheric Administration (NOAA), Commerce Department, is the principal federal agency for producing and distributing nautical and aeronautical charts. Nautical charts illustrate the nature and form of the coast, water depths, character of the ocean bottom, aids to navigation such as channel landmarks, navigation hazards, magnetic variations, port and harbor facilities, and cultural details. Aeronautical charts depict communications facilities, navigational charts, airport landing patterns, safe operating procedures, and air traffic rules. International charts (standard small scale) are produced in cooperation with the International Hydrographic Organization program for charts covering the world's oceans. These products are available free of charge from the Distribution Branch of the NOS, Riverdale, MD 20737-1199.

NOS grew out of the nation's oldest scientific agency, the Survey of the Coast, established in 1807 by President Thomas Jefferson to chart the coast and its harbors. Indeed, the former name of NOS was the National Ocean Survey. Today, 50 percent of the population of the United States lives within 50 miles of the coast, and NOS has a good Web site that furnishes information on its products and services (**http://www.nos.noaa.gov**). The home page links to pages that feature a State of the Coast Report, Products and Services information, National Marine Sanctuaries, and many other useful and related services, including information on ordering *Turning the Tide,* an interactive multimedia CD-ROM guide to some of today's coastal issues.

The *List of Classes* notes more than 100 series available to Title 44 depository libraries. One major series is the *Nautical Chart Catalogs.* Issued as index maps in NOS's Charts and Publications series, the catalogs show which nautical charts are available. *Catalog 1* covers the Atlantic and Gulf Coasts, including Puerto Rico and the Virgin Islands. *Catalog 2* includes the Pacific Coast and Hawaii, Guam, and Samoa. *Catalog 3* covers Alaska and the Aleutian Islands. *Catalog 4* comprises the Great Lakes and adjacent waterways. *Catalog 5* consists of bathymetric and fishing maps, including topographic/bathymetric maps. Moreover, NOS generates the well-known *Tide and Tidal Current Tables, Coast Pilots* series by regions, and *Helicopter Route Charts* for cities such as Los Angeles, New York, Baltimore, Washington, Boston, and Atlanta.

NOS had its own separate map depository program by which it distributed most of its nautical and aeronautical charts to selected designated libraries. However, in the late 1970s it closed its depository program to new applicants and, in the mid-1980s, was forced to reduce the number of charts distributed due to budgetary constraints. Throughout the 1980s, the Government Printing Office (GPO) and NOS staff met to negotiate a merger. In December 1987 NOS gave the Library Programs Service (LPS) samples of maps and charts, which were assigned SuDocs classification and depository item numbers; distribution was initiated in 1989 under the Title 44 program. Librarians in charge of these collections were reminded by the LPS to ensure that superseded maps and charts, which are revised monthly or bimonthly, be discarded immediately so that customers do not use them for navigation purposes.[5]

National Imagery and Mapping Agency

The predecessor of the National Imagery and Mapping Agency (NIMA) was the Defense Mapping Agency (DMA), which was established in 1972 to produce topographic, nautical, and aeronautical maps and charts needed by the military services for defense purposes. NIMA was established October 1, 1996, to address the expanding requirements in the areas of imagery, imagery intelligence, and geospatial information. A member of the intelligence community, NIMA is a Department of Defense (DoD) combat support agency that has the statutory mission of supporting policymakers and government agencies. It was formed through the consolidation of the DMA and other units of DoD as well as the imagery dissemination elements of various entities including the CIA. This structure of commands, services, departments, and agencies, in cooperation with foreign governments and private-sector organizations, forms what is known as the Imagery and Geospatial Community (IGC), which fosters partnerships with, among others, commercial and academic institutions, to share information. Highlights of this NIMA strategic plan are announced in the pages following the NIMA home page (**http://www.nima.mil**), which notes that, subject to national security classification, the public is able to secure copies of world maps; maps of Vietnam produced during the Vietnam War era; maps of military installations; a Vector Smart Map, which is a digital chart of the world on CD-ROM; hydrographic charts; gazetteers; declassified imagery; technical reports; and miscellaneous publications.

The *List of Classes* contains more than thirty-five series issued by NIMA to Title 44 depository libraries. Most maps produced by NIMA are available to depositories and the public, so long as the international agreements under which they are produced allow their distribution. The DMA depository program had its origins in the Army Map Service (AMS) depository system, which began following World War II. In the early 1940s, the army found that it did not have large-scale maps of areas expected to be theaters of military operations. The academic community supplied not only maps but also geographers and cartographers. By war's end, the army found itself with a large number of maps, both captured and army produced. Partly out of gratitude to the academic community and partly out of a desire to dispose of the maps, the AMS established a specific depository program that eventually enrolled 245 designated libraries. Most of the materials were maps distributed during the immediate postwar years; revisions were only occasionally supplied.

The AMS program became the DMA depository program, but few shipments were made in the 1970s, and those consisted primarily of aeronautical and nautical charts with scarcely any topographic maps.[6] In 1982, DMA joined with the United States Geological Survey to participate in the Title 44 depository program, and DMA discontinued its own depository arrangements.[7] In late 1998, after DMA had become NIMA, a notice was sent to all Title 44 depository libraries selecting NIMA series, stating that henceforth maps and other materials formerly distributed by NIMA would be shipped from the Library Programs Service (LPS) directly to the subscribing libraries.[8] Among the many items available to depository libraries are significant publications such as the JNC-Jet Navigation and GNC-Global Navigation and Planning Charts; List of Lights series, which includes Sailing Directions, Loran Tables, Radio Aids and Fog Signals, and Omega Tables; the quarterly *Navigator;* and the *Digital Chart of the World* (DCW) on CD-ROM.

United States Geological Survey

The United States Geological Survey (USGS), Department of the Interior, is the nation's primary provider of earth and biological science information related to natural hazards; certain aspects of the environment; and mineral, energy, water, and biological resources. USGS prepares maps and digital and cartographic data; collects and interprets data on energy and mineral resources; conducts nationwide assessments of the quality, quantity, and use of the nation's water resources; and publishes thousands of maps and reports each year. Established by an act of March 3, 1879 (20 Stat. 394; 43 U.S.C. § 31), the agency's mission to produce topographic maps and conduct chemical and physical research was authorized in subsequent legislation. Currently, authorizations for publication, sale, and distribution of material prepared by USGS are contained in 43 U.S.C. §§ 41–45 and 44 U.S.C. §§ 1318–1320.

USGS produces several thousand new and revised maps and reports annually. Many thematic maps are included in its book series, such as its Bulletins, Numbered Circulars, Professional Papers, and Water Supply Papers. Geologic maps are also published as folded sheets in envelopes in the following series: geologic quadrangle maps; miscellaneous field studies maps; investigations of mineral resources; oil and gas, coal, and geophysical maps series; and miscellaneous investigations maps. In addition, USGS prepares multicolor geologic maps in cooperation with many states, but the majority of states have geologic agencies that also prepare their own maps. Hundreds of USGS titles are announced in the *List of Classes* and are made available to depository libraries in print, fiche, and CD-ROM. Moreover, the agency supports a splendid Web site (**http://www.usgs.gov**) with links and buttons galore (more of which later).

National Cartographic Information Center

The National Cartographic Information Center (NCIC) was established by USGS in 1974 to serve as the central source for federal, state, local, and private-sector cartographic and geographic information. It accepts orders for the full range of maps, map by-products, and other cartographic information. For example, NCIC publishes the *Catalog of Cartographic Data* and digital representations of terrain elevations produced by NIMA's Topographic Center. It maintains third-order horizontal and vertical geodetic control information established by USGS. Vertical control lists are available with descriptions, locations, and elevations of benchmarks. Horizontal lists contain geodetic and/or geographic positions of transit traverses, triangulations, and electronic traverse stations, covering the United States from 1900 to the present. Perhaps NCIC's best-known collection is its millions of aerial photos and space images. NCIC produces the Aerial Photography Summary Record System, which describes existing aerial photography projects from various federal, state, and commercial sources. The System gives geographic location, date of acquisition, scale, and information about the film and camera, and identifies the holding organization for approximately 500,000 aerial photography projects. Fifty-three microfiche sets are available for the fifty states, the District of Columbia, Pacific Islands, Puerto Rico, and the Virgin Islands. Each entry consists of a summary record for an aerial photography project that is located by longitude and latitude and sorted by date. Located at the USGS National Center in Reston, Virginia, NCIC has regional offices in several states. In addition, cooperative agreements have been made with many state governments to operate NCIC-affiliated offices. Indeed, the agency works in cooperation with nearly 2,000 local, state, and federal agencies.

USGS Topographic Maps

Topographic maps (known affectionately as "topogs") are the best-known and most widely used USGS series. A topographic map is defined as a "line-and-symbol representation of natural and selected man-made features of a part of the Earth's surface plotted to a definite scale. A distinguishing characteristic of a topographic map is the portrayal of the shape and elevation of the terrain by contour lines."[9]

Another characteristic of topographic maps is their use of color and symbols to represent features. Water features are blue, human-made objects are black, built-up areas are red, the color green distinguishes wooded areas from clearings, and contour lines are brown. Some maps also contain symbols (pictographs) resembling the objects they represent. Of the several topographic series, perhaps the most used is the 7.5 minute, 1:24,000 scale, where 1 inch represents 2,000 feet. These quadrangle maps cover 7.5 minutes of longitude and latitude on each side. Indexes prepared by the agency permit users to "read" the maps, which are produced for every state, the District of Columbia, outlying areas, and a U.S. Summary.

The National Atlas of the United States of America

The National Atlas of the United States, a 400-page, oversized, 12-pound collection of maps, was published as a sales item and made available to depository libraries in 1970. In 1997 the USGS and commercial firms began work on a new edition with a lengthier title. It is now called *The National Atlas of the United States of America.* USGS and its business partners have been able to take advantage of technologies that did not exist in 1970, most notably CD-ROM and the Web, to produce the new edition. On CD-ROM it differs from the 1970 edition in several ways. In addition to having high-quality, small-scale maps, the atlas includes authoritative digital national geospatial and geostatistical data sets. The former include soils, boundaries, volcanoes, and principal aquifers. The latter include crime patterns, population distribution, and incidence of disease. These data are tied to specific geographic areas and categorized and indexed using different methods, such as county, state, and zip code boundaries or geographic coordinates like latitude and longitude. The atlas also includes software for data display, query, and custom information and mapmaking. Moreover, the product includes links to atlas sites on the Web, permitting more current real-time and regional data. Descriptive information, marketing products, and software programs are also delivered via the Web (**http://www-atlas.usgs.gov**), while information on maps released and distributed through the Federal Depository Library Program (FDLP) is announced at **http://www-atlas.usgs.gov/atlasmap.html**.

Unfortunately, the CD-ROM edition of the *National Atlas* will not be available to depository libraries. Although the USGS is concentrating its efforts on developing Web-based GIS tools for the display and analysis of federally collected geospatial information, it is mandated to continue publishing paper maps as part of the new atlas. All digital cartographic data collected for the atlas can be downloaded free from **http://www-atlas.usgs.gov/atlasftp.html**. However, cooperative arrangements with USGS and the private sector to develop digital products on CD-ROM will be marketed and retailed by the latter, thus precluding shipments to depository libraries. The distinction has become as settled as black-letter law: All products that are solely generated by the federal government are sent to Title 44 libraries and other libraries that participate in the USGS map library depository program. Cooperative ventures between the private sector and an agency of government, unless otherwise allowed by contractual agreements, are not open to depository distribution.

USGS and Microsoft

> If Microsoft made cars, we'd all have to buy Microsoft gas.
>
> —Old Silicon Valley joke

When the nation's largest civilian mapping agency joins in a partnership with the world's most successful computer company, one is tempted to paraphrase Freud's famous question about women in this context, "What does Bill Gates want?" Microsoft joined with USGS to make detailed images of local neighborhoods available free to the public via the Internet. Under a Cooperative Research and Development Agreement entered into May 20, 1997, the United States Geological Survey and Microsoft will make about 3 terabytes of mapping data (that's a 3 followed by 12 zeroes) produced by USGS available and readable over the Internet using Microsoft technology and software. In a news release from the agency's Office of Outreach on the above date, USGS Associate Director Barbara Ryan said, "We now sell and distribute about 3 million paper copies of our maps every year. . . . We will continue to produce the paper topographic maps long used by planners, scientists, hikers and hunters. But there is a growing demand for digital products, for maps and images that can be downloaded and manipulated to meet special needs. Microsoft is giving us a great opportunity to test and develop our ability to meet these growing needs." The news release went on to say that the Agreement signed by USGS and Microsoft will run "at least 18 months." Among the stated goals:

- present over the Internet vast amounts of USGS geospatial data;

- present an easy-to-use interface available to the general public over low-speed connections, such as 18.8 kbps;

- increase the public awareness of and access to USGS information;

- involve private-sector expertise in the marketing, public access and distribution of USGS data and information;

- streamline the process of finding, ordering, and purchasing USGS products.

USGS National Mapping Information

Within the USGS Web site is the home page of the USGS National Mapping Information site (**http://mapping.usgs.gov**). Here one finds a cornucopia of content links to several large topics which in turn are subdivided into more specific categories. Under the heading "Mapping Products and Services," there are links to the Geographic Names Information System (discussed below); Global Land Information online system; National Spatial Data Infrastructure Clearinghouse; and Map and Other Product Ordering, with prices and lists of USGS map dealers and a site map (literally) of the United States, which, by clicking on a particular state, will display a list of retailers that sell USGS maps in that state. The page titled "Ordering U.S. Geological Survey Products" gives you the information needed to order topogs, digital data derived from topogs, aerial photographs, satellite images, books (for example, Professional Papers, Bulletins, etc.), CD-ROMS (of which there are more than forty available), Open-File Reports, and various software such as Biological, Geologic Sciences, Mapping Sciences, and Water Resources Applications.

The National Spatial Data Infrastructure (NSDI), noted above, merits comment. Click on that button and you are transported to the USGS node of the National Geospatial Data Clearinghouse, a component of NSDI (**http://nsdi.usgs.gov**). This node provides pathways to information about geospatial data (in other words, metadata). One pathway is called "Browsing," which is "like going to a section of the library and looking at what's on the shelf." It's a good way to get a general idea of the types of information available. By clicking on buttons you are sent to metadata such as "Best Sellers," a guide to the most popular USGS geospatial data products; "Product Category," an alphabetical listing of all major categories of USGS geospatial data; and "Theme," data organized by topic. "Searching," the other pathway, "is the equivalent of using the library's card (sic) catalog" (the USGS techies may know their html's, but it appears that they haven't been in a library lately). The narration goes on to say that searching is "the most efficient method of examining available online USGS geospatial data holdings to find the information you want. Use the search capability if you can identify your interest by keyword or if you can identify an area by its latitude and longitude boundaries." The next menu-driven screens tell you how to view and/or obtain the data sets you want. Once you have successfully pushed all the right buttons, the universe of USGS products and services invites you to partake of its manifold bounties.

Depository Library Procedures

Like NOS and NIMA, there are a large number of USGS series available to Title 44 depository libraries. The separate depository arrangements that the three agencies formerly entered into with libraries have been incorporated into the Federal Depository Library Program (FDLP). Chapter 3 of the November 1993 revision of the *Federal Depository Library Manual* offers a useful summary of the various ways in which Title 44 depository institutions can select, process, sort, catalog, and shelve maps and charts produced by or for USGS, NOS, and NIMA. In addition, instructions for claiming replacement copies of missing publications are found at the end of the chapter. Librarians should, moreover, take advantage of Mary Lynette Larsgaard's third edition of *Map Librarianship: An Introduction* (Englewood, CO: Libraries Unlimited, 1998), which is designed to help spatial-data librarians become more competent in working with map collections. The author focuses upon the practical methods of handling both hard-copy and digital forms of atlases, maps, remote-sensing images, globes, and so forth. The third edition also adds significant new material on selection, cataloging, and reference.

SERIAL SET MAPS

Part XIV of the *CIS US Serial Set Index, 1789–1969,* discussed in chapters 4 and 5, is a product that provides detailed access to more than 50,000 maps that are embedded in the several executive and congressional publications included in the United States Congressional Serial Set through the decades. Often folded inside the published volumes, the maps were difficult for researchers to locate in the absence of an index. With the publication of the *Index and Carto-Bibliography of Maps, 1789–1969,* these hidden treasures are now readily accessible.

Produced under the editorial direction of Donna P. Koepp, with support from the University of Kansas, the *Index* is issued in three chronological segments, 1789–1897, 1897–1925, and 1925–1969.

In each segment, four separate index sections in two volumes give access by geographical areas and subjects, by map titles, by personal names, and by corporate names. A separate two-volume carto-bibliography annotates each map, providing a description of any special features. Included are map title, cartographer, surveyor, publisher name, date, number of sheets, size, scale, relief, and coordinates derived from the maps. Citations reference the numbered Serial Set volume where the map is located, the individual document or report number, the exact page (or facing page) on which the map appears, and the number of the CIS microfiche card on which the map is found. The maps cover a wide range of topics: inland transportation, battlegrounds, economic conditions, navigational features, information on Native Americans, and so forth. The *Index and Carto-Bibliography* is the definitive source for these historical maps.

LIBRARY OF CONGRESS PANORAMIC MAPS

Among the many links found on the home page of the Library of Congress's Web site (**http://www.loc.gov**) is a segment called "Panoramic Maps, 1847–1909," the provenance of LC's Geography and Map Division. The panoramic map, according to the information on this page, "was a popular cartographic form used to depict U.S. and Canadian cities and towns during the late nineteenth and early twentieth centuries. Known also as bird's-eye views, perspective maps, and aero views, panoramic maps are nonphotographic representations of cities portrayed as if viewed from above at an oblique angle. Although not generally drawn to scale, they show street patterns, individual buildings, and major landscape features in perspective." This site, searchable by keyword, geographic location, or subject, is based upon John R. Hebert and Patrick E. Dempsey's *Panoramic Maps of Cities in the United States and Canada,* 2d ed. (1984). "Hebert and Dempsey compiled a checklist of 1,726 panoramic maps of U.S. and Canadian cities, the bulk of which were done by Albert Ruger, Thaddeus Mortimer Fowler, Lucien R. Burleigh, Henry Wellge, and Oakley H. Bailey who prepared more than fifty-five percent of the panoramic maps in the Library of Congress."

MrSID and LizardTech

Certain kinds of detailed maps involved digital files too large to publish on the Internet; that is, until 1998. Enter MrSID, an acronym that stands for Multi Resolution Seamless Image Database. Originally developed by the image technology group at Los Alamos National Laboratory, MrSID is compression software designed to store and retrieve large digital images. Unlike other compression software that relies on tiling, MrSID gets all its sharp resolution from within a single compressed image, and it does not require any special hardware. File size doesn't matter: MrSID allows immediate access to any part of an image, of any size, at any resolution.

The unique feature of MrSID is its ability to decompress only that portion of the image requested by the user. The compression ratio is about 22:1, depending on image content and color depth. Because fast access is furnished via networks and the Internet to vast amounts of geographic information, MrSID is ideal for viewing maps, orthophotos, terrain models, and satellite data. For example, with MrSID one can view 64 USGS Digital Orthophotoquads (DOQs; also a depository series) at 512 pixels per meter all the way down to 1 pixel per meter within a single file, using just a megabyte or two of RAM. This approach permits one to access any portion of an image quickly and easily: no more tiles, no more seams, and no more searching through hundreds of files looking for a particular location. In other words, you no longer have to load multiple files to view large maps, satellite imagery, or aerial photo sets.

A small company named LizardTech took the core code developed by Los Alamos National Laboratory and produced a commercial version of MrSID using a process called "wavelet compression technology." LizardTech entered into a contract with the Library of Congress for delivery of the panoramic maps that have been scanned into raster image files and has a cooperative research agreement with USGS to publish their maps and aerial photos. For more details about MrSID and LizardTech, visit **http://www.lizardtech.com/mrsid.html**.

LANDVIEW III

Issued by the Bureau of the Census, LandView III is a set of CD-ROMs that contains database extracts from the Environmental Protection Agency (EPA), Census Bureau, USGS, Nuclear Regulatory Commission, Department of Transportation, and the Federal Emergency Management Agency. Essentially a desktop mapping system, LandView III consists of two software programs: the LandView database system and the MARPLOT mapping system. The two systems communicate with each other, allowing the user to make map inquiries based on a selection of database records and to make database inquiries based on a selection of map objects.

LandView had its roots in the CAMEO system (Computer-Aided Management of Emergency Operations) developed by the EPA and the National Oceanic and Atmospheric Administration (NOAA) to make easier the implementation of the Emergency Planning and Community Right-to-Know Act, a law requiring local governments to develop emergency response plans for public knowledge of chemical hazards in their communities. CAMEO DOS, first released in 1991, contained a mapping program called MARPLOT, which provided access to computerized street maps based on the Census Bureau's TIGER/Line files (see chapter 9). Later, MARPLOT was enhanced to include Census boundaries and demographic statistics and was included as one of the TIGER/Line 1992 CD-ROM products under the name of LandView.

With the addition of EPA-regulated sites and more detailed demographic data, LandView became a CD-ROM product in itself, released in 1995 as LandView II. Being a DOS-based program, LandView II was limited by the DOS memory restrictions and was difficult to run in memory-intensive environments such as local area networks (LANs). To solve that problem, two programs were developed, MARPLOT for Windows (the mapping engine) and LandView (the database search and query engine). Both programs were converted to run on the Macintosh platform. This Windows-Macintosh cross-platform system, with the inclusion of updated data from the several entities noted above, was released on CD-ROMs as LandView III.

The beauty of LandView III is that it is capable of showing census geographic boundaries down to census tract and block group level and locate EPA "brownsites," schools, public buildings, and other important community locations. The CD-ROMs match information on hazardous wastes in a community and include census statistics for populations affected by these sites and matches addresses to census tracts displaying official 1990 tract boundaries over the network of streets. Moreover, LandView III permits coding of rural addresses, streets without numbers, and new construction. Comprising eleven CD-ROMs sold individually and as a set, LandView III is also available to Title 44 depository libraries. Ordering information is available at **http://www.census.gov/geo/www.tiger**.

GEOGRAPHIC INFORMATION SYSTEMS

MrSID and LandView III are examples of Geographic Information Systems (GIS), defined by the General Accounting Office as a "digital computer system that captures, stores, analyzes, and models natural and artificial environments using data referenced to locations on the earth's surface." GIS has also been described as a term or concept encompassing the entire field of computerized mapping and has been used to mean a specific subset of the field, referring to a high-end computerized mapping system. GIS data are usually described by a geographic position and attributes in a computer-readable form. "For example, spatial data representing a building would identify the building; the geographic position, such as its longitude-latitude coordinates; and attributes, such as its name and use."[10]

Most government data relate to geography, as Woody Guthrie must have intuited when he wrote the song quoted at the beginning of this chapter. "Land is the issue in most citizen-government interactions—zoning disputes, the designation of areas in need of more crime-prevention resources, the re-drawing of election districts, controversies over siting a new landfill." But for decades producing and managing geographic information have been among the most labor-intensive, time-consuming, and expensive government tasks. Today, technology has come to the rescue. Computer hardware and software, combined with GIS, can generate precise graphic displays and analyses, providing citizens and their governments with new ways of looking at problems and envisioning solutions.

Today's GIS basically consist of a computer hardware/software system, a database, and an electronic base map. The GIS database consists of spatial and attribute information. Spatial data, in the form of graphic symbols, refer to the geographic location of, for example, a parcel of land, a water pipe, or a fire station. Such data usually are stored in a hierarchical database, with information arranged in layers ranging from general concepts to specific details. Attribute data, usually words and numbers, may describe that same parcel or pipe or station. As a rule, attribute data are stored in a relational database, one that arranges a particular piece of information according to the way it relates to other information. For example, the plot number for a particular parcel of land would be stored along with the address of that parcel and the name of its owner. An electronic base map is a computerized coordinate map that can be displayed on a terminal screen. It has been converted from existing paper or electronic maps of a metropolitan area, county, a state or its subsections. These spatial and attribute data are fed into the GIS, which store, manipulate, analyze, and display the information on top of the base map in ways specified by the programmed instructions. In response, each system produces on the screen a graphic display that is the base map, with multiple layers superimposed on it, "the electronic equivalent of layering several plastic transparencies in front of an overhead projector to produce a composite image."[11]

GIS and Global Change

There are myriad uses for GIS technology for federal, state, county, and municipal governments and for the private sector. One example from the GIS node of the USGS Web site (**http://www.usgs.gov/ research/gis**) will suffice to illustrate its potential. Maps have been used for centuries to explore the Earth and to exploit its resources. GIS technology, as an expansion of cartographic science, has enhanced the efficiency and analytic power of traditional mapping. As individuals, corporations, and governments become increasingly aware of the environmental consequences of human activity, GIS technology is becoming an essential tool in the effort to understand the process of global change. The condition of the Earth's surface, atmosphere, and subsurface can be examined by feeding satellite data into GIS, thus giving researchers the ability to examine the variations in Earth processes over days, months, and years. For instance, the changes in vegetation vigor through a growing season can be animated to determine when drought was most extensive in a particular region. The resulting graphic, known as a normalized vegetation index, represents a rough measure of plant health. Working with two variables over time allows researchers to detect regional differences in the lag between a decline in rainfall and its effect on vegetation. In sum, GIS greatly assist in the analysis of large volumes of data, allowing for better understanding of terrestrial processes and better management of human activities to maintain world economic vitality and environmental quality. Moreover, the layered images thus achieved and displayed can be equally helpful in conveying technical concepts of GIS study subjects to the interested layperson.

A useful Web resource is the "GIS FAQ" page located at the Census Bureau home page (**http://www.census.gov**), where resides an index with buttons for definitions; colleges and universities that offer course work in GIS; data formats and map products, including how to order USGS maps; selected journals that carry GIS articles; information on subscribing to listservs such as GIS-L and MAP-L; and many other links.

GIS Private and Public Sector Uses

A large number of federal agencies use multiple GIS applications. As noted in chapter 9, the Census Bureau's Topologically Integrated Geographic Encoding and Referencing (TIGER) databases have revolutionized census geography. For the 1990 decennial count, the Bureau consulted private-sector GIS experts and joined forces with the USGS to develop a "single, integrated geographic data base for the entire Nation." USGS's role in this effort consisted of scanning or manually digitizing its most current 1:100,000-scale maps covering the country's land area. USGS supplied the Census Bureau with computer tape files containing digital descriptions of water and transportation features as well as major power lines and pipelines; the Bureau in turn merged these data into a seamless map database. The result was an acceleration of map production and a dramatic demonstration of the manifold advantages of computer mapping.[12]

Other examples of federal agency use of GIS include managing natural resources; environmental assessment and monitoring, as noted in the example above; tracking hazardous and toxic waste; analyzing tactical and strategic defense data; and assessing nuclear safety, health care, and narcotics. State and local governments and the private sector derive benefits from advances in GIS and the development of national-level spatial data sources such as TIGER and the Geological Survey's Digital Line Graph (DLG). These technologies are combined to include applications in logistical operations such as police dispatching, parcel delivery, and emergency vehicle routing.[13]

Major vendors that produce and sell workstation software include Environmental Systems Research Institute, Inc. (ESRI), Intergraph Corporation, and Earth Resources Data Analysis Systems (ERDAS). Software packages for personal computers divide into IBM and Macintosh GIS software. Companies that supply both IBM and Apple include Strategic Mapping, Inc., MapInfo, and Tactics International. Because it is estimated that "as much as 80% of all information held by business and government may be geographically referenced," the field of Geographic Information Management (GIM) has become a growth industry. GIM focuses upon policy issues and technology. The former include "assessment, design, planning, and cooperation among users of geographic information." The projected growth rate for GIS "is a minimum of twenty-five to forty percent per year" for the remainder of the twentieth century. "This means the number of users will move from tens of thousands to hundreds of thousands and perhaps millions" by the advent of the millennium.[14]

GAZETTEERS

A gazetteer is a geographic dictionary or index containing geographic names and descriptions arranged alphabetically. The United States Board on Geographic Names (BGN), an agency within the Interior Department, is responsible for establishing and maintaining uniform geographic name usage throughout the federal government. Its purpose is to resolve name problems and to eliminate duplication of effort by agencies responsible for the production of maps and other publications that use geographic names. Its membership consists of representatives of several federal entities who are appointed for a two-year term; and it has developed principles, policies, and procedures governing the use of both domestic and foreign geographic names as well as underseas and Antarctic feature names. The members of the BGN may not, like Shakespeare's poet, give "to airy nothing / a local habitation and a name," but they are indisputably thorough.

With respect to domestic names, the Board's policy is to recognize present-day local usage or preferences when possible. To carry out this policy, the Board maintains close cooperation with state geographic names authorities, state and local governments, and the general public. When confusing duplication of local names exists, or when a local name is derogatory to a particular person, race, or religion, BGN may disapprove such names and seek alternate local names for the features. In instances where local usage is conflicting or weak, well-established documented names and names with historical significance are given strong consideration. Moreover, the Board has a policy of disapproving new domestic geographic names that commemorate or may be construed to commemorate living persons. Any person or organization, public or private, may make inquiries or request BGN to render formal decisions on proposed new names, proposed name changes, or names that are in conflict.[15]

Decision Lists

Decisions on Geographic Names in the United States bears the subtitle *Decision List* followed by the year of issuance. It was published on a quarterly schedule through 1989, when it became an annual. The current issues follow the format of the earlier quarterly serials. The contents are organized alphabetically by state and, within state, alphabetically by name. Entries define the spellings and applications of the names for use on maps and other publications of federal agencies. Unapproved variant names, spellings, or applications are listed following the word "Not"; these may include former names or spellings no longer used, names derived by the application of policies other than those approved by BGN, misspellings, and names misapplied to all or part of the subject features.[16] For example, "Dripping Vat Reservoir" (Arizona) is "Not: Merlyn Lake, Merlyn Reservoir, Merlyn Tank."

In each entry, coordinates are given for the mouth of a stream, valley, or any other linear feature; the center of areal features such as a bay, lake, island, or populated place; the dam of a reservoir; the summit of a mountain, peak, or hill; the tip of a point of land; and each end of a certain linear feature such as a ridge, range, canal, or channel. The information following the coordinates supplies the name of a USGS topographic map or National Ocean Service chart on which the features can be located. If the feature is on more than one map or chart, the map cited is the one on which the primary coordinate is located, such as the mouth of a linear feature or the center of an areal feature. And if a populated place is incorporated under the laws of its state, its legal designation (city, town, borough, village), as the date of the decision, is specified in parentheses. A populated place without such a designation is not incorporated. An alphabetical index of all names listed in that issue rounds out the contents. Figure 12.1 shows a page from *Decision List 1998*, which contains names approved by BGN during that year.

Geographic Names Information System

> The world is so full of a number of things
> I'm sure we should all be as happy as kings.

> —Robert Louis Stevenson

The author of *Treasure Island* and other classics might have added that all these things have been given names. The Geographic Names Information System (GNIS), developed by the USGS in cooperation with the BGN, is the nation's official repository of information on domestic geographic names. "What's in a name?" Juliet asks Romeo. How about 2 million names? That is roughly the size of the GNIS database, located at a wonderful Web site within the USGS Mapping Information site (**http://mapping.usgs.gov/www/gnis**). The database consists of two parts: United States and Territories and Antarctica. The former contains the following information about a specific geographic feature: federally recognized feature name, feature type (stream, dam, populated place, and so forth), elevation (where available), recent estimated intercensal population of incorporated cities and towns,[17] state and county

Figure 12.1. Page from *Decisions on Geographic Names in the United States: Decision List 1998.*

10

West Fork Woodland Grade Creek: stream, 1.4 km (0.9 mi) long, on the Nez Perce Indian Reservation, heads at 46°15'55"N, 116°02'14"W, flows S to Woodland Grade Creek, 6.8 km (4.2 mi) SSE of Woodland; Idaho Co., Idaho; Sec 26, T34N, R3E, Boise Mer.; 46°15'10"N, 116°02'23"W; USGS map - Woodland 1:24,000. (Docket 357)

Woodland Grade Creek: stream, 183 m (600 ft) long, on the Nez Perce Indian Reservation, heads at 46°15'10"N, 116°02'23"W at the confluence of West Fork Woodland Grade Creek (q.v.) and East Fork Woodland Grade Creek (q.v.), flows SW into Clearwater River, 6.8 km (4.2 mi) SSE of Woodland; Idaho Co., Idaho; Sec 35, T34N, R3E, Boise Mer.; 46°15'06"N, 116°02'30"W; USGS map - Woodland 1:24,000. (Docket 357)

Wye Creek: stream, 3.7 km (2.2 mi) long, in the Selway-Bitterroot Wilderness, Nez Perce National Forest, heads at 46°10'52"N, 114°48'41"W, flows NNW to East Fork Moose Creek; Idaho County, Idaho; Secs 16,21&22, T33N, R13E, Boise Mer.; 46°12'07"N, 114°50'16"W; USGS map - Freeman Peak 1:24,000. (Docket 354)

INDIANA

Clouse Lake: lake, 100 m (328 ft) by 61 m (200 ft), 3.5 km (2.2 mi) SE of Merriam; Noble County, Indiana; Sec 32, T33N, R10E, Second Principal Mer.; 41°16'13"N, 85°23'53"W; USGS map - Merriam 1:24,000. (Docket 366)

MAINE

Floods Cove: bay, 0.8 km (0.5 mi) by 0.3 km (0.2 mi), on the E shore of Muscongus Bay, 2.6 km (1.6 mi) WSW of the community of Friendship; named for Dr. Everett Flood (d. 1935), the former owner of the land around the cove; Knox County, Maine; 43°58'39"N, 69°22'03"W; USGS map -Friendship 1:24,000; Not: Ames Cove. (Docket 366)

Grays Island: island, 152 m (500 ft) by 122 m (400 ft), one of three small islands off the N end of Cape Rosier, at the mouth of Bagaduce River, opposite the community of Castine; named for the Gray family, 200-year owners of the island; Hancock County, Maine; 44°22'43"N, 68°47'41"W; USGS map - Castine 1:24,000; Not: Cree Island, Ina Grays Island, Jarvis Island, Javes Island, Mill Island. (Docket 364)

Kays Ledge: bar, located 1.6 km (1 mi) SE of the center of the Town of Camden, on the mainland opposite Curtis Island, between Dillingham Point and Ogier Point; named for Katherine "Kay" Aldridge Tucker (1918-1995), former local resident; Knox County, Maine; 44°12'00"N, 69°03'15"W; USGS map - Camden 1:24,000. (Docket 366)

Killdeer Point: cape, located on E shore of China Lake, 3.2 km (2 mi) NE of South China, 24 km (15 mi) NE of Augusta; named for the Killdeer bird; Kennebec County, Maine; 44°25'19"N, 69°33'16"W; USGS map - China Lake 1:24,000; Not: Kildeer Point. (Docket 364)

MASSACHUSETTS

Peaked Hill: summit, elevation 95 m (311 ft), located near the SW end of Martha's Vineyard, 19 km (11.8 mi) W of Edgartown, 6.4 km (4 mi) W of Tisbury Great Pond, 1.6 km (1 mi) NE of Chilmark, includes three distinctive unnamed summits; descriptive name; 1989 description revised; Dukes County, Massachusetts; 41°21'23"N, 70°44'22"W; USGS map - Squibnocket 1:25,000. (Docket 366)

Peskeomskut Island: island, 150 m (492 ft) by 75 m (246 ft), located at a bend in the Connecticut River, just N of the community of Turners Falls, between Canada Hill and Riverside; named "Place of Great Waters" by the American Indian tribe which once fished from this island; Franklin County, Massachusetts; 42°36'46"N, 72°33'14"W; USGS map - Greenfield 1:24,000. (Undocketed) in which the feature is located, latitude and longitude of the feature location, list of USGS 7.5-minute x 7.5-minute topographic maps on which the feature is shown, and names other than the federally recognized name by which the feature may now be or has been known. For specific Antarctica geographic features, the information includes all the elements described above except the state and county and list of topogs. However, Antarctica has a description of the feature, including name origin and history, an element lacking in the information on domestic names.

The GNIS Web site has links to information about foreign geographic feature names, which can be obtained from the GEONet Names Server developed by the National Imagery and Mapping Agency, discussed above; GNIS products; related products; and other information. The entire database is available on a compact disk titled *The Digital Gazetteer of the U.S.,* and information on how to acquire gazetteers of foreign lands and other NIMA products is given. One of the products made possible by the existence of the GNIS database is the *National Gazetteer of the United States of America,* discussed earlier in this chapter. Gazetteers for only a few states have been produced in print, but the *Digital Gazetteer* covers the entire country and is available to Title 44 depository libraries. It is far more expensive for the federal government to produce these large state gazetteers in print. Volumes need to be revised periodically, and with CD-ROM and, best of all, Internet access, the printed gazetteers become superfluous.

Suppose that you want to know where Nowhere is. Far from being a metaphysical conundrum or cosmological conceit, a Kodak moment at the GNIS domestic database displays several Nowheres, much as some cosmologists have postulated multiple universes. Only one Nowhere is a populated place, in Caddo County, Oklahoma. The rest consist of five streams, a dam, a meadow, and a ridge, in various states other than Oklahoma. Because Nowhere, Oklahoma, is an unincorporated entity, GNIS did not provide an intercensal population figure, but all other information was duly recorded. And you can link to the Census Bureau's TIGER Map Server, which shows a map of the United States and the location of Nowhere on it. Another link leads to the Environmental Protection Agency's "Surf Your Watershed" page, at which you can find out about environmental, economic, and demographic conditions; trends; uses; impacts; and natural resources associated with the feature you are researching. And there are yet other related links and buttons sufficient to make the most fastidious topographers as happy as kings.

NIMA Gazetteers

The National Imagery and Mapping Agency produces and distributes foreign gazetteers as part of its overall mission of supporting foreign-area scientific studies. Even though different agencies may have been responsible for the content of the NIMA gazetteer series, the provenance is NIMA. In 1990, when NIMA was still the Defense Mapping Agency, the Library Programs Service (LPS), in reviewing the agency's Public Sales Catalog, discovered that DMA had not sent a number of gazetteers to depository libraries. When LPS notified DMA of this discrepancy, the Agency filled the request and also gave LPS one copy of nearly every gazetteer listed in its catalog. In turn, LPS converted these volumes to microfiche and made a "one-time special distribution" of the fiche. These gazetteers continue to be distributed to depository institutions in a microfiche format under the earlier SuDocs classification D 5.319 (Depository Item 0617).[18]

The NIMA gazetteer series is based on the work of linguists, geographers, and cartographers; and, wherever possible, the compilation is carried out with the cooperation of the concerned country. With German reunification, the upheavals in Eastern Europe, and the dissolution of the former Soviet Union, name changes occurred with unusual alacrity. Consequently, during 1990 and 1991, officials of the agency met with greater frequency to assign new names to countries and cities, with the approval of the Department of State and the country involved.

The Romance of Names

The names we give to places are digitized images of mere words, vibrations transmitted through the ambient air, or squiggles impressed on papyri, composed on plates, or flickering on monitors. Yet they evoke an almost numinous response in the souls of those who love language. In Stephen Vincent Benét's celebrated poem "American Names" (1927), the author expressed his preferences for domestic names while acknowledging the enchanted connotation of names foreign:

> I have fallen in love with American names,
> The sharp names that never get fat,
> The snakeskin-titles of mining-claims,
> The plumed war-bonnet of Medicine Hat,
> Tucson and Deadwood and Lost Mule Flat.

I shall not rest quiet in Montparnasse.
I shall not lie easy in Winchelsea.
You may bury my body in Sussex grass,
You may bury my tongue at Champmédy.
I shall not be there. I shall rise and pass.
Bury my heart at Wounded Knee.[19]

NOTES

1. William A. Katz, *Introduction to Reference Work, Volume I: Basic Information Sources,* 6th ed. (New York: McGraw-Hill, 1992), p. 401.

2. *The Random House Dictionary of the English Language,* 2d ed., unabridged (New York: Random House, 1987), p. 320.

3. Ken Rockwell, "Privatization of U.S. Geological Survey Topographic Maps: A Survey," *Government Publications Review* 17: 200 (1990).

4. Charles A. Seavey, "Collection Development for Government Map Collections," *Government Publications Review* 8A: 17 (1981).

5. *Administrative Notes* 9: 21 (February 1988).

6. Seavey, "Collection Development," pp. 19–20.

7. Gary W. North, "Maps for the Nation: The Current Federal Mapping Establishment," *Government Publications Review* 10: 352 (1983).

8. *Administrative Notes* 19: 6–7 (November 15, 1998).

9. Theodore D. Steger, *Topographic Maps* (Washington: Government Printing Office, 1986), p. 3.

10. U.S. General Accounting Office, *Geographic Information Systems: Information on Federal Use and Coordination* (GAO/IMTEC-91-72FS), September 1991, p. 7.

11. *An Introduction to Geographic Information Systems (GIS): A Reader for Local Governments* (New York: State Archives and Records Administration, 1995), pp. 7, 8.

12. Bureau of the Census, *TIGER: The Coast-to-Coast Digital Map Database,* November 1990, pp. 2, 5.

13. GAO, *Geographic Information Systems,* pp. 7, 11–12.

14. Carl Franklin, "An Introduction to Geographic Information Systems: Linking Maps to Databases," *Database,* April 1992, pp. 13–14, 19.

15. *Decisions on Geographic Names in the United States: Decision List 1998* (Reston, VA: U.S. Board on Geographic Names, 1998), p. iii.

16. Ibid., p. iv.

17. For example, a 1999 display of a populated place showed an estimated population as of 1994.

18. *Administrative Notes* 12: 2 (January 30, 1991).

19. The first and last stanzas of "American Names" in William Harman, ed., *The Oxford Book of American Light Verse* (New York: Oxford University Press, 1979), p. 413.

THE IMPEACHMENT AND TRIAL OF THE PRESIDENT: A CHRONOLOGY OF PRIMARY SOURCE MATERIALS

> Government is a trust, and the officers of the government are trustees; and both the trust and the trustees are created for the benefit of the people.
>
> —Henry Clay

> Guilt and crimes are so frequent in the world, that all of them cannot be punished; and many times they happen in such a manner that it is not of much consequence to the public whether they are punished or not.
>
> —John Adams

BEGINNINGS

Ironies abound in this story. The genesis of the legislation that led to the impeachment and trial of William Jefferson Clinton, 42nd President of the United States, is the Ethics in Government Act of 1978, as amended (Public Law 95-521, October 26, 1978; 92 Stat. 1867). Section 601(a) et seq. of the act pertained to the duties of the Independent Counsel and was codified at 28 U.S.C. §§ 591–599, whereas the rest of the 1978 Act is codified in 5 U.S.C. Appendix and other titles and sections because it covers other ethical matters such as obligating financial disclosure of federal personnel. That portion of the statute dealing with the Independent Counsel has had several reauthorizations because of its sunset provision. In the enactment of the Independent Counsel Reauthorization Act of 1994, a piece of legislation that President Clinton supported and signed into law, the events leading to his impeachment, trial, and acquittal have their origins.

431

FOR ALL TO READ

Fast forward to 1998, the year of the discovery of Reckless Bill's folly precipitating media feeding frenzy ad nauseam. When the Independent Counsel's Report (not including, thank goodness, the thirty-six boxes of salacious and other evidence) was made available to the public, network and cable television and the Internet conspired to ensure that every person in the world would not be denied access to the lascivious details of Clinton's dangerous liaison. Dozens of Web sites carried the contents, paragraph by paragraph, including the Government Printing Office, which began providing access to the "Starr Report" (named after Independent Counsel Kenneth W. Starr) pursuant to House of Representatives Resolution 525, September 10, 1998, authorizing public disclosure. GPO went live with the report on September 11 within a half-hour of obtaining a CD-ROM containing certified HTML files from the House. Because of heavy Internet traffic, GPO set up a special URL solely for the report, at **http://icreport.access.gpo.gov/report/ 1cover.htm**. On September 11 and 12, there were more than 569,000 visitors to the site. GPO also made the White House preliminary and initial responses to the Starr Report available on September 11 and 12 at the special URL above.

THE OFFICIAL VERSIONS

In addition to placing the Starr Report online, GPO was requested by the House to provide 500 looseleaf copies of the report for House members. These were delivered as they were completed, with the final copies dispatched by the early evening of September 11. In accordance with the House Resolution, GPO printed the Starr Report as House Document 105-310, titled *Referral from Independent Counsel Kenneth W. Starr in Conformity with the Requirements of Title 28, United States Code, Section 595(c)*. It was distributed to all federal depository libraries in paper copy under Item Number 1004-E, SuDocs classification notation Y 1.1/7:105-310 (part of the Serial Set) on Shipping List 98-0050-S, dated September 14, 1998. The "S" stands for "Separates" (see chapter 3); the report was not sent in the regular shipment box but rather arrived in a white jiffy bag. The Starr Report was also a GPO sales item, bearing the stock number S/N 052-071-01271-1 at a price of $14 (several commercial publishers rushed the report into print faster and sold their books for less money, a common practice for hot-ticket items from the government, typically involving scandal).

Later that month, House Document 105-311, *Appendices to the Referral to the United States House of Representatives Pursuant to Title 28, United States Code, Section 595(c) Submitted by the Office of Independent Counsel Report* (Isn't it fortunate our rules of language permit short titles and popular names?), was shipped in two parts classed as Y 1.1/7: 105-311/PT.1 and Y 1.1/7: 105-311/PT.2 in paper copy to those depositories selecting Items 996-A and in microfiche to those libraries selecting 996-B (see chapter 5). The price for the sales copies of the paper edition of the Appendixes was $68 (S/N 052-071-01274-5). A "CD-R" edition of H. Doc. 105-311 was also made available from the SuDocs sales program. CD-R is like CD-ROM but is produced one at a time instead of in bulk quantities. The CD-R disk was produced on demand in small quantities and was sold only at the Main GPO Bookstore in Washington, DC. This edition of the Appendixes was not sent to depository institutions; it duplicates the information available in paper, on microfiche, and in online formats. The two volumes furnish documentation of Bill and Monica's shenanigans.

SUNSET AND EVENING STARR

All the materials in the following "Chronology of Impeachment Documents" are, or were in 1998–1999, available via GPO Access, THOMAS, and several unofficial Internet sites. 28 U.S.C. §§ 591–599 is available on GPO Access. Section 599, titled "Termination of effect of chapter," states that "This chapter [Chapter 40—Independent Counsel] shall cease to be effective five years after the date of the enactment of the Independent Counsel Reauthorization Act of 1994, except that this chapter shall continue in effect with respect to then pending matters before an independent counsel." Keep in mind that Starr is not, nor need not be, the only Independent Counsel pursuing official malfeasance under the statute. The effective date of this sunset provision was June 30, 1999.

Some of the information in these prefatory remarks was excerpted from GOVDOC-L and GPO Press Releases. My apologies to Alfred, Lord Tennyson, for that last heading, but I could not resist it. The main event follows.

CHRONOLOGY OF
IMPEACHMENT DOCUMENTS

Date	Event	Citation
9 Sep. 98	Communication from Independent Counsel. The House received a communication from Independent Counsel Kenneth Starr that notified the House that his office delivered thirty-six sealed boxes containing two complete sets of a Referral to the House of Representatives.	*Congressional Record* (daily edition), v. 144, n. 118, p. H7468 (Sep. 9, 1998).
10 Sep. 98	House Resolution 525 reported to the House. Resolution providing for deliberative review by the Committee on the Judiciary of a communication from the Independent Counsel and for release thereof. Referred to House Calendar.	*Congressional Record* (daily edition), v. 144, n. 119, p. H7583 (Sep. 10, 1998).
10 Sep. 98	House Report 105-703, pursuant to House Resolution 525.	House Report 105-703, Sep. 10, 1998 (**http://thomas.loc.gov**)
11 Sep. 98	House Resolution 525 considered by the House. Debate and vote. Roll Call number 425: Yeas 363/Nays 63. House agreed to House Resolution 525.	*Congressional Record* (daily edition), v. 144, n. 120, pp. H7587-H7608 (Sep. 11, 1998).

Date	Event	Citation
7 Oct. 98	House Resolution 581 reported to the House. Resolution authorizing and directing the Committee on the Judiciary to investigate whether sufficient grounds exist for the impeachment of William Jefferson Clinton, President of the United States. Referred to House Calendar.	*Congressional Record* (daily edition), v. 144, n. 139, p. H10010 (Oct. 7, 1998).
7 Oct. 98	House Report 105-795 pursuant to House Resolution 581.	House Report 105-795, Oct. 7, 1998 (**http://www.house.gov/ judiciary/increport.htm**)
8 Oct. 98	House Resolution 581 considered by the House. Debate and vote. Roll Call number 497: Yeas 258/ Nays 176/Not Voting 1. House agreed to House Resolution 581.	*Congressional Record* (daily edition), v. 144, n. 140, pp. H10015-H10032; H10084-H10119 (Oct. 8, 1998).
15 Dec. 98	House Resolution 611 reported to the House. Resolution impeaching William Jefferson Clinton, President of the United States, for high crimes and misdemeanors. Referred to House Calendar.	*Congressional Record* (daily edition), v. 144, n. 153, p. H11768 (Dec. 17, 1998).
15 Dec. 98	House Report 105-830 pursuant to House Resolution 611.	House Report 105-830, Dec. 16, 1998 (**http://www.house.gov/ judiciary/icreport.htm**)
18 Dec. 98	House Resolution 611 called up for and read.	*Congressional Record* (daily edition), v. 144, n. 154, pp. H11774-H11775 (Dec. 18, 1998).

Date	Event	Citation
18–19 Dec. 98	House considered House Resolution 611. Debate and vote. Article 1 Passed (Yeas 228/Nays 206/NV 1) Article 2 Defeated (Yeas 205/Nays 229/NV 2) Article 3 Passed (Yeas 221/Nays 212/NV 2) Article 4 Defeated (Yeas 148/Nays 285/NV 2)	*Congressional Record* (daily edition), v. 144, n. 154-155, pp. H11755-H11870; H11879-H11965; H11968-H12042 (Dec. 18-19, 1998).
19 Dec. 98	House Resolution 614 reported and read. Resolution appointing and authorizing managers for the impeachment trial of William Jefferson Clinton, President of the United States.	*Congressional Record* (daily edition), v. 144, n. 155, pp. H12042-H12043 (Dec. 19, 1998).
19 Dec. 98	Roll call vote number 547 on House Resolution 614. Passed (Yeas 228/Nays 190).	*Congressional Record* (daily edition), v. 144, n. 155, p. H12043 (Dec. 19, 1998).
6 Jan. 99	House Resolution 10 called up, considered and passed. Resolution appointing and authorizing managers for the impeachment trial of William Jefferson Clinton, President of the United States. (Continuation of authority conferred in House Resolution 614.)	*Congressional Record* (daily edition), v. 145, n. 1, pp. H211-H217 (Jan. 6, 1999).
7 Jan. 99	Senate Proceedings, Day 1. Administration of Oath	*Congressional Record* (daily edition), v. 145, n. 2, p. S41 (Jan. 7, 1999).

Date	Event	Citation
8 Jan. 99	Senate Proceedings, Day 2. Senate Resolution 16 read and agreed to. Resolution providing for the issue of a summons and for related procedures concerning the articles of impeachment against William Jefferson Clinton, President of the United States.	*Congressional Record* (daily edition), v. 145, n. 3, p. S50 (Jan. 8, 1999).
13 Jan. 99	Senate Document 106-2. Impeachment of President William Jefferson Clinton— Constitutional Provisions; Rules of Procedure and Practice in the Senate When Sitting on Impeachment Trials; Articles of Impeachment Against President William Jefferson Clinton; President Clinton's Answer; and Replication of the House of Representatives.	Senate Document 106-2, Jan. 13, 1999. (**http://www.access.gpo. gov/congress/senate/ miscspub.html**)
14–16 Jan. 99	Senate Proceedings, Days 3-5. House managers presented case.	*Congressional Record* (daily edition), v. 145, n. 4-7, pp. S221-S251; S259-S279; S281-S300 (Jan. 14–16, 1999).
19–21 Jan. 99	Senate Proceedings, Days 6-8. White House Counsel presented President's case.	*Congressional Record* (daily edition), v. 145, n. 8-10, pp. S483-S495; S810-S830; S832-S848 (Jan. 19–21, 1999.
22–23 Jan. 99	Senate Proceedings, Days 9-10. Senate questioned House managers and White House Counsel.	*Congressional Record* (daily edition), v. 145, n. 11-12, p. S870-S892; S933-S956 (Jan. 22–23, 1999).

Date	Event	Citation
25 Jan. 99	Senate Proceedings, Day 11. Trial continued. House managers and White House Counsel presented arguments. Motion to dismiss debated in closed session.	*Congressional Record* (daily edition), v. 145, n. 13, pp. S961-S974 (Jan. 25, 1999).
26 Jan. 99	Senate Proceedings, Day 12. House managers and White House Counsel presented arguments regarding subpoenaing of witnesses and taking depositions. Motion debated in closed session.	*Congressional Record* (daily edition), v. 145, n. 14, pp. S991-S1010 (Jan. 26, 1999).
27 Jan. 99	Senate Proceedings, Day 13. Roll call vote on Motion to Dismiss. Motion rejected. Roll call vote on Motion for Appearance of Witnesses at Depositions. Motion agreed to.	*Congressional Record* (daily edition), v. 145, n. 15, pp. S1017-S1018 (Jan. 27, 1999).
28 Jan. 99	Senate Proceedings, Day 14. Senate Resolution 30 offered. A resolution relative to the procedures concerning the articles of impeachment against William Jefferson Clinton. (Regarding deposition of witnesses.) Considered and agreed to, as amended.	*Congressional Record* (daily edition), v. 145, n. 16, pp. S1070-S1073 (Jan. 28, 1999).
4–8 Feb. 99	Senate Proceedings, Days 15-17. Trial continued. House managers and White House Counsel made presentations.	*Congressional Record* (daily edition), v. 145, n. 20-22, pp. S1199-S1254; S1290-S1318; S1337-S1365 (Feb. 4–8, 1999).

Date	Event	Citation
9 Feb. 99	Senate Proceedings, Day 18. Senate began final deliberations on articles of impeachment. Deliberations closed.	*Congressional Record* (daily edition), v. 145, n. 23, pp. S1385-S1388 (Feb. 9, 1999).
10 Feb. 99	Senate Proceedings, Day 19. Senate resumed closed session to allow members to continue to deliberate the articles of impeachment.	*Congressional Record* (daily edition), v. 145, n. 24, pp. S1411-S1412 (Feb. 10, 1999).
11 Feb. 99	Senate Proceedings, Day 20. Senate resumed closed session.	*Congressional Record* (daily edition), v. 145, n. 25, p. S1437 (Feb. 11, 1999).
12 Feb. 99	Senate Proceedings, Day 21. Vote on articles of impeachment Article 1: 45 guilty/ 55 not guilty Article 2: 50 guilty/ 50 not guilty	*Congressional Record* (daily edition), v. 145, n. 26, pp. S1458-S1459 (Feb. 12, 1999).

TITLE/SERIES INDEX

patent searches, 348
presidential documents, 182
    executive orders and proclamations,
        178
    Reorganization Plans, 216
private bills, 145
public laws, text of, 141
reorganization plans, 216
reports from congressional commit-
        tees, 122
search strategies, 278
Shepardizing, 263
trade secret law, 335
trademark information, 358
treaty information, 199, 207
United States Law Week, 271, 279
USCA, 141
voice recognition software, support
        for, 278
votes, Committee recorded, 122
voting records, congressional, 130
WIN, 278
West's Encyclopedia of American Law,
    255
West's Federal Digest, 4th, 259
West's Federal Practice Digest, 2d, 259

West's Federal Practice Digest, 3d, 259
West's Veterans Appeals Reporter, 266
White House Virtual Library
    executive orders and proclamations,
        178
Whole Earth Catalog, 9
Wholesale Prices and Price Indexes, 292
WILSONDISC, 257
WILSONLINE, 257
Wind Energy, 382
Words and Phrases, 255
Work Unit Information System, 386
World Factbook, 256, 380, 394
World Wide Web Sites Reported by Fed-
        eral Organizations, 72
World Wide Web Virtual Library, 280
    Web site, 280
WorldCat, 33, 34, 56
    search mechanisms, 34

X-Search User Manual, 358

Yahoo! Government, 6, 71
    links to bills and resolutions, 113

SUBJECT/NAME INDEX

Top secret documents. *See* Declassified
materials, access to
Topographic maps
defined, 412
USGS topographic maps, 412–13
Tower Commission Report, 193
Trade dress, 353
Trade names, 353
distinctive names, 353
Trade secrets, 333–35
defined, 333–34, 335
factors used to determine status, 334
federalization of, 335
sources of law, 335
theft, activities treated as, 334
Department of Justice prosecution
of, 335
Internet, misappropriation through
use of, 335
Trademark treaties
Madrid Agreement Concerning the
International Registration
of Marks of 1891, 362
Stockholm Act of 1967, 362
Trademark Trial and Appeal Board, 354
Trademarks, 333, 352–61
appeals, 361
Trademark Trial and Appeal Board,
354, 361, 366
authority, 352
basic information sources, 354
categories of marks, 362
on CD-ROM, 355–56, 357
classification of, 355
commercial online databases, 358–59
depository libraries, 342–43
Federal Depository Library System
logo, 354–55
description of the mark, 355
design phrase, 355
disputes, procedures for, 361–62
domain names, issues regarding,
359–61
cybersquatting, 361
cyberpiracy, 361
high-profile disputes, 360
duration, 352
electronic data, protection of, 354
Internet sites, 357–58
law on trademarks, 361–62
obtaining registration, 352
protection of, 353
general rule, 353
on Internet, 359–61

search library, 358
service marks, 353–54
surnames, 353
symbol, 352
term, 352
trade dress. *See* Trade dress
trade names. *See* Trade names
treaties. *See* Trademark treaties
types of, 353
unprotectable trademarks, 353
weak marks, 353
Transport Control Protocols/Internet
Protocols (TCP/IPs), 2, 4
Treasury Department. *See* Department
of the Treasury
Treaties and agreements
agreement and treaty compared, 197
commercial sources, 206–9, 211
Internet sites, 212–13
multilateral treaty, 202(fig)
official supporting series, 205–6
Senate's shared partnership in the
process, 197
Shepard's United States treaty series,
140
treaty defined, 197
useful publications regarding,
198–211
Trenwith
collection of treaties, 204
Trial courts, 245
Trial of President, 431–39
Truman, Harry, 182, 328
presidential library, 196
Tull, Pamela M., 74
Twain, Mark, 5, 171, 303, 336
Tyler, Thomas J., 49

Unemployment figures, 297–99
Uniform Code of Military Justice, 246
Uniform Resource Locator (URL), 6
Uniform Trade Secrets Act, 335
extraterritorial provisions, 335
United Nations, 190, 289, 344
United States Agency for International
Development, 212
United States Archivist, 106
United States Board on Geographic
Names, 423
purpose, 423
United States Botanic Garden, 102
United States Court of Appeals for the
Armed Forces, 245